DISCARDED

S0-AHD-418

Valuation and the Environment

ADVANCES IN ECOLOGICAL ECONOMICS

General Editor: Robert Costanza, *Director, University of Maryland Institute for Ecological Economics and Professor, Center for Environmental and Estuarine Studies and Zoology Department, USA*

This important series makes a significant contribution to the development of the principles and practices of ecological economics, a field which has expanded dramatically in recent years. The series provides an invaluable forum for the publication of high quality work and shows how ecological economic analysis can make a contribution to understanding and resolving important problems.

The main emphasis of the series is on the development and application of new original ideas in ecological economics. International in its approach, it includes some of the best theoretical and empirical work in the field with contributions to fundamental principles, rigorous evaluations of existing concepts, historical surveys and future visions. It seeks to address some of the most important theoretical questions and gives policy solutions for the ecological problems confronting the global village as we move into the twenty-first century.

Titles in the series include:

Transition to a Sustainable Society
A Backcasting Approach to Modelling Energy and Ecology
Henk A.J. Mulder and Wouter Biesiot

Modelling Global Change
The Art of Integrated Assessment Modelling
Marco Janssen

Valuation for Sustainable Development
Methods and Policy Indicators
Edited by Sylvie Faucheux and Martin O'Connor

Sustainability and Firms
Technological Change and the Changing Regulatory Environment
Sylvie Faucheux, John Gowdy and Isabelle Nicolaï

Valuation and the Environment
Theory, Method and Practice
Edited by Martin O'Connor and Clive Spash

Sustainability in Question
The Search for a Conceptual Framework
Jörg Köhn, John Gowdy, Fritz Hinterbergr and Jan van der Straaten

Valuation and the Environment

Theory, Method and Practice

Edited by

Martin O'Connor

C3ED, Université de Versailles-Saint Quentin en Yvelines, France

and

Clive Spash

Department of Land Economy, University of Cambridge, UK

ADVANCES IN ECOLOGICAL ECONOMICS

Edward Elgar

Cheltenham, UK • Northampton, MA, USA

© Martin O'Connor and Clive Spash 1999

All rights reserved. No part of this publication may be reproduced, stored in a retrieval system or transmitted in any form or by any means, electronic, mechanical or photocopying, recording, or otherwise without the prior permission of the publisher.

Published by
Edward Elgar Publishing Limited
Glensanda House
Montpellier Parade
Cheltenham
Glos GL50 1UA
UK

Edward Elgar Publishing, Inc.
6 Market Street
Northampton
Massachusetts 01060
USA

A catalogue record for this book
is available from the British Library

Library of Congress Cataloguing in Publication Data
Valuation and the environment: theory, method, and practice / edited
    by Martin O'Connor, Clive L. Spash.
        (Advances in Ecological Economics)
        Includes bibliographical references.
        1. Environmental policy—Evaluation. 2. Environmental economics.
    I. O'Connor, Martin, 1958–   . II. Spash, Clive L. III. Series.
    GE170.V34 1998   98–28491
    363.7'05—DC21   CIP

ISBN 1 85898 538 2

Printed and bound in Great Britain by Bookcraft (Bath) Ltd.

Contents

Figures

Tables

1. Introduction

Martin O'Connor and Clive Spash

1.1 ECONOMIC SCIENCE AND ENVIRONMENTAL VALUES

In civilizations over many centuries people have represented natural beauty and have portrayed their respect for the natural powers. But the current vogue for 'environmental valuation' is very recent. It has grown up in 'modern' societies — those dominated by industrial commodity production — roughly in proportion with the perceived scale of 'environmental degradation' being brought about by these same societies. In this respect we can note two things. First, a place or ecosystem or resource or any other cherished thing will be explicitly defended as valuable only when it is felt to be under threat. Second, the defence of nature will take the form of monetary 'valuation' only where the society is already organized by principles of economic valuation.

Economics, although having roots in the analysis of agricultural subsistence economies (such as the Physiocrat school in France), developed primarily for the analysis of the 'produced' wealth of human societies — in particular the goods and services produced by industrial processes for exchange in markets. The key variables for this economic science were, thus, quantity and price for produced goods and services. In this scheme of things, value theory refers primarily to the sphere of 'produced' economic wealth, underpinned by the 'free gifts of nature'. The non-produced or 'pre-existing' domain of nature receives a simplified treatment, as a set of exogenous 'givens' such as freely available air, rainwater and sunshine, open seas for fishing and productive land.

Although the politics of distribution determined the sharing out of the fruits of productive effort on the sea or land, the productive powers of nature were, themselves, given from God. Through labour and technology and advances of human knowledge, the stocks of produced wealth would grow and, over time, the productivity of these original natural endowments would also be improved. This is termed material progress. From this point of view, the natural environment was placed outside the economic valuation problem, and concern for value was, in most economic analysis, synonymous with 'produced' economic value.

Why is nature suddenly in need of protection? The diagnosis broadly stated is that we have failed to take adequate account of the impact of human economic activity upon our milieu. This impact now puts at risk the present and future quality of life. The particular forms of impact can vary a lot — industrial stench and emissions of chemical pollutants, amenity loss, noise, climate destabilization, deforestation and other ecosystem destruction, acid rain, dioxins, large-scale species extinction. These are the 'negative environmental externalities' of current industrial production and consumption on a world scale.

Changing social perceptions are gradually translated into changed academic and institutional priorities. Such a process of institutional change is exemplified in the European Community's successive Environmental Action Programmes. The first of these was put in place in 1973 following on from the 1972 Paris Summit of Heads of State and the Stockholm 'Habitat' Conference, with particular emphasis on environmental protection (habitat quality and the reduction of pollution and nuisance) as a determinant of quality of life. The Fifth Environmental Action Programme, put in place in 1993, seeks to integrate environmental concerns into all facets of Community policy through the objective of sustainable development. The call for sustainable development thus has the same piquancy as the call for environmental valuation: it is fuelled by the perception that current trends of economic activity, described in shorthand as 'growth', may simply not be sustainable for very long. Practices formerly perceived as benign aspects of the human project — forest clearance for agricultural production, for example — are no longer unambiguously seen as paths towards the Good.

What is needed, according to this new diagnosis, is to 'balance' economic and technological advances with a care and attention for the environmental domain. The demand is for an enlarged scope for valuation practices that encompasses the ecological dimensions of human experience, recreation and life support as well as the domain of produced commodity values. Established economic science, which initially sidelined the problem, has responded to the environmental concerns by enlarging its notion of an optimum. If there are bads as well as goods, and production of goods also entails by-production of bads, then for this there is the theory of negative externality, explaining the divergence between market equilibrium and social optimum, and thus the prospects of correction through a Pigovian tax or, more recently, a Coasian solution based on establishment of tradable property rights. If there is natural resource exhaustion, then for this there is the theory of intertemporal optimal resource use, whereby the correct estimation of opportunity costs in the use of produced and non-produced resources should take into account the willingness-to-pay of future generations. If there are stocks of produced capital and (more problematically) human capital, then nature can be assimilated within enlarged economic rationality through the notion of natural capital.

These are honourable attempts to address the issue. But the environmental valuation problematic requires more than incremental adjustments to the toolkit of market-system economic science. The traditional economic valuation methodology is being proposed for extensions into an arena very different from that for which it was originally devised, namely: (a) extension spatially and materially to the non-produced and largely non-commodified natural environment; and (b) extension temporally to the long term of ecological change, future generations and sustainability concerns. These extensions bring qualitatively new problems for scientific analysis, for economic analysis and for decision-making judgement (Passet, 1979; Hueting 1980; Martinez-Alier, 1991; O'Neill, 1993). Charting a course in this new problem domain is the preoccupation of this book.

1.2 WHAT ARE ENVIRONMENTAL VALUES?

We can learn a lot about environmental values by a catalogue of the things that are being lost. The term 'environmental damage' can have a range of applications. Most obviously it refers to harm inflicted, or potentially inflicted, on creatures whose interests, existence or livelihoods we might or should respect. These include other humans but not only humans. Polluted rivers are a threat to human health, but also to the fish that live in them and to the other animals that may drink from them. The depletion of fisheries stocks in turn, whether due to pollution or to overexploitation, poses a threat to the many communities who depend directly on the sea for subsistence and to the economic livelihood of many others involved in commercial harvesting and processing of fish.

So the term damage may refer to far-reaching changes in the physical environment that adversely affect human life and economic activity, prospects for future generations of life, and also the flourishing of non-human life. This may register, most simply, a sense of loss, as when we learn that there are only a few hundred giraffes left living in the wild. Neither human existence nor economic productivity are likely to be much effected by the loss of the blue whale or the red raft spider, or the disappearance of marshland. So the concern is not only about the conservation of nature as a resource but about the moral considerability of the natural world. Such terms as 'intrinsic value' signal the direct and heartfelt alarm of many people, all around the world, at the seemingly thoughtless destruction of sources of delight, awe and wonderment in the non-human world.

We touch here on sentiments of what is right, respectful and good; of human coexistence with other forms of life in the natural world (Holland, 1997). When people speak of the intrinsic value of nature and of ecosystems, this expresses a feeling that, in some sense, the world is good the way nature made it. Human appreciation of nature takes many different forms. A woodland or mountainside can be a place to walk in with a lover, a favoured area for hunting, a child's delight, a domain of botanical fascination, a source of firewood, a tourist destination. It can become a symbol of a way of life (as in the French *patrimoine naturel*), or a jumble of rocks and weeds that is a piece of God's creation. People thus speak of delighting in nature, of an intimate bond, also of fear, horror and wonderment at nature. Consideration of environmental values in all these different ways raises a range of questions, touching on foundations of ethics and of human perception.

The environment is more than just a physical precondition for human life and productive activity or a habitat for other species, it is also the place and space of meanings where humans lead their lives. Further, these spaces are not merely a playground or spectacle, such as might have substitutes in a local gym, or art gallery. Particular places such as woodlands or coastal fisheries or bathing areas can matter deeply to individuals and communities by virtue of embodying their history and cultural identities. For example, the public significance attached to the damage to forests and lakes in Scandinavia and Germany due to atmospheric pollution reflects their cultural as much as their economic importance. This sense of value of a cherished place or landscape often has a very localized dimension, in the importance local communities place on the ordinary places in or near which they live — a pond or copse of woods — places that from the economic or biological point of view have limited significance. The cultural dimension is also expressed in issues concerning the quality of the urban environment: in the kinds of social life that different urban environments make possible, the effects of the car not only on the quiet of the city, but also on the (in)capacity of individuals to meet and converse in public spaces.

1.3   THE INTERNALIZATION OF ENVIRONMENTAL VALUES

Often the demand for taking the environment into account has been formulated by economists and policymakers in monetary terms, which potentially allows environmental impact and protection questions to be included through an extension of traditional cost–benefit analysis techniques. Yet, many reasons may be given for the difficulty or inappropriateness of monetary valuation, and the corresponding need for decision support techniques that do not depend exclusively on monetary valuation. This divergence in valuation perspectives can be introduced in terms of two differing conceptions of *internalization*. The diagnosis in both versions is that decisionmakers have failed to take proper account of the impact of human economic activity upon the natural environment and the remedy is taking the environment properly into account. The two formulations are:

- Internalization of environmental damages in a narrow sense, referring to an ideal of Pareto efficiency in resource allocation.
- Internalization in a broad sense, referring to political processes and institutions for expressing and resolving or accepting conflicts over environmental concerns.

Environmental valuation perspectives and methods may then be categorized according to which of these concepts of internalization — narrow or broad — they affirm.

In conventional economic terms, internalization requires: (a) developing ways of estimating in monetary terms the opportunity costs associated with alternative uses of economic and environmental resources, which means placing monetary values on environmental goods and services (and also environmental bads); and (b) choosing the course of action that is judged to be best for society in terms of a sum of values. This approach depends on a combination of analytical and normative premises. First, the act of costing environmental damage is taken to mean finding a way of comparing environmental with non-environmental goods and services in monetary terms. We refer to this as *the assumption of monetary commensurability*. Second, the monetization of environmental costs and benefits would provide the basis for maximizing the balance of benefits over costs for society, through applying *the criterion of Pareto efficiency* for project selection decisions.

In slightly simplified terms, the procedure for pursuit of an efficiency goal in the use of an environmental amenity or natural resource is as follows. Before choosing to demolish one more unit of, say, tropical forest, an assessment should be made of whether the benefits to society of the demolition (perhaps to convert the land into farmland, or to make computer paper from the wood pulp) are greater than the costs (such as aesthetic appreciation of trees, or habitat loss for tribal peoples, or contribution to carbon dioxide absorption and to hydrological cycle stability). If the gains on-the-margin outweigh the losses, on we go. This principle of valuation on-the-margin can be applied everywhere and, if it is so applied, it will lead (under certain assumptions) to a 'highest value to society' in the use of economic and environmental resources.

This notion of 'highest value to society' is treacherous and must be treated with care. In formal cost–benefit terms, it corresponds to a state of affairs that is *Pareto efficient* — meaning a situation in which, under the defined constraints on opportunities and actions, all the opportunities for improving the welfare of some individual(s) without lowering that of any other(s) have been exhausted. A policy is thus said to offer a *potential Pareto improvement* if those who gain from the policy could fully compensate the losers and still be better off. Cost–benefit analysis is intended to offer signposts for the directions in which to move to achieve potential Pareto improvements.

Yet, on the one hand a *potential* Pareto improvement can mask a situation where, in reality, some people are left worse off because the theoretically indicated compensation goes unpaid. On the other hand, many (if not most) environmental policy problems are largely about (re)distribution of costs and benefits, not about efficiency gains. Where concerns are about ownership, entitlements or access rights, the fights might indeed be between two (or more) contrasting Pareto efficient resource use situations.

For these reasons and others, Pareto efficiency is insufficient (and perhaps unnecessary) as a criterion for policy. A society that has placed all wealth in the hands of a rich and highly mobile elite, while the others grind and starve, might be Pareto efficient. A society that engages in a consumption extravaganza while leaving future generations to fend for themselves (tyranny of the present) might also be Pareto efficient (Samuels 1972a, 1972b; Samuels and Mercuro, 1979). So notions of justice, honour or fair play may also enter into the scene, as elements of principled policy design, political process or negotiation procedure.

These limitations just mentioned are inherent to the conceptual framework of cost–benefit analysis. They coexist with (and reinforce) the methodological issues that arise in relation to monetary evaluations. A basic presupposition for environmental cost–benefit analysis is that although we cannot introduce all ecological goods and services into actual markets, it is nevertheless possible to extrapolate in various ways from actual market transactions so as to get an estimate in money terms of the value of some environmental good, or the cost of some environmental harm. Environmental good or damage may be assessed in terms of its impact (direct or indirect) on other sectors of activity, for example the production of goods having a market price, or it may be assessed on the basis of substitute or complementary goods that do have a price (for a comprehensive presentation see, for example, Hanley and Spash, 1993).

Operationally, the costing of environmental damage in money terms can be approached in two distinct ways: (i) on the 'supply side' for environmental improvements, by estimates of economic costs that are or might be incurred in abating or repairing damage; and (ii) on the 'demand side' by estimates of the monetary value of the lost or damaged environmental amenity or service itself. Examples of the 'supply side' approach are:

- *Restoration costs* paid (or potentially to be paid) by individuals, firms and state institutions in response to environmental pollution, to maintain or restore buildings, rivers and lakes to certain levels of water quality, fishery stock, and so on, or to remedy human health problems due to pollutants.
- *Avoidance costs* incurred (or potentially incurred) by individuals, firms and state authorities to avoid environmental damage: for example, the costs incurred in introducing traffic calming and noise buffer measures in town; of installing catalytic convertors; of improving safety measures against toxic chemical spills in storage, factory use, and transportation; of diverting a road out of a site of special environmental value.

Note, the monetary figures obtained with these approaches relate to expenditures to achieve improvements in environmental quality or to avoid degradations in quality. So they do not, in themselves, provide an estimate of the monetary value of the benefits gained (or the loss forestalled). Further hypotheses about 'optimal' investment behaviour have to be introduced. The requirement in conventional environmental cost–benefit analysis is to compare the costs of obtaining further environmental improvement (or avoiding further damage) with the benefits obtained. So the implementation of this optimization approach requires money estimates also on the 'demand side' — that is, of the marginal benefits of the environmental protection or enhancement action. The most commonly used methods for quantifying environmental benefits are:

- *The travel cost method,* which estimates a money value on the basis of the amount that people actually pay (in money and time) to gain access to beauty spots, wilderness and so forth.
- *Hedonic pricing,* which correlates the environmental good or bad with some actual market item such as houses, so that variations in the price of houses from one locality to another can be correlated with the presence or absence of some desirable or undesirable environmental feature, for example, a view. How much people are willing to pay is then assumed to reflect their preference for the environmental good in question, or their aversion to a bad.
- *Contingent valuation methods (CVM),* usually conducted through survey or interview of a sample of the interested population. People

are presented with *hypothetical situations* (or, in some cases, simplified laboratory choices) designed to elicit statements about what they would be *willing to pay (WTP)* for a specified environmental improvement, or the *compensation that they would find acceptable (WTA)* in the case of environmental degradation.

The travel cost method and hedonic pricing are often described as revealed preference valuation techniques, which involve deducing a money value on the basis of (a) observed time and money expenditures for goods in a complementary relationship, and (b) underlying hypotheses about optimizing behaviour. They are sometimes referred to as indirect methods. In the case of CVM, by contrast, the worth of environmental features is elicited directly through the questionnaire procedures. Application of these sorts of approaches has received a strong boost by emergence of legal frameworks, notably in the United States, which have promoted CVM as a basis for deciding compensation for natural resource damage due to industrial accident or waste spillage (see NOAA/Arrow et al., 1993).

The environmental cost–benefit analysis in its most simple formulations aims at matching the 'supply' for environmental quality with the 'demand' — thus achieving the highest balance of benefits over costs for the project selected (for example, maximizing net present value, or having marginal abatement cost equal to marginal benefit of pollution abatement). As we have already said, this simple formulation leaves unanswered several important issues, notably concerning the distribution of the costs and benefits, the ways that the valuations (however elicited) might depend on prevailing arrangements of power and property, and the likely inequities in exposure of different groups or different generations to environmental damages, major risks and hazards. The extension of 'valuation' concerns to the environment has, thus, added new dimensions to established distributional concerns (Howarth and Norgaard, 1992; Martinez-Alier and O'Connor, 1996; O'Connor, ed., 1996). These concerns then extend to future generations and their ethical considerability in the face of such problems as the enhanced greenhouse effect (see Spash, 1994a, 1994b).

So in theory and in reality the internalization achieved through CBA procedures is strongly dependent on specific institutional forms and social power relations. The irreversible character of much ecosystem damage (species loss, deforestation, salination of soils, and so on) and of health risks occasioned by accidental release or stockage of durable toxic wastes, raises issues of worsening social inequalities through time (Spash, 1993). Finally, the wholesale destruction of non-human life-forms brings to the fore a range of ethical concerns that the cost–benefit approach cannot very adequately take into account. From this point of view, the citizen or policymaker is faced not with a clear-cut decision between protection and damage, but rather with the distribution of different kinds of damage and benefit across different dimensions of value. There can be conflicts between the avoidance of environmental damages and other social, economic and cultural objectives. There can be conflicts between different timescales of concern. In human reality, criteria of choice are multiple and simultaneous accommodation of divergent principles is not always possible. Compromises must often be made, and finding acceptable compromises for effective policy implementation and robust commercial strategies may require complex processes of negotiation. These are the justifications for adopting the second, broader and institutional perspective on internalization mentioned earlier (O'Neill, 1993; Jacobs, 1997; O'Connor, 1997a; Spash,1997).

These considerations imply the importance of interdisciplinary work for effective environmental policy support and policy assessment analyses. They imply the need to integrate different timescales of significance for quantifying ecological changes, appraising economic opportunities and constraints, and human concerns. They imply the need to integrate explicitly the standard economic concern for produced value with the value dimensions of 'pre-existing' nature. They imply the need to rethink the ways that analyses based on monetary units of measure and imputation can be cross-cut with analyses using non-monetary forms of description and quantification. This is a complex intellectual, cultural and institutional terrain which, even after thirty years of public environmental concern, is still only just beginning to be explored. Many new perspectives are being evoked, alongside modifications of established views. This book gives a selection of current work in the field. All the papers are explorations of perspectives that the authors believe or hope can prove useful in the new preoccupation for 'taking the environment into account'.

1.4   ORGANIZATION OF THE BOOK

The papers brought together in this volume occupy various points on a continuum. For presentation purposes it is useful to identify three points of reference: (1) the *conception* of a valuation exercise (what does it do, or try to do, what should it try to do?); (2) the *tool box* of methods, empirical enquiry procedures and analytical procedures that might be implemented; (3) the *situations* or socio-institutional contexts in which valuation practices may be envisaged.

- Early papers, Chapters 2 to 5 of the book, explore valuation issues essentially at conceptual and methodological levels. The primary concern is with establishing a view about the nature of the problem/process of environmental valuation. What is valuation seeking to do as a measurement and decision support practice? Inevitably this means addressing the question as to what are the important social as well as ecological features of the situations being addressed, so scientific measurement and socio-institutional context issues interact — they cannot be maintained as isolated methodological compartments.

- Papers in the middle of the book, Chapters 6 to 10 are primarily empirical in character, being attempts at discovering, eliciting or appraising or resolving conflicts over environmental values. They are state-of-the-art examples, in quite diverse contexts, that grapple with the real dilemmae of quantification and interpretation of multidimensional realities.
- Papers towards the end, Chapters 11 to 16, represent a return to methodological themes, where the emphasis is on the formulation of evaluation practices that are adequate for particular sorts of environmental problems and institutional (policy, decision-making) contexts.

This division is, of course, a bit artificial. The various methodological discussions are supported by empirical illustrations, and the empirical studies are themselves the sites for methodological reflection (in some cases after the fact, in other cases intentionally). The selection as a whole represents, thus, a good spectrum — principally of European origins — of contemporary thinking and environmental valuation practice. In the following sections of this chapter the contents are outlined.

1.5 CONCEPTS AND PERSPECTIVES FOR ENVIRONMENTAL VALUATION

JOAN MARTINEZ-ALIER, GIUSEPPE MUNDA AND JOHN O'NEILL, in the opening contribution on *Commensurability and Compensability in Ecological Economics*, start from the standpoint of the environment as a site of conflict between many competing values or interests and, more precisely, between the different groups and communities that claim them. How are the conflicts between different dimensions of value and between the different groups who stand to bear gains or losses to be resolved? The traditional approaches grounded in neoclassical economics, such as cost–benefit analysis, attempt resolution through the use of a common measure (marginal monetary valuation) so that losses in one regard can be compared with gains in another. This presumes what we may call *value commensurability*. Yet, as this contribution recalls, the debate on possible incommensurability of values and of different dimensions of value has a long tradition in economics.

These authors argue that the assumptions of value commensurability and interpersonal compensability do not provide adequate foundations for rational environmental choices. In some situations these assumptions deny application of a choice criterion, for example, choosing between two different Pareto efficient situations, which requires introduction of further criteria such as social distribution rules. This inadequacy is especially plain where uncertainties, distributional conflicts and long-term sustainability are major decision-making concerns. Attention is then turned to alternative foundations for environmental evaluation and decision support analyses. They argue that accepting incommensurability does not necessarily entail total incomparability, but can be dealt with in terms of a postulate of *weak comparability* (according to which values or valuation dimensions are irreducibly plural and cannot be uniquely ordered along a single scale). Weak comparability can be considered as a natural epistemological base for multicriteria evaluation, and is proposed by the authors as an appropriate foundation for framing choice problems in the ecological economics domains.

MICHAEL TOMAN IN *Sustainable Decision-making: the State of the Art from an Economics Perspective,* poses the question: what sort of practical guidance on sustainable development can be offered at the present time to decisionmakers on the basis of economic analysis? The multiple time-frames and existential dimensions of environmental significance mean that monetary valuation as proposed by standard economics — in support of traditional cost–benefit analysis — cannot easily be applied to environmental space, amenity and life support functions. On the one hand it can be argued that the search for 'social efficiency' is largely misplaced and that monetary information is anyway as much a matter of power and institutional arrangements as an estimate of relative utility (this is a theme of the contribution by Peter Söderbaum later on in the book). On the other hand it can be argued that monetary valuation is unnecessary and generally inappropriate for achieving rational resource management. Toman adopts a middle position. Starting from the observation that there is no consensus on the definition of sustainability from a policy point of view, he rejects approaches based on mechanistic application of a 'rule' for sustainability in favour of processes and procedures that can bring together the range of information and viewpoints in political decision-making. In particular he suggests a variety of reasons for seeking to embed the insights from established economic analyses — such as perspectives on opportunity costs and on the potential roles of markets and other institutions to provide for efficient use of resources — in a wider sociological perspective on information for sustainability. He notes how increasing numbers of economists are coming to accept that a simple cost–benefit perspective on policy options is insufficient to address the complexity of distributional, ethical and scientific issues inherent in the domain. Moreover, community values such as social solidarity and the importance attached to a 'sense of place' can reinforce the importance of procedural issues, such as inclusion of stakeholder participation, for effective policy design and implementation. Toman also emphasizes that, in this context of scientific uncertainties, complexity and controversies, it is impossible to insulate science practice — including economic analysis as well as natural sciences enquiry — from value debates. While integrity of scientific enquiry is important, the links between the priorities of scientific enquiry and social preoccupations must be reassessed regularly and openly. This permanent debate would be a crucial part of the 'pluralistic' approach that Toman advocates.

BEAT BÜRGENMEIER in *Environmental Protection: Towards a Socio-Economic Policy Design,* brings out the inadequacy of mechanistic perspectives on valuation in another way. One traditional justification for environmental valuation is the establishment of pollution taxes. Yet, the argument that information provided by economists can be the basis for setting an optimal tax would seem to have been discredited some time ago because of difficulties of establishing marginal cost and benefit functions. Cost–benefit case studies normally give a point estimate of environmental damages (the benefit from pollution reduction) at current pollution levels rather than a functional relationship between pollution and damages. The iterative tax approach suggested by Beckerman in the 1970s is politically impractical and inefficient due to lost capital investments generated.

Thus, the appropriate focus for economists would seem to be contributing to the design of socially acceptable taxes. Yet the widespread use of cost–benefit analysis as the central indicator of the best tax level continues (for example, in debates about carbon dioxide taxation) and putative efficiency remains the unique criterion in the economists' contribution. As Bürgenmeier points out, one of the effects of this straitjacket is that economists generally have neglected to analyse the aspects of tax design which would make them socially acceptable, and this has contributed to ill-framed environmental tax options rejected by the public. For example, the attempts by the British government to introduce an energy tax in the mid-1990s failed largely because equity issues were ignored and the old and poor would have suffered. Bürgenmeier presents some evidence on the types of concerns Swiss businesses have about the introduction of ecological taxes, which has particular pertinence in light of the rejection of carbon dioxide taxation in Switzerland after a consultation process. He uses factor analysis to group concerns into four categories. Of these two relate to neo-classical economic arguments and would be addressed by standard models.

However the remaining two factors relate to wider concepts of the institutional setting and uncertainty about objectives. This example is used to introduce a deeper problem underlying economics which is the necessity to use value judgements in all economics and the inseparability of normative and positive issues. Thus, Bürgenmeier emphasizes the need for economics to take on a wider perspective in accepting ethical and social insights, and for policy recommendations to pay attention to moral issues. He rejects the 'objective' scientific approach which has been portrayed as the only way to view economics by most mainstream economists and some ecological economists. The importance of socio-economic aspects such as changing institutions and the role of different 'actors' is then brought to the fore.

PETER SÖDERBAUM addresses himself to *Valuation as Part of a Microeconomics for Ecological Sustainability*. His institutionalist perspective builds on the observation that some actors in society are more powerful than others, and, more particularly, that this inequality is manifest partly in the currency given to some ideas about economic and ecological management at the expense of others. Söderbaum seeks to offer an alternative to the neoclassical utility-maximizing paradigm at the heart of neoclassical economics, an alternative 'ideological orientation' that he refers to as an 'actor–network model' emphasizing the complexity of relationships and interactions.

This view, which builds on Söderbaum's earlier published expositions, is then fleshed out in order to offer an interpretation of valuation as an institutional process where what counts most is the power struggle to maintain or change the dominant ideological orientation — not just the identification of opportunity costs in the monetary sense alone. This places emphasis on the complex tissue of social interactions, and on the process of conflictual change to the institutions, perceptions and commitments of actors in society. For example, in relation to a productive sector such as agriculture there are consumers who place high priority on 'green' products, and others who don't care. There may be farmers who are receptive to ecological concerns, including those who seek to implement organic farming practices, and there will be some bureaucrats in administrative roles who also have 'green' sympathies. The amount of time needed for the efforts by committed actors to bring about change in consumers' perceptions and in administrative arrangements cannot be deduced by mechanistic models of supply and demand. So 'valuation' in this context is a dynamic disequilibrium concept, a matter of perception and power before becoming translated (in part) into monetary manifestations. Valuation refers partly to the commitments of social actors — that is, their ideological orientations that are translated into efforts to preserve parts of the status quo or to bring about change. From this point of view the application of cost–benefit analysis techniques to environmental problems is, in itself, a matter of ideological orientation, and the institutional economist would focus not just on the numbers that can be produced but more paticularly on the relative power of the various actors involved in the policy scene and the ways that the CBA numbers may serve or obstruct the interests and commitments of these actors. This is an intuitively appealing socio-economic analysis perspective, but whose real value might only be seen through some in-depth future case studies.

1.6   EMPIRICAL ENQUIRIES INTO ENVIRONMENTAL VALUE

If the essentially methodological contributions of the opening chapters establish some elements of conceptual order in relation to the complexity of the valuation domain, the group of contributions that follow bring out this same complexity through a confrontation of valuation concepts with difficulties of empirical implementation. We see here the interface between the difficulties of definition of the policy problem, of formulation in operational terms of a management approach, and of obtaining meaningful quantifications that can serve the specified management purposes.

DOUGLAS MACMILLAN, DAVID HARLEY and RUTH MORRISON discuss *Cost-Effectiveness Analysis of Forest Biodiversity Enhancement* as an example of the application of expert judgement in the environmental evaluation field. In the area of project decision analysis the difficulty of estimating benefits is often seen as the major problem with the use of cost–benefit analysis. This has led to an interest in using political processes or scientific experts to establish a set of goals which are then to be achieved at the lowest cost. Thus, cost-effectiveness is offered as a perspective by which tools developed for cost–benefit analysis can be used while avoiding the criticism levelled against attempts to establish monetary valuation of environmental benefits.

Macmillan et al. present a study of forest biodiversity enhancement to show how this cost-effectiveness approach can be made operational. Their case study looks at the extent to which an individual pinewood created under a current British government grant scheme could recreate a range of natural features including species composition, structural diversity, and ecological processes. Eleven criteria, relating to woodland and landscape ecology, were used as indicators of effectiveness in ecosystem restoration. These criteria were weighted to express relative importance as judged by experts, and these same experts were used to attribute scores to individual schemes for each criteria. For some criteria, direct measurement of pinewood characteristics was possible and some such data was available directly from grant applications. The more difficult criteria to score were genetic integrity, species composition, and tree density, and for these expert judgement was fully employed. The scores from twelve experts were then averaged for each pinewood. Costs were taken as the payment from the government grant which would be made to each forest. Results are then given for forests at 10 and 100 years. The success of the application can be judged from the useful insights the authors are able to make into the necessity to redesign the grant scheme.

Although the cost-effectiveness analysis has been successfully used by these analysts, some interesting questions for valuation procedures are left unresolved (see also Spash 1997). A fundamental aspect of their approach is the use of scientific experts. The selection procedure for establishing this panel will determine the criteria used and scores attributed to a specific project. This would quickly become an issue where environmental projects are operating in areas of complexity and controversy and there is no agreement on directly measurable criteria. In addition, the use of experts alone may be inappropriate for some environmental projects where wider social issues are relevant.

Another unresolved issue is the extent to which quantification of costs in monetary terms can itself pose problems. In the case study reported here, costs are narrowly defined and given by a current institutional framework that is, grant costs. However, in order to generalize the approach the definition of what is to be regarded as a 'cost', to be evaluated in monetary terms, is required. Cost-effectiveness has an apparent advantage over cost–benefit analysis in that one of the controversial aspects of monetary valuation is removed when an environmental performance goal or criterion is set by experts or by a public policy negotiated process rather than determined by reference to net benefits generated. However, some projects will involve environmental costs which are identical to the benefits of other projects. For example, choosing the least-cost strategy for carbon dioxide reduction might involve a comparison of carbon sequestration via reforestation with introducing alternative heating technologies. The costs of the reforestation option must be estimated as a net social cost, that is, taking into account any benefits such as biodiversity or recreation. Similarly, the social costs of alternative heating technologies will be reduced by the extent to which, say, other air pollutants or particulates are removed as a result; so improving human health. The cost-effectiveness approach can either ignore all the wider social costs around which there is controversy, or include them as an additional objective (which would need to be defined, for example by experts), or treat them as a monetary cost. In adopting either the second or third option, cost-effectiveness is transformed effectively into a constrained cost–benefit analysis.

Finally, one interesting aspect of the cost-effectiveness approach is that it highlights the requirement for an understanding of the institutional constraints and political objectives, and then working within them. To some extent this can mean accepting those constraints as appropriate. Yet this has become questionable in many areas of environmental policy, and so — as emphasized in the contributions by Toman, Burgenmeier and Söderbaum already discussed — the cost-effectiveness approach needs, like the cost–benefit approach, to be situated explicitly in a broader perspective of institutional change, conflict resolution and political negotiation.

GAIE MENDELSSOHN, in *The Relevance of Economic Valuation for Species Conservation Policy: The Case of the African Elephant,* provides a striking illustration of the problem of inadequate institutional arrangements for environmental valuation and management. Direct regulation without adequate funding for enforcement is a continuing feature of species loss. This type of approach also has the effect of removing problems from popular media attention (at least in the short term) on the assumption that blanket regulation has effectively solved the problem. In addition, regulation has created protected areas without working to integrate local communities with conservation goals, and the violation of the areas has become a major problem for endangered species preservation. Meanwhile pressures are rising for the operation of markets to exploit various aspects of species such as whales, elephants, and tigers. Disaffected local communities wish to exploit stocks, and politicians can gain from supporting the right to 'development' and equal treatment amongst nations to 'unlock' natural resources. Freedom of choice on the demand side of the equation also has considerable weight in the debate. At present CITES seems to be moving towards trade in ivory with the sale of stocks by selected African countries to Japan. The International Whaling Commission is also under pressure to increase the absurdly named and thinly disguised 'scientific whaling', which supplies Japanese meat markets. Those recommending species conservation driven by scientific considerations have begun to realize socio-economic issues cannot be ignored in policy formation.

Both species loss and, more generally, biodiversity loss have been regarded by some environmental economists as problems of optimal depletion and incorrect pricing (for example, Swanson). This familiar pricing approach requires the non-market aspects of a species such as the elephant be included in policy calculations if not actual markets. The efficient and effective way to proceed with optimal preservation or extinction will then be forthcoming. Preservation requires that elephants, for example, be evaluated as a sound investment giving a good market rate of return relative to other assets. Social optimality requires capturing the role of elephants in such aspects as maintaining the ecosystem of which they are a part, and assessing whether this enduring value (suitably discounted) outweighs the commercializable benefits that can be obtained in the more short term. As Mendelssohn points out there are considerations of uncertainty and complexity here which defy cause–effect analysis. Furthermore, this purely economic approach reduces the value of the species (and its individual members) to their currently identifiable human usefulness. A fundamental assumption in the pricing approach is that conservation values can be equated to monetary amounts.

Mendelssohn appraises the relationship between economic exploitation and conservation values by reviewing a range of studies on elephant valuation. She argues that a new approach is required which unifies the two broad dimensions of value, but which also accounts for the social, political and cultural dimensions of environmental policy. In particular, relatively unsophisticated ranking approaches are recommended as offering potentially useful opportunities for interdisciplinary collaboration amongst experts. The central issue here is seen to be the need to discuss the range of values relevant to the policy debate rather than the creation of sophisticated models which distract attention away from the broader issues in the guise of quantification/objectivity. (Both economists and ecologists can be found guilty of this diversion.) One aspect of the discussion which is required but currently neglected is to identify clearly the various qualitatively different goals being sought from conservation policy. These goals vary from economists to ecologists but also from developed to developing countries and national governments to local communities — and also, as Söderbaum would say, according to the different ideological orientations of the stakeholders involved. The problem which remains is how to design institutional processes which allow acceptable decisions to be made which account for all these various interests.

Amongst the fundamental issues of valuation methodology is the question of entitlements, as for example expressed in the various claims on property rights made by different groups. This applies both within and across generations. It seems common sense to say that the application of valuation methods should be conducted so as to respect accepted property rights where they are well defined, or to make explicit propositions about new rights structures to be introduced. One of the currently most popular tools of cost–benefit analysis is contingent valuation. However, the contingent valuation method as recommended for use by the NOAA panel, is conceived solely with a willingness-to-pay format. This implies attributing a particular set of property rights a priori, namely that those asked their WTP do not have prior entitlement. In addition, the exclusion of willingness to accept has been identified as imposing biases that, in some cases at least, imply underestimation of environmental benefits from the points of view of some of the interested parties involved.

ERKKI MÄNTYMAA, in *Willingness-to-pay, Willingness to Accept: a CVM Field Study of Environmental Commodities,* brings into focus these several issues. The study concentrates on the specific problem of trying to explain the discrepancy between WTP and WTA in terms of substitution effects, as proposed by Hanemann, yet the issues raised are quite far-reaching. Mäntymaa uses both open-ended and dichotomous choice formats in a postal survey of the Finnish public. This gave a sample of 1,622 responses which were split into four subsamples (that is, WTP and WTA for each of the open-ended and dichotomous choice samples). Respondents were also asked to give a score on a five-point scale of the extent to which the two 'commodities' were to them seen as substitutes for each other. These scores were used to categorize respondents by 'substitutability group'. Despite the relatively large sample, some of the high substitutability groups had low or zero respondents. Mäntymaa generally confirms the divergence by substitutability and that WTP < WTA. However, some of the specific results are interesting and provoke reflection on the study design.

First, it may be recalled that the dichotomous choice format has been recommended by the NOAA panel as giving 'conservative' values relative to open-ended questions. But here the reverse is generally the case, with the divergence strongest between the two WTA survey results.

Second, Mäntymaa has followed the general tradition of environmental economists by expanding the concept of 'commodity', but introduces a design innovation. Two institutional contexts with their associated property rights are the 'environmental commodities' between which individuals are required to chose. This results in asking WTP and WTA for the property rights associated with access to the countryside in Finland. The extension of market pricing to many aspects of the environment has proved controversial and the attempted development of existence values as a utilitarian concept has created some confusion in the literature. This additional extension by Mäntymaa seem no less controversial or problematical. Here property rights over access are described for the survey without reference to any specific environmental quantity or quality change in any specific site, species or other aspect of the environment. The respondents' reactions to the survey would therefore be of particular interest and particularly the occurrence of and motivations behind positive bids, protest bids and outliers.

The treatment of outliers and zero bids for reasons besides zero valuation are in fact a problem for all CVM studies. In the case of the Mäntymaa study a process of exclusion of bids is performed using a variety of often arbitrary criteria (this is noted in a footnote by the author). For example, bids exceeding 5 per cent of an individual's annual income are excluded. This kind of procedure is common enough amongst CVM studies but is methodologically questionable and becomes of concern when a large proportion of the sample is thusly removed from analysis. For example, Mäntymaa reports reviewing 74 zero bids and defining 59 as protests, while a further 7 bids were removed for other reasons, which resulted in 66 out of 273 responses of that subsample being removed (that is, 25 per cent of the sample).

The concern of Mäntymaa to identify 'real' zero bids is similar to the occupation of many CVM studies with the concept of 'true' values. This implies that valuation is essentially a process of discovery and inference about features of the objective world (namely, the preferences of people, the opportunity sets and substitution possibilities open to people, the intertemporal opportunity costs, and so on). The scientific enquiry into possible consequences of human choices for the future of biological and physical systems on the one hand, and into people's perceptions and value commitments on the other hand, is unquestionably a foundation of good environmental valuation practice. Yet, as we have already seen with reference to early chapters of this book, the extent to which this enquiry can satisfactorily be conducted as a process of 'discovering the truth' is very much a matter of debate.

SANDRA GOODMAN, SHABBAR JAFFRY and BILL SEABROOKE, in their discussion of *Conservation Quality of the British Coast*, raise many of these methodological issues. They provide an empirical example of an increasingly typical use to which CVM is now being put, namely prioritizing public expenditure and so helping policy formation. This is at least the theoretical aim of such CVM work, although the extent to which government administrations actually make use of the results is highly uncertain. (In the UK, a proposed tax on aggregates has specifically sought to employ a CVM study as guidance, but there are few if any other examples to date.)

The researchers defined the British coastline as their 'environmental commodity'. A sample of 806 in-house interviews was obtained using an open-ended WTP format. The environmental change was described in terms of avoiding a catastrophic and irreversible loss of species and habitat over 75 years. Respondents were asked whether they were prepared to pay in principle and then, if affirmative, asked the amount for the entire coastline. This amount was then used as the budget from which they would draw for projects designed to protect 10 per cent of the coastal zone. A semi-log linear bid curve was estimated, as well as a probit model with the payment in principle question used as dependent variable.

One of the cited reasons for choosing CVM as opposed to other tools of cost–benefit analysis is the ability to estimate non-use or indirect use values. Despite the relatively unadventurous starting points of the study, it develops into an interesting exercise of evaluation of the validity and limits of the CVM approach itself. In the formulation of the study the authors adopted without much question the notion of 'total economic value' (being defined as the sum of marginal use and non-use valuations for the environmental resource or feature in question). They also display clearly at several points their adherence to the idea of a true value premised on an underlying stratum of individual preferences and substitutability. This leads to deep methodological waters. When it comes to analysing the survey results, they look closely at those refusing to pay and classify 161 out of 238 as protests, this being 76 per cent of the refusal responses. In addition, 17 per cent of those giving positive WTP bids were designated as invalid estimates of 'respondents' true WTP'. Probing into the possible reasons for both zero and positive bids — more than in most CVM studies — the authors suggest that respondents constructed their value statements during the CVM, rather than retrieving a previously formed preference. They then conclude that individuals' environmental preferences are multidimensional and difficult to assess monetarily.

Some other features of the results are also noteworthy. In the study, natural and cultural features were stated by respondents to be a dominant reason for valuing coastlines. Motives relating to option, existence and bequest values were identified amongst 86–92 per cent of the sample desiring coastal protection. Individuals were thus found to express a preference for conservation quality, yet this failed to translate systematically into monetary valuation statements.

A central hypothesis of the study was that such non-use values could be related back to physical characteristics of environmental quality used by scientists as indicators for the protection of conservation values. This hypothesis was not validated by the study, and the authors conclude that public notions of coastal value may diverge from what conservation scientists would identify as the object of an ecologically preferred management strategy.

These features corroborate empirically the propositions about plurality of perceptions and ideological orientations, and can be taken as evidence for incommensurabilities. The observed divergence between public and scientific perceptions is interesting to reflect upon in relation to proposals for the use of experts to guide policy (as in the procedures suggested in the chapters by Macmillan et al. and Mendelssohn).

Generalizing, this sort of result suggests that CVM type enquiries might effectively be used as a tool for investigating environmental values in a broad sense. Methodologically an open mind as to the psychology of individuals — their perceptions, commitments, and concern for economically or 'scientifically' important features — is called for, rather than an imposed model as suggested by the NOAA panel (which rejects on an *a priori* basis any unfavourable and non-conformist behaviour). The focus of research attention may in this way be broadened to include environmental attitudes and social institutions as explanations of behaviour (including survey response).

Behavioural psychology is the dimension specifically explored by EIJA MOISSEINEN in her analysis of *Behavioural Intentions in the Case of the Saimaa Seal*. As can be seen in the other CVM studies reported in this book, economists have often regarded motivational research as non-economic but then, confronted by their inability to explain their survey results, have been struggling with explanations of observed behaviour. Using the case of protecting an endangered seal species, Moisseinen investigates the attitude–behaviour research and the interdisciplinary area between economics and psychology. The work was stimulated by a CVM survey which found a large discrepancy between support for a species protection programme and the stated WTP for that programme. A second CVM was then conducted in association with behavioural questions, and this is the study whose results are reported here.

The second survey attempted to apply Fishbein and Ajzen's theory of reasoned action to explain respondents' WTP. This theory regards an initial behaviour as a function of social norms and the individual's attitude, interpreted as a judgement over the importance of consequences related to the requested behaviour. A combination of dichotomous choice and open-ended payment questions were used in a mail survey. This yielded 215 responses for use in the behavioural analysis.

The attitudinal aspects of the intention to pay model were found to be related to the standard socio-economic variables used in a bid function. A model combining some socio-economic variables with an attitudinal and a social norm variable was statistically superior. However the socio-economic variables seem to add little in terms of explanatory power. A comparison of a standard bid curve model with the one presented here would have aided this direct comparison of the benefits of adopting a different psychological interpretation of CVM results. Despite the absence of this comparison the results are suggestive of how standard economic models give a narrowed a priori interpretation of human behaviour.

An additional finding by Moisseinen is that private actions to protect the environment are more likely to be undertaken than a WTP action. That is, individuals stated a willingness to respond by private action rather than paying to a government scheme. Moisseinen suggests that this is self-protection as a reaction to endogenous risk, and that such self-protection is an important aspect to be taken into account when designing environmental protection schemes.

1.7   VALUATION METHODOLOGY AND
INSTITUTIONAL CONTEXTS

Despite their methodological variety, all of the empirical studies just reviewed reinforce the observation that establishing monetary commensurability for natural systems features is a problematical business. Thus, while both produced (economic) and pre-existing (ecological) goods/services contribute fundamentally to human welfare, there is more to environmental valuation than a search for a single unit or index of this human welfare.

Environmental quality is a psychological and also material requirement for human welfare and for sustainable economic activity. The recognition of this need may doubtless be considered as a kind of social demand for maintenance of environmental functions, however, a demand curve in the traditional neoclassical sense can be a poor representation of this (Hueting, 1980; Brouwer, et al., 1996).

For example the approach may be taken that economic resource management for sustainability should fulfill two complementary functions: the delivery of an ecological welfare base through assuring maintenance of critical environmental functions; and the delivery of an economic welfare base through production of economic goods and services (cf. Faucheux and O'Connor, eds, 1998). The supply of and demand for ecological goods and services (natural resources, amenities, waste reception, environmental life support functions) is here analysed as *complementary to and interdependent with* economic goods and services, but this is not a symmetrical relationship of complementarity. The geophysical cycles (including ocean and atmospheric currents), landscapes and ecosystems are, notwithstanding long centuries of human influence, essentially pre-existing (they are not purely human artifacts and are not produced solely by human hand). Appraisal of their human significance involves cultural and psychological dimensions of a quite different sort from the assessment of a produced commodity's value. The change processes for the systems in question are complex and marked by irreversibilities. So the quantification of the damage that may be done to ecosystems and the opportunity costs of exploitative use, is a matter of much scientific uncertainty. Finally, the resolution of social conflicts over conservation and development policies requires that a wide range of divergent ethical and cultural sensibilities, as well as economic interest claims, be addressed.

One way to analyse this social demand, in economic terms, for environmental quality is from the point of view that economic resources must be committed (directly or indirectly) in order to maintain a desired level of environmental quality functions. This economic resource allocation can, in some respects, be quantified, so that a link is made between the social demand for environmental services and its economic costs. The evaluation process then typically involves:

- description in social, aesthetic and scientific terms of environmental functions as currently understood, with acknowledgement of uncertainties and scientific controversies;
- identification of alternatives — that is, of visions of possible and desirable futures, and of the resource management choices that would be entailed by them;
- appraisal of the vulnerabilities of identified features and systems of value, and hence of the significance of the damages/ hazards through social processes of value articulation.

In effect, as suggested in the contribution, by Toman and Macmillan et al., the environmental policy objectives may be identified based on scientific information and socio-political processes, and economic analysis may then be brought to bear to identify cost-effective responses and to assess the distribution of benefits and burdens of the different options for achieving the goals. A variety of approaches are being developed for systematizing valuation work in this way. Some are primarily methodological, others centre more on institutional and social process aspects. The contributions making up the third part of this book give examples of these sorts of explicitly multidimensional and multidisciplinary perspectives.

ANDREW GIBBONS, in *Sustainable Development and Appraisal Methodology*, looks at options available for environmental policy appraisal in the context of the United Kingdom's new Environment Agency charged with an integrated environmental regulatory role for England and Wales. This chapter offers an insightful overview of how pre-existing appraisal and regulatory practices now grouped under the Agency are being adapted to respond to new legislative requirements. Gibbons discusses especially the case of Integrated Pollution Control (IPC) applied to seriously polluting industries, including Best Practicable Environmental Option appraisal (BPEO), and also looks more briefly at cost–benefit issues in water resource management.

Created under the Environment Act 1995, the UK Environment Agency is charged with a range of functions having for their principal aim 'attaining sustainable development'. According to the provisions establishing the agency, the approaches to be adopted should be consistent with precepts of social cost–benefit analysis and environmental assessment, while also meeting other leglislative and political requirements. The agency has to reconcile the divergences that can exist between perspectives on sustainable development emerging from scientific and environmental viewpoints, official government perspectives on policy for sustainable development, and the conventions of social cost–benefit analysis in neoclassical economics. This tension is made explicit in the ministerial guidance issued by the Environment, Agriculture, Fisheries and Food ministries in 1996 to the new agency, which specified (inter alia) the following contributions: to take a long-term perspective, especially for irreversible impacts or those affecting intergenerational equity; to maintain biodiversity; to maximize the scope for cost-effective investment by business in improved technologies and management techniques; and others. Also, it is stated that the agency must 'take into account the likely costs and benefits' in the exercise of its powers.

As Gibbons discusses, these provisions can be regarded as implying a form of appraisal in the spirit of cost–benefit analysis. Yet, the legislation makes no explicit requirement about the weight that should be given to any particular kind of impact (damage or benefit). So the agency is left with a certain freedom, and also the necessity to determine its own approach. The official guidance does recognize that in many contexts 'prices' for environmental benefits and damages will be absent. The question of how to adapt or reconcile cost–benefit perspectives to the objective of sustainability is, however, less clearly articulated.

The discussion of the BPEO procedures is particularly revealing. Under this approach, the environmental 'externalities' of an existing or prospective industrial activity are appraised for each option available to the industry operator, and comparisons are made in terms of the identified physical and social impacts, not generally in monetary terms. According to Gibbons, the underlying ambition is to identify an option for which the marginal costs of abatement is somewhere close to the marginal social benefit of the environmental protection. This would approximate the 'first-best' optimization criterion of social cost–benefit analysis, except that in the absence of 'complete information' this can only be a matter of judgement which, he asserts, should be made as consistent and transparent as possible.

This official ideological formulation seems opaque. It can be agreed that 'complete information is rarely available' and establishing a commensurability of the various sorts of impacts is difficult. Yet, the judgements in question are decisions bearing much more directly on the distribution (including intertemporal distribution) of economic and environmental benefits and costs — including judgements about what sorts of environmental and technological risks the society accepts and who will bear these risks — than on the equalization of costs and benefits on the margin. In other words (and this is indeed at the heart of neoclassical welfare theory: see Samuels, 1992; Howarth and Norgaard, 1993; Schnaiberg et al., 1986; O'Connor and Muir, 1995; Muir, 1996 ; Faucheux, Muir and O'Connor 1997), the so-called 'social optimum' is not identifiable through mere technical estimations of opportunity costs on-the-margins. Rather it can more properly be understood as an outcome of the social arbitration of distributional issues which establishes the 'property rights' framework within which efficient resource uses might be pursued.

Although not discussed by Gibbons as such, these distributional dimensions of regulatory judgement and the related ambiguities attached to the formulation and pursuit of the 'sustainable development' objective are brought out sharply in reference to the BPEO procedures. The basic rule under the current legislation is that, for any 'prescribed' industrial process (as designated in the legislation), authorization for operations should be granted subject to the application of BATNEEC — that is, the implementation of Best Available Techniques Not Entailing Excessive Cost. Technological performance refers to the prevention or reduction of releases into a given environmental medium of the noxious substance(s) in question. In cases where the process is likely to involve many different substance releases and/or more than one environmental medium, the application of BPEO and of BATNEEC in particular becomes multidimensional. Views about what is 'best' will inevitably involve judgements about compromises or trade-offs between different dimensions of environmental risk and performance. These judgements will in practice, says Gibbons, tend to focus around identifiable discontinuities or 'steps' in the relevant marginal cost functions. So, for example, society may deem the reasonable acceptance of a level of abatement effort beyond which the (economic) costs to firms rise steeply, and avoidance of severe and irreversible (environmental) impacts that would result when noxious releases go beyond critical environmental thresholds. Through the use of these tangible 'proxies' for marginal cost and benefit information, a kind of fuzzy 'social negotiation space' would be identified within which acceptable solutions may be found.

Two comments can be made in this context. First, referring to the search for 'satisfactory' performance would have been better — recalling Herbert Simon's concept of 'satisficing rationality' — rather than preserving the reference point of a 'first best' social optimum. Second and more important, the existence of a technological option that will, simultaneously, satisfy the criteria of 'non-excessive costs' for the economic sector in question and minimal damage for the environmental media in question, cannot be guaranteed. This is crucial, because in cases where the trade-off between economic viability and environmental performance is sharp, the risk is that the 'social compromise' implied by the judgement processes of the agency's operations might, in reality, devalue the long-term environmental performance goals established in the legislation. The *de facto* 'social optimum' may be biased excessively towards present economic interests (echoing the famous status quo bias of conventional cost–benefit analysis procedures) and the 'sustainable development' objective of the legislation will be undermined.

TOM CROWARDS, in *Combining Economics, Ecology and Philosophy : Safe Minimum Standards of Environmental Protection*, gives a discussion that is more overtly methodological than Gibbons, and which brings out exactly this set of tensions about the formulation of the goal of sustainable development as a 'balancing' act between economic and environmental interests. The concept of safe minimum standard (SMS) was originally introduced by Ciriacy-Wantrup (1952) as a way of coping with uncertainties and irreversibilities in environmental policy. The idea is to avoid courses of action that entail risks of serious and irreversible damages to natural features or to future economic interests (there is a parallel with the more recent enunciation of the Precautionary Principle); the way proposed to achieve this is the respect of safe minimum standards such as non-invasion of sensitive wildlife ecosystems or avoidance of toxic waste dispersal in biological systems.

Croward presents SMSs as a policy instrument in the general spirit of environmental cost–benefit analysis, that is, as a way of seeking to consider benefits of a proposal in comparison with costs — the appraisal being extended to *possible (uncertain) but unquantifiable costs*. He notes, however, that the treatment of unquantifiable risks essentially involves the question of ethical attitudes, and as such the rule of respect for SMS can be interpreted as a social judgement about appropriate intertemporal distribution of environmental risks. The application of SMSs is thus — although Crowards does not say this explicitly — a pragmatic way of shifting the distribution of entitlements so as to furnish an improved economic and ecological endowment for future generations. However, we would emphasize, more than Croward himself does, that this intertemporal (re)distribution dimension is logically distinct from efficiency of resource use. The arbitration being proposed between benefit opportunities foregone by the present generation and dangers being generated for future generations is based on such considerations of morality rather than optimality in the Pareto sense (see Spash 1993). (In situations of possible severe and irreversible damage, the notion of a potential Pareto improvement loses meaningful application, and to quantify compensation payments on the basis of fractional percentages of nasty death makes little sense.)

Croward reviews meticulously the different formulations of SMSs in the environmental policy literature and discusses the various categories of costs and benefits and the issues associated with their quantification. In effect he ends up formulating the sustainable development objective as a dilemma. Whereas Ciriacy-Wantrup presented the respect of SMSs as a binding criterion and considered that the costs imposed on society would be relatively minor, more recent commentators (notably Bishop, 1978) pointed to the possibility that avoidance of *all* serious ecological risks associated with technological and economic development might be strictly speaking impossible and, at the very least, could impose very severe costs on present society. So Bishop proposed an important modification, recommending that SMSs be adopted unless the social costs involved are unacceptably large. This is a non-trivial modification!

First, who decides what is acceptably or unacceptably large? This is inevitably a social judgement, and will have long-term implications raising concerns over intergenerational equity.

Second, if the SMS relates to notions of critical thresholds, the effect of the Bishop modification is to introduce a countervailing critical threshold concept on the side of current economic interests. In effect a compromise must be sought between between two fundamentally distinct commitments — that towards present economic interests, and that towards future security interests (to avoid imposing potentially disastrous hazards).

This suggests that the famous Brundtland formulation of sustainable development as meeting the needs of the present without compromising the interests of the future, is more a formula of hope than a rigorous policy guideline. What happens when the conflict between respect for the two principles is sharp, and one or other of the principles will have to be compromised? Indeed, is this already the case with fundamental technological hazards such as nuclear technologies, genetic engineering releases, climate system perturbations and species losses? (If so, then for the offending already-generated hazards we are already in the domain of fatality rather than rationality, and the Precautionary Principle cannot be applied.)

As Crowards concludes, no simple calculation process will resolve these policy tensions. Scientific and economic cost–benefit information can be marshalled, but the role of power, ideology and interests in modulating commitments of principle cannot be avoided. Crowards refers to the need for a kind of supraeconomic decision-making process that would involve mediation, negotiation and participation.

One might wonder whether, in these circumstances, the distinction that Crowards makes between the economic and supraeconomic becomes a bit strained. What is most required, perhaps, is for economists to become more competent and aware of the significance of their own value commitments and involvement in the processes of real-power arbitration of conflicts.

The need to tackle head-on the limits to monetization as a basis for ecological economics decision-making is the theme of HÉLÈNE CONNOR's contribution *Taking Non-Monetizable Impacts into Account in an Eco-Development Strategy*. In situations marked by long timescales of ecological change, uncertainties, social conflicts and complex interactions of ecosystem components, making meaningful money value estimates for

the significance of environmental change becomes difficult. The figures
can become quite arbitrary. Yet, remarks Connor, the unquantifiable
elements of economic and ecological change have often been placed in the
basket of 'too difficult' and simply excluded from consideration.

Connor sets out to offer a typology of non-monetizable impacts (NMIs)
and to identify effective ways of dealing with them, taking the energy
sector as an example. Her starting point, taking inspiration from René
Passet (1979) is to insist that NMIs exist as phenomena or possible
phenomena that are unquantifiable and not monetizable *as an expression
of the very logic of nature*. That is, NMIs are a manifestation of the
complexity of ecosystem processes, they defy rationalization in
conformity with the economic concepts of marginal productivity,
opportunity cost and so on. So NMIs are no longer a residual category due
to our ignorance, they are a feature of our world constructed dialectically
at the interface of economic calculation and natural complexity.

NMIs can be partly categorized, she suggests, according to the degree
of knowledge we have about them. Some impacts reveal themselves
quickly and their causes can readily be identified. Other impacts reveal
themselves only over long periods of time (even though the triggering
event may be very short, such as a single accident), and cannot be
definitively described. In this category are some deadly diseases or
deformation effects induced by chemical and biological accidents. Some
impacts may be difficult to isolate from the cumulative ecological change
processes, such as vegetation changes that may be due partly to human-
induced climate change. Some impacts may be partly non-material, such
as the significance of disappearance of ethnic or cultural groups. NMIs
can also be categorized by spatial dimensions (local, regional, global), the
timescales of their manifestations and the degree of their irreversibility
(for example as measured by time and energy that would be required to
undo the impact, if that is possible at all).

What does taking NMIs into account mean? For Connor as for many of
the other contributors to this volume, the action of taking the environment
into proper account cannot be reduced to a practice of precise
measurement and optimization. Internalization must, under these
circumstances, be given different meaning, referring to the emergence of
political processes and institutional arrangements through which concerns
for environmental quality and conservation are expressed, and conflicts
resolved. Valuation practice then becomes more than just scientific and
economic analysis of opportunity costs and consequences of alternative
resource management actions. It is also a matter of practical ethics and
political philosophy for the understanding of norms and rules of proper
social conduct and conflict resolution.

As approaches that can have usefulness, Connor mentions multicriteria
analyses (following the spirit of weak comparability enunciated by

Martinez-Alier, Munda and O'Neill in the opening contribution of this volume), qualitative criteria of acceptability and non-acceptability (for example, veto rules), and also Delphi consultations that seek to elicit expert insights and judgements. In addition or as complements, various institutional approaches need to be developed that improve the capacity of people in society to identify and assess the NMIs that affect them. These approaches are illustrated discursively by Connor with reference to energy options — the NMIs of nuclear and fossil fuel energies being considered in relation to options for large-scale renewable energy such as hydro, wind, biomass and direct solar capture. She makes the concluding observation that NMIs constitute some of the worst and most real threats to collective human wellbeing, and that their unquantifiable character is one of the reasons why their significance is still neglected in many corridors of power. Faced with the possibilities that so-called safe minimum standards for reducing energy-sector impacts could easily imply reductions by more than 50 per cent of current energy utilizations, explains why the call for sustainable development does indeed represent a profound human dilemma.

TIM JENKINS and PETER MIDMORE in *Towards an Integrated Understanding of Environmental Quality* offer a less apocalyptic view of the challenges of environmental management but also place the emphasis on the integration of qualitative judgement dimensions into decision support analysis. They discuss the prospects of establishing indicators for environmental quality, and the challenges involved in efforts to link scientific measurement approaches to ethical and psychological dimensions of human action. They use insights from cognitive psychology in order to develop the view of environmental quality not as an objective property of the physical world but as something arising and evolving with and through human relationships within society and with the natural world. A broader understanding of human–environment coevolutionary interaction offers hope for influencing change in people's attitudes and perceptions in directions away from current unsustainable patterns of risk creation and environmental resource use.

These authors thus reinforce the idea expressed already in several other contributions, that valuation research can be undertaken which specifically sets out to identify and indeed to design elements of the social context for decisions or for sustainability policy advice. This approach deliberately internalizes the fact that the character of valuation statements and decisions reached depends on the process itself. The research instruments in these cases can include discursive processes such as focus groups, or participative hearings, and deliberative procedures such as mediation and citizens' juries. In addition Jenkins and Midmore propose that education for ecological awareness, integrated where possible within communal processes of learning, debate and decision-making, should be a fundamental part of environmental policy. The social process aspects of formal and informal learning are complementary to the more instrumental procedures of environmental assessment and systems analyses that seek to quantify processes of environmental change and biophysical requirements for sustainability.

Valuation here is not merely the quantitative outcome of an analytical procedure, it is indissociable from negotiation and the wider institutional context of individual and collective decision-making action. The valuation judgements are embodied in the agreements reached (or the disagreements made more plain) and in the decisions taken. Underlying ideological orientations are established not just in the choice of methods but in the design of political institutions and social conventions for conflict resolution.

DOROTHEE BECKER SOEST and RÜDIGER WINK emphasize this collective institutional design dimension in their contribution *Institutional Solutions for Sustainable Management of Global Genetic Resources*. Adopting what they call a 'constitutional economics approach' and adapting some well-known ideas about 'procedural justice', they argue that the search for solutions to environmental management problems should focus primarily on the rules and principles governing decision-making procedures — that is, on the conventions of governance adequate for the new challenges. They argue that the task of economists is not to produce images of false precision with models of optimization, but rather to contribute to procedures for resolving conflicts arising from differing value orientations and competing interests. More particularly, they put their faith on the possibilities of 'liberal constitutions' (drawing from Buchanan, Hayek, J.S. Mill, among others) which provide a large place for the exercise of individual freedom subject (only) to the requirement to respect the freedoms of others. This provides a departure point for expressions of individual creativity in the emergence of new knowledge, innovation processes, and the search for creative solutions to conflicts over scarce resources.

Taking the example of genetic resources (the global gene pool), they then discuss the problem of how to avoid irreversible losses that, at present, are the result of short-sighted competitive use of these now-scarce environmental functions. They distinguish three broad categories of functions linked to global genetic resources: regulatory functions relating to stability and resilience of ecosystems, productive functions contributing to the satisfaction of human demands for agricultural and pharmaceutical products, and carrying functions relating to the assimilative capacities of ecosystems in the face of human use, waste disposal and other perturbations. They note that private coordination through contractual (marketlike) procedures reaches a limit when individual (tradable) property rights cannot be defined and allocated precisely. This is particularly significant in relation to the 'regulation' functions of biodiversity where, according to the authors, collective commitment towards biodiversity is needed as a component of the enlarged liberal constitution.

In effect this would mean collective agreements to limit the unsustainable pressures being placed on these resources. Given the avowedly 'procedural' thrust of their argument, this raises the question of how to avoid the requirement to establish binding quantitative constraints on exploitation. By insisting that, in order to avoid perverse effects of political patronage and rent-seeking (and so on) such treaties or other collective agreements should arise out of 'liberal' processes between individuals and between sovereign nations, the authors displace but not yet resolve the question of how to provide for sustainability. In effect, they advocate 'Coasian' recipes for offering maximum scope to individual initiatives, but they do not advise how the Coasian remedies can, in reality, be expected to overcome the problems of cost-shifting by powerful actors onto vulnerable members of society and actors absent from the bargaining table (for discussions of this problem see Samuels 1972a, 1972b; Dragun and O'Connor, 1993). The authors do emphasize the importance of investigating why people use resources without regard to the implications for future generations. They identify economic pressures for survival, including demographic pressures, and also the ways that commercial agriculture (the world food market) and forestry have operated to place pressure on local subsistence societies. This is a sign in needed debate. Yet, their proposals for measures of 'flexible capacity-building' that will pave the way for individuals to develop adaptation pathways through original solutions to the new natural scarcity — an honourable rhetoric that has been a mark of development literature for several decades — are at risk of becoming pathways for opportunistic profit-oriented and *non*-sustainable exploitation.

Other lacunae are noticeable in the authors' proposals. For example they identify prospects for the 'establishment of local networks for managing local networks on a collective basis' which seems indeed to open the way towards exploration of 'common property' solutions. Yet these latter may in some cases be parochial and tribal rather than 'liberal' in their motivation. In sum, the authors assert rather than demonstrate the basis for their faith in 'open social structures that induce permanent research and discovery of new techniques and rules'. In this respect there is profit to be had from a rereading of John Stuart Mill (*On Liberty* and *Utilitarianism*) for his original ideas on the limits to individual freedoms. Mill perceived plainly the excesses and limits of competition per se, and foresaw the need for the emergence of an enlarged social sentiment of reciprocity and humanitarianism as a basis for a durable decent society (see discussions in O'Connor, 1997b). Adding a valuable dimension to the sustainability debate through insisting on the social preconditions for the creation and application of new knowledge, the authors certainly add weight to the call for new expressions of social ethics and institutions for the long-term governance of the market order, but the authors case for the liberal constitutional solution in particular is less convincing.

NURIA CASTELLS AND GIUSEPPE MUNDA, who in *International Environmental Issues: Towards a New Integrated Assessment Approach*, give the closing contribution to this volume, approach the problem of negotiation in the face of large-scale problems, conflict, irreversible processes and complexity along quite a different plane. Their concern is the emerging practice of Integrated Assessment (IA), meaning the attempt to bring together natural science, economic and social–political dimensions of information together for an integrated problem-solving approach. Sometimes this integration is postulated through a model, in which case we may speak of Integrated Assessment Modelling.

Castells and Munda offer a critical appreciation of the roles that can potentially be played by IAM as a decision support procedure for the political resolution of large-scale environmental problems. They insist on developing a strong dimension of reflexivity in addressing complex environmental problems. This means an appreciation of the interplay of the difficult to quantify human and social dimensions of perception, purpose and judgement with the material dimensions of economic and ecosystem change. Societies are not clockworks, and histories are made through incessant processes of adaptation and negotiation.

They take the example of the use of the RAINS model as a support for establishment of the Second Sulphur Protocol between European countries (signed in Oslo 1994). Not only were the results of the scenario modelling inevitably the focus of dispute between interested parties — in this case between representatives of sovereign states and their scientific advisers concerned about the sharing of abatement burdens between states and within industrial sectors — but how biases of perspective enter into any IAM procedure became clear, for example, through the design of the model, the formulation of the problem to be addressed, the treatment (or non-treatment) of uncertainties, and so on. Removing these biases completely is neither necessary nor possible, rather the role of reflexivity is to let them be perceived and debated along with other elements of the assessment process.

In this context, the authors make an argument for the appropriateness of *value pluralism* as a perspective for Integrated Assessment. This means recognition that the appraisal of problems and solution alternatives can involve not merely different methods but also diferent social criteria and perspectives of evaluation. Here they suggest the pertinence of multiple criteria decision aid (MCDA) methods as tools to help organize scientific as well as economic information as a basis for environmental decision making. MCDA methods can avoid the need for the commensurability of different dimensions of value. They do not, of themselves, provide a unique criterion for choice, but rather help to frame the problem of arriving at social–political compromise solutions. They delineate alternative courses of action and judge them on the basis of different evaluation criteria — economic, social and environmental — and by their relevance for different affected interest groups. The integration of analytical (quantitative and qualitative) multicriteria procedures within social processes of problem appraisal, is one way of structuring value pluralism as an approach to environmental problem-solving. As such, this affirmation of an irreducible plurality of perspectives on a problem and of the need for an enlarged decisionmaking process that allows the range of stakeholder perspectives to be expressed, can be seen as having political philosophy dimensions — these are decision support perspectives that afirm an idea of the 'open society'.

1.8   WHAT IS ENVIRONMENTAL VALUATION?

We would be rash to try to offer a definitive summing up of the variety of propositions to be found in the papers making up this volume. What the reader will find is that, as environmental scarcity comes onto the centre stage, environmental valuation is not merely the application of traditional economic analysis tools to the hitherto externalized (natural) domains, but involves new challenges of bringing scientific understanding into decision-making arenas, of resolving social conflicts, and of reconciling disparate ethical principles concerning individual and collective responsabilities in society and towards absent parties.

In a synthetic way, we can say that the *validation* of a valuation method depends not only on standards of theoretical rigour and internal coherence, but also on external considerations. In this respect, at least four broad interlocking sets of considerations for environmental valuation work can be identified:

- *scientific adequacy:* the description and evaluation methods should deal well with the important features of the natural world and its characteristic processes of change
- *social adequacy:* the methods should furnish information in ways that respond to identified needs and that support social processes of decisionmaking
- *economic efficiency:* the suggested courses of action that emerge from the valuation process should respect economic efficiency, in

the sense of arriving at the envisaged outcome without wasting scarce resources

- *statistical adequacy:* the empirical measurement and subsequent aggregation procedures should be consistent with the guiding theoretical precepts, and conform to norms of reliability, coverage and representativeness

The bringing together of scientific, social, institutional and economic considerations in real time, as a sort of interdisciplinary dialogue and social learning process, furnishes a basis for prioritizing and revising actions in the environmental domain (O'Neill, 1993; Munda, 1995; Brouwer, et al., 1996; O'Connor, 1997a). There are many ways of laying out the issues. Analytical work in support and evaluation of environmental policies needs to proceed in recognition of social controversy, uncertainties, and plurality of decision criteria.

We have seen that the call for environmental valuation is one expression of the broad dilemma of sustainable development — that is, of the tension of trying to achieve simultaneous respect for contrasting principles of right action. In practice, priorities for policy action are established and revised iteratively, depending partly on estimates of the economic and social costs of responses, and partly on judgements made by those with decision-making power on the basis of scientific information, commercial interests, and ethical concerns about the urgency of responses. The criteria of social choice are multiple and simultaneous accommodation of divergent principles is often impossible. Compromises must often be made, and finding acceptable compromises for effective policy implementation and robust commercial strategies may require complex processes of negotiation. This means that analytical work in support and evaluation of environmental policies needs to proceed in recognition of social controversy, uncertainties, and plurality of decision criteria. In part the quality of the decisions may depend on the courage of those involved to face up to the real moral tensions and conflicts of interests.

REFERENCES

Bishop, R.C. (1978), 'Endangered species and uncertainty. The economics of a safe minimum standard', American Journal of Agricultural Economics, 60, 10–18.
Brouwer, R., M. O'Connor and W. Radermacher (1996), 'Defining Cost Effective Responses to Environmental Deterioration in a Periodic Accounting System', in *Proceedings of the Third Meeting of the London Group on Natural Resource*

and Environmental Accounting (May 1996), Stockholm: Statistics Sweden, pp. 397–422.

Ciriacy-Wantrup, S.V. (1952), *Resource Conservation: Economics and Policies*, Berkeley: University of California Press.

Dragun, A.K. and M. O'Connor (1993), 'Property Rights, Public Choice and Pigovianism', *Journal of Post-Keynesian Economics*, 16, 127-52.

Faucheux, S. and M. O'Connor (eds, 1998), *Valuation for Sustainable Development: Methods and Policy Indicators*, Cheltenham: Edward Elgar.

Faucheux, S., E. Muir and M. O'Connor (1997), 'Neoclassical Theory of Natural Capital and Weak Indicators for Sustainability', *Land Economics*, 74, 528–52.

Hanley, N. and C.L. Spash (1993), *Cost–Benefit Analysis and the Environment*, Aldershot: Edward Elgar.

Holland, A. (1997), 'The foundations of environmental decisionmaking', *International Journal of Environment and Pollution*, 7(4), 483-96.

Howarth, R.B. and R.B. Norgaard (1992), 'Environmental Valuation Under Sustainable Development', *American Economic Review Papers and Proceedings*, 80, 473–7.

Howarth, R.B. and R.B. Norgaard (1993), 'Intergenerational Transfers and the Social Discount Rate', *Environmental and Resource Economics*, (3) 337–58.

Hueting, R. (1980), *New Scarcity and Economic Growth: More Welfare through Less Production?*, Amsterdam: North-Holland.

Jacobs, M. (1997), 'Environmental Value, Deliberative Democracy and Public Decision-Making Institutions' in J. Foster (ed.), *Valuing Nature? Economics, Ethics and the Environment*, London: Routledge.

Martinez-Alier, Juan (1991), 'Environmental Policy and Distributional Conflicts', pp. 118–36 in Robert Costanza (ed., 1991), *Ecological Economics: The Science and Management of Sustainability*, New York/Oxford: Columbia University Press.

Martinez-Alier, J. and M. O'Connor (1996), 'Distributional Issues in Ecological Economics', pp. 153–84 in R. Costanza, O. Segura and J. Martinez-Alier (eds, 1996), *Getting Down to Earth: Practical Applications of Ecological Economics*, Washington DC: Island Press.

Muir, E. (1996), 'Intra-Generational Wealth Distributional Effects in Global Warming Cost Benefit Analysis', *Journal of Income Distribution*, 6, 193–214.

Munda, G. (1995), *Multicriteria evaluation in a fuzzy environment. Theory and applications in ecological economics*, Berlin: Physica-Verlag.

NOAA (K. Arrow, lead author) (1993), *Report of the NOAA Panel on Contingent Valuation*, Washington DC: Resources for the Future.

O'Connor, M. (ed., 1996), *Ecological Distribution*, Special Issue of the *Journal of Income Distribution*, 6(2), 1996.

O'Connor, M. (1997a), 'The internalization of environmental costs: implementing the Polluter Pays Principle in the European Union', *International Journal of Environment and Pollution*, 7, 450–82.

O'Connor, M. (1997b), 'J.S. Mill's Utilitarianism and the Social Ethics of Sustainable Development', *European Journal of the History of Economic Thought*, 4, 478–506.

O'Connor, M. and E. Muir (1995), 'Endowment Effects in Competitive General Equilibrium: A Primer for Policy Analysts', *Journal of Income Distribution* 5, 145–75.

O'Neill, J. (1993), *Ecology, Policy and Politics. Human Well-Being and the Natural World*, London: Routledge.

Passet, R. (1979), *L'économique et le vivant*, Paris: Payot.

Samuels W.J. (1972a), 'Welfare Economics, Power, and Property', Reprinted pp. 9–75 in W.J. Samuels and A.A. Schmid (eds), *Law and Economics: An Institutional Perspective*, Boston: Martinus Nijhoff, 1981.

Samuels W.J. (1972b), 'Ecosystem Policy and the Problem of Power', *Environmental Affairs*; 2, pp. 580–596; reprinted pp. 111–27 in: W. Samuels and A. Schmid (eds, 1981), *Law and Economics: An Institutional Perspective*, Boston: Martinus Nijhoff.

Samuels W.J. (1992), *Essays on the Economic Role of Government: Vol.I Fundamentals; Vol.II Applications*, London: Macmillan.

Samuels W.J. and N. Mercuro (1979), 'The Role of the Compensation Principle in Society', *Research in Law and Economics* 1, pp. 157–94; reprinted pp. 210-47 in: W. Samuels and A. Schmid (eds, 1981), *Law and Economics: An Institutional Perspective*, Boston: Martinus Nijhoff.

Schnaiberg, A., N. Watts and K. Zimmerman (eds, 1986), *Distributional Conflicts in Environmental Resource Policy*, Aldershot: Gower.

Spash, C.L. (1993), 'Economics, ethics and long-term environmental damages', *Environmental Ethics*, 15, (2), 117–32.

Spash, C.L. (1994a), 'Trying to find the right approach to greenhouse economics: some reflections upon the role of CBA', Analyse & Kritik: Zeitschrift für Socialwissenschaftens 16, 186–99.

Spash, C.L. (1994b), 'Double CO_2 and Beyond: benefits, costs and compensation', *Ecological Economics*, 10, 27–36.

Spash, C.L. (1997), 'Reconciling different approaches to environmental management', *International Journal of Environment and Pollution*, 7, 497–511.

2. Commensurability and Compensability in Ecological Economics

Joan Martinez-Alier, Giuseppe Munda and John O'Neill

2.1 INTRODUCTION

The environment is a site of conflict between competing values and interests and different groups and communities that represent them. Biodiversity goals, landscape objectives, the direct economic services of different environments as resource and sink, the historical and cultural meanings places have for communities, the recreational options environments provide are a source of conflict. The different dimensions of value can conflict with each other and within themselves. Moreover, any decision will distribute different goods and bads across different groups both spatially and temporally. How are conflicts between different dimension of value and the between the different groups who stand bear gains or losses to be resolved?

One approach that has its roots in utilitarianism attempts resolution through the use of a common measure through which different dimensions of value can be traded off one with another, so that losses in one dimension of value can be compensated for in gains in others: monetary measures are the most commonly used measure invoked for this purpose. The approach assumes the existence of value commensurability. The possibility of trading off gains and losses is not confined to different intrapersonal dimensions of value. Within the neo-classical tradition, where options have losers and gainers, such trade-offs are extended across persons without interpersonal comparisons of utility through the compensation test: 'How are we to say whether a reorganization of production, which makes A better off, but B worse off marks an improvement in efficiency? ... If A is made so much better off by the change that he could compensate B for his loss, and still have something left over, then the reorganization is an unequivocal improvement' (Hicks 1941, p.105). The approach assumes interpersonal compensability in this special sense.

Do the assumptions of value commensurability and interpersonal compensability provide adequate principles for rational environmental choices? In the following we argue that they do not.

2.2 HISTORICAL INTRODUCTION TO THE CONCEPT OF INCOMMENSURABILITY

The arguments about economic commensurability and its place in decision-making about the environment are not new to economic debate. It was precisely the relation between rational decision-making and economic commensurability which was the main point in the opening stage of the famous debate of the 1920s and 1930s on economic calculus in a socialist economy. The debate, started in central Europe (Hayek, ed. 1935, repr. 1970), focussed on disagreement on how an economy could work, when the means of production were socialized, and therefore were not in the market. The question seemed practically relevant in the aftermath of the First World War in virtue of the wave of revolutions in central and eastern Europe.

Both Max Weber (in *Economy and Society*, vol. 1) and Hayek (see above, p. 30) credited Otto Neurath, the analytical philosopher cofounder of the Vienna Circle, with the seminal contribution to the debate, although there had been previous contributions to debate on economic calculus in a socialist economy, in the form of exercises in economic theory (Barone, in Hayek, ed. 1935). Neurath has been recently claimed, with reason, as one of the founders of ecological economics, not only for his part in this debate of the 1920s and 1930s, but also because of his work on the 'unity' — or rather, the 'orchestration'— of the sciences in the study of specific issues in social, economic, ecological history (Martinez-Alier and Schluepmann 1987, 1991; O'Neill, 1995a). Neurath's articles on the economics of socialism had a practical bent, since they were reports addressed to revolutionary groups. He was himself inspired by work of authors such as Ballod-Atlanticus and Popper-Lynkeus, who had written what would be called now scenarios of an ecological economy, particularly Popper-Lynkeus (1912) who carefully counted the energy and material throughput in the German economy, suggesting the introduction of renewable energies and also of new social and economic institutions. Neurath thought of such scenarios as practical Utopias (Martinez-Alier, 1987, 1992).

Neurath explained the essence of economic incommensurability by means of the following example (Neurath, 1919). Let us consider two capitalist factories, achieving the same production level of the same type of product, one with 200 workers and 100 tons of coal, the second one with 300 workers and only 40 tons of coal. Both would compete in the market, and the one using a more 'economic' process would achieve an advantage. However, in a socialist economy (where the means of production are socialized), in order to compare two economic plans, both of them achieving the same result, a present value should be given to future needs for coal (and, we would now add, a present value should be given also to the future impact of carbon dioxide emissions). We must not only decide, therefore, a rate of discount and a time horizon, but also guess the changes in technology: use of solar energy, use of water power, use of nuclear power. In Neurath's own words (1928, p. 263), the answer to whether coal-intensive or labour-intensive methods should be used

> depends for example on whether one thinks that hydraulic power may be sufficiently developed or that solar heat might come to be better used. If however one is afraid that when one generation uses too much coal thousands will freeze to death in the future, one might use more human power and save coal. Such and many other non-technical matters determine the choice of a technically calculable plan ... We can see no possibility of reducing the production plan to some kind of unit and then to compare the various plans in terms of such units.

Elements in the economy were not commensurable, hence the need for a *Naturalrechnung*. Summarizing Neurath's ideas, Hayek wrote that Neurath tried to show 'that it was possible to dispense with any considerations of value in the administration of the supply of commodities and that all calculations of the central planning authorities should and could be carried out *in natura*, i.e. that the calculations need not be carried out in terms of a common unit of value but that they could be made in kind'. Hayek added (1935, p. 31), 'Neurath was quite oblivious of the insuperable difficulties which the absence of value calculations would put in the way of any rational economic use of the resources'. Thus commensurability of values was a condition of rationality. Or, as Von Mises had put it (Von Mises, 1920, in Hayek, ed. 1935, p. 111), 'Where there is no free market, there is no pricing mechanism; without a pricing mechanism, there is no economic calculation'.

Certainly, the market would sometimes fail to give a 'correct' economic value to environmental amenities, thus, the calculation of the profitability of a hydroelectric scheme would not include 'the beauty of the waterfall which the scheme might impair', except that attention could be paid 'to the diminution of tourist traffic or similar changes, which may be valued in

Valuation and the Environment

terms of money' (Von Mises, in Hayek, ed. 1935, p. 99). Through what is now called the 'travel-cost method', or similar methods, the market mechanism could be extended in a capitalist economy to positive or negative externalities. But in a socialist economy, the issue was not whether the externalities produced by a tractor could be internalized into the price system, but rather that the tractor itself had no price. Socialism, Von Mises concluded, was 'the abolition of rational economy'.

As it is well known, the debate on economic calculus in a socialist economy took a new turn with the proposals from both Lange and Taylor (1938), according to which the decisions by socialist managers would be guided by a tentative vector of prices which would fulfil a parametric function. Such prices would be periodically adjusted by the planning commission, by trial and error. The Lange and Taylor position assumed with Von Mises that rational choices required commensurability (O'Neill, forthcoming). The debate continues to this day (Brus, 1991; Roemer and Silvestre, 1994; Roemer, 1994), in the direction of a market socialism able to cope (theoretically) with the problems of missing markets, and also of lack of incentives and the dispersal of information — recent contributions wishing to demonstrate how a socialist economy could be as efficient as a capitalist economy (by the use of actual markets for most goods and services, and of surrogate markets only for externalities), and at the same time more egalitarian.

Our intention here is not to make our own contribution to the economics of socialism. It is rather to remind the reader that the question of incommensurability of values (which we take to be a foundation stone for Ecological Economics) had already been the centre of analysis in the important debates on economic calculus in a socialist economy earlier this century.[1]

2.3   COMMENSURABILITY AND COMPENSABILITY IN COST–BENEFIT ANALYSIS

From a philosophical perspective, it is possible to distinguish between the following concepts: strong commensurability according to which there exists a common measure of the different consequences of an action based on a cardinal scale of measurement; weak commensurability according to which there exists a common measure based on an ordinal scale of measurement; strong comparability, according to which there exists a single comparative term by which all different actions can be ranked; and weak comparability according to which values are irreducibly plural and cannot be uniquely ordered along a single scale — rational choice given incommensurable values is however possible (O'Neill, 1993). In our view, ecological economics rests most happily on a foundation of weak comparability.

Cost–benefit analysis (CBA), the conventional neo-classical approach to project evaluation, aims to achieve strong comparability, that it is always possible to find a set of conversion factors able to transform all dimensions underlying a given action into a single composite measure (Hanley and Spash, 1993; Mishan, 1982; Pearce and Nash, 1981). In order to be consistent with the objective of maximizing social welfare, it is necessary that the prices attached to the physical benefits and costs reflect society's valuations of the final goods and resources involved. A variety of methods are employed to extend the measuring rod of money to environmental goods that currently come unpriced in the market, most notably, hedonic pricing, travel-cost methods and contingent valuation.

In the subsequent aggregation of several dimensions it assumes *compensability* between values and the preferences of persons. Intuitively, compensability refers to the existence of trade-offs, the possibility of offsetting a disadvantage on some attribute by a sufficiently large advantage on another attribute, whereas smaller advantages would not do the same. Thus a preference relation is noncompensatory if no trade-off occurs and is compensatory otherwise.

The way each aggregation procedure transforms information in order to arrive at a preference structure can be called its aggregation convention, which is generally well illustrated by the numerical transformation used. Clearly, the convention underlying the additive utility model is completely compensatory (Munda, 1996). Let us start with the mathematical formal definition of the case of *complete compensability*. An attribute i, $i \in \Omega$, consists of a set X_i of at least two elements expressing different levels of some underlying dimensions, and of a total strict order P_i on X_i. Given any nonempty disjoint subsets of attributes I and J, I strongly compensates J if for all x, $y \in X$ such that $x \mid y$, $P(x,y) = J$, $P(y,x) = I$, there is a $z \in X$ such that $z \mid x$ or $z = x$ and $z_i = y_i$ for all $i \notin I$. Therefore, a notion of complete compensability is at hand if we ask for strong compensability to hold both ways between any two disjoint (nonempty) subsets of attributes (Bouyssou, 1986; Vansnick, 1986). The concept of complete compensability underlying conventional CBA has great significance on both distributional and environmental sides (Munda, 1996).

The use of compensability to make choices between states of affairs in which some lose and others gain is commonly realized in CBA through the *compensation principle* or 'potential improvement criterion' usually associated with the names of Hicks (1939) and Kaldor (1939). This seeks to allow aggregative choices across persons while avoiding interpersonal comparison of utility. If the monetary value of benefits exceeds the monetary value of costs, then the winners can hypothetically compensate the losers and still have some gains left over. The excess of gains over compensation is equal to the net benefits of the project. Given a choice of projects we choose that which yields the highest net benefit.

In the following we argue that the basic assumption of value commensurability, and the employment of compensation tests across persons, both fail. We begin with the latter.

2.4 COMPENSATION, DISTRIBUTION AND PARETO-INCOMPARABILITY

Since the compensation principle was formulated, it has been attacked from several sides. Amongst the most important contributions to the debate are those of Scitowsky (1941, 1954) who first noted the possibility that the undertaking of a project without the payment of compensation may redistribute income in such a way that an ex post application of the compensation test yields a different answer from an ex ante one, and Little (1950) who stressed the value content of the approach and the need to take distributional factors into account. 'The compensation principle is either redundant — if the compensation is actually paid then there is a real Pareto improvement and hence no need for the test — or unjustified — it is no consolation to losers, who might include the worst off members of society, to be told that it would be possible to compensate them even though there is no actual intention to do so' (Sen, 1987, p. 33). Generally, it is said that cost–benefit analysis focuses in the first instance on *efficiency* criteria; *equity* problems are often ignored. But, any policy decision affects the welfare positions of individuals, regions or groups in different ways; consequently, the public support for a certain policy decision will very much depend on the *distribution effects* of such a decision.

A standard response to this objection is to claim that the compensation test for efficiency does not preclude the later introduction of independent criteria for determining the distribution of wealth. The potential Pareto criterion allows us to determine which of a set of possible sets of projects produces the greatest benefit over cost for society as a whole: it determines which choice maximizes the total consumer surplus. Having thus ascertained the maximum surplus the decision-maker can then go on to an ex post consideration of how it should be distributed between different groups, employing whatever principle of equity is given by political processes. Distributional considerations are not ruled out by the compensation test. They are merely bracketed (Katz and Rosen, 1991, p. 397; Mishan, 1982, p. xxi).

However the treatment of efficiency as if it were logically independent of distribution is at best misleading, for the determination of efficiency already presupposes a given distribution of rights. For a given initial distribution of rights, one can derive a Pareto-optimal outcome, but Pareto optimality is always relative to an initial starting point, and cannot tell us what that should be. Different property right regimes are themselves not Pareto comparable. If property rights are changed so also (except in special cases) is what is efficient. Hence, the opposition between distributional and efficiency criteria is misleading. Existing costs and benefits themselves are the product of a given distribution of property rights. Since costs are not independent of rights they cannot guide the allocation of rights. Different initial distributions entail differences in whose preferences are to count. Environmental conflicts are often about who has rights to environmental goods, and hence who is to bear the costs and who is to bear the benefits. Policy choices often have significant consequences on the distribution of the rights and incomes of affected parties. Where this is the case one cannot treat distributional issues as a distinct item to be treated ex post once efficiency has been met. Hence, environmental policy and resource decision-making cannot avoid making normative choices which include questions of resource distribution, income distribution, and relationships between conflicting rights claims (Nijkamp, 1986; O'Connor and Muir, 1995; Samuels, 1972; Schmid, 1978).

Any claim to efficiency has always to be read, 'given this distribution of property rights, this is the efficient policy'. Unqualified statements employing Paretian efficient outcomes are elliptical. This dependency of efficiency claims on prior distribution of rights is normally implicit and tends to disappear in policy recommendations. Hence, in practice, CBA tends to a conservatism by assuming a status quo distribution of rights that is actually or potentially contestable, but which in the policy recommendation is rendered invisible. Hence from an intra/inter-generational point of view, the compensation model has particular strong distributive impacts; the monetary value of a negative externality depends on social institutions and distributional conflicts (willingness to pay measures consider preferences of the higher income groups more important than the lower ones). If the people damaged are poor or of a future generation, the monetary measure of the cost of internalization will be lower ('the poor sell cheap') (Martinez-Alier, 1994; Martinez-Alier and O'Connor, 1996).

2.5 MONETARY MEASURES AND COMMENSURABILITY

In order to be consistent with the objective of maximizing social welfare, in CBA it is necessary that the prices attached to the physical benefits and costs reflect society's valuations of the final goods and resource involved, that is, the opportunity costs and trade-offs on the margin in the use of resources and production of goods. Two questions immediately arise:

(1) If markets do exist, to what extent will observed market prices reflect social valuations?
(2) If markets do not exist (as happens for most environmental goods and services), how are surrogate prices to be derived which, in turn, reflect social valuations?

For environmental problems the Kaldor–Hicks compensation principle assumes that it is always possible to find an amount of money in terms of willingness to pay for environmental quality improvements or of willingness to accept for environmental quality deterioration that keeps utility constant. The optimization and compensation models[2] can be regarded as crucial tools in conventional economics, because only in this way may one assign an amount of money to environmental decay. However, it has to be noted that such models do not aim at achieving a better environmental quality, but only at incorporating the environmental impacts in the traditional price and market system. It has to be noted that since the objective is to keep utility constant, substitution between environmental quality and economic growth is always allowed, then a *weak sustainability* philosophy is implied (Pearce and Atkinson, 1993).

In neoclassical welfare economics, prices resulting from a competitive equilibrium can be considered to be a measure of social opportunity costs. Deviations from this situation were thus the so-called *market failures*. Some set of prices, called *shadow or accounting prices*, which reflect the true social opportunity cost of using resources in a given project need to be computed. As a first approximation, shadow prices are assumed to reflect marginal costs. However, the use of marginal cost pricing in the public sector with prices elsewhere diverging from marginal costs involves the 'second best problem'. The essential argument is that setting prices equal to marginal cost in one sector only may actually move the economy away from a Pareto optimum (Lipsey and Lancaster, 1956).

Clearly, if market prices are to be corrected so that they reflect marginal costs, there is a *practical* problem of estimating marginal costs and a *conceptual* problem of justifying the procedure in the face of the second-best theorem. Furthermore, marginal private cost will still not fulfil the role of a proper shadow price if private and social cost diverge. An important cause of divergence is the presence of an important category of market failures contributing to environmental degradation, namely, *externalities* (Ayres and Kneese, 1990; Baumol and Oates, 1975; Mishan, 1971).

The standard neoclassical account of microeconomic environmental policy is based on partial equilibrium analyses, which are underpinned by commensurability and compensability and where these problems of second-best and of distribution are simply neglected. Thus, the standard account makes the marginal profits of a polluting firm commensurable with the (monetized) marginal external costs, in order to establish a 'social optimum'. A Pigouvian tax is equal to the marginal external cost at the 'optimum' pollution level. The environmental policy applied to reach the social optimum is then based on a compensation principle, such as 'the polluter pays principle'.

Some economists (such as Baumol and Oates, 1975) and many non-economists have expressed doubts on the possibility of giving present money values to future, cumulative, uncertain, irreversible externalities. Hence, the recommendation to focus environmental policy on the issue of *cost-effectiveness* rather than social optima. For instance, in order to curb emissions down to a norm or level set from outside economic reasoning, what is cheaper (or more cost-effective), a tax or marketable pollution permits? Cost-effectiveness analysis (CEA) thus implies weak commensurability. But the environmental limits or norms themselves are set by practical judgements, not so much by pure scientific expertise as by a process of 'extended peer review' or social evaluation (Funtowicz and Ravetz, 1994; O'Connor et al., 1996). Kapp (1970) wrote:

> To place a monetary value on and apply a discount rate (which?) to future utilities or disutilities in order to express their present capitalized value may give us a precise monetary calculation, but it does not get us out of the dilemma of a choice and the fact that we take a risk with human health and survival. For this reason, I am inclined to consider the attempt at measuring social costs and social benefits simply in terms of monetary or market values as doomed to failure. Social costs and social benefits have to be considered as extra-market phenomena; they are borne and accrue to society as a whole; they are heterogeneous and cannot be compared quantitatively among themselves and with each other, not even in principle.

Economists who wish to go beyond CEA, and apply CBA, need often to place monetary values on non-market goods such as clean air, clean water and wilderness areas. Several methodologies have been developed to cope with such estimation requirements, the principal ones being contingent valuation, the travel cost method, hedonic pricing, and the shadow project approach. Among these contingent valuation is the only method which can claim to capture all preferences for environmental goods. The method has a series of well-discussed internal validity problems: the existence of strategic and protest bids; design effects — the way a bid is elicited can effect the outcome; presentation and information effects — changes in the quantity and quality of information will alter responses; payment vehicle biases — the vehicle used to elicit bids in a CVM can effect the WTP value; embedding and part/whole effects; ordering effects — the order in which options are presented to the individual can effect the payments; compliance bias — individuals may respond in order to please the interviewer. Much work has been done to attempt to resolve such problems. However, further refinement points to the uncomfortable conclusion that valuation results may be ultimately an artifact of the survey: the price you get out depends on what you put in, the information and presentation you offer, the way the question is framed, how you define options, the vehicle of payment you use, the order you present options and so on. Many of the 'biases' themselves point to problems in the assumptions that underlie the contingent valuation procedures. The question needs to be raised whether they turn out not to be simply internal problems which with technical developments could be solved, but rather examples of deeper external problems with the attempt to arrive at public policy on the environment through the use of a single monetary metric measuring preferences for environmental goods. Moreover, willingness to pay depends upon the *ability to pay*, thus projects which benefit higher income groups would generally be considered to be the best. An extensive discussion of the limits of contingent valuation can be found in Holland et al., (1996) and Vatn and Bromley, (1994).

Cost–benefit analysis is committed to the existence of a single measure that orders all objects and states, on the personal basis of persons' willingness to pay at the margin for the satisfaction of preferences. Hence, it is committed to weak commensurability. Under some welfare interpretations it is understood — wrongly — to involve strong commensurability, that is, it is taken to presuppose that there is a single source of value, and willingness to pay provides a cardinal measure of different amounts of that value. But, neither pleasure nor preference will do the trick of reducing a plurality of values to a single value which provides a unique ordering of objects and states of affairs. Even if pleasure were the ultimate and only intrinsic value, it could not provide a single value to order goods, since pleasures themselves are plural in character: the pleasure of drinking beer and that of good conversation are different in kind and are not measurable on a single scale. Preferences, on the other hand, answer to values, not values to preferences. I prefer A because of its value, I do not value it because it is preferred. Hence, given a plurality of values, our preferences merely record our judgements in resolving conflicts between them. They do not provide the supreme value through which they are to be resolved.

Cost–benefit analysis treats all preferences as identical save in the 'intensity' with which they are held. It is blind to the reasons and arguments that individuals have for or against different proposals. Standardly, environmentalists appeal to features of the site on which a development is to take place, to its aesthetic merits, its landscape qualities, to its value as a habitat, to the variety of species it holds, to its value as a place, its history and so on. Cost–benefit analysis is blind to such reasons. The strength or weakness of the intensity of a preference count, but the strength or weakness of the reasons for a preference do not.

2.6   INCOMMENSURABILITY OF VALUES AND MULTICRITERIA EVALUATION

There is great pressure for research into techniques to make larger ranges of social value commensurable. Some of the effort should rather be devoted to learning — or learning again, perhaps — how to think intelligently about conflicts of value which are incommensurable (Williams, 1972, p. 103).

Incommensurability, that is, the absence of a common unit of measurement across plural values, entails the rejection not just of monetary reductionism but also any physical reductionism (for example, eco-energetic valuation). However it does not entail incomparability. It allows that different options are weakly comparable, that is comparable without recourse to a single scale of value. In terms of formal logic, the difference between strong and weak comparability, and one defence of weak comparability, can be expressed in terms of Geach's distinction between attributive and predicative adjectives. (Geach, 1967). An adjective A is predicative if it passes the following logical tests:

(1) if x is AY, then x is A and x is Y;
(2) if x is AY and all Ys are Zs then x is AZ.

Adjectives that fail such tests are attributive. Geach claims that 'good' is an attributive adjective. In many of its uses it clearly fails (2): 'X is a good economist, all economists are persons, therefore X is a good person' is an invalid argument. Correspondingly, statements of the form 'X is good' need to be understood as elliptical. They invite the response 'X is a good what?'. If 'good' is attributive, then its comparative form will have its scope limited by the particular noun it qualifies. 'X is a better economist than Y, all economists are persons, therefore X is a better person than Y' is an invalid argument.

That a comparative holds in one range of objects does not entail that it holds in the wider range. Given a claim that 'X is better than Y' a proper response is 'X is better what than Y?'. Similar points can be made about the adjectives 'valuable' and 'is more valuable than'. If evaluative adjectives like 'good' and 'valuable' are attributive in standard uses, it follows that their comparative forms have a limited range. That does not however preclude the possibility of rational choices between objects that do not fall under the range of a single comparative. Weak comparability is compatible with the existence of such limited ranges.

It is under such descriptions that evaluation takes place. A location is not evaluated as good or bad as such, but rather, as good, bad, beautiful or ugly under different descriptions. It can be at one and the same time a 'good W' and a 'bad X', a 'beautiful Y' and an 'ugly Z'. The use of these value terms in such contexts is attributive, not predicative. Evaluation of objects under different descriptions invokes not just different practices and perspectives, but also different criteria and standards for evaluation associated with these. It presupposes value-pluralism. Appeal to different standards often results in conflicting appraisal of an object: as noted above, an object can have considerable worth as a U, V, and W, but little as an X, Y and Z.

In general, a multicriteria model presents the following features (Munda et al., 1994; Munda, 1995):

(1) There is no solution optimizing all the criteria at the same time and therefore the decision-maker has to find compromise solutions.
(2) The relations of preference and indifference are not enough in this approach, because when an action is better than another one for some criteria, it is usually worse for others, so that many pairs of actions remain incomparable with respect to a dominance relation.

The main advantage of these models is that they make it possible to consider a large number of data, relations and objectives which are generally present in a specific real-world decision problem, so that the decision problem at hand can be studied in a multidimensional fashion. On the other side, an action a may be better than an action b according to one criterion and worse according to another. Thus when different conflicting evaluation criteria are taken into consideration, a multicriteria problem is mathematically ill-defined. The consequence is that a complete axiomatization of multicriteria decision theory is quite difficult (Arrow and Raynaud, 1986).

Acknowledging that the problem is mathematically ill-structured, two simple 'ways out' immediately present themselves:

(1) leave the decision-maker entire liberty for the decision (decisionism),
(2) introduce consciously or not restrictive hypotheses, so that the problem can be solved by a classical method (rationalism).

Decisionism in practice maintains that decisions are blind actions, inspired by the subconscious and by the instincts, so that the act of reasoning over a decision is meaningless. On the contrary, rationalism assumes that in any decision problem an optimal or precise solution always exists and that it is possible to find it by reasoning over the problem. Thus, using Socrates' words, 'ignorance is the only cause of foolish or evil acts'.

The methods used in multicriteria analysis lie between these two extremes: they are based on (necessarily restrictive) mathematical assumptions as well as on information gathered from the decision-maker. Thus the concept of 'decision process' has an essential importance. According to Simon (1972, 1978, 1983), a distinction must be made between the general notion of rationality as an adaptation of available means to ends, and the various theories and models based on a rationality which is either substantive or procedural. This terminology can be used to distinguish between the rationality of a decision considered independently of the manner in which it is made (in the case of substantive rationality, the rationality of evaluation refers exclusively to the results of the choice) and the rationality of a decision in terms of the manner in which it is made (in the case of procedural rationality, the rationality of evaluation refers to the decision-making process itself) (Froger and Munda, 1997).

Thus, in ecological economics, instead of focussing on 'missing markets' as causes of allocative disgraces, we focus on the creative power that missing markets have, because they push us away from false hope for economic commensurability, towards multicriteria evaluation of evolving realities.

2.7   MULTICRITERIA EVALUATION AND ECOLOGICAL ECONOMICS

Weak comparability can be considered to be the philosophical base of the so-called *fundamental partial comparability axiom* (Roy, 1985). The concept of partial comparability is the base of the so-called *outranking methods*. These are based on the understanding that, in general, in multicriteria problems the dominance relation is poor because it is based on a consensus of points of view. Thus, an action *a* outranks an action *b* only if *a* is at least as 'good' as *b* on all the criteria considered. The concept behind the outranking methods is that the enrichment of the dominance relation can be done only if information is available; so there is a formal structure between the dominance relation which is too weak and the utility functions complete preorder. By using outranking methods some incomparable actions become comparable because realistic information exists, but other actions remain, nevertheless, incomparable. For an extensive discussion of the epistemological and methodological foundations of these methods, see Arrow and Raynaud, (1986), Munda (1993), Roy (1985).

In this framework, it is important to clarify the concept of *non-compensability* (Bouyssou and Vansnick, 1986). Let $P(x,y)$ be the set of attributes for which there is a partial preference for x on y. A preference structure (X,f) is generalized noncompensatory if $\forall\ x, y, z, w \subset\vee X$:

$$\{[P(x,y),P(y,x)] = [P(z, w), P(w, z)]\} \Rightarrow [x\ f\ y \Rightarrow z\ f \text{ or } = w] \qquad (2.1)$$

and

$$[P(x, y) \neq \varnothing \text{ and } P(y, x) = \varnothing\ ] \Rightarrow x\ f\ y \qquad (2.2)$$

This definition allows to have at the same time $(P(x,y),\ P(y,x)) = (P(z,w),\ P(w,z))$, $x\ f\ y$ and $z \approx w$. This possibility of an absence of preference between z and w aims to encompass the notion of discordance between evaluations, introduced whenever there is an attribute j in $P(x,y)$ for which $y_j \vee x_j$ which can be interpreted as 'y_j is far better than x_j'.

An important consequence of noncompensability is that it is possible to operationalize the concept of strong sustainability. Systemic approaches to environmental issues consider the relationships between three systems: the economic system, the human system and the natural system (Passet, 1979). From the ecological economic perspective, the expansion of scale of activity of the economic subsystem is limited by the size of the overall finite global ecosystem, by its dependence on the life support sustained by intricate ecological connections which are more easily disrupted as the scale of the economic subsystem activities grows relative to the biosphere (Daly, 1991). As a consequence, the scale of the economy has a limit defined either by the regenerative or absorptive capacity of the ecosystem; thus the concept of *strong sustainability* is used. Such a definition is based on the assumption that certain sorts of 'natural capital' are deemed critical, and not readily substitutable by man-made capital (Barbier and Markandya, 1990). In particular, the characterization of sustainability in terms of the 'strong' criterion of non-negative change over time in stocks of specified 'natural capital' is based on *direct physical measurement* of important stocks and flows (Faucheux and Noël, 1995; O'Connor et al., 1996).

In the strong sustainability perspective, we are left with bio-physical indicators, or 'satellite accounts' of variations in natural patrimony, not integrated in money terms within national income accounting. However, behind a list of indicators there would always be a history of scientific research and political controversy (Funtowicz and Ravetz, 1994). Moreover, one should note that a list of indicators is far from being a list of agreed targets and lower limits for those indicators. Then a question arises, how could such indicators be aggregated? Often, some indicators improve while others deteriorate. For instance, when incomes grow, SO_2 might go down while CO_2 increases. It has to be noted that this is the classic conflictual situation studied in multicriteria evaluation theory. Of course, the possibility of limiting the compensability among indicators and to put lower bounds of acceptability (for example, by the notion of a veto threshold) is of a fundamental importance to operationalize the strong sustainability concept. A first application of these ideas can be seen in Faucheux and O'Connor, (1994), see also Faucheux and O'Connor (eds, 1997).

2.8   CONCLUSIONS

Traditional economic theory is based on optimizing principles aiming at finding a precise 'best' solution. CBA is based on strong or weak commensurability thus implying strong comparability. The most important thing is the quality of the final decision not the quality of the decision process. At the same time, complete compensability and commensurability imply the inseparability between efficiency, equity and environmental issues, as a consequence optimization of a monocriterion type cannot be 'objectively value free'.

Ecological economics explicitly recognizes that economy–environment interactions are also characterized by significant institutional, political, cultural and social factors through which action is carried out. The use of a multidimensional approach seems desirable. This implies that in the framework of ecological economics, the strong comparability assumptions of neo-classical economics have to be changed. Since multicriteria evaluation techniques are based on a 'constructive' rationality and allow one to take into account conflictual, multidimensional, incommensurable and uncertain effects of decisions, they look as a promising assessment framework for ecological economics.

As a conclusion, we will try to synthesize the main differences between multicriteria evaluation and cost–benefit analysis by means of some comparison criteria (see also Munda et al., 1995).

Cost–benefit analysis is a traditional evaluation instrument used in economics both at a micro and macro level of analysis. It is based on the neo-classical maximization premise on behaviour stating that rational decisions coincide with utility maximization. According to the scarcity principle, the most efficient allocation of resources is considered the most important objective of economic analysis.

Multicriteria decision theory is based on different concepts and types of rationality according to the models used. The only one similar, to some extent, to the concept of rationality assumed in neo-classical theory is the value and utility function approach. In general, models based on satisfycing behaviour, bounded and procedural rationality principles are considered. No one-dimensional monetary performance indicator has across-the-board application. Efficiency is not considered the only aim of the analysis but many different conflictual heterogeneous points of view are considered.

In CBA, economic votes expressed on the market are in principle taken into account. However, one has to note that it is not possible to escape from value judgements since, if no weighting system is used, the assumption that current distribution of income is optimal needs to be accepted. From an intragenerational point of view, the compensation model has major distributive impacts; the monetary value of a negative externality depends on social institutions and distributional conflicts. From an intergenerational equity point of view, since future generations are not on the market, their preferences do not count; the simple summation of today's individual preferences may imply the extinction of species and ecosystems.

Multicriteria evaluation explicitly recognizes that the identification of the preference system of the decision-maker(s) is a very important step of the overall analysis. We think that in an evaluation exercise, the presence of a subjective component has to be accepted. The advantage of multicriteria methods is that the subjectivity is made explicit. In multicriteria evaluation, generally the decision-makers to whom one can ask the weights or with whom the interaction can be carried out are political authorities in charge of a given decision. From this point of view multicriteria decision theory can be considered more elitist than CBA. However, equity problems can explicitly be considered in three different ways:

- as specific evaluation criteria,
- by means of different sets of weights,

- by integrating multicriteria methods with conflict resolution techniques (see Munda, 1995).

Finally, is CBA consistent with a goal of sustainable development? The optimization and compensation models do not aim at achieving a better environmental quality, but only at incorporating the environmental impacts in the traditional price and market system. A weak sustainability philosophy is always implied, since substitution between man-made capital and 'natural capital' is a direct consequence of the compensation model.

Is multicriteria evaluation consistent with sustainable development? Since multicriteria evaluation is multidimensional in nature, it allows to take into account economy–environment interactions in a variety of different ways. According to the aggregation procedure chosen, weak or strong sustainability concepts can be operationalized. This depends on the degrees of compensability allowed by the aggregation procedures. An important consequence of noncompensability is that it is possible to operationalize the concept of *strong sustainability,* in terms of direct physical measurement in different units.

ENDNOTES

1. For readers who have wide philosophical interests, this article could have started with a reference to Aristotle's distinction in the *Politics* between oikonomia and chrematistics (Daly and Cobb, 1989; Martinez-Alier, 1987; Meikle, 1995; O'Neill, 1995b; Polanyi, 1957; Soddy, 1922).
2. An externality is *optimized* when its level is consistent with Pareto efficiency according to the Kaldor–Hicks criterion; an externality is *compensated* when a (financial) transaction takes place between the supplier and the receiver of the effect.

REFERENCES

Arrow, K.J. and H. Raynaud (1986), 'Social choice and multicriterion decision-making', USA: MIT. Press.

Ayres, R.U. and A.V. Kneese (1990), 'Externalities: economics and thermodynamics', in F. Archibugi and P. Nijkamp (eds), *Economy and Ecology: towards sustainable development*, Dordrecht: Kluwer, 89–118.

Barbier, E.B. and A. Markandya (1990), 'The conditions for achieving environmentally sustainable growth', *European Economic Review,* 34, 659–69.

Baumol, W.J. and W.E. Oates (1975), *The Theory of Environmental Policy,* Englewood Cliffs: Prentice-Hall.

Bouyssou, D. (1986), 'Some remarks on the notion of compensation in MCDM', *European Journal of Operational Research,* 26, 150–60.

Bouyssou, D. and J.C. Vansnick (1986), 'Noncompensatory and generalized noncompensatory preference structures', *Theory and Decision,* 21, 251–66.

Brus, W. (1991), 'Market socialism', in *Palgrave Dictionary of Economics,* London.

Daly, H.E. (1991), 'Elements of environmental macroeconomics', in R. Costanza (ed.), *Ecological Economics: the science and management of sustainability,* New York: Columbia University Press, 32–46.

Daly, H.E. and J.J. Cobb (1989), *For the Common Good: Redirecting the economy toward community, the environment and a sustainable future,* Boston: Beacon Press.

Faucheux, S., G. Froger and G. Munda (1994), 'Des outils d'aide à la decision pour la multidimensionalité systémique: une application au développement durable', *Revue Internationale de Systémique,* No. 15.

Faucheux, S. and J.F. Noël (1995), *Economie des ressources naturelles et de l' environnement,* Paris: Armand Colin.

Faucheux, S. and M. O'Connor (eds) (1997), *Valuation for Sustainable Development: Methods and policy indicators,* Aldershot: Edward Elgar.

Froger, G. and G. Munda (1997), 'Methodology for environmental decision support', in S. Faucheux and M. O'Connor (eds), *Valuation for Sustainable Development: Methods and policy indicators,* Aldershot: Edward Elgar.

Funtowicz, S.O. and J.R. Ravetz (1994), 'The worth of a songbird: ecological economics as a post-normal science', *Ecological Economics,* 10, 197–207.

Geach, P. (1967), 'Good and Evil', in P. Foot (ed.), *Theories of Ethics,* Oxford: Oxford University Press, 66–73.

Hanley, N. and C. Spash (1993), *Cost–benefit Analysis and the Environment,* Aldershot: Edward Elgar.

Hayek, F.A. (ed.) (1935), *Collectivist Economic Planning,* reprinted New York: Augustus M. Kelley, 1970.

Hicks, J.R. (1939), 'The foundations of welfare economics', *Economic Journal,* 49 reprinted in Hicks, 1981, 59–79.

Hicks, J.R. (1941), 'The rehabilitation of consumers' surplus', *Review of Economic Studies* reprinted in Hicks, 1981, 100–113.

Hicks, J.R. (1981), *Wealth and Welfare,* Oxford: Blackwell.

Holland, A., M. O'Connor and J. O'Neill (1996), 'Costing Environmental Damage', Report for the Directorate General for Research, European Parliament, Luxembourg: STOA.

Hueting, R. (1993), 'Calculating a sustainable national income: A practical solution for a theoretical dilemma', in J.C. Dragan, E.K. Seifert and M.C. Demetrescu (eds), *Entropy and Bioeconomics,* Milan: Nagard.

Kaldor, N. (1939), 'Welfare comparison of economics and interpersonal comparisons of utility', *Economic Journal,* 49, 549–52.

Kapp, K.W. (1970), *Social Costs, Economic Development, and Environmental Disruption,* in J.E. Ullmann (ed.), London: University Press of America, reprinted 1983.

Katz, M. and H. Rosen (1991), *Microeconomics,* Hoomewood, IL: Irwin.

Lange, Oskar and Fred M. Taylor (1938), *On the Economic Theory of Socialism*, edited by Benjamin E. Lippincott, reprinted, New York: McGraw-Hill, 1966.

Lipsey, R.G. and K. Lancaster (1956), 'The general theory of second-best', *Review of Economic Studies*, vol. 7.

Little I.M.D. (1950), *A Critique of Welfare Economics*, Oxford: Oxford University Press.

Martinez-Alier, J. and Klaus Schluepmann (1987), *Ecological Economics*, Oxford: Blackwell.

Martinez-Alier, J. (1992), 'Ecological economics and concrete utopias', *Utopian Studies*, 3 (1), 39–52.

Martinez-Alier, J. (1994), 'Distributional conflicts and international environmental policy on carbon dioxide emissions and agricultural biodiversity', in J.C.J.M. van den Bergh and J. van der Straaten (eds), *Toward Sustainable Development*, Washington: Island Press/ISEE, 235–63.

Martinez-Alier, J. and M. O'Connor (1996), 'Ecological and economic distribution conflicts', in R. Costanza, J. Martinez-Alier, and O. Segura (eds), *Getting Down to Earth: Practical applications of ecological economics*, Washington DC: Island Press/ISEE.

Meikle, S. (1995), *Aristotle's Economic Thought*, Oxford: Clarendon.

Miller, D. (1992), 'Deliberative democracy and social choice', *Political Studies*, 40, 54–67.

Mishan, E.J. (1971), 'The postwar literature on externalities: an interpretative essay', *Journal of Economic Literature*, 9 (1), 1–28.

Mishan, E.J. (1982), *Cost–Benefit Analysis: An Informal Introduction*, 3rd edition, London: George Allen and Unwin.

Munda, G. (1993), 'Multiple criteria decision aid: some epistemological considerations', *Journal of MultiCriteria Decision Analysis*, vol. 2, 41–55.

Munda, G. (1995), *Multicriteria Evaluation in a Fuzzy Environment. Theory and applications in ecological economics*, Heidelberg: Physica-Verlag.

Munda, G. (1996), 'Cost–benefit analysis in integrated environmental assessment: some methodological issues', in *Ecological Economics*, 19, (2), 157–68.

Munda, G., P. Nijkamp and P. Rietveld (1994), 'Qualitative multicriteria evaluation for environmental management', *Ecological Economics*, 10, 97–112.

Munda, G., P. Nijkamp and P. Rietveld (1995), 'Monetary and non-monetary evaluation methods in sustainable development planning', *Economie Appliquée*, XLVIII, (2), 145–62.

Neurath, Otto (1919), *Through War Economy to Economy in Kind*, in Neurath, 1973.

Neurath, Otto (1925), *Wirtschaftsplan und Naturalrechnung*, Berlin: Laub.

Neurath, Otto (1928), *Personal Life and Class Struggle*, in Neurath 1973.

Neurath, Otto (1973), *Empiricism and Sociology*, Dordrecht: Reidel.

Nijkamp, P. (1986), 'Equity and efficiency in environmental policy analysis: separability versus inseparability', in A. Schnaiberg, N. Watts and K. Zimmermann, *Distributional Conflicts in Environmental Resource Policy*, Aldershot, UK: Gower, 59–108.

O'Connor, M. and E. Muir (1995), 'Endowment effects in competitive general equilibrium: a primer for paretian policy analysts', *Journal of Income Distribution*, 5, 145–75.

O'Connor M., S. Faucheux, G. Froger, S.O. Funtowicz and G. Munda (1996), 'Emergent complexity and procedural rationality: post-normal science for sustainability', in R. Costanza, J. Martinez-Alier and O. Segura (eds), *Getting Down to Earth: Practical Applications of Ecological Economics*, Washington D.C: Island Press/ISEE.

O'Neill, J. (1993), *Ecology, Policy and Politics*, London: Routledge.

O'Neill, J. (1995a), 'In partial praise of a positivist', *Radical Philosophy*, 74, 29–38.

O'Neill, J. (1995b), 'Policy, economy, neutrality', *Political Studies* XLIII, 414–31.

O'Neill, J. (1995c), 'Public goods, environmental goods, institutional economics', *Environmental Politics*, 4, 197–218.

O'Neill, J. (1996), 'Value pluralism, incommensurability and institutions', in J. Foster (ed.), *Valuing Nature?: Economics, Ethics and Environment*, London: Routledge.

O'Neill, J. (forthcoming), 'Who won the socialist calculation debate?', *History of Political Thought*.

Passet, R. (1979), *L'économique et le vivant*, Paris: Payot.

Pearce, D.W. and C.A. Nash (1981), *The Social Appraisal of Projects*, London: Macmillan.

Pearce, D.W. and G.D. Atkinson (1993), 'Capital theory and the measurement of sustainable development: an indicator of "weak" sustainability', *Ecological Economics*, vol. 8, 103–8.

Polanyi, K. (1957), 'Aristotle discovers the economy', in K. Polanyi, C.W. Arensberg and H.W. Pearson (eds), *Trade and Market in the Early Empires*, New York: Free Press, 243–70.

Popper-Lynkeus, Josef (1912), *Die allgemeine Naehrflicht als Loesung der soziale Frage*, Dresden: Reissner.

Roemer, J.E. and J. Silvestre (1994), 'Investment policy and market socialism', in P.K. Bardhan and J.E. Roemer (eds), *Market Socialism: The Current Debate*, New York.

Roemer, J.E. (1994), *A Future for Socialism*, London: Verso.

Roy, B. (1985), *Méthodologie multicritere d'aide à la decision*, Paris: Economica.

Samuels, W. (1972), 'Welfare economics, power and property', reprinted in W. Samuels and A. Schmid (eds) (1981), *Law and Economics: An International Perspective*, Boston: Martin Nijohoff.

Schmid, A. (1978), *Property, Power and Public Choice*, New York: Praeger.

Scitowsky, T. (1941), 'A note on welfare propositions in economics', *Review of Economic Studies*, 9.

Scitowsky, T. (1954), 'Two concepts of external economies', *Journal of Political Economy*, 58, 143–51.

Sen, A. (1987), *On Ethics and Economics*, Oxford: Blackwell.

Simon, H.A. (1972), *Theories of Bounded Rationality. Decision and Organization*, edited by C.B. Radner and R. Radner, Amsterdam: North Holland.

Simon, H.A. (1978), 'On How to Decide What to Do', *The Bell Journal of Economics*, 9, 494–507.

Simon, H.A. (1983), *Reason in Human Affairs*, Stanford: Stanford University Press.

Soddy, F. (1922), *Cartesian Economics: The bearing of physical science upon state stewardship*, London: Hendersons.

Turvey, R. (1963), 'On divergences between social cost and private cost', August, *Economica*.

Vansnick, J.C. (1986), 'On the problem of weights in multiple criteria decision-making (the noncompensatory approach)', *European Journal of Operational Research*, 24, 288–94.

Vatn, A. and D.W. Bromley (1994), 'Choices without prices without apologies', *Journal of Environmental Economics and Management*, 26, 129–48.

Williams, B. (1972), *Morality*, Cambridge: Cambridge University Press.

3. Sustainable Decision-Making: The State of The Art from an Economics Perspective

Michael A. Toman

3.1 INTRODUCTION

Government, corporate and other decision-makers are more and more often being urged to 'act sustainably' and to pursue policy paths toward 'sustainable development'. These admonitions and instructions appear to express a significant societal commitment to alter current practices. And yet these widely supported admonitions provide little guidance to policy makers and other actors, because the term 'sustainable' embodies deep conceptual ambiguities. These ambiguities cannot be easily resolved because they rest, in turn, on serious theoretical disagreements about the interactions of humans with their environment that transcend disciplinary boundaries.

In this paper I attempt to summarize the current state of knowledge on sustainable development from the perspective of what practical guidance is offered by economic analysis to decision-makers. I begin with the obvious point that there is no consensus about what constitutes sustainability, and such a consensus may be long in the future. I further argue that this is not a question that can be addressed solely through an improvement in scientific knowledge. These observations lead me to express skepticism about the capacity of *any* more or less mechanistic rule, economic, scientific or otherwise, to provide definitive and reliable answers about sustainable policies or conduct.

However, I do suggest that the past several years of research and debate about sustainability have begun to identify *processes and procedures* that can guide decision-making. I underscore the need for a methodologically pluralistic approach to addressing sustainability issues, and the need to recognize the range of different values at issue in sustainability debates. In making these points, however, I also underscore the importance of addressing economic costs and benefits as one important element of sustainability assessment, and I note that practicioners of cost–benefit analysis are increasingly recognizing the need for embedding their findings in a broader set of information. I further note that a pluralistic approach, without mechanistic decision rules, only increases the need to have greater quantity and maturity of political discussion and education about sustainability than seems often to prevail.

3.2   THE LACK OF CONSENSUS ON SUSTAINABILITY

I do not propose here to review the plethora of sustainability definitions that has emerged over the last few years (for example, Pezzey, 1989 and Toman, 1994). Instead, I attempt to identify several broad and somewhat overlapping categories of interpretation which in practice have quite different policy implications, and to provide a fair description of some of the more controversial underlying assumptions.

Perhaps the most familiar definition to economic theorists is that sustainability requires nondecreasing well-being, or potential well-being, over time.[1] Two very large loose ends remain in this understanding of sustainability, however. The first concerns the kinds of endowments that must be provided to future generations to achieve a quality of life at least the equal of our own. Economists tend to assume that degradation of some resources can be ameliorated by increases in other kinds of social investment (in people, machines, or ideas). This *weak sustainability* concept (Solow, 1986; Pearce and Atkinson, 1993) draws particular attention to the total level of saving provided for the future, with less emphasis on the particular components of the endowments (for example, nature versus human constructs). This perspective is by no means universally accepted in the sustainability debate.

The other major loose end is addressed by the question 'Whose well-being?' Most sustainability discussions implicitly or explicitly seem to emphasize the well-being of all future generations. However, there are respectable philosophical arguments that would put much greater emphasis on the well-being of the immediate future, the people with whom we arguably have the most identification (for example, Golding, 1972; Parfit, 1983; Passmore, 1974).[2] The emphasis on future generations in sustainability debates also puts less emphasis on other pressing questions related to the distribution of well-being and opportunities within the current generation, and how efforts to help safeguard the future are related to our current obligations to the world's destitute.

This point leads us to a second broad category of sustainability interpretations that also lies largely within the realm of economics. This view combines observations about the inefficiency of current economic policies and practices with theorems about the economically efficient management and protection of the environment to argue that correction of market failures (externalities) and policy failures is a key element of sustainability. According to this view, there is a substantial 'win–win' opportunity for increasing economic well-being as conventionally measured and the level of environmental protection. One of the most articulate versions of this argument can be found in World Bank (1992). The set of policy recommendations emerging from this argument combines standard prescriptions of environmental economics (correct open access and underpricing of collective environmental goods, tax or otherwise restrict the productions of bad spillovers) with standard prescriptions of economic growth and development theory (reduce economic pricing and management distortions, expand international trade and investment opportunities, develop stable macro policies and a secure regime of property rights).

Many economists and other experts heartily endorse these recommendations for expanding economic activity and environmental protection. Yet, critics can argue that even if one accepts these prescriptions as necessary for sustainability (and there is not unanimity on that point), they are not sufficient. By essentially reinventing environment and development economics, this conception of sustainability does not address whether more efficient market behavior will provide either adequate provision in general for future generations, or adequate provision of specific forms of capital that may be needed to maintain future well-being. Like the weak sustainability view, the environmental and development efficiency perspective tends to assume a relatively high degree of substitutability among resources. Moreover, it generally tends to be relatively 'presentist' in its orientation, focusing on expanding opportunities for the current poor and the next generation.

There is a variant of the 'win–win' which holds that there are significant untapped opportunities for technological innovation that will protect the environment and promote economic activity (see especially Porter and van der Linde, 1995). By embracing regulations and other policies that spur this innovation, the argument continues, the parties involved (firms or nations) can further expand economic gains by increasing shares of domestic and foreign markets in the relevant technologies.

The part of the argument which holds that innovation can and will occur if policies are correctly designed, and that this innovation will reduce the cost of protecting natural and environmental resources, is widely accepted among economists and others. However, the argument that there are sufficient untapped opportunities as to make environmental protection the source of increased economic activity depends on the existence of a pretty deep well of low-cost untapped technical potential, which is much more controversial (for example, Palmer et al., 1995). Moreover, the argument that expanding markets can provide an offset to the economic costs of environmental protection needs to take into account the fact that if there is widespread demand for such protection, these markets likely will quickly become as competitive as other technology markets, with success less assured even for the early innovators.

The economic perspectives just discussed contrast with other disciplinary perspectives. Some ecologists, for example, emphasize ecological concepts of system function and resiliency that do not appear in the standard economic representation of production and consumption opportunities (see Holling, 1986, 1993; see also Common and Perrings, 1992 and Arrow et al., 1995). This view holds that ecological systems are only malleable within limits, beyond which they may abruptly transform into a new state. The new state may be very unlike the prior condition and not necessarily as friendly to human interests that were adapted to the status quo ante. Such transformations are ubiquitous naturally, but generally at a smaller scale than the stresses that can arise from human activities on a regional or global scale and overcome the redundancy of natural systems. Moreover, the threat of discontinuous unwelcome natural transformations can arise from a myriad of small stresses on component ecological systems that are individually less noticeable.

This argument raises questions about the substitution hypotheses underlying much economic analysis of sustainability and leads in turn to much greater emphasis on the need for ecological protection (Daly, 1990, 1992). In a number of cases, however, the argument for preservation is based on a scientific assessment of ecological consequences from the status quo, without a connection being drawn explicitly from the ecological to the human consequences. There is a presumption that humans cannot live with the ecological consequences — that substitution is not easy or even possible — and this presumption is used to justify a strong (in some cases, almost lexicographic) presumption in favor of ecological preservation. These presumptions are as hotly debated as the economists' perspectives and prescriptions. Their plausibility is a function of the scale of the potential impacts, since smaller-scale impacts generally are more readily ameliorated than larger-scale ones. The ecological and economic uncertainties surrounding the functions of natural systems, the contributions of those functions to human well-being, and the impacts of human intervention make firm scientific conclusions difficult to draw (Carpenter, 1992).

Social perspectives on sustainability provide yet another set of views. Cultural theorists have attempted to describe people's values in terms of various 'social solidarities' to which they hew. In this approach, different social world views affect, among many things, the extent to which nature is seen as robust, fragile or somewhere in between, and the types of solutions prescribed for environmental threats (for example, regulations or market outcomes). For example, Rayner (1994) argues that the position one takes on these issues could be described as depending on the extent to which one identifies with a world view that is 'hierarchical' (implying a duty to act in the larger interest), 'egalitarian' (implying a duty to be fair to others), or 'competitive' (implying a duty to seek self-interested outcomes with peers). Perspectives like this emphasize the endogeneity of individual values to the cultural context in which they are formed, thereby admitting the possibility that as cultures change through exposure to new ideas, so will the individual values and preferences of its members. Economists also have wrestled with how to connect ethical concerns and endogenous values with models of individual preferences (Woodward and Bishop, 1995 ; Spash et al., 1995 ; Stern, 1997).

Related to these broad ideas of community values is the concept that humans attach great importance to a sense of place. This value may be seen by proponents of this perspective as transcending market values (see, for example, Norton and Hannon, forthcoming). Such a perspective can be used to support the minimization of spillovers that would disrupt the identity people derive from their connections to place and community. Critics of this view, while conceding that a sense of place has value, would again question the quasi-lexicographic view that loss of that value is so inherently noncompensable, and whether the exercise of a sense of place could disrupt a larger community by transferring large amounts of power to small disaffected groups.

Both economic and social arguments can be used to underscore the importance of procedural issues — in particular, the degree of inclusiveness of social decision-making and the sense of fair play people have about the process — in evaluating sustainability policies. For example, people may accept an outcome that seems a priori to treat them unfairly if they believe it has been arrived at through due process as part of a larger social compact; they may more readily accept government actions they believe reflect their own concerns. This argument has been expanded by advocates of 'place-based policymaking' to embrace a variety of economic, social, and environmental concerns (see, for example, PCSD, 1996).

This perspective on sustainability makes process a central concern, with, for example, an emphasis on participatory stakeholder forums for addressing contentious policy issues. While procedural fairness seems an undeniable virtue, it is also the case that for social agreements to be lasting and to contribute to meeting affected parties' needs, they need to reflect solid substance as well as process. In addition, they must reflect the views of all affected parties, including those not adequately organized to participate in stakeholder dialogues. Even advocates of place-based policy-making acknowledge that these are significant challenges to overcome.

3.3   SUSTAINABILITY AND SCIENCE

The discussion in the previous section reveals a wide range of different conceptions of sustainability, emphasizing substantive economic, ecological and social concerns and procedural issues. These various conceptions are based in turn on various sets of values, for example, perceived differences in the importance of economic well-being, ecological integrity, and social legitimacy. It therefore seems obvious on its face that debate on sustainability cannot be resolved solely by recourse to scientific inquiry. For example, substantial progress in resolving uncertainties about the effects of greenhouse gases on the world's climate system, and the effects of climatic changes on ecological systems and human well-being, will not in itself address basic disagreements about the importance of humans versus nature.

Governments and other decision-makers continually seek to reduce factual uncertainties in order to support 'better' decisions. This can be seen in the attention paid to the quality of science underlying major regulatory and other policy decisions (witness the controversy during the 104th Session of the US Congress over legislation that would attempt to prescribe standards for scientific assessments and peer reviews before government regulated). It can also be seen in the surge of recent interest in 'sustainability indicators' that would seek to provide a snapshot view of whether sustainability is being achieved (PCSD, 1996). Proposed indicators include both corrections to national income and product accounts to reflect depletion and degradation of natural endowments, and parallel measures of ecological and social conditions (for example, flows of materials and wastes, sociological data such as poverty statistics, and so on).

Efforts to improve scientific understanding are important contributions to better decision-making. However, such efforts also can mask deeper and more complex disagreements about social values. Even in the refuge of scientific inquiry, moreover, value judgments are not absent. Prior assumptions about what is important implicitly guide the structuring of scientific inquiry. For example, if one takes the view that ecological systems are organized hierarchically according to scale, the study of these systems at the micro scale (the function of a single leaf) will differ from the study of these systems at a macro scale (the biome), and there is no scientific basis for preferring one level of inquiry over another (Norton, 1992a).

The fact that science is not and cannot be entirely value-free does not imply that science must be subservient to values in sustainability, or that established measures to test and validate scientific hypotheses must be discarded. Instead, I would argue that science and values need to be seen as two sides of a recurring process in which increased information about the natural world and human impacts leads to a reconsideration of values, which in turn leads to a refocusing of science as needed to address emerging policy issues. This recursive process ensures not only that scientific inquiry is focused on issues that need to be addressed in forming policies, but also that new scientific insights find their way into the policy debate and stimulate constructive reevaluations of existing positions.

3.4   THE NEED FOR A PLURALISTIC APPROACH

The plethora of different conceptions of sustainability, and the inability of these issues to be resolved through some 'silver bullet' scientific breakthrough, underscore the need for a pluralistic approach to sustainability. Knowledge from the ecological sciences about the physical consequences of different management regimes (including laisser faire), their scale and duration, clearly is important in an economic assessment. Similarly, information from other social sciences about determinants of values and how values might change in different circumstances is useful in its own right and useful for economists in considering the robustness of willingness to pay estimates. By the same token, information about economic and other values can help guide scientists in determining how studies of the natural world should be focused.

However, my argument goes beyond the relatively innocuous assertion that interdisciplinary enrichment in resource assessment is useful. A pluralistic approach to evaluation of options also is needed. Consider first the use of economic assessment; the role of other disciplinary perspectives is discussed below.

There are several reasons why a narrow cost–benefit approach to sustainability evaluation is in itself inadequate (see, for example, Toman, 1994). Such an approach does not adequately address important distributional concerns, both within and across generations. It also does not address concerns people may have with decision-making procedures themselves, for example, how fair they are. In addition, sole reliance on monetary measures of benefits and costs cannot adequately address important impacts that are not easily monetized.[3] It may further be problematic when, as is often the case with environmental issues, there is a high level of nonquantifiable uncertainty (in other words, there is limited information about underlying processes rather than just statistical uncertainty about key parameter values), and the possibility of very adverse effects. In these kinds of situations there is not just the problem of quantifying expected values and other moments of probability distributions; there also is concern that the standard model of expected utility maximization does not work very well — for example, that people have asymmetric attitudes toward different kinds of risks (Machina, 1987).

To overcome these limitations, decision-makers must supplement economic information with information on the physical consequences (in space and time) of different decisions, information on the incidence of various effects, and other sources of information about social values and priorities, such as information from political processes. This information helps provide a broader context in which economic calculations of benefits and costs can be evaluated, especially significant uncertainties and irreversibilities can be identified, and conflicts with values like fairness can be explored. In this approach, the policy decision ultimately will rest with the judgment of the decision-makers, and thus will be inherently a political question. However, while there are no magic formulae for these decisions, various kinds of sensitivity and multicriteria analytic techniques may be useful complements to the economic assessment.[4]

Just as one can express doubt about the usefulness of a rigid benefit–cost criterion for sustainability, one can just as strongly question the possibility of other disciplines having a unique capacity to settle such policy issues. In particular, ecological information — even if more of it were available than today — could not in itself establish a course of action. Some combination of information and assumptions about social values must give context to that information. This is why, for example, efforts to establish 'sustainability indicators' can only be meaningful with a set of explicit or implicit axioms about what is important to measure and why; without this context, only a mass of data is provided. Similarly, to argue that certain norms for ecological protection must be met, and to confine socioeconomic assessment entirely to an evaluation of which means might be cost-effective, can only be justified by nonscientific value judgments that can and should be debated. In addition, the elaboration of moral precepts accomplishes little toward guiding actual management decisions unless one has some idea of the extent to which the precepts actually animate decision-makers, and the actual consequences of the precepts for management (for example, the need to protect certain 'key' resources or alleviate another problem like child poverty).

It may be surprising to some critics of conventional environmental economics that there already is a growing recognition within that group of the need for the sort of pluralism described here. For example, Kopp et al., (1997) describe an expansive approach to cost–benefit analysis that combines intensive efforts to monetize environmental damages with the requirement to provide detailed information on the nature of physical effects and the incidence of benefits and costs. They argue that such information should have broad standing in public policy assessments and decision-making, but that its weight should not be overriding (as would be the case with a rigid benefit–cost decision criterion).[5]

Similar reasoning underlies the approach to regulation enunciated by the Clinton Administration under a September, 1993 presidential action, Executive Order 12866. Under that approach, benefits are to 'justify' costs, rather than outweighing them, a conscious departure from earlier cost–benefit mandates which emphasize a more pluralistic approach. The list of impacts to consider in the Executive Order includes a number of concerns (environmental protection, distribution, and equity) that can partly or entirely transcend economic calculations. The Executive Order also emphasizes the need for procedural fairness and transparency and inclusiveness in seeking out information and views on values affected.[6]

'Two-tier' conceptual frameworks provide one basis for structuring a pluralistic approach (see Norton, 1992b ; Toman, 1994, and Norton and Hannon, forthcoming for discussions). In this sort of framework, decision-makers must first consider what criteria and management tools to apply to a particular issue. It is presumed in the framework that human impacts on the environment that are larger in scale and longer in duration give rise to greater concerns about the opportunities for well-being available to future generations (as well as to ourselves), and about the opportunities for amelioration of adverse effects through the conventional channels of resource substitution and innovation. Impacts that are smaller in scale and shorter in duration give rise to less concern and thus are more amenable to being treated through conventional cost–benefit tools, supplemented with information about nonmonetizable impacts and distributional consequences. In other cases, standard economic calculations are more likely to need supplementing with information about the physical robustness of underlying ecological systems and the potential consequences over time, and by information about social norms (for example, basic presumptions about fairness to existing communities and future generations) that might be affected.

We can briefly illustrate these ideas in the context of climate change. Climate policies undertaken by the current generation will impose costs (and generate some ancillary benefits, like air quality improvements) for the current generation. These costs should be assessed to the extent possible using the best state of the art in economic analysis, including procedures for intragenerational discounting that reflect the opportunity costs of changes in consumption and investment streams. The benefits of action or the costs of inaction, on the other hand, are more complex to assess since they involve significant redistributions of income between current and future generations; they will accrue globally, not just to our own heirs; they are difficult to estimate; and they will depend on the actions taken — for example, actions to reduce future risks by limiting greenhouse gas emissions, versus actions to promote adaptability to future climate change that can also provide more immediate economic development benefits. Simply calculating the present value of these effects as they appear to the current generation does not provide an adequate basis for evaluating different outcomes. An alternative is to provide a description of the effects (monetary and otherwise) and their timing, and allow decision-makers to weigh these effects and their costs against a variety of ethical criteria and the expressed wishes of various stakeholders.

The approach thus uses multiple disciplines in the first tier to assess how an issue should be judged, and then in the second tier in evaluating the issue and decisions (though the mix of disciplines will vary depending on the first tier outcome). The fact that this is not just an application of 'scientific' policy analysis can be underscored by the fact that value judgments will permeate the first tier categorization decision-making as well as guiding the second tier evaluation. The process thus can operate only if it is superimposed on a mature ongoing social discussion about which values matter in which contexts. With this superimposition, the interaction between science on the one hand and the process of values formation and education on the other hand can operate.

3.5   CONCLUSIONS: A CONCEPTUAL BLUEPRINT FOR SUSTAINABILITY DECISION-MAKING

Based on the discussion in the previous sections, we can now sketch the following conceptual blueprint for action to promote sustainability:

(1) Prior assessment of what criteria and evaluation tools should apply to the issue. In the two-tier model sketched above, this amounts to assessing where the issue lies on a continuum between a simple analysis of economic tradeoffs and an analysis more circumscribed by physical limits on substitution and the operation of broader social norms, which themselves must be identified.

(2) Assessment of physical impacts from different courses of action to the extent possible, with particular attention to their scale, to the

identification of impacts that are difficult to evaluate in monetary terms and to distributional issues across space and time.

(3) Assessment of economic benefits and costs from different courses of action to the extent possible, as well as their incidence in space and time.

(4) Further identification of whether and how social values or norms beyond the quantified benefits and costs may be affected by a decision.

(5) Engagement of public discourse about both the consequences of different actions and the applicable social values, especially where operable norms are not clear-cut or are conflicting. This is the step which explicitly acknowledges that the decision process cannot be purely scientific. The public engagement can take various forms, from educational programs to multiple-stakeholder negotiations to interagency debates with disclosure and electoral accountability.

(6) Decision-making based on the pluralistic approach and criteria outlined above.

(7) Using the results of the decision process to consider what new information and uncertainties have been revealed about both science and social values, and plugging these insights back into both the values discourse and scientific research agendas.

As noted at the beginning of the chapter, this blueprint is long on process and short on concrete decision rules. Such rules may be very helpful in certain circumstances that are more clear-cut and where decision shortcuts are useful. This could be the case, for example, for a number of regulatory decisions on issues without large-scale and enduring ecological consequences (though there will be debate on these points too, indicating the provisional nature of policy evaluation). For decisions in this category, a rough cut on economic benefits and costs combined with information to screen out excessively adverse distributional consequences may be more than adequate. Not all actions will be completely efficient or fair, but actions with very unfair or inefficient consequences can be sieved out. For more complex issues, on the other hand, the more complex process sketched above would be needed.

Practical experience will be needed to flesh out this. Success in gaining this experience will be aided by a greater commitment to pluralism by analytical practicioners. It will also be aided by a greater commitment by decision-makers and analysts alike to the use of analysis in policy determination, to exposing and evaluating hidden value judgments, and to the recursive interactions between policy determination and scientific assessments mentioned previously.

ENDNOTES

1. The emphasis on potential well-being, while often sluffed off in simple models, is important in that the current generation cannot guarantee how the future will turn out, either in terms of its opportunities or its proclivities. However, the current generation can take steps to make sure that the future generation is able to have opportunities to do as well as we are, at least as reckoned given our limited insights into future ecological conditions, technology, wants, and tastes.

2. One of the interesting philosophical points to emerge from the sustainability debate has been an understanding that while neoclassical economics is strongly utilitarian, there are utilitarian constructs that put much more emphasis on future generations than the neoclassical model with discounting (see, for example, Broome, 1992). The debate is better cast as one over teleological (effects-based) approaches, deontological (rights-based) approaches, and contractarian (for example, stewardship) approaches to intergenerational responsibility (Norton and Toman, 1997).

3. This is an important consideration whether one believes that full monetization of impacts is possible in principle and that the handicap is empirical, or that some impacts are inherently incommensurable with individual monetary measures of well-being and thus defy monetization.

4. Faucheux et al. (1997) address these issues in the context of what they call 'procedural rationality'. The idea here is that when knowledge is limited, optima are hard to identify, and irreversible consequences may ensue, decision-making should seek to preserve options, identify measurable subgoals, and choose 'satisfactory' outcomes based on these goals. They advocate a particular form of multicriteria analysis to help identify such policies, with tradeoffs among subgoals mediated by certain imperatives (for example, no reduction in biodiversity below a certain level) that must be satisfied.

5. Adams (1995) argues that the only appropriate response to the limitations of cost–benefit analysis is to discard the method. While I agree that CBA techniques can be and are misused, and the CBA cannot determine social policy, I do not agree with his prescription.

6. The fact that this conceptual parallel exists does not mean that the US government's decision-making apparatus is doing a good job in practice of generating sustainable outcomes. Critics express concern about the quality of the economic assessments done by agencies; the assessments may fall short because of statutory constraints on the scope of economic analysis in rulemaking or lack of agency commitment (that is, too little spent too late on assessment with too little impact on agency decisions). As Kopp et al. (1996) point out, analysts such as Ludder and Morrall (1994), Congressional Budget Office (1995), and Hahn (1996) have identified very inconsistent economic assessments (for example, very different levels of expenditures to reduce similar levels of risk, or greater expenditures to reduce lesser risks, as well as costs that seem very much in excess of benefits). This information suggests that the economic component of regulatory assessment often does not function well.

REFERENCES

Adams, J. (1995), 'Cost–Benefit Analysis: Part of the Problem, Not the Solution', revised version of a paper presented at Green College Centre for Environmental Policy and Understanding, Oxford, UK, on December 9, 1994.

Arrow, K., B. Bolin, R. Costanza, P. Dasgupta, C. Folke, C.S. Holling, B. Jansson, S. Levin, K. Maler, C. Perrings and D. Pimentel (1995), 'Economic growth, carrying capacity, and the environment', April, *Science*, 268, 520–21.

Broome, J. (1992), *Counting the Cost of Global Warming*, Cambridge: White Horse Press.

Camerer, C.F. and H. Kunreuther (1989), 'Decision processes for low probability events: policy implications', *Journal of Policy Analysis and Management*, 8 (4), 565–92.

Carpenter, R.A. (1992), 'Can Sustainability Be Measured', paper presented at the 2nd Meeting of the International Society for Ecological Economics, Stockholm University, Stockholm, Sweden, August 3–6.

Common, M. and C. Perrings (1992), 'Towards an ecological economics of sustainability', *Ecological Economics*, 6 (1), 7–34.

Congressional Budget Office (1995), *The Safe Drinking Water Act: A Case Study of an Unfunded Federal Mandate*, Washington, DC: Congress of the United States, Congressional Budget Office, September.

Daly, H. (1990), 'Toward some operational principles of sustainable development', April, *Ecological Economics*, 2, 1–6.

Daly, H. (1992), 'Steady-state economics: concepts, questions, policies', *GAIA*, 6, 333–8.

Faucheux, S. and M. O'Connor (eds) (1997), *Valuation for Sustainable Development: Methods and Policy Indicators*, Cheltenham: Edward Elgar.

Faucheux, S., G. Froger and G. Munda (1997), Chapter 8 in S. Faucheux and M. O'Connor (eds), *Valuation for Sustainable Development*, Cheltenham: Edward Elgar.

Golding, M.P. (1972), 'Obligations to future generations', *The Monist*, 56, 85–99.

Hahn, R.W. (1996), 'Regulatory reform: what do the government's numbers tell us?', in R.W. Hahn (ed.), *Risks, Costs, and Lives Saved*, Washington, DC: The AEI Press.

Holling, C.S. (1986), 'Resilience of ecosystems: local surprise and global change', in W.C. Clark and R.E. Munns (eds), *Sustainable Development of the Biosphere*, Cambridge, MA: Cambridge University Press.

Holling, C.S. (1993), 'New science and new investments for a sustainable biosphere', in R. Costanza, C. Folke, M. Hammer and A.M. Jansson (eds), *Investing in Natural Capital: Why, What, and How?*, Solomons, MD, ISEE Press.

Kopp, R., A. Krupnick and M. Toman (1997), 'Cost–benefit analysis and regulatory reform', *Journal of Human and Ecological Risk Assessment*, 3 (5), 787–852.

Lutter, R. and J.F. Morrall III (1994), 'Health–health analysis: a new way to evaluate health and safety regulation', *Journal of Risk and Uncertainty*, 8 (1), 43–66.

Machina, M. (1987), 'Choice under uncertainty: problems solved and unsolved', *Journal of Economic Perspectives*, 1 (1), 121–54.

Norton, B. G. (1992a), 'A new paradigm for environmental management', in R. Costanza, B.G. Norton and B.D. Haskell (eds), *Ecosystem Health: New Goals for Environmental Management*, Covelo, CA: Island Press.

Norton, B. G. (1992b), 'Sustainability, human welfare, and ecosystem health', *Environmental Values*, 1 (2), 97–111.

Norton, B.G. and Bruce Hannon (forthcoming), 'Environmental values: a place-based theory', *Environmental Ethics*.

Norton, B.G. and Michael A. Toman (1997), 'Sustainability: ecological and economic perspectives', *Land Economics*, November 3 (4), 553–68.

Palmer, K., W.E. Oates and P.R. Portney (1995), 'Tightening environmental standards: the benefit–cost or the no–cost paradigm?', *Journal of Economic Perspectives*, 9 (4), 119–32.

Parfit, D. (1983), 'Energy policy and the further future: the identity problem', in D. MacLean and P.B. Brown (eds), *Energy and the Future*, Totowa, NJ: Rowman and Littlefield.

Passmore, J. (1974), *Man's Responsibility for Nature*, New York: Scribner's.

Pearce, D.W. and G.D. Atkinson (1993), 'Capital theory and the measurement of sustainable development: some empirical evidence', *Ecological Economics*, 8 (2), 103–8.

Pezzey, J. (1989), *Economic Analysis of Sustainable Growth and Sustainable Development*, World Bank Environment Department Working Paper No. 15 (now reprinted as Pezzey, J. (1992), *Sustainable Development Concepts: An Economic Analysis*, World Bank Environment Paper No. 2, Washington, DC: World Bank.

Porter, M.E. and Claas van der Linde (1995), 'Toward a New Conception of the Environment–Competitiveness Relationship', *Journal of Economic Perspectives*, 9 (4), 97–118.

President's Council on Sustainable Development (PCSD) (1996), *Sustainable America: A New Consensus for Prosperity, Opportunity, and a Healthy Environment for the Future*, Washington, DC: President's Council on Sustainable Development, February.

Rayner, S. (1994), 'Governance and the Global Commons', Discussion Paper 8, London: London School of Economics, Centre for the Study of Global Governance, January.

Solow, R.M. (1986), 'On the intergenerational allocation of natural resources', June, *Scandinavian Journal of Economics*, 88, 141–9.

Toman, M.A. (1994), 'Economics and "Sustainability" : Balancing Tradeoffs and Imperatives', *Land Economics*, 70 (4), 399–413.

World Bank (1992), *World Development Report 1992: Development and the Environment*, New York: Oxford University Press.

4. Environment Protection: Towards a Socio-Economic Policy Design

B. Bürgenmeier

The theory of environmental policy stresses the use of economic instruments (Baumol and Oates 1988). These instruments are well known and their efficiency widely recognized. However, they are not widely applied and raise a social acceptability problem.

This paradox is discussed here in three parts. The first part recalls the main results of a study about the introduction of ecological taxes in Switzerland. The second part discusses the conceptual problems raised by a purely economic approach to environmental protection. As these problems are downplayed by policy recommendations exclusively based on the promotion of economic instruments, it seems to be useful to show, in the third part, how social policies should be integrated in a global policy design.

4.1 SOCIAL ACCEPTABILITY OF ECOLOGICAL TAXES

The dilemma between theoretical demonstration and social acceptability of economic instruments can be illustrated by an inquiry conducted among 300 Swiss firms which are asked about the importance of the major objections raised in the public debate about the introduction of ecological taxes (Bürgenmeier et al. 1996). Though the majority of the answers were overwhelmingly positive (see Table 4.1), a recent CO_2 tax has been rejected in the preliminary consultation process which precedes any new legislation in Switzerland.

It is difficult to understand why the majority of firms agree on an ecological tax, but reply through their professional organizations have to protect the weakest members and reflect, therefore, the firms which replied negatively. Another explanation is linked to the conditions in which ecological taxes are introduced. If these taxes are accepted in principle only, they will raise many objections in practice where very different individual situations become relevant.

Table 4.1 Introduction of environmental taxes

Question: Are you favourable to taxes promoting a better environment protection?			
	YES %	NO %	NO ANSWER %
All firms	66.7	27.5	5.8
Polluting firms	63.6	27.3	9.1
Non-polluting firms	69.0	27.6	3.4

Table 4.2 regroups the ten main objections which have been mentioned by a majority of the firms questioned. This table shows that economic objections rank very high, but there are also arguments which have a strong normative content. This is the case for rank No. 3 where 'uncertainty about conflicting goals' means that ecological taxes may not only be used as incentives but also as fiscal revenues. Rank No. 6, No. 7 and No. 8 refer to objections which are rooted in the political rather than in the economic sphere.

Table 4.2 The main ten objections to ecological taxes

Rank	Questions	Average	Standard deviation
1	increased investments	0.77	0.67
2	supplementary production costs	0.63	0.77
3	uncertainty about conflicting goals	0.62	0.88
4	international competition	0.57	0.86
5	displacements	0.47	0.83
6	administrative costs too high	0.45	0.87
7	increasing influence of the State	0.41	0.97
8	problems of fiscal competence	0.39	0.97
9	uncertainty according to economic sectors	0.37	0.72
10	supplementary costs for consumers	0.36	0.92

In order to group the different objections, a factor analysis was performed. This analysis has the following result for all firms questioned:

factor one: objections linked to the production process
factor two: institutional setting
factor three: uncertainty about conflicting objections
factor four: uncertainty about the repercussion on prices

Factors one and four can be easily related to economic arguments. Factors two and three, however, refer to political and social conditions which stress the need for enlarged policy design. Instead of promoting exclusively ecological taxes, a more complex strategy should be implemented. That is, in addition to income redistribution policies and clearly targeted information accompany an ecological tax reform, a negotiation process should be employed. The main justifications for such a strategy are found in the fundamental conceptual problems raised by an economic approach to the environment.

4.2 CONCEPTUAL PROBLEMS OF ECONOMIC APPROACHES TO THE ENVIRONMENT

Economics considers the natural environment as a free good, having no monetary cost until its over-exploitation due to 'free-riding' makes it scarce and converts it into an economic good. The theory that tries to model this transformation subjects this process to the market as the analytical referent, and thus considers the environment as an externality to the economic sphere. This surprises most researchers in the other social sciences. Robert Hettlage expresses this astonishment as follows: 'Externalities are built, whose exploration can be delegated to other sciences lest they contaminate the model (this would at once clean the theory), if this explanation effort were necessary' (Hettlage, 1993, p. 84). Instead of accepting the intellectual limitations of every economic theory built on a 'pure' model, most economists continue to recommend the efficient market — albeit corrected by internalizing the externality — as a theoretical reference point and the practical means of better environmental protection. In our opinion, this recommanded procedure is the origin of social acceptability problems (Jeanrenaud, 1996).

The conceptual aspects arising in the economics environment relationship concern the notion of externality, the determination of non-market values and the social learning process which has to legitimate any policy in environmental protection.

4.2.1 The Environment: an Externality?

When it treats the environment only as an externality, economics is subject to criticism, particularly with respect to the concept of social cost which originates in reasoning that attempts to give a scientific basis to income transfers by relying on internalization techniques rooted in welfare economics. The externality argument admits that market failures can arise, where private benefits from some economic activity impose a cost on someone else. Such a case directly pertains to pollution, but has a more general scope. Every time there is an immediate benefit from an economic activity whose marginal cost is less than the expected marginal revenue, because a third party bears part of the total costs, we are confronted with market failure. No incentive to reduce or to stop such an activity exists. The total cost to society is greater than the cost borne by those who receive the private benefit. This situation calls for government intervention. The recommended policy is to ask the government to invoice the individual for the social cost created, for example through a tax on the polluting activity. This method of justifying government intervention consistent with market rules raises a daunting question: to what degree can the private marginal cost be compared to the social one? Such a comparison would only be conceptually acceptable if the costs could be measured objectively (Buchanan, 1969).

In the opinion of Robbins, the narrow interpretation of the market confronted with an externality has no scientific foundation. In 1933, in his famous essay about the nature and the meaning of economics, Robbins criticized Pigou for formulating concrete policy recommendations. The economic policy recommended by Pigou was based on welfare theory, that is, on the assumption of a decreasing marginal utility function. Indeed, for Pigou (1918), as each monetary unit of supplementary income is worth less for a rich person than for a poor person, transferring income between both is enough for global economic welfare to increase. In more popular terms, this means that a dollar does not have the same value for everybody and that fiscal transfers can correct this inequality.

This conclusion has been considered for many decades as the result of scientific reasoning. It has also been at the root of the theoretical concept of an ecological tax, compatible with the smooth operation of markets facing social costs because of pollution. Thus, it deals with the scientific foundation of values. Yet Robbins' challenge deals precisely with this point. According to him, all values are subjective, thus excluding any interpersonal utility comparison. Since the market faces external costs calling for environmental protection, no scientific response is possible and the debate remains primarily a normative one. We cannot objectively add numbers about individual valuations. According to this view, economists have no scientific criteria by which to evaluate the variation of a social value. If pollution reduces this value and requires a tax to be introduced, it is followed by income transfers which ultimately cannot be evaluated without value judgements. To our knowledge, this argument has never been refuted. No economist belonging to the marginalist school has ever proposed a theory that takes Robbins' objection into account. Accordingly, the whole dream of scientific economic policy recommendations based on theoretical modelling vanishes.

Although it is widely acknowledged by now that welfare theory is based on value judgements (Feldmann, 1983), many economists feel comfortable with the microeconomics modelling of the kind proposed in widespread textbooks (for example, Varian, 1992). According to this kind of modelling, any exchange in competitive markets increases global economic welfare, whatever the initial income distribution is, notwithstanding Robbins' warning. They follow Roy Harrod, who, in turn, criticized Robbins, explaining in 1938 that if Robbins were right, this would destroy any applied economics, because any policy favours some people to the detriment of others. If no subjective interpersonal utility comparisons can be made, economists should remain forever silent on the valuation of a society's economic welfare following any decision, be it individual and private or collective and public. According to Harrod, such a conclusion is too radical and therefore cannot be justified (Harrod, 1938). This position led Robbins to recant his own criticism of Pigou's welfare theory (Robbins, 1938); however, like all economists after him, he never gave arguments justifying this retraction. Perhaps Robbins followed Harrod with a view to perpetuating economists' influence in the formulation of political recommendations. Yet, this withdrawal was motivated by strategic, not scientific arguments. It was a question of protecting a discipline that experienced great difficulty in dissociating itself from a past where it formed a part of moral and social philosophy. This scientific ambition carefully separates positive from normative aspects of economics.

   In the field of environmental protection, market logic still has to be defended at any price. Among more recent authors, we found one of the sole expressions of this epistemological concern in the writings of James Buchanan (1969). If the debate on the most appropriate means to protect the environment is normative, it cannot be supported by a logic that purports to be scientific, neutral and free of values. Economists have to be more explicit about the norms and values underpinning their discipline.

4.2.2 Non-Market Values

The value of the environment as determined by a market refers to an economic use of it. Yet the value of the environment is also determined outside the market and independently of any economic use. The beauty of a landscape, amazement before scientific and artistic creation and inspiration are but a few examples of the value of the natural environment outside any exchange value. Because the natural environment has an intrinsic value, its worth cannot be determined exclusively by the market. Likewise, failure to subject the natural environment to economic use — albeit possible on both a technological and a normative plane — can give the environment a 'non-use' value that economists readily associate with an opportunity cost. This cost is part of every economic choice, and is defined by the fact that any economic decision related to managing scarce productive resources necessarily implies giving something up. Preventing the transformation of a mountain pasture into a tourist resort is evaluated economically in terms of loss of an alternative use. Yet such a decision also expresses values defined outside the economic field, where the concept of opportunity cost is inapplicable, and therefore hinges on society's perception of nature. The fact that we have progressively replaced the word 'nature' by the word 'environment' may be a sign of the current change in this perception (Baudrillard, 1972). An environmental protection policy essentially finds its legitimacy in such a change, itself determined by the social perception of non-market values. This change takes place over a long time, and is codified in laws, regulations, morals and customs which reflect the fact that people are increasingly aware of problems related to the protection of the environment, despite the fact that the intensity of this awareness can vary. Social concern about an undamaged environment can be supplanted by other, temporarily more worrying problems such as unemployment. However, this growing awareness has set in motion a process that influences all the symbols expressing the values to which our society adheres.

Finally, the change in these symbols also influences the behaviour of economic actors. It is therefore illusory to think that changing social perceptions of the natural environment will only change the institutions of a society and leave its perceptions of the economy untouched. Accordingly, we cannot observe constant and inalterable economic behaviour, but rather a permanent interaction between social values and human behaviour. The origin of changing motivations in individual as well as collective behaviour thus becomes crucial to the building of an operational environmental protection policy. Here, mainstream economic theory sees no more than an optimization problem subject to the constraint of satisfying new needs. This problem is addressed through an improved ability to solve environmental problems, which can be expressed, in terms of the standard economic rationale, by a change in the utility function. This time, however, the problem can no longer be treated identically from an individual and a collective point of view, due to the reasons set out above. There is no scientific criterion that enables us to move from an individual to a collective level. Society's economic welfare cannot be defined by simply adding up individual behaviour, and then treated as a simple allocative problem. A change in the social utility function ignores the factors which induced it. This brings us back to an old question in the history of economic thought: the definition of the 'right' price.

This question cannot be solved by simply referring to a price determined by supply and demand in a competitive market. It also implies the normative valuation of social values and costs. If economic theory fails to recognize this dilemma, that theory lays itself open to the criticism of removing its normative reference, and thus of serving a market ideology. Instead of pursuing the difficult path to more scientific accuracy, it becomes the main obstacle to the analysis of current economic practices. After all, a discipline that rejects questioning must remain suspicious, because scientific debate has always progressed through a critical dialectic and continuous questioning of fundamental hypotheses (Bürgenmeier, 1994). Under the pretence of having answered once and for all the question of the 'right' price with a market model, mainstream economic theory resists a much-needed renewal. It thus continues to treat the environment as an externality that has to be internalized in monetary terms in the market. The economic optimality calculus required by a cost–benefit analysis can then be applied to the pollution problem, in which case the environment is considered as a public good revealed by market failure. Tasks not fulfilled by the market are, in practice, handed over to the government; this strengthens the widespread conflict between the market and the State, between individualism and collectivism and between market society and civil society.

The public choice school points out that government failures also exist. Correcting market failures through government is often illusory. This concern has led us to favour a normative approach once again. If market and government failures exist, we might as well trust the market. Before handing over a task to the government, a case has to be clearly established that the task cannot be achieved by market forces. If from the standpoint of externality theory, the market alone is no safeguard for the protection of the environment and public intervention is therefore justified, the latter has to be implemented in accordance with market rules. Our discussion of the fundamental problems raised by interpersonal comparisons and their aggregation into social values and costs shows that the opposition between the market and the state is nonsensical, because the evaluation criteria cannot be the same for the market and the state. Therefore, market failures cannot be compared with government failures either. If we nevertheless try to make this comparison and conclude that markets are superior, we have to use the trick of public choice theory, and credit political actors with the same motivations as economic actors. If economic rationality is taken to be the unique behavioural norm, a comparison can only be made with economic criteria. In this case, nobody is surprised by the conclusion of the market's superiority, and the argument becomes perfectly circular.

From a scientific standpoint, the foregoing cannot be justified. An operational environmental protection policy is ill served by the simplistic opposition between the market and the state, or between individual competition and collective planning, and would benefit from a process which, in the end, leads to institutional changes in the market as well as to an increased consumer awareness motivating a new behavioural pattern. All values cannot be economic in nature.

4.2.3 Environmental Protection: a Social Learning Process

The supposition that social costs related to increased awareness of environmental protection can be considered as economic values, in terms of growth, raises daunting problems for evaluation. As any new economic activity over a certain size is subject by law to an environmental impact assessment in many countries, the consequences on the natural environment are, as a matter of fact, very difficult to determine. Mainstream economic theory recommends addressing this problem with a valuation based on a cost–benefit analysis reflecting the optimization concept. A large-scale investment project such as drilling a new tunnel through the Alps may increase economic growth and provide a means of reducing pollution, but may also add to existing environmental costs. Accordingly the valuation of a new investment project's environmental consequences must meet many criteria, where the question is to evaluate not only new costs, but also new expected benefits.

In practice, however, cost–benefit analysis, despite its theoretical foundations, is rarely applied. The research departments in charge of studying the environmental impact of some economic activity mainly rely on engineering expertise. Even if, due to the complexity of the criteria used, impact assessments are made by teams which also include social scientists, most analyses use a multicriteria approach, where the weighting of the different explanatory factors becomes essential. Engineers apparently prefer the weighted sum approach, which does not differentiate between explanatory factors on a qualitative level. Thus, if one variable is considered less important, the low weighting assigned to it cannot do justice to cases where this variable — for example above a certain emission level and sometimes only in relation to another variable — can, during the valuation procedure, take on a totally different meaning. Thus, considering new costs for the protection of the environment therefore requires analytical methods more sophisticated than those of cost–benefit analysis or the weighted sum.

Although the relevant literature offers many other methods for weighting the variables entered in an evaluation procedure, it should be stressed that none of them attaches sufficient importance to the fact that an impact assessment is a process that also includes a learning aspect. This element not only makes it likely that the value function of the criteria will be changed, but also increases the information of the actors concerned by the project and their knowledge of possible interactions between different variables. Consequently, we encounter a problem that has become familiar by now, namely the estimation of the social values and costs submitted to normative judgements, which varies according to the changing social perception of environmental problems over time. In other words, taking new environmental protection costs into account is a normative process, dependent on a politico–legal context which is also supposed to reflect these changes. This conclusion thus rules out any allegedly objective valuation method.

In order to take these objections into account, Jean Simos (1990) proposes an original approach that combines a multicriteria analysis with a negotiation procedure that includes a cognitive process for the actors concerned by the project evaluated. Therefore, not only does the actors' information improve during the negotiation, but the learning function is clearly taken into account. The normative dimension of any impact assessment then becomes part of the analysis. Important economic actors such as private firms and special interest groups have long stressed that any assessment must be combined with a negotiation process. They expect increased transparency in applying valuation criteria, as well as a learning effect for all the partners concerned by a project, in order to improve the instruments that are to be introduced with a view to enhancing environmental protection.

Thus, the future of impact assessments lies in going beyond approaches inspired by economic theory. Cost–benefit analysis is unable to dispel the ambiguity field to the economic treatment of social costs which could be considered beneficial in terms of growth. It cannot solve the conceptual problem of defining social costs as the aggregation of individual costs. Consequently, the definition of new costs will require increasingly complex analytical techniques that not only refer to socio-economic aspects such as the changing institutional frame provided by legislation but also give more importance to the actors concerned. Such a trend is clearly interdisciplinary (see Brown, 1994). It explicitly takes into account the fact that, ultimately, the positive aspect of an analysis cannot be separated from its normative aspect. On the contrary, these two aspects interact directly with each other and cannot be separated for analytical needs, as economic theory tries to do.

Taking a normative dimension into account in any valuation of new environmental costs is also justified from the point of view of the economic theory of welfare, which shows income distribution to have a normative content. Yet internalizing social costs into the market necessarily implies a redistribution which, when converted into monetary units, generates income transfers between different actors in the market. Hence, cost distribution is subject to normative judgements, which concern not only the distribution between actors of the same generation but also distribution between generations. Accordingly, consideration of new costs is subject to the collective perception of social justice. We saw that the growing awareness of environmental problems also depends on the evolution of this perception. The importance of social costs is therefore valued through a normative interactive process.

This conclusion applies to concrete markets. The weight of new environmental costs for the collectivity and their distribution among different actors depend upon the structure of these markets. Among the elements that define these structures, we find not only price elasticities of supply and demand linked to the internalization of external costs but also imperfect competition. Therefore, the environmental costs expressed in monetary units are more or less borne by producers or by consumers according to these prevailing conditions. The resulting prices thus reflect the market structure and value judgements with respect to distributive aspects.

If new environmental costs are taken into account in the markets, for example by means of a fuel tax, the expected result is usually an increase in fuel prices. Yet whether this increase is fair is uncertain. As any price increase has an exclusion effect dependent on income and wealth, this increase may reduce demand from low income earners while probably having very little impact on high income earners. In so far as market structures are strengthened by coalitions, fixing the price influences the cost distribution between both current producers and consumers and current and future generations. A standard economic analysis requires separating the positive and the normative aspect and necessitates a strict separation between economic policy — in our example, it would take the form of a fuel tax — and social policy. An environmental protection policy should be accompanied by a distinct social policy with corrective income transfers, for example in the form of a subsidy or direct payments for low incomes. Such a strategy again follows the illusion that the internalization of social costs can be objectively subjected to markets.

4.3   THE NEED FOR SOCIAL POLICIES

The debate about values, the internalization of social costs and the explicit recognition of ethical aspects confront economic theory with conceptual issues as soon as it tries to apply modelling to the physical and biological environment. New approaches are being brought to bear on this theoretical debate. Today, we can no longer refer to a single, exclusive economic approach. Many research strategies are being followed. We can basically distinguish to two groups of models.

The first group consists of conventional models which take the environment into account, either through public goods theory or through property rights theory. These two theories cover the main issues in environmental economics. The second group refers to more wide-reaching models, which try to feature relationships between economics and the biosphere. In the same way, models which add a social dimension in order to come closer to the concept of sustainable development (where these three levels: economic, environmental, social are included) also belong to this group, and cover the field of ecological economics. The first difference between environmental economics and ecological economics is one of methodology. Whereas environmental economics mainly refers to a mechanistic vision of the working of our societies and treats social institutions as an exogenous factor in its models, ecological economics refers to a more evolutionary perception of our societies and treats their institutional changes as important endogenous variables in its theoretical representations.

This methodological difference has an important consequence for the behavioural hypothesis underlying theoretical representations. Environmental economics explicitly refers to economic rationality, crediting social actors with only one type of behaviour, that is, maximizing either profits or utility, under the constraint of production costs or income respectively. On the contrary, ecological economics reminds us that the market, already in its temporal dimension, is short-sighted with regard to the ethical responsibility of individuals of the same generation and especially of one generation to another. Table 4.3 shows that value judgements are behind the economic approach to the environment at each stage.

At the first stage, the theory of public goods, defined by the criteria of non-rivalry and non-exclusion, implies a collective social decision in order to consider the environment as an economic good. At the second stage, the State and the environment are both external to the market, but have to interact in order to internalize the social costs to the market. At the third stage, the simple question 'who was first' in the economic use of the environment leads to conflicting positions about the 'polluter pays' principle. The fourth stage also gives rise to newly defined property rights. At the fifth stage, a theory of value cannot be solely built on the 'willingness to pay' principle ; moral considerations continue to ask for the 'just price' of the environment. Finally, at the sixth stage, the theory of welfare shows the necessary references to normative criteria in order to settle the case for equal income distribution.

Valuation and the Environment

4.4   CONCLUSIONS

The crucial point is the integration of the ethical dimension in the traditional theoretical representations of the economy that society has adopted (Bürgenmeier, 1993). The trend is to delegate ethical questions to the human sciences and thereby to 'clean' the economic model, which then constitutes the main reference. Ethics, as well as the environment, are then to be treated as external to the market. This distinction makes it possible to work on a 'scientific' level and root criteria in a positive basis. Theology and moral philosophy are assigned the task of maintaining the social representation of the workings of the economy as intact as possible, treating these aspects outside the economic sphere. The intellectual challenge lies not only in preventing such a development (which is already well under way if one is to judge by the many institutes specialized in economical ethics), but also in integrating ethical considerations in economic reasoning itself. The assumption of behaviour guided by a single motivation cannot be maintained, and has to be replaced by social representations which view economics with its entire ethical dimension. The promotion of economic policies of environment protection has to be completed by social policies in order to catch this dimension. Such social policies include both transfers of income redistribution, and basic values of the institutional setting of the market, such as legal regulation of 'fairness' and non-discriminatory practices. This extension inevitably exposes economics to a dilemma.

If, in competitive markets, actors act rationally, they contribute to the best possible resource allocation. Their activities follow an ethical logic that also seems to help preserve the environment. However, perfect competition rules out any action on non-economic grounds. In contrast, in situations of imperfect competition some room is made for other objectives, but economic efficiency is reduced. Yet such situations are put in the same category as market failures that become a prerequisite for the pursuit of non-economic objectives. For example, the possibility of taking the ethical dimensions of intergenerational responsibility into account is dependent on market failures. This conclusion reveals the ambiguity inherent in an exclusively economic treatment of environmental problems.

The following two modes of reasoning cannot be easily reconciled. Economic reasoning tries to reduce pollution at the lowest possible cost. It proposes an optimization calculus that equalizes the marginal cost with the marginal benefit of any economic activity. If many actors in a market are responsible for a given polluting emission, it recommends a policy reducing these where the marginal costs of doing so are smallest.

Table 4.3 Economics of the environment: different stages of value judgements

1) Theory of public goods	Non-exclusion for normative reason
2) Theory of externalities	Market failures corrected by incentives decided outside of the market place
3) 'Polluter pays' principle	Reciprocal nature of environmental uses
4) Theory of property rights	Attribution of property rights
5) Theory of value	How to determine values outside of the economy? (for example, non-use and intrinsic values)
6) Theory of welfare	How are the new costs distributed between individuals and generations?

Following the efficiency criterion, economic reasoning therefore allows for a differentiated treatment of actors in a market according to their cost or utility functions. In contrast, moral reasoning, often legally codified, is concerned with equality of treatment, which originates in a normative judgement (for example, through the collective memory of a community). This normative judgement may also come out of a political process. If this process is democratic, it is supposed to express the opinion of a majority. Once economic theory recognizes that there may be as many normative judgements as actors in the markets (and as many individual actions), legal reasoning only refers to collective preferences. As has been showed, an economic theory cannot be derived from individual preferences (Arrow, 1977), and we have no common criteria to evaluate these two logics. Economic instruments are supposed to obey the first, social policies the second, logic. They are complementary by nature, the one does not go without the other.

REFERENCES

Arrow, K.J. (1977), 'The organization of economic activity issues pertinent to the choice of market versus non-market allocation', in R.H. Haveman and J. Mangolis (eds), *Public Expenditure and Policy Analysis*, Chicago: Rand MacNally College Publishing Company.

Baudrillard, J. (1972), *Pour une critique de l'économie politique du signe*, Paris: Editions Gallimard.

Baumol, W.J. and W.E. Oates (1988), *The Theory of Environmental Policy*, Cambridge: Cambridge University Press.

Brown, G. (1994), 'Estimating non-use values requires interdisciplinary research', in B. Bürgenmeier (ed.), *Economy, Environment and Technology, A Socio–Economic Approach*, NY : M.E. Sharpe Inc. Armonk.

Buchanan, J. (1969), *Cost and Choice, An Inquiry in Economic Theory*, Chicago: Chicago University Press.

Bürgenmeier, B. (1993), 'Ethical aspects of environmental protection', in J.P. Vernet (ed.), *Environmental Contamination, Studies in Environmental Sciences*, 1, 55, Amsterdam, London, New York and Tokyo: Elsevier.

Bürgenmeier, B. (ed.) (1994), *Economy, Environment and Technology: A Socio-Economic Approach*, NY : M.E. Sharpe Inc. Armonk.

Bürgenmeier, B., T. Butare, Y. Harayama and N. Wallart (1996), *Taxes écologiques et réforme fiscale*, Final Report to the Swiss National Science Foundation, Bern.

Feldmann, A.M. (1983), *Welfare Economics and Social Choice Theory*, Boston, London and Amsterdam: Kluwer Academic Publisher.

Harrod, R.F. (1938), 'Scope and method of economics', *Economic Journal,* XLVIII.

Hettlage, R. (1993), 'Ökonomie auf dem Weg zur Sozialwissenschaft?' *Revue Suisse de Sociologie*, (19), 1.

Jeanrenaud, C. (ed.) (1996), 'Environmental policy between regulation and market'.

Pigou, A.C. (1918), *Economics of Welfare*, London.

Robbins, L. (1933), *An Essay on the Nature and Significance of Economic Sciences*, New York : St-Martin, 2nd edition.

Robbins, L. (1938), 'Interpersonal comparisons of utility: a comment', *Economic Journal*, XLVIII.

Simos, J. (1990), *Evaluer l'impact sur l'environnement*, Lausanne: Presses polytechniques et universitaires romandes.

Varian, H.R. (1992), *Microeconomic Analysis*, New York and London: W.W. Norton & Co., 3rd edition.

5. Valuation as Part of a Microeconomics for Ecological Sustainability

Peter Söderbaum

5.1 INTRODUCTION

Some actors in society are more powerful than others. In their thinking and practice, all these actors refer to specific images of man, of business, of markets and so on. Where do these ideas and images come from and what do they look like? Which images are most influential? John Maynard Keynes argued that many important ideas stem from the work of economists:

> The ideas of economists and political philosophers are more powerful than commonly understood. Indeed the world is ruled by little else. Practical men, who believe themselves to be quite exempt from any intellectual influences, are usually the slaves of some defunct economist. (Fusfelds, 1994, p. 1)

Examples of such ideas that play a role in public debate and in decision-making and the practice of politicians, bureaucrats and businessmen is the mechanistic interpretation of markets in terms of supply and demand with associated beliefs in 'the invisible hand', a concept used by Adam Smith, but older in origin. Other examples of ideas that have become common include the view of firms as profit maximizing machines and of human beings as consumers who maximize utility.

But why is it that specific ideas get a strong hold on the thinking habits of many scientists and practical men? According to one view, economists and perhaps also the 'political philosophers' referred to by Keynes seek the truth, and when successful disseminate their knowledge to various actors within society and to the public at large. It is believed that the best knowledge will automatically gain acceptance in society.

In this paper, a second model will be illustrated, referred to as an actor–network model, or alternatively, an interaction model. According to this view, models, theories and conceptual frameworks, especially in the social sciences, should not exclusively be seen as a matter of science but also of ideology. Concepts and theories are, at least in part, socially constructed to serve specific scientific and ideological purposes. Ideology is here defined in broad terms, as referring to 'ideas about means and ends'. Supply and acceptance of specific conceptual simplifications (or more complex conceptual frameworks) such as the aforementioned invisible hand is as much a matter of ideology as science.

Thinking in terms of 'supply' and 'demand' of specific thought patterns and ideas may be of help in understanding why a particular view of the firm becomes quite popular among practical men, while competing ideas find fewer supporters. On the 'supply' side we have inter alia all the universities who teach economics, often in a monistic way; and on the 'demand' side practitioners and often powerful organizations, who may prefer specific views of the firm as a way of legitimizing their own well established thought patterns and valuational orientations. A focus on the financial and monetary aspect of business practice may facilitate life for business actors, at least in the short run, when compared with a view of the firm where non-monetary (social, environmental and so on) impacts are systematically made visible in accounting systems and in other ways. Within the scope of a focus limited to profit maximizing, a kind of monetary reductionism, issues such as the social responsibility of business can effectively be played down. In the last few decades, a 'demand' for new ideas concerning management of natural resources and ecosystems has been articulated in some circles and specific versions of 'ecologism' have even been offered as an ideology meeting such demands (Eccleshall et al., 1994). The role played of such alternative views and of ecological economics is not only a matter of the strength of the scientific foundations, but as much a matter of a power game in relation to established interests.

In the vision of textbook neoclassical economics, 'demand' and 'supply' generally refer to homogenous commodities. Our interest here, by comparison, is in a complex written or oral dialogue about perspectives in economics and in society. Each actor may contribute to society presenting ideas and learning about ideas. (In a sense each actor may at the same time 'supply' and 'demand' ideas.) I believe that viewing interaction in society as a process of mutual learning, where science as well as ideology is involved, is a better representation of reality than the traditional 'truth dissemination' model. But, according to the very logic of our second model — which sees science and ideology as interconnected — it also serves my ideological purposes in searching for a microeconomics that may help us deal with environmental problems in a fruitful manner.

Ecological economics is an interdisciplinary field of study which to a large extent is value driven (see Krishnan et al., 1995). Ecological sustainability is widely espoused as an essential norm, and the ambition is to move the economy and society closer to this norm. Following in the wake of more than 20 years of activism, much of it by non-governmental organizations, the Rio conference in 1992 and Agenda 21 have stimulated work in organizations as well as municipalities to improve environmental performance. Ongoing activities are exemplified by environmental management systems (ems), environmental auditing, environmental Labelling and systems of environmental standards such as ISO14000. Various tools have been developed such as environmental impact assessment and life cycle analysis which are recommended for use within individual countries and throughout the European Community. Reference is often made to green marketing, green consumerism, greening of business and so on. At issue in this paper is whether neoclassical economics is a useful conceptual framework to understand and illuminate these phenomena or whether other theories and models more in line with social sciences such as sociology, political science, educational science, management science and so on have something more to offer.

In what follows, I will not question that different parts of neoclassical microeconomics can be used in attempts to deal with environmental problems, but I will argue that it would be unwise to rely exclusively on the neoclassical approach. Neoclassical microeconomics was mainly constructed for other purposes, for instance monetary policy at the national level. It should perhaps not be expected that it is at the same time 'optimal' or even 'satisficing' for environmental management purposes. Other theoretical perspectives in economics, for instance institutionalism, and other social sciences appear to have a lot to offer to facilitate the understanding of the greening phenomena referred to and contribute to the further development of tools and practices.

Essential components in neoclassical microeconomics are a view of man, usually referred to as economic man, a view of organizations, usually seen as firms, a view of markets in terms of supply and demand, a view of decision-making and valuation and a view of social change. The idea here is not to find alternative views for each phenomenon with the promise to do the same job, but better. What is proposed is rather a conceptual framework that partly focuses on different phenomena and which can do a different job from that usually attributed to neoclassical economics.

The alternative view to be presented includes the following elements:

- Man is seen as a socio-psychological and political being and referred to as political economic man (or woman). This political being is assumed to be led by a specific valuational or 'ideological orientation' in his or her behaviour. He or she can also be seen as an actor.

- Actors engage in activities and are connected in relationships and networks. Relationships may be of a non-market or market kind. Interaction outside markets, for instance public dialogue, may be as important for social and economic change as market behaviour.
- Markets, organizations and social change are interpreted in actor–network terms.
- A holistic view of economics and efficiency. 'Holistic' here refers to a multidimensional (and disaggregated) idea of resources and impacts as well as an analysis in terms of patterns and profiles (see Figures 5.3 and 5.4). A holistic idea of economics (efficiency) is then seen as opposed to one-dimensional reductionism, for instance the 'monetary reductionism' of cost–benefit analysis.
- A view of valuation and rationality as being a matter of 'ideological orientation' and a disaggregated approach to decision-making in business and at the societal level.

5.2 POLITICAL ECONOMIC (WO)MAN

There is a political element in all kinds of social science, economics included. No paradigm and no research project can claim value neutrality in any final sense. 'Valuations are always with us' as argued by Gunnar Myrdal (1978, p. 778). 'Disinterested research there has never been and can never be. Prior to answers there must be questions. In the questions raised and the viewpoint chosen, valuations are implied' (ibid., p. 779).

I will here go one step further by arguing that the political element is an important aspect of all human roles and all behaviour and thus not limited to the professional role as scholar in economics or other social sciences. It is assumed that man is a political being and to make this clear I will suggest that economic man is replaced by political economic man. Or, to put it in the vocabulary of the actor–network model, man is seen as an actor who is embedded in a web of social relationships.

A symbolic representation of political economic man (or woman) is given in Figure 5.1. It is assumed that for each individual, there is a set of relevant roles, R_1 to R_k, a set of relevant activities, A_1 to A_m and a set of relevant motives or interests, M_1 to M_n. The role R_1 is assumed to be connected with the activity (or set of activities) A_1 and with the motive(s) M_1. For the individual, the total set of roles is integrated as part of an 'identity', whereas the total set of activities form a pattern referred to as a 'life-style'. The total set of motives or interests in turn combine to a valuational or 'ideological orientation'. Even 'world view' or 'Weltanschauung' is a relevant description for such a holistic orientation, comprising cognitive as well as valuational elements.

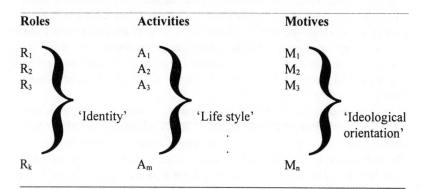

Roles	Activities	Motives

R_1 A_1 M_1
R_2 A_2 M_2
R_3 A_3 M_3

'Identity'   'Life style'   'Ideological orientation'

R_k A_m M_n

Note: a holistic and integrated view of an individual with his or her various roles, activities and interests

Source: Söderbaum, 1993, p. 396

Figure 5.1 Symbolic representation of political economic man

R_1 may represent the role of market actor, A_1 market related activities of buying, selling, investing and so on, M_1 motives and interests related to this role and these activities. Market roles, relationships and activities may be very important as exemplified above by reference to green consumerism and so on, but Figure 5.1 reminds us that other roles are as relevant in relation to environmental issues. R_2 may refer to man as a parent, R_3 as a member of an environmental organization, R_4 as a professional, R_5 as a citizen. In order to understand the behaviour of an individual, all these roles, activities and motives are potentially relevant.

The individual is seen as a social being, that is a person embedded in a web of social relationships. In spite of tensions between various motives and interests, the individual is somehow held together through ideas of his or her role or identity in relation to each specific socio-cultural context. Dissonance theory, learning theories and other parts of social psychology are seen as relevant and useful in understanding behaviour. The individual strives for some congruence and balance between roles, activities and interests, and may experience such balance, but incongruence and tensions are equally characteristics of the human existence.

Egoistic versus other-related (or community-oriented) motives are an example of such tensions. This points to a view of man as a moral being where responsibility in relation to others and society at large becomes a potential issue. Amitai Etzioni, for instance, has propounded an 'I & We Paradigm' (Etzioni, 1988). According to him, the fact that there is a strong ego in each healthy individual is not sufficient reason to denigrate or exclude the social and ethical aspects of human life. Each individual plays a part in many groups, 'we-contexts' and such relationships involve a number of tensions and ethical issues. (Ethics is, of course, also relevant for 'we–they' relationships, for instance in situations of conflict.) Similarly Amartya Sen, an open-minded, mainly neoclassical economist, has argued in favour of explicit consideration of ethics in economics (1987).

In their models, neoclassicists tend to present individuals as robot-like, instant optimizers. Institutionalists and many representives of other social sciences tend to point to the important role of habits in human behaviour. The individual is largely 'locked into' specific habits of thought and specific habitual activities that together form a pattern, here referred to as a life-style. Herbert Simon's early arguments about selective perception, limited cognitive capacity and search costs are relevant here (Simon, 1945). As humans we tend to stick to familiar environments and use various rules of thumb to deal with complexity. The development of a habit can be expressed in terms of increases in the probability of a specific behaviour (like purchasing a specific brand A of coffee among available alternatives A, B and C) for successive trials, that is, purchasing situations of a similar kind (see Howard, 1963). Emphasis on habitual behaviour does not exclude the possibility of 'problemistic search' and conscious decision-making. At times the individual perceives a problem and alternative courses of action. Habits are reconsidered and behaviour may change. Such decision situations can be discussed in conventional terms of maximizing an objective function, subject to various constraints. In what follows, a more holistic idea of rationality, related to the ideological orientation of an actor, will be emphasized.

The theory of the consumer as part of neoclassical microeconomics is of some interest when discussing environmental policy issues, for instance expected impacts of eco-taxes. Neoclassical public choice theory is similarly useful for understanding possible behaviour of individuals in professional roles. But a more holistic attempt to integrate various human roles seems warranted. The theory of the consumer is limited not only in the sense that one human role is emphasized at the expense of all others; in addition consumer tastes or preferences are taken as given. As part of an imagined value-neutrality, the neoclassical scholar regards it as external to his/her role to problematize the values and life-styles of consumers. But if, as many suggest, environmental problems are connected with present consumer tastes and life-styles and more generally with dominating world-views in industrialized countries, then the neoclassical approach implies that essential aspects of the problems faced are overlooked. Focusing instead on political economic man and 'ideological orientation' means that the different consumer preferences and life-styles of two individuals are no longer regarded as equally justified. Supported by a simultaneous, facilitating public policy or not, individuals may move in a step-by-step manner away from life-styles that are environmentally destructive toward those that are environmentally more beneficial. But again, whether such moves represent an advance is a matter of ethics and ideological orientation of the observer.

Political economic woman or man will play a key role throughout the present essay. Reference will be made to political economic relationships, political economic networks, political economic organizations or management regimes, and political economic valuation of activities, projects or policies on the basis of ideological orientation.

5.3   RELATIONSHIPS AND NETWORKS

Individuals with their roles, activities and ideological orientation relate to each other as suggested by Figure 5.2. For each actor resources and power have been added as important factors in understanding interaction. Resources and power in turn are related to the knowledge of an actor and his or her control over property of various kinds, for example, financial and physical property.

All kinds of relationships between actors are potentially of importance in understanding environmental policy issues and environmental performance. Public and private debate may be as relevant as market relationships or relationships within an organization. Not all organizations are business companies, some organizations are universities, others can be described as environmental organizations. What goes on within universities, or among intellectuals more generally, may be as decisive for the sustainability issue as anything else.

The importance of public and private debate is emphasized here since it is more or less neglected in neoclassical theory. Neoclassical discourse — if there is discourse at all — tends to be limited to prices. To interpret relationships in terms of price signalling is a bit meagre in relation to many 'real world' situations. But also, to presume that 'prices' reflect actors' opportunity costs (marginalist theory of values) without paying attention to the institutional-power features that have a bearing on the observable prices, is an unnecessarily narrow approach to the economic analysis of price formation.

Figure 5.2 should thus be understood as a general model of relationships, whereas a market relationship becomes one, admittedly important, special case. In the case of a market relationship, actor A is replaced by market actor A and actor B by market actor B in Figure 5.2. Also when referring to markets, a broad frame of reference is needed. Remember Alfred Hirschman, the economist who became well known for his rather trivial observation that in addition to 'exit' there is voice as an option in communication and which attempts to influence a company or other market actors (Hirschman 1970).

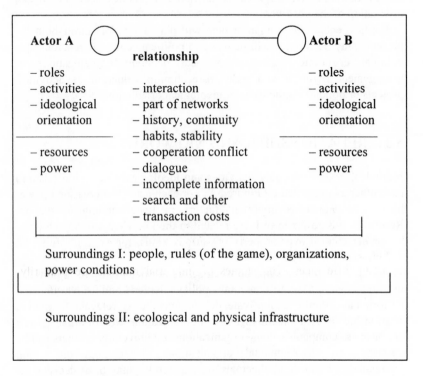

Figure 5.2 Essential aspects of a relationship between two actors

As suggested by Figure 5.2, actors interact, that is engage in mutual learning as previously mentioned. They may influence each other and coordinate their activities. A relationship is normally a link in a larger set of relationships that may be referred to as a network. Each actor has a history which will influence a specific relationship and the relationship itself has a history or development pattern from birth to maturity and perhaps decay. Many relationships relevant in relation to environmental issues have a certain continuity which sometimes can be explained by a similar ideological orientation of the two actors. The actors have their habits and this may be reflected in the relationship, whereby interaction and cooperative activities may be routinized. While actors tend to look for opportunities of cooperation, conflicts of interest in relation to details or broader issues are equally a normal condition of human relationships. Dialogue is part of cooperation and can be of help in dealing with conflicts. Each actor is endowed with some knowledge and information, but this information is normally incomplete. Search efforts could add to the available stock of knowledge and information, for instance about relationships. To search for new relationships and to move from one relationship to another will incur transaction costs.

Figure 5.2 also suggests that no relationship could be seen in isolation. In addition to other actors and institutional arrangements, a physical and ecological infrastructure belongs to these surroundings. Ecosystems are here seen as a kind of infrastructure, since they deliver goods and services to humans. Building a road then no longer necessarily means that existing infrastructure is enlarged or improved, but rather that one kind of infrastructure is substituted for another.

The importance of relationships and networks has been stressed before, especially in the study of industrial markets. An example is provided by the Industrial Marketing and Purchasing Group with its centre at the Department of Business Studies, Uppsala University (Ford, 1990, see for instance illustration of relationship on p. 20); for further reading in relation to relationships within business networks see Håkansson and Snehota (1995). While many of the aspects of relationships mentioned here are similar in the studies of industrial markets, there are also some important differences. The studies of industrial markets are primarily carried out at the level of companies, that is where the companies are seen as the actors. Individuals as actors may appear but are less visible than in the context of reference here suggested. When reference is made to 'environment' in the studies by Håkansson and Snehota and their coauthors (1995), this refers to market structure, position in the marketing channel and internationalization, and less to the kind of 'environment' discussed in this essay. Value issues are furthermore largely avoided and concepts referring to private roles, roles as citizens, life-style or 'ideological orientation' do not appear in these studies. But many soft variables are there such as the 'image' of a corporation or its 'goodwill' in relation to customers. In spite of the differences mentioned, the two approaches appear largely mutually supportive and compatible.

5.4   A POLITICAL ECONOMICS VIEW OF ORGANIZATIONS, MARKETS AND SOCIAL CHANGE

In neoclassical microeconomics, the principal kind of organization that is recognized is the profit maximizing firm. As part of the present approach, reference will more generally be made to 'political–economic organizations'. The monetary aspect will presumably be important for all organizations, but its role in relation to non-monetary considerations may vary. An organization is a collectivity of individuals and the ideological orientation of the organization (business concept or mission statement)will

depend on its socio-institutional context and the preferences and relative power of various actors and stakeholders related to the organization.

While the neoclassical firm is described as an entity controlled from a single centre, our organization is composed of individuals who differ more or less in their ideological orientations· and behaviour. Business economists and organization theorists have introduced a stake-holder model of the firm or other organization, which at least in some of its versions breaks with the monistic, equilibrium thinking of the neoclassical theory of the firm. In relation to a specific organization, an attempt is made to identify all interested parties, that is those who have something 'at stake' in relation to the functioning and performance of the organization. Employees, shareholders, other investors, suppliers, customers and neighbours (who may suffer from pollution) are among the interest groups normally identified.

It is interesting to note that as part of the stakeholder model, each category is assumed to be relatively homogeneous. Our present model built on political economic man assumptions, where the individual is seen as an actor, could rather be described as a polycentric model. The organization has many centres rather than one, each individual with his or her ideological orientation representing such a potential centre. While a specific business concept may be largely accepted in an organization at any point in time, there may also be tension between actors. Such tension may be a precondition for creativity and the success of an organization which is not necessarily a negative thing.

As an example, some actors in the employee category may be 'green' in orientation while others are not. Similarly some shareholders in the company may prefer a green orientation and strategy for the company, while other shareholders are less interested. In this way green employees, green shareholders, green suppliers, green customers, green investors have something in common and that is their ideological orientation. Similarly, actors belonging to the non-green category have something in common which represents a potential force in modifying the operations of the company. Changes in the business concept and image of an organization will often cause tension. One network of individuals within, or otherwise related to the company in stakeholder terms, may differ in their views from those of another network, and each actor within such networks may exert his or her power to influence the course of events.

Markets can similarly be seen in the light of polycentric networks of individuals as actors. The idea is simple. For example green consumers will prefer green producers or companies. Green producers in turn will look for green suppliers and so on. Market segmentation along green lines will occur and green networks will compete with those that are less green or non-green. As suggested by the Uppsala school, a relationship between one customer and one supplier could sometimes be seen as an 'organization' of its own in the case that the two market actors enter into technological cooperation.

Reasoning in terms of ideological orientation, business concepts and mission statements leads to a conditional view of the functioning of organizations and markets. Some scholars and 'practical men' have a very optimistic idea of organizations such as multinational corporations and of the market. All problems, environmental problems included, will be solved by the invisible hand. Others like David Korten (1995) warn against such dogmatic views. The 'conditional view' advocated here simply states that the functioning of organizations and markets to a large extent depends on individuals as actors in organizations and market places, their knowledge, morals and ideological orientation. Also of importance certainly are the rules of the game and other elements of the institutional context. The rules of the game are not only a matter of laws at the national level, the actors themselves exert influence on the system of governmental rules and in addition they create their own rules. The rules formed as part of the 'self-regulation' of business may be less permissive than the rules implemented through the state. Compliance with present laws is no longer sufficient for many companies.

Our reasoning in terms of actors and networks also leads to criticism of neoclassical public choice theory or perhaps to a different and extended version of this theory (Söderbaum, 1992a, 1992b). When ideological orientation is taken into consideration it becomes unrealistic to see farmers or bureaucrats as a homogeneous category. Some farmers are engaged in ecological agriculture or are green in some other sense, others are not concerned much about environmental issues. Green farmers may find that they have interests in common and work together, their interests will differ from non-green farmers. In addition, green farmers may find that they have something in common with green bureaucrats and may therefore engage in network building or lobbying activities with them. Predictions made on the basis of the assumptions of conventional public choice theory – for instance about a pale future for environmental interests – can be questioned along these lines.

5.5   A HOLISTIC AND IDEOLOGICALLY OPEN CONCEPTION OF ECONOMICS AND EFFICIENCY

In everyday language, and to a somewhat lesser extent in neoclassical economics, there is a tendency to associate 'economics' with 'monetary thinking'. Money and prices are at the heart of the analysis. Money is considered as a common denominator and it is assumed that it is possible to reduce impacts expressed in non-monetary terms to a monetary equivalent. No-one can deny this possibility of putting a price tag on every impact. What is at issue, however, is the theoretical interpretation(s) that might be given to such a monetary figure, and whether such a way of proceeding is wise or unwise under different circumstances. Wisdom in this case is as much a matter of ideology and world–view as science. My personal belief is that the 'monetary reductionism' of much neoclassical theory (for example, cost–benefit analysis) is part of the problems faced by the present society. The main philosophy should be one of holism in the sense of disaggregation and irreducibility, that is, keeping different impacts separate from each other. (This emphasis does not, as we shall see, contradict the usefulness of a *partial* analysis in terms of monetary calculus or the use of prices, for example, eco-taxes, as part of environmental policy.)

The use of the terms 'holism' and 'holistic' here needs further clarification. Holism can be seen as being opposed to 'atomism' which then refers to a broadening of the scope of an analysis, for instance analysis should not be limited to the micro level. The broader macro connections might be of interest. Analysis can furthermore be broadened from one sector of the economy to all sectors affected using systems thinking, holism can, however, also be seen as opposed to 'reductionism'. In cybernetics and early systems theory, the reduction and understanding of biology in terms of the laws of physics was questioned. Along these lines, the reduction of complex patterns or images perceived by human beings to one-dimensional analysis can be questioned. The response suggested here is a multidimensional approach and analysis in terms of patterns or profiles. Here, something else other than the one-dimensionality and 'monetary reductionism' of cost–benefit analysis (CBA) is proposed.

Thus economics refers to the management of all kinds of resources. Non-monetary resources (natural resources, human resources, cultural resources) are not regarded as less 'economic' than monetary ones. In other words, non-monetary resources are economic, irrespective of whether we put a price tag on them or not. Whenever we refer to the monetary price of a natural resource, only a monetary aspect is taken into account. Other aspects of the same resource can be described in non-monetary (but equally 'economic') terms. It is equally relevant to speak of 'resource management' in situations where no money prices are invoked in the attempt to arrive at wise decisions.

The difference between a reductionist and a holistic view of economics is illustrated in Figure 5.3. When comparing alternative courses of action or alternative development paths, all economists would agree that there are monetary as well as non-monetary impacts or indicators. As part of the reductionist view, it is proposed that non-monetary impacts and indicators can meaningfully be transformed to numerical money. This is usually done in the framework of a cost–benefit analysis and the purpose is to make comparison between alternatives or between development paths simple. The monetary language is said to be accepted already in society, making the approach very practical.

Those who, like the present author, are in favour of the holistic view would say that the idea of trading one impact against another in monetary terms, while simplifying things, is at the same time dangerous. At what prices should different impacts be traded against each other?

What is the price of a specific irreversible negative environmental impact? At a societal level, prices and their interpretation are in large measure a matter of politics and ideology, and the role of science should be limited to one of illuminating an issue. Rather than the technocratic role of dictating 'correct' prices for societal valuation, the scholar or analyst could choose a more democratic role. If reality is complex, why should it be treated as simple? A better strategy might be to live with some complexity.

Aggregation is less questionable at the micro level. An individual may choose his or her own weights or prices as part of an aggregation procedure. For a business company some degree of consensus about values may similarly be assumed. But even in the case of business, the disaggregative philosophy seems to be gaining ground. Monetary calculation of investment alternatives and monetary success indicators in terms of profits will be of importance as long as present institutional arrangements will remain. Institutions change gradually, however. One example is the growing importance of a company's environmental performance. Monetary accounting and auditing will continue but environmental accounting and auditing procedures are now gaining ground. Those who are limited in their thinking to one-dimensionality will interpret non-monetary indicators exclusively in monetary terms, while others will see a value within separate but complementary perspectives.

As part of the latter more holistic view, impacts or indicators may be categorized as in Table 5.1. In addition to the distinction between monetary and non-monetary impacts or indicators, a distinction can be made between those impacts that are expressed in terms of flows (referring to periods of time) and those that are expressed as state variables or positions (referring to points in time). This will give us four categories as indicated in Table 5.1.

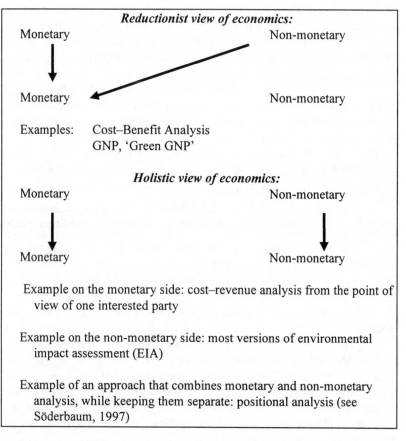

Figure 5.3 An attempt to illustrate the difference between a reductionist and a holistic view of economics

The turnover of a business company and GNP exemplify monetary flows (category I), while the assets and liabilities of a corporation or the liquidity of an individual at a specific day and hour exemplify monetary positions. On the non-monetary side, pollution of cadmium from a factory per year exemplify a flow and the content of cadmium in the soil at a specific place and point in time, a position. The number of species in a forest ecosystem is another example of a non-monetary position.

Table 5.1 Four categories of economic impacts (indicators)

	Flow (referring to a period of time)	Position (referring to a point in time)
Monetary	I	II
Non-monetary	III	IV

All kinds of impacts are potentially relevant and analyses of non-monetary flows can certainly help to explain what happens to non-monetary positions. If one has to economize in measurement on the non-monetary side, measurements in terms of positions is often a good idea. A series of positions over time may be compared to make judgements about whether a lake (or the soil in some area) is in a 'healthy' condition. Such an interest in a series of non-monetary positions or states is very different from the discounting procedure and 'present values' as part of CBA, where it is assumed that future impacts somehow can be pressed together to a point in time.

5.6 VALUATION AS BEING A MATTER OF IDEOLOGICAL ORIENTATION

For the cost–benefit analyst, 'value' refers exclusively to money value as expressed in a set of prices or shadow prices. According to our premises in terms of political economic man, ethics and ideology are seen as the primary basis of valuation of past, ongoing or future activities, projects or policies. According to this view, monetary valuation, and aggregation in monetary terms, become special cases which are practical and useful only under certain circumstances.

'Valuation' is then grounded in the ideological orientation of individuals in specific roles and contexts, as depicted in Figure 5.4. One of our strengths as human beings is the ability to recognize patterns (Simon, 1983). Decisions can be thought of in terms of matching the multidimensional ideological orientation or profile of each decision-maker with the likewise multidimensional impact profiles of each alternative.

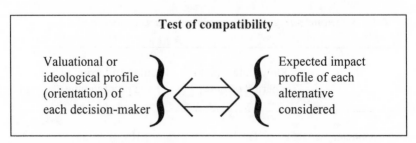

Test of compatibility

Valuational or ideological profile (orientation) of each decision-maker

Expected impact profile of each alternative considered

Note :   A holistic idea of the decision act is suggested, where the ideological profile of each decision-maker is matched against the expected impact profile of each alternative.

Figure 5.4 Test of compatibility

This view opens the way for multidimensional thinking and thinking in terms of pictures and 'gestalts', in addition to one-dimensional numbers. According to this view, an alternative is attractive for an individual if a 'good fit' between his or her ideological orientation and the impact profile of the alternative is expected or experienced. As part of a conscious decision process, individuals may reconsider their ideological orientation. In this sense the values or even the principles of valuation are not seen as constant and given.

To illustrate this idea of viewing the relationship between the decision-maker and each alternative considered in terms of a 'pattern recognition' or 'matching' process, an example from private life may be of help. Complex decision situations do not only exist in organizations and at a public level but also, as most of us have realized, in the realm of private affairs. The members of a family may have taken a decision to move to another location and buy a new house. A number of alternatives are considered. Each family member is assumed to refer to an ideological orientation, in this case an idea of what might constitute a 'good', 'satisfactory', or even the 'best' solution to the problem faced. When visiting one of the houses considered in its specific context and when learning about its functional, aesthetic and other qualities, each family member might test the compatibility between his/her image(s) and other ideas of a good solution and the impact profile of the particular alternative at hand. If all family members experience a 'good fit', then they may be ready for a purchasing decision or continue the search in the hope of finding an even better alternative.

Whether applied at the level of private or public affairs, or something in between, the above idea of rationality does allow for pictures and images, that is visual thinking (or seeing) in addition to partial quantitative analysis, for instance of monetary costs or physical space. There are systematic approaches to decision-making other than those ending with one-dimensional numbers and experiences from private life suggest that individuals often prefer the holistic or non-reductionist idea of rationality here indicated.

5.7   POSITIONAL ANALYSIS AS A DISAGGREGATED APPROACH VALUATION

Approaches to decision-making and 'valuation' can be classified as follows:

(A) Highly aggregated approaches
    (a) ideologically closed
    (b) ideologically open
(B) Highly disaggregated approaches
    (a) ideologically closed
    (b) ideologically open

Cost–benefit analysis belongs clearly to the A category, since it is highly aggregated. CBA is furthermore 'ideologically closed' in the sense that the scientist or analyst claims to provide correct rules of societal valuation (see category A.a). A highly aggregated, ideologically open version of monetary calculation (see A.b) might be one where each politician or other decision-maker has his/her particular idea(s) of a good society, on this basis provides his/her particular price list for different kinds of impacts and makes his/her particular calculation of present values or internal rates of return.

The discussion in this paper points rather in the direction of a highly disaggregated, ideologically open approach to valuation of projects, programmes and policies (see the B.b category). Positional analysis is one such approach. This method can be characterized as follows:

- Political economic man assumptions and the associated actor, relationship, network approach

- Investigation of the history and institutional context of an issue. What can be learnt from previous studies? What are the rules of the game, for instance who is making the study and according to what rules will interested parties and citizens be involved and heard? How is the present decision situation related to policy issues or other decision situations?
- Listening to interested parties and other actors with respect to problem images and ideas about alternatives and relevant values or ideological orientations. Involvement of parties and actors in a search for possible solutions
- A holistic (non-reductionist) idea of economics and efficiency
- Systems thinking
- Positional thinking
- Conflict analysis and management
- Conditional conclusions in relation to possibly relevant ideological orientations

Of these characteristics, only the last four need further clarification. Systems thinking is an attempt to broaden the scope of an analysis from one sector (for example, transportation) to all sectors affected. On the basis of a given set of alternatives, the analyst tries to identify those systems of various kinds that will be affected differently depending on the specific alternative chosen. The systems identified will then be helpful for the later steps of identifying differences between alternatives with respect to impacts and interests.

As already made clear non-monetary impacts are no less important than monetary ones and it is suggested that non-monetary positions are of special significance in attempting to assess the 'healthiness' of a lake or other ecosystem or the welfare of an individual. Is the position of a natural resource improving or being degraded as a result of specific measures or projects considered? It is argued also that issues of inertia, for instance irreversibility, is best illustrated in positional terms. Actions today will influence future options.

As in the case of systems discussed above, activities for individuals and organizations that will be influenced differently depending on the alternative chosen can be identified. For each activity identified, an assumption is made about goal direction which in turn can be used for a ranking of alternatives from the point of view of the activity. For individuals living close to a road, one may assume that they prefer a level of environmental disturbances from the road (noise, pollution and so on) that is as low as possible. On the basis of this assumption, an alternative which includes the building of a new road, which diverts some part of the traffic, will be preferred to a situation (zero–alternative) with no new transportation facilities. A matrice can then be constructed with alternatives as columns and the identified activities with connected interests as rows facilitating identification of conflicts of interest. It is seldom the case that one alternative is the best from the point of view of all interests identified.

Conditional conclusions are stated on the basis of matrices where alternatives are compared at the two levels of impacts and interests. Ecological sustainability (defined in a specific way) as a possible ideological orientation will then point to one alternative as preferable whereas some other valuational basis may point in a different direction. As a special case, concensus may exist among decision-makers about ideology. In this case, the analysis can be more closed with respect to ideology (category B.a in the above classification) and it becomes presumably easier to recommend one best alternative.

A number of other alternatives to CBA exist, for instance some forms of policy analysis, systems analysis, environmental and comprehensive impact assessment and multicriteria approaches. Most versions of environmental impact assessment (EIA) are 'highly disaggregated' in the sense given above, but the tradition of expertness and technocracy also often leads to aggregation in terms of points, indexes and the like. Similarly, multicriteria approaches exist which belong to each of the four categories according to our classification scheme. As with EIA, multi-criteria approaches should better be understood as a tool-box and set of methods rather than a single approach.

Among disaggregated approaches, positional analysis (PA), has been emphasized in the present essay. Experience of this approach dates back to the early 1970s (for example, Söderbaum 1973) and are largely limited to the Scandinavian countries and languages. The method has been applied in student papers and PhD-theses (for example, Leskinen 1994, Brorsson 1995) and has been developed to include control of ongoing activities and ex post valuation, so called retrospective studies (Hillring 1996). PA is one of the approaches that represent a movement away from a technocratic role for the analyst. The idea is one of involving actors and interested parties in a search for consensus while, at the same time, acccepting the existence of conflicting views (see Dinar and Loehman, eds 1995).

5.8 CONCLUSIONS

At this stage it may be clear to the reader that even the choice of approach to valuation in itself becomes a matter of ideological orientation. Do the analysts, decision-makers and interested parties share an idea of a working democracy? Do they share a view that various non-monetary impacts, such as environmental impacts and social impacts, and various conflicts of interest should be made visible within the decision base or not? Are they even ready to discuss issues of power relationships, world views, ethics or paradigms in economics? Among ecological economists, Stephen Viederman (1995) has reminded us about Friedrich von Hayek, who in his Nobel address in 1975, noted the irony that economists of his time were being called upon to solve the very problems that they had helped to create. Einstein had remarked years before that 'we cannot solve the problems that we have created with the same thinking that created them'.

Those who hold the view that public debate is important and that values cannot be dealt with in monetary reductionist terms will presumably vote for one or other of the alternatives to CBA. In relation to the environment, it becomes especially important that the more fundamental issues become part of the agenda, and that a sufficient number of 'establishment actors' reconsider their world views to open up for a sustainable development path.

Such establishment actors can be found not only in business and government but also, for instance, at the universities. Will the universities be able to rearrange their strategies to play a significant role in a necessary transformation process? Will departments of economics allow a certain amount of pluralism or continue on their monistic path? Will interdisciplinary cooperation and international research cooperation in associations, such as the International Society for Ecological Economic, and its branches, contribute to a sustainable development?

REFERENCES

Brorsson, Kjell-Åke (1995), *Metodutveckling av positionsanalysen genom tillämpning på Assjö kvarn. Hållbar utveckling i relation till miljö och sårbarhet* (Positional analysis applied to Assjö water mill. Sustainable development in relation to environment and vulnerability), Swedish University of Agricultural Sciences, Department of Economics, Dissertations 14. Uppsala.

Dinar, Ariel and Edna Tusak Loehman (eds) (1995), *Water Quantity/Quality Management and Conflict Resolution. Institutions, Processes, and Economic Analyses*, Westport: Praeger.

Eccleshall, Robert (1994), *Political Ideologies. An Introduction* (second edition), London: Routledge.

Etzioni, Amitai (1988), *The Moral Dimension. Toward A New Economics*, New York: The Free Press.

Ford, David (ed.), (1990), 'and the Industrial Marketing and Purchasing Group', *Understanding Business Markets. Interaction, Relationships, Networks*, London: Academic Press.

Fusfeld, Daniel R. (1994), *The Age of the Economist*, New York: Harper Collins.
Hillring, Bengt (1996), 'Forest fuel systems utilising tree sections. System evaluation and development of evaluation methodology', Swedish University of Agricultural Sciences, Faculty of Forestry, *Studia Forestalia Suecica*, 200, 1–17, Uppsala.
Hirschman, A.O. (1970), *Exit, Voice, and Loyalty*, Cambridge, Mass.: Harvard University Press.
Howard, John A. (1963), *Marketing Management. Analysis and Planning*, Homewood, Ill.: Irwin.
Håkansson, Håkan and Ivan Snehota (eds) (1995), *Developing Relationships in Business Networks*, Routledge.
Korten, David C. (1995), *When Corporations Rule the World*, West Hartford: Kumarian Press.
Krishnan, Rajaram, Jonathan M. Harris and Neva R. Goodwin (eds) (1995), *A Survey of Ecological Economics*, Washington DC: Island Press.
Leskinen, Antti (1994), *Environmental Planning as Learning: The Principles of Negotiation, Disaggregated Decision-making Method and Parallell Organization in Developing the Road Administration*. University of Helsinki, Department of Economics and Management, Environmental Economics Publications No. 5, Helsinki.
Myrdal, Gunnar (1978), 'Institutional economics', December, *Journal of Economic Issues*, 12 (4), 771–83.
Sen, Amartya (1987), *On Ethics and Economics*, New York: Basil Blackwell.
Simon, Herbert (1945), *Administrative Behavior*, New York: Free Press.
Simon, Herbert (1983), *Reason in Human Affairs*, London: Basil Blackwell.
Söderbaum, Peter (1973), *Positionsanalys vid beslutsfattande och planering. Ekonomisk analys på tvärvetenskaplig grund* (Positional analysis for decision-making and planning. Economic analysis on an interdisciplinary basis), Stockholm: Esselte Studium/Scandinavian University Books.
Söderbaum, Peter (1992a), 'Neoclassical and institutional approaches to development and the environment', *Ecological Economics*, 5, 127–44.
Söderbaum, Peter (1992b), 'Environmental and Agricultural Issues: What is the Alternative to Public Choice Theory?' in Partha Dasgupta (ed.), *Issues in Contemporary Economics, Volume 3, Policy and Development,*. London: Macmillan, pp. 24–42.
Söderbaum, Peter (1993), 'Values, Markets and Environmental Policy: An Actor–Network Approach', *Journal of Economic Issues*, 27 (2), pp. 387–404.
Söderbaum, Peter (forthcoming 1997), 'The Political Economics of Sustainability. Positional Analysis as an alternative to Cost–Benefit Analysis', in Sylvie Faucheux, Martin O'Connor and Jan van der Straaten (eds), *Sustainable Development: Concepts, Rationalities, and Strategies*, Dordrecht: Kluwer.
Viederman, Stephen (1995), ISEE Newsletter, April 1995.

6. Cost-Effectiveness Analysis of Forest Biodiversity Enhancement: An Application of Expert Judgement

Douglas C. Macmillan[1], David Harley[2] and Ruth Morrison[1]

The conservation of biodiversity is rapidly becoming an important keystone of sustainable development policy in Europe. Member states of the European Community (EC) are obliged to protect rare species and restore habitats under the Habitats Directive (92/43/EEC), and environmental enhancement is viewed as central to the reform of the Common Agricultural Policy (CAP). Implementation of biodiversity initiatives involves considerable sums of public and private expenditure. In the UK, for example, fourteen 'Habitat Action Plans' for conserving biodiversity under Article 6a of the Earth Summit's Convention on Biological Diversity, are expected to require additional public funding of about £40 million (48 million ECU) by 2010 (Biodiversity Steering Group, 1995). Evaluating the benefits in economic terms is, however, extremely difficult and thus poses a problem not just for economists, but also for policy makers anxious to portray expenditure as 'value for money'.

Economic appraisal of conservation policies through cost–benefit analysis (CBA) is difficult because the benefits, such as species protection and maintenance of genetic resources, are public goods. Application of the contingent valuation method, or other non-market techniques, is controversial and costly. Since it does not rely on monetary valuation, cost-effectiveness analysis (CEA), provides an alternative form of economic appraisal which selects projects on the basis of cost and effectiveness in meeting a pre-determined objective (Gittinger, 1982).

In this paper the range of situations where CEA may provide a more appropriate method of analysis than CBA are described. The particular problems of applying CEA to biodiversity policies are discussed and, as a case study, the approach is applied to the restoration of native pinewoods in Scotland. The expansion of native pinewoods is an important objective of the UK's Biodiversity Action Plan (HM Government, 1994a) and, under the Woodland Grant Scheme (WGS), the government aims to restore a natural pinewood ecosystem by providing a range of grant options to landowners for creating new pinewoods. The cost-effectiveness of this grant aid depends on the rate of grant paid and a number of locational and site factors which contribute to environmental output. By comparing government cost with a measure of effectiveness for individual pinewoods it is possible to assess 'value for money' from the different WGS options.

6.1   ADVANTAGES OF CEA OVER CBA

Cost-effectiveness analysis seeks to identify the most cost-effective way of meeting a pre-determined objective from a range of options. This objective is usually set outside the CEA process by legal constraints or a policy commitment. In the UK, CEA has been applied to a wide range of environmental issues. The Department of the Environment commissioned a study of the cost-effectiveness of two main options (water treatment and restrictions on agricultural practice) for meeting the EC Directive on nitrates in drinking water (DoE and MAFF, 1989). Colman et al. (1992) used a CEA approach to assess the conservation effectiveness of options such as management agreements and land purchase using cost efficiency, targetability and timeliness criteria. London Economics (1992) used CEA to compare the potential use of market mechanisms with legal regulations in the control of acid rain emissions. However, the small number of CEA-type studies in the environmental literature contrasts with the situation in health economics. (See Bina et al., 1995 for a brief review of the CEA literature).

Cost–benefit analysis, by contrast, can be used to identify the best way of meeting a number of pre-determined objectives or to help set objectives in the first place. For each objective it weighs up all the costs and benefits to society and assesses which is in the public interest on the basis of economic welfare. CBA is appropriate particularly where the pre-set objectives appear to conflict with each other (where they are complementary a CEA approach may still apply) or where there are no constraining objectives.

An important difference between CEA and CBA is that while CEA specifies the benefits of different options by non-monetary measures, CBA requires that benefits (and costs) are measured in monetary terms. Monetary valuation is in a subordinate role in CEA because the benefits (effectiveness) and the costs need not be expressed in common (monetary) units. This is an important distinction because the monetary valuation of non-marketed environmental benefits is controversial.

In the environmental field there are a range of situations where CEA is a more appropriate form of analysis than CBA. These include the following:

- Legal or Political Agreements. The UK Department of the Environment has advocated the use of CEA where policy is 'constrained by existing environmental targets or objectives', such as 'previous political choices, domestic legislation, EC directives or international agreements' (DoE, 1991).
- Sustainable Development. CEA takes as its starting point a pre-determined environmental objective. If one views sustainable development as requiring the conservation of certain key natural assets, such as biodiversity, irrespective of economic welfare considerations, then CEA becomes more appropriate.[3]
- Environmental Complexity. Benefit valuation using public survey methods (for example contingent valuation) may be difficult to apply in instances where changes in environmental quality are complex, and require a level of understanding of scientific and technical issues beyond the average member of the general public.
- Site-specificity. Where the benefits of an environmental scheme are site-specific (for example, woodland establishment) benefit estimates can only be obtained by *de novo* investigation or through benefit transfer. The former may be impractical on the basis of cost, while the conditions for the latter are rarely, if ever, met (Desvouges et al., 1992).[4]

6.2   APPLICATION OF CEA TO CONSERVATION PROJECTS

All of the situations above apply to a certain extent to biodiversity and other conservation policies and CEA can therefore be seen as a potentially useful and important form of analysis. For example, UK forestry policy includes a commitment 'to promote research into the measurement and cost-effective enhancement of biodiversity' (para 3.34, HM Government, 1994a), while the Helsinki guidelines for sustainable forestry call for 'specific, practical, cost-effective and efficient biodiversity appraisal systems' (Resolution 2, 2 in HM Government, 1994b).

One of the major problems for CEA in relation to biodiversity is the measurement of effectiveness. In many applications of CEA the objective can be simply defined in terms of a scientific standard (for example, air and water quality levels) which can be easily interpreted and measured. In these cases CEA chooses the least-cost option which meets the objective and there is no need for a separate measure of effectiveness (either an option meets the objective or it does not). However, in the case of conservation projects, the extent to which the objective is met is more difficult to assess and a measure of effectiveness is required. For example, where the objective is the maintenance of lowland heathland for nature conservation, options may include grazing, mowing, controlled burning, and chemical control. The effectiveness of each option will depend on how the conservation objective is interpreted, and the physical characteristics of the site under analysis. CEA must therefore assess effectiveness as well as cost before recommending a particular option. Gittinger (1992) has termed these two forms of CEA as the constant effects method and the constant cost method. In the next section we describe an application of CEA to the restoration of the native pinewood ecosystem in Scotland where both the costs and effectiveness of different options vary.

6.3   A CASE STUDY: RESTORATION OF NATIVE PINEWOOD HABITAT IN SCOTLAND

In the UK, native 'Caledonian' pinewoods are restricted to the Highlands of Scotland. They are relict indigenous forests dominated by self-sown Scots pine, and are an important western representative of the European boreal forest. Although they now only occupy about 16 000 hectares, (around 1 per cent of their former range in pre-historic times) they support many rare species including the Scottish crossbill (*Loxia scotica*), Britain's only endemic bird species, the capercaillie (*Tetrao urogallus*), and many insect and plant species (Biodiversity Steering Group, 1995).

The UK government's forestry policy includes biodiversity objectives, as part of multipurpose forestry (HM Government, 1994b). The government is committed to the Rio forestry principles, which include the conservation of natural forests and biodiversity, and have adopted the Helsinki guidelines which require the conservation of primary and climax forests. Caledonian pinewoods are also recognized as a priority habitat in the EU habitats directive which requires the UK government to designate Special Areas of Conservation, to enable the habitat (and associated species) to be maintained or, where appropriate, restored to a 'favourable conservation status'.[5]

The government has concentrated on the expansion of the area of native pinewoods through new planting or natural regeneration, mainly by providing grants to private landowners under the Woodland Grant Scheme.[6] Established in 1988, the general objective of this grant aid is 'to encourage the creation of new pinewoods which emulate the shapes, distribution and ultimately the structure of a natural pinewood system' (Forestry Commission, 1994b). Secondary aims include the enhancement of aesthetic value, the maintenance of genetic integrity of populations of native species, and the production of utilizable timber.

Since 1989 over 12 000 hectares of new pinewoods have been created on bare land, through either new planting or extension by natural regeneration, with the assistance of government grant aid worth approximately £10 million (ECU 12 million). The rate of grant varies according to the restoration option selected, with higher payments available for planting[7] and for smaller schemes (Table 6.1). The extent to which a new pinewood can recreate a natural pinewood also varies, depending on attributes such as its area, method of establishment, location and maturity (age). We compare the cost to central government of pinewood restoration under different grant options with the extent to which new schemes can effectively restore a native pinewood ecosystem in order to determine whether the current policy provides value for money.

Table 6.1 Current grant rates available for native pinewoods under the Woodland Grant Scheme

Options	Rate per hectare (£ ha^{-1})	
New Planting	less than 10 ha	10 ha or more
	£1350	£1050
Natural Regeneration	£525 plus 50% of agreed cost for work to encourage regeneration	

6.3.1 Effectiveness Criteria

The extent to which an individual pinewood created under the WGS can recreate the characteristics of a natural pinewood depends on a range of factors. These include internal features of a scheme such as area, species composition, and structural diversity, which will influence the restoration of ecological processes (for example, nutrient cycling), and locational attributes (for example, its position in the landscape) which affect colonization rates of specialist pinewood species.

In order to establish a reliable measure of effectiveness for individual new pinewoods, which takes account of these factors, a panel comprising 12 leading national experts in woodland ecology, was established. Each expert was asked to develop an ex ante system for measuring conservation effectiveness of new natural woodlands based on an agreed set of criteria. Criteria selection was confined to characteristics which could be measured from the data available for the new native pinewoods. This data came from two sources. The Forestry Authority supplied maps for each pinewood and supporting information on silvicultural methods, while locational information on land cover data was obtained from MLURI's land cover data base (MLURI, 1993). Both sets of data were stored in a geographic information system (GIS) to facilitate subsequent analysis.

The criteria are intended to reflect a holistic approach to the question of ecosystem restoration rather than measure the effectiveness of new pinewoods for restoring populations of individual species.

However, experts were asked to pay particular attention to attributes which are relevant to the requirements of the rarer and more specialists pinewood species. Eleven criteria, drawn from concepts of woodland and landscape ecology, were selected and included internal features of the scheme, such as size, and species composition, and locational characteristics relevant to habitat fragmentation and extinction processes. The agreed criteria are described in Table 6.2.

In order to measure the relative importance of the criteria to overall effectiveness, the pinewood experts were asked to weight them from 0 (little or no importance) to 10 (very important). Opportunity was also given to adjust these weights through time in order to reflect their relevance to the ex-ante assessment of effectiveness as the new pinewoods mature. For example, the weighting attached to criteria associated with colonization and support of specialist populations of pinewood flora and fauna might increase with time because immature schemes, regardless of their location and size, are unlikely to be colonized by the full range of plants and animals. On the other hand, the weight attached to precursor ground vegetation may decrease over time because almost all schemes will eventually develop a more natural ground flora. Two time periods were selected: year 10 and year 100.

The second component of the effectiveness measure was concerned with how well individual schemes performed under each criterion. The range of possible values each pinewood could achieve under each criterion was identified and experts were asked to provide an appropriate scoring system within the range 0 (no contribution) to 10 (maximum possible contribution). For most of the criteria scoring could be based on the direct measurement of individual characteristics of the pinewood. In the cases of Criteria 5 (deer control) and 6 (area) this information was available from the grant application, while for Criteria 7 to 11 the relevant characteristics had to be calculated from the land cover data in a 5km radius around the new pinewood.

Criteria 1 (genetic integrity), 2 (species composition), and 3 (tree density) were considerably more difficult to measure because no information was available for the relevant characteristics. Scoring based upon this was therefore the percentage of natural regeneration within the new pinewood. Experts were asked to establish a scoring system for these criteria which reflected the extent to which they considered that natural regeneration was 'better' than new planting under these criteria. If any of the experts considered this characteristic to be an inadequate measure for these criteria then they could express this by awarding a similar score to all schemes. Figure 6.1 shows an example of a new native pinewood and the values for the relevant characteristics of each criterion.

The effectiveness score for an individual pinewood under each criterion was calculated by multiplying the score by the criterion weight. The total effectiveness score for the pinewood for each expert was then obtained by adding up the scores under all of the criterion. An average effectiveness score for each pinewood was obtained by averaging across all 12 experts.

6.3.2 Costs

Grant costs are shown in Table 6.1. The relevant rate for each pinewood was derived from its area and the proportion of natural regeneration involved. Discretionary payments available for natural regeneration (to cover the costs of operations to encourage regeneration) such as scarification and fencing, were predicted from supporting information available for each scheme in the GIS.

6.3.3 Results

The costs and effectiveness of each new woodland were compared by correlating the grant cost with average effectiveness. Grant costs and effectiveness were negatively correlated in both year 10 and year 100 ($r = -0.52$ and -0.56 respectively). In other words, woodlands which attracted the greatest level of public funding were least effective in meeting the policy's objective. Table 6.3 presents the average grant cost and average effectiveness score for the three grant options at 10 and 100 years. At both time periods small new woodlands (less than 10 ha) were least effective and most expensive, while woodlands predominately established through natural colonization were cheapest and most effective. Woods established through natural regeneration, were, on average, more effective than new planting.

Valuation and the Environment

Table 6.2 Effectiveness criteria

	Criteria
1	Genetic Integrity: An important feature of the WGS new pinewoods is the requirement to use either natural regeneration or planting stock of local origin.
2	Species Composition and Distribution: Species distribution and composition within a native pinewood reflects local conditions, and can be highly variable. New planting under the WGS is required to reproduce an irregular distribution of trees and a mix of species suitable for the site.
3	Tree Density and Patchiness: Variable tree densities and patches of open habitat are distinctive features of natural pinewoods.
4	Precursor Vegetation: New pinewoods can be established on a range of semi-natural habitats. The ground vegetation at time of establishment influences the extent to which a characteristic pinewood flora will develop through time.
5	Method of Deer Control: In the absence of natural predators grazing has to be controlled by exclusion (fencing) or by maintaining deer numbers at low levels by shooting. The method used will influence the composition and structure of the habitat (tree regeneration, ground flora etc.), with shooting most likely to emulate the effects of low grazing expected under natural conditions.
6	Area of the Scheme: The Caledonian forest was once an extensive ecosystem covering many thousands of hectares. Certain specialist pinewood species require relatively large areas of pinewood (for example, capercaillies, red squirrels).
7	Area of Native Pinewoods surrounding a new pinewood: New schemes located in a region containing a significant proportion of mature native pinewoods are more likely to be colonized by specialist pinewood species. These schemes are also likely to provide important additional habitat for existing populations of pinewood species.
8	Distance to Surrounding Native Pinewoods: The closer existing native pinewoods are to the scheme the greater the possibility of colonization by pinewood specialists, and for the restoration of ecosystem processes and energy flows.
9	Number of Surrounding Native Pinewoods: Several studies have shown that due to differences in composition, structure and management, the combined species total from several small patches may be more than the total present on one patch of equivalent area (Kirby, 1995).
10	Area of Associated Habitat surrounding a new pinewood: The extent to which a new scheme will be colonized by specialist pinewood species and can contribute to the support of regional populations of pinewood flora and fauna will also be influenced by the matrix of non-pinewood habitats in the surrounding area. Each expert was asked to define the range of associated habitats from the Land Cover classification.
11	Adjacent Habitat: This criterion is related to Criteria 10 but highlights the importance of the habitat which is adjacent to a scheme. For example, a new scheme which is bordered by an existing pinewood is more likely to contribute to the support of pinewood species than one bordered by arable fields. This criterion uses the same definition of associated habitat as above.

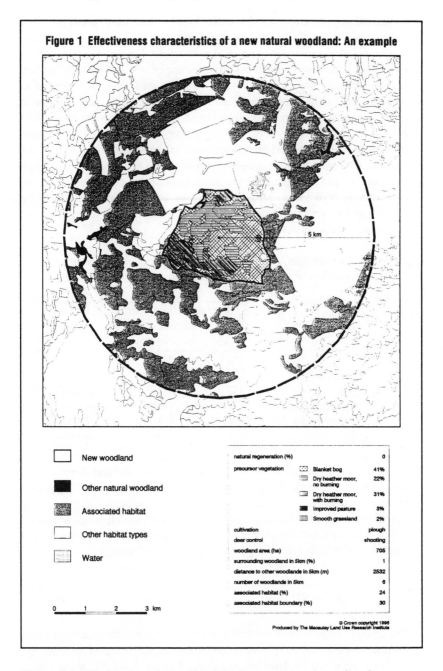

Figure 6.1 Effectiveness characteristics of a new natural woodland: an example

Natural regeneration scored more highly than new planting for a number of reasons. It was the preferred method with respect to woodland structure and composition, and it also involved less ground cultivation, which was considered to be a negative feature of new schemes. As natural regeneration can only occur close to existing seed sources, it tended to score higher on locational criteria. The schemes which had the lowest effectiveness score were typically planted schemes below 10 hectares in area, protected from deer by fencing rather than shooting, and remote from other pinewoods and other associated habitats.

After 100 years the average effectiveness score for natural regeneration was only 42 per cent greater than for new planting, compared to 52 per cent after just 10 years. This is a result of lower weightings placed on criteria which were considered to be less relevant to the appraisal of restoration effectiveness at year 100.

Table 6.3 Average effectiveness score and grant cost for different grant options (10 and 100 year comparison)

WGS Option	Average Effectiveness Score		Grant Cost ($£\ ha^{-1}$)
	10 years	100 years	
New planting (avg)	281	272	1101
less than 10 ha	265	259	1350
10 ha or more	317	309	1050
Natural regeneration (avg)	427	386	986
less than 10 ha	426	393	1276
10 ha or more	427	379	823

As a pinewood matures, woodland structure and ground flora evolve rapidly in response to changing environmental conditions and, regardless of initial conditions (such as tree density and patchiness and precursor vegetation), new woodlands begin to develop the characteristics of natural woodland over time[8]. Smaller schemes remained less effective than larger schemes under both natural regeneration and new planting.

6.4   CONCLUSIONS

The results suggest that the current grant options, which encourage small schemes established by planting, are inefficiently designed to meet the scheme's principal biodiversity objective. Natural regeneration and large schemes qualify for lower per hectare rates of grant aid because they incur lower per hectare costs of establishment. The principle of compensation for costs incurred is well established in other land use policies in the UK, such as the Farm Woodland Premium Scheme and Nitrate Sensitive Areas, and can be justified on the basis that landowners and farmers will only enter voluntary schemes if adequate compensation is available.

Setting aside the question of uptake for a moment, it is clear that the application of the compensation principle fails to produce value for money with respect to the delivery of environmental benefits. In the case of new pinewoods created under the WGS a more efficient grant structure would award higher grants to woodlands created using natural regeneration. By placing a far greater emphasis on natural regeneration the WGS payments accord with the Helsinki guidelines which encourage silvicultural practices which emulate nature, and with the Forestry Commission's own guidance which states that for the creation of new native woodlands 'natural colonization of unwooded sites is theoretically preferable to planting' (Rodwell and Patterson, 1994).

While ecological effectiveness should influence the rate of grant available for native woodland restoration, the actual grant paid will also be determined by other concerns of the policy-makers including the funding available and policy targets in terms of uptake. For example, the Biodiversity Steering Group (1995) have indicated a target level of expansion of 25 000 hectare of new pinewoods on unafforested land by 2005. If the grant rates are appropriately designed with respect to the effectiveness, but too low to attract landowners, the scheme will fail to meet this target. Conversely, if grant rates are set well above the actual cost of establishment landowners might be thought to be making excessive profits at the tax-payers, expense.

CEA focuses on the evaluation of policies where there is a clearly stated objective. Many government policies contain a range of objectives. Other aims of the pinewood scheme, for example, include the enhancement of aesthetic value, the maintenance of genetic integrity of populations of native species, and the production of utilizable timber. In this study it was not considered necessary to investigate these other objectives because they were considered to be secondary to the overall biodiversity objective. Additionally, in the case of timber, since financial support for woodland creation is justified on the basis of public benefits (Forestry Commission, 1991) seem inappropriate to include a private market good in the appraisal of the grant system.

Where there are competing multiple objectives, for example in other agricultural and environmental policies, CEA becomes more complex. Weightings could be attached to the different outputs, to reflect the importance experts, or policy-makers, attribute to the different objectives. In this form of application CEA becomes more or less analogous to CBA, with the weights replacing prices, except that the eventual option selected is not determined by economic efficiency (OECD, 1989). CEA, since it includes a measure of value for money, and incorporates expert judgement concerning conservation benefits, should be appealing to both policy-makers and environmental interest groups.

ACKNOWLEDGEMENTS

The authors would like to thank the Forestry Authority for supplying the maps and information on the new pinewoods. We would also like to thank the members of the expert panel for their assistance in this study. These were R. Turner, U. Urquhart, S. Taylor, and D. Beaumont (all RSPB), A. Hampson and E. Cameron (Scottish Natural Heritage), G. Patterson, J. Humphrey and G. Tuley (Forestry Commission), A. Hester and P. Dennis (MLURI) and T. Clifford (Caledonian Partnership). Helpful comments were also given by I. Ross, C. Taylor, R. Callender, and B. Crabtree.

ENDNOTES

1. Macaulay Land Use Research Institute, Craigiebuckler, Aberdeen AB15 8QH, UK
2. Royal Society for the Protection of Birds, Sandy, Bedfordshire, SG19 2DL,UK
3. If one prefers a 'weak' form of sustainable development, without any environmental limits, then CBA is more appropriate because it allows the trade-off of natural capital for man-made capital. The concepts of strong and weak sustainability are discussed in Pearce (1993).
4. The Stated Preference approach may, however, provide some potential for benefit transfer (Adamowicz et al., 1994).
5. Favourable status being defined by ecological criteria, including a stable or increasing natural range and a structure and functions ensuring long-term maintenance (Fry, 1995).
6. Although the rest of this paper focuses on the WGS, other public and private agencies have a very important role in expanding pinewoods.
7. All native pine expansion by planting must use native (that is, Highland) sources, with guidance given on the use of local sources and the use of other native tree species (Forestry Commission, 1994a).
8. No further intervention in the woodland was assumed during this period.

REFERENCES

Adamowicz, W., J. Louviere and M. Williams (1994), 'Combining revealed and stated preference methods for valuing environmental amenities', *Journal of Environmental Economics and Management,* 26, 271–92.

Bina, O., D. Harley, N. Marshall, M. Rayment and R. Turner (1995), *Cost Effectiveness Analysis and Caledonian Pine Forests,* Sandy : RSPB.

Biodiversity Steering Group (1995), *Biodiversity: the UK Steering Group Report.* 2 Volumes, London: HMSO.

Colman, D., J.R. Crabtree, J. Froud and L. O'Carroll (1992), *Comparative Effectiveness of Conservation Mechanisms,* University of Manchester, Department of Agricultural Economics.

Department of the Environment and Ministry of Agriculture, Fisheries and Food (1989), *The Nitrates Issue,* London: HMSO.

Department of the Environment (1991), *Policy Appraisal and the Environment,* London: HMSO.

Desvouges, W.H., M.C. Naughton and G.R. Parsons (1992), 'Benefit transfer: conceptual problems in estimating water quality benefits using existing studies', *Water Resources Research,* 28, 675–83.

Forestry Commission (1991), *Forestry Policy for Great Britain,* Edinburgh : Forestry Commission.

Forestry Commission (1994a), *The Woodland Grant Scheme Applicant's Pack,* Edinburgh: HMSO.

Forestry Commission (1994b), 'Native Pinewoods', *Forestry Practice Guide 7,* Forestry Commission, Edinburgh: HMSO.

Fry, M. (1995), *A Manual of Conservation Law,* Oxford: Clarendon Press.

Gittinger P. (1982), *Economic Appraisal of Agricultural Projects,* second edition, John Hopkins University Press, EDI.

HM Government (1994a), *Biodiversity: The UK Action Plan,* Cm 2428, HMSO.

HM Government (1994b), *Sustainable Forestry: The UK Programme,* Cm 2429. HMSO.

Kirby, K. (1995), 'Rebuilding the english countryside: habitat fragmentation and wildlife corridors as issues in practical conservation', *English Nature Science Series,* 10, Peterborough : English Nature.

London Economics (1992), *The Potential Use of Market Mechanism in the Control of Acid Rain,* Report to DoE. London : HMSO.

MLURI (1993), *The Land Cover of Scotland 1993,* Aberdeen : The Macaulay Land Use Research Institute.

OECD (1989), *Environmental Policy Benefits: Monetary Valuation,* Paris : OECD.

Pearce, D. (1993), *Blueprint 3 — Measuring Sustainable Development,* London : Earthscan.

Rodwell, J. and G. Patterson (1994), 'Creating new native woodlands', *Forestry Commission Bulletin 112,* London: HMSO.

7. The Relevance of Economic Valuation for Species Conservation Policy: The Case of the African Elephant

Gaie Mendelssohn

From an economic perspective, biodiversity is thought to be declining because the real value of wildlife resources is not reflected in the market place. This chapter examines whether the rigorous application of economic valuation to land-use decisions, and policy and project analysis could result in an optimum (or, at least, an increased and more targeted) level of investment in conservation. A case study of elephant conservation is presented to highlight the theoretical and practical problems associated with the application of economic valuation for determining policy using tools such as cost–benefit analysis (CBA) and market analysis. It suggests that these techniques are unable to capture a range of considerations that are central to conservation and that conflicts may emerge between priorities based upon conservation value and those based upon economic value. Furthermore, the methods prevent meaningful interaction with ecologists regarding the basis for priority setting. The conclusions go beyond the case of elephants and apply to species conservation in general.

What role, if any, can economic valuation play in influencing wildlife conservation policy? Economics is relevant both to understanding the way in which governments can influence private sector investment in conservation and to considering the most effective ways of allocating limited public sector resources to conservation. It allows for an analysis of the distribution of costs and benefits between actors at the local, national and global level, and for a distinction to be drawn between private and social-interests. In the context of a single species, it is relevant to selecting appropriate conservation and use strategies.

While economic valuation is relevant, it represents only one of a range of considerations that need to be taken into account. This chapter's examination of the relationship between economic and conservation value indicates that there is a need for new approaches that bring together these two perspectives. However, in order to contribute to decision-making, analyses need also to take into account the range of social, political and cultural values that in practice influence policy actions. Both conservation and economic value are only elements of a broader set of values upon which decisions are based.

This chapter suggests that for species conservation relatively simple tools such as ranking systems offer good opportunities for interdisciplinary collaboration. These types of tools will more readily allow for a broader discussion of values. More sophisticated joint modelling exercises, while attractive in their capacity to integrate approaches, may be impracticable given the state of our knowledge of ecosystems. They may also be more limiting in the extent to which they can incorporate other forms of values.

7.1   INTRODUCTION

This chapter considers how economic valuation can contribute to the development of conservation policy and practice in ways that are theoretically sound, practicable and politically relevant. It particularly examines the extent to which current approaches to policy and project analysis capture ecological concerns and looks at the prospects and need for more integrated approaches. A case study of elephant conservation is presented in order to consider these issues in the context of a single, high profile species. The lessons learned are considered relevant to a range of species and conservation issues.

Elephants are classified as an endangered species due to a rapid decline in numbers in the 1980s and as a result are relatively well researched. They have a high public profile due to their charismatic nature and economic importance. In ecological terms, they are considered a keystone species because of their significant impact on their environment.[1] They share much in common with other large endangered mammals that have significant economic value such as rhinos, gorillas, pandas and whales. Experiences drawn from the application of environmental economics to elephant conservation are also likely to be relevant to other species of economic value and/or rarity such as other game animals, butterflies and birds. These types of species face economic pressures due to the demand for use rights, the opportunity costs of land and the limited availability of public sector funding for conservation. The issues facing lower life forms are likely to be somewhat different because they generally have less direct-use value and are less well researched.

Elephants, like other species of economic value, can be considered as a natural resource in which the public and private sector may choose to invest in order to earn a return. As for other natural resources, policy analysis can be carried out to determine the extent to which market imperfections and government policy may be resulting in a level of investment which is suboptimal. This may be due to government pricing and investment policies that favour other sectors and due to the failure of market prices to reflect the ecological benefits of elephants. It may also be asked if a social optimum will ensure wildlife conservation or, more widely, ecological sustainability. Although historically decisions regarding species conservation and protected areas (PAs) were not analysed in this way, there is increasing interest both in demonstrating that wildlife conservation can be an economically viable investment option and in promoting private sector and community involvement in wildlife conservation.

There are a growing number of studies on the economics of single species. Natural resource use models have been developed to examine the conditions under which the extinction of species or decline in population size would be optimal for society as a whole or for private operators (Clark, 1973; Barbier, 1989; Barbier et al., 1990). While no one is likely to suggest that allowing elephants to become extinct is desirable, this kind of analysis can help to determine the incentives facing the private sector and the appropriate role for the public sector.

Market analysis has been carried out for wildlife products such as rhino horn and ivory (Sas-Rolfes, 1995; Barbier et al., 1990). Other studies have examined the economic potential for producing various wildlife products and reviewed alternative use options (Thresher, 1981a,b). Another group of studies has sought to estimate various components of economic value such as existence values, consumer surplus and opportunity costs (Munasinghe, 1992; Brown and Henry, 1993; Hampicke, 1993; Hyde et al., 1994). Since there are a number of difficulties associated with isolating the ecological and economic importance of a single species, the role and usefulness of such approaches needs to be assessed.

This chapter examines studies that have addressed the economic value of elephants or conservation areas that contain elephants. Most of this research adopts an environmental economics approach which is based upon neo-classical economics but seeks to place values on various environment costs and benefits that were traditionally excluded from economic valuation. This approach is probably not the most effective way of contributing to conservation policy. We question the claim that the rigorous application of environmental economics to land-use decisions results in levels of protection for the African elephant that would ensure its survival. This relates to a central concern of this book, namely, the respective roles of economics and ecology and in the current context how they compete in determining the number and location of a species to be conserved. Priorities calculated on the basis of environmental economics may be in accordance with or conflict with those based purely on conservation interests. Thus, here the focus is upon the role of valuation for a new ecological economics paradigm that integrates and expands the scope of economics and ecology.

7.2 ECONOMIC ASPECTS OF ELEPHANT CONSERVATION POLICIES

In 1989, tentative estimates reported that there were approximately 616 000 African elephants occupying land area of 5.8 million square kilometres (Cobb, 1989); an area equivalent to 27 per cent of the total land area in the elephant range states as shown in Table 7.1. More recent estimates (Said et al., 1995) suggest that following a decline in the 1980s, elephant populations have stabilized.

Table 7.1 Elephant conservation status

Region	No. of range states	Elephant population 000's				PAs as % of total land area	Elephant range as % of total land area
		1979	1989	% of total	% change		
Central Africa	7	496	286	46	−42	3.5	51
Eastern Africa	7	547	111	18	−79	6.8	28
Southern Africa	8	282	201	33	−29	6.8	22
Western Africa	14	17	18	3	+8	2.4	5
Totals:	36	1,342	616	100	−54	4.7	27

Note : The figures are tentative because of the considerable difficulties with estimating elephant numbers, particularly in forest environments, and determining range.

Sources: Cobb (1989), WRI (1992)

While the total population size suggests that the species is being afforded a reasonable level of protection, the rapid decline in elephant range and numbers during the 1980s was cause for serious concern. This crisis was precipitated by a period of intense poaching in the 1980s and resulted in an international debate about the wisdom of maintaining a legal ivory trade. Economists advised that some form of controlled trade should be permitted in order to raise revenue and provide an incentive for conservation (Barbier et al., 1990). Contrary to this advice, the African elephant was transferred to Appendix 1 of the Convention on International Trade in Endangered Species (CITES) in January 1990, thereby all but stopping legal international trade in ivory and other elephant products. While there is still debate about the extent to which the ivory trade ban is limiting poaching (Dublin et al., 1995; EIA, 1994) and whether it is acting as a disincentive to elephant conservation, it is thought to have played a role in bringing the situation under control. There are, however, demands that the trade be reopened and these are likely to increase as ivory stocks held by African governments steadily grow due to confiscation, problem animal control and deaths from natural causes. Indeed, the June 1997 meeting on CITES saw the agreement to allow some sale of these stocks by selected African countries to Japan.

The future of the African elephant is also threatened by commercial pressure to convert land to uses incompatible with elephant conservation. These pressures are being particularly felt in some communal areas in southern and eastern Africa experiencing high population growth rates and in-migration, but are also likely to apply increasingly to PAs, particularly in zones with high agricultural potential. The tensions are marked by an increased awareness of conflicts between elephants and humans, which is at least in part due to increased loss of human life and elephant damage to property.

Elephant range currently includes both PAs and significant areas of communal and private land. Twenty six per cent of elephants have been classified as being within PAs, although some of these afford minimal levels of protection (Douglas-Hamilton et al., 1992). The importance of PAs for elephant conservation varies widely in different countries; the two extreme cases are South Africa, where 91 per cent of elephants live within PAs and Botswana where the comparable figure is only 30 per cent. The trend to limit elephant populations to relatively small fenced PAs raises a number of concerns. Some populations have relied upon access to varied ecosystems and have used land outside PAs for water and grazing in the dry season. There is a related concern, particularly apparent in parts of eastern and southern Africa, about rising elephant populations in PAs and the impact that elephants at high densities are having on other parts of the ecosystem (Western, 1989; Hoft and Hoft, 1995). In order to have any influence on changing land-use patterns, there is a need for a better understanding of the economic incentives and their relationship to the political, social and cultural factors that influence decisions.

The impact of poaching and land-use pressure is being compounded by declining government budget allocations for protected area management in many range states; aid budgets have not been rising to meet the shortfall. This is intensifying the need to ensure that available funds are used efficiently to meet conservation priorities identified for elephants and other species. There is also an incentive to promote conservation on private and communal lands, if this can be done at a lower overall cost. Declining funds also fuel demands for reopening the international trade in elephant products in order to provide an additional source of revenue.

These key policy concerns need to be considered in assessing the potential role of valuation. This theme is further developed in Section 7.4 which addresses how recent studies have interacted with the policy environment. As background to an examination of how economists and ecologists can interact to influence conservation policy (Sections 7.5 and 7.6), the next section explores the different analytical approaches employed by economists and conservationists.

7.3   ANALYTICAL BASIS FOR ECONOMIC AND CONSERVATION VALUE

While economists and conservationists broadly agree on the policy issues outlined above, their analytical approaches can differ markedly.[2] While environmental economics has broadened its scope to address the role of the ecosystem and man's dependence upon environmental services, it still maintains a utilitarian perspective where natural resources are considered in terms of the goods and services they can provide to people both now and in the future. This underlying basis of value is radically different from a conservationists' or deep green viewpoint where species have intrinsic value in their own right regardless of their usefulness to mankind and where all species are of significance.

In practice, for management purposes, conservationists distinguish between species and habitats. They focus on keystone species or those with a high public profile to help achieve education, recreation or community development goals. They also consider the diversity and rarity of species in an ecosystem. While conservationists consider a range of social, economic and ecological factors, they lack a theoretical framework on which to base priorities and have no common currency with which to assess the importance of different considerations.

Historically, economists have been concerned with much shorter time frames than conservationists. Due to the growing interest in sustainability issues, economists increasingly acknowledge the importance of maintaining resources to provide goods and services for both current and future generations. There remains, however, considerable debate about what this means in practice. For example, should all elephants be conserved or just enough to ensure the survival of the species?

Although there has been much debate about whether discounting is appropriate for environmental projects and at what rate (Pearce et al., 1988; Johansson, 1993; Spash, 1993; Hanley and Spash, 1994), discount rates are still generally applied to allow for consumers' preferences for consumption now rather than in the future and for the interest that can be earned when capital is saved. This has the effect of reducing the value of natural resource use in the future and may lead to a situation where it is economically sound to cull an elephant population now and invest the income earned in an another type of economic activity. This is in direct contrast with a conservation approach which tends to suggest that elephant populations should be maintained without regard to opportunity costs.

Approaches to considering risk and uncertainty also differ markedly between the two disciplines. While economics traditionally considered lack of information as a market imperfection, in the environmental economics field the precautionary principle has been advocated to address situations where mistakes may be made through ignorance, particularly when the damage may be irreversible (O'Riordan, 1994). In selecting an appropriate degree of restraint, economists generally take account of the costs involved. Conservationists tend to advocate stricter controls and are less concerned with the costs and forgone income earning opportunities.

In seeking to explain the way ecosystems function, ecologists have developed a number of concepts which have not featured in economic analysis. They consider the potential impact of catastrophic events and thresholds which when reached may result in damaging consequences. There is particular interest in the resilience of ecosystems to accommodate external shocks. For example, periodic droughts are taken into account in ecological models that explore the minimum viable population size for elephants (Armbruster and Lande, 1993).

The relative weight given to these differences will determine the kind of integrated approach deemed feasible and desirable. Two options are: (i) improving existing valuation methods and using them, as suggested by Randall (1991) and Perrings et al., (1992), within the constraint of safe minimum standards (SMS), or (ii) developing radically new models that reflect both ecosystem functions and socio-economic forces. In order to assess the appropriateness of these alternatives, the next section considers the lessons to be learned from recent economic studies and the factors currently influencing policy decisions.

7.4   ECONOMIC ANALYSIS AND ELEPHANT CONSERVATION

7.4.1   Introduction to Recent Studies

Various types of analyses are summarized in Table 7.2; these have been carried out both specifically on elephants and more generally on wildlife areas containing elephants. Although none of the studies have attempted to determine the total economic value of elephants, those exploring components of their value, studies A, B and C in Table 7.2, have supported the view that elephants are an economically valuable resource in which it is worthwhile to invest. Studies B and C provide a financial rationale for promoting the consumptive use of elephants.

The location specific studies of land-use options, that include elephants, are referred to as study E in Table 7.2 and have been reviewed in Mendelssohn (1996). These studies suggest that, in certain conditions, land-use options with elephants can compete with alternative uses, but that there are a large number of situations where this is unlikely to be the case. Favourable settings include small to medium-sized PAs, with a capacity for large numbers of tourists, and forest areas, where there are far-reaching environmental benefits which may have little to do with elephants.

The market analyses of the impact of government policy, study F, have considered wildlife in general rather than elephants specifically. They draw a useful distinction concerning benefits and costs as they accrue privately as opposed to socially. This shows that aspects of government policy, such as heavy public sector investment in competing rural sectors, may limit private sector investment, while others, such as low world prices for beef, may favour wildlife. Studies on the impact of the international trading bans on both ivory, studies B and D, and rhino horn (Sas-Rolfes, 1995) highlight how these policies can influence private sector incentives to conserve. There may, of course, be other reasons why trading bans are justified.

Study G include models developed in order to examine the factors contributing to poaching and the decline in elephant numbers Africa-wide over the last 200 years and poaching in Luangwa Valley in Zimbabwe in the 1980s. The results have implications for the type of policies that are likely to be most effective in preventing further declines in elephant numbers.

Together these studies address, in various ways, the central policy concerns outlined earlier regarding declining elephant populations, land and budgetary pressures, and the wisdom of promoting the consumptive

Table 7.2 Application of environmental economics to elephant conservation

Studies	Method Of Analysis	Results	Comments
A. Valuing elephant viewing in Kenya (Brown and Henry, 1993)	Estimating consumer surplus and loss of revenue associated with decline in elephant population using travel cost method and contingency valuation survey.	Estimated annual value of consumer surplus of elephant viewing at US$25 million. A 25% fall in elephant numbers would lead to a fall in wildlife tourism revenue of between US$52 million and US$63 million.	Widely quoted as showing the value of wildlife tourism but of little direct relevance to decision-making. Some concerns about the data due to questions asked and small sample size.
B. Comparisons of alternative elephant-use strategies in Botswana (Barnes, 1990)	CBA of elephant use strategies before and after a ban on ivory trading. Considered the impact of different levels of government investment.	Positive NPV with a 6% discount rate. A combination of wildlife viewing, safari hunting and culling would be the most viable form of elephant use provided culling did not deter tourists.	Analysis provides useful tool for reviewing options and costs associated with restricting trade. Methodological difficulties isolating contribution of elephants.
C. Financial and economic viability of investing in elephant fencing (Hoare, 1992)	Outline of how to use CBA for assessing viability of elephant fences.	Example produced a positive IRR of 55%. Most significant benefits were value of elephant used for safari hunting and savings on staff patrol costs.	Analysis helpful in considering financial implications. There will, however, be other political and public relations considerations. So far, approach has not been used in the field.
D. Analysis of ivory market and advisability of imposing international trading ban (Barbier et al, 1990)	Regression analysis to explore factors influencing the demand for ivory and a review of options for introducing controlled ivory trade.	A ban was considered inadvisable because of the loss of revenue and probable growth of illegal markets. Due to demand inelasticity, a cartel type trading arrangement was considered workable.	Useful approach for exploring implications of alternative marketing options. Recommendations were not adopted but options remain relevant. Some criticism of model specification (Milner-Gulland, 1993)
E. Financial and economic viability of wildlife areas with elephants (for example, Norton-Griffiths, 1994, Douglas-Hamilton, 1988, Engelbrecht and Van der Walt, 1993, Davies and Matebesi, 1993, ODA, 1992, Ruitenbeek, 1990)	A number of studies of wildlife areas with elephants have included a CBA or a comparison of income from wildlife with that from other sources.	Some conservation areas with elephants, particularly small areas with high volume tourism and forested areas with significant environmental benefits can compete with alternative land-uses. There are, however, many that although considered important for elephant conservation are unlikely to be viable.	These types of analysis allow for a rigorous review of costs and benefits. They have so far tended to rubber stamp projects rather than influence the use of investment funds. They are unable to capture many ecological considerations.
F. Analysis of how government macroeconomic, pricing and investment policy impacts on private investment in wildlife conservation in elephant range states. (Bojo, 1994 ; Byrne et al., 1993 ; Jansen et al., 1992a, b)	Some studies have explored whether government policies are discouraging investment in the wildlife sector. In Zimbabwe detailed financial and economic analysis has been carried out based on surveys of private ranches. Modelling incorporating both ecological and economic factors.	There are various market distortions such as overvalued exchanged rates, subsidies to the agricultural sectors and government investment in agriculture and livestock rather than wildlife which may serve to deter investment in wildlife/elephant conservation. Other factors such as the low world price of beef may have the opposite impact, so case by case analysis is required.	Further work in this area is critical in order to better understand the factors influencing private sector investment. While not specifically related to elephants, the results are relevant.
G. Modelling of trends in elephant numbers and incentives for illegal use (Milner-Gulland and Leader-Williams, 1992, Milner-Gulland and Beddington, 1993)		One model highlights the importance of both poaching and reduced habitat in the long-term decline of elephant numbers. The other indicates that the probability of detection is likely to have a greater effect on poaching levels than the penalty imposed. Local economic development appears to reduce the incentives facing local poachers but not to influence the activity of organized gangs.	Models address key policy concerns. The academic presentation may limit the use of results by policy makers.

use of elephants. Although very difficult to measure, the influence of these various studies on policy decisions so far appears to have been relatively limited. Possible reasons for this are explored below with reference to the policy environment and methodological issues.

7.4.2 The Policy Environment

A research activity will generally have greater influence if it is undertaken in response to a specific policy decision, and if decision-making bodies commission the study and are involved in its design. Amongst the studies reviewed in Table 7.2, the analysis of the ivory market (Barbier et al., 1990) was the one most directly linked to a policy decision, albeit at an international level. It was prepared for the seventh CITES conference of parties, with funding from two international conservation bodies. It informed the 1989 decision to ban the international trade in ivory, although the economists' recommendation that some form of controlled trade be allowed went unheeded. The study's recommendations were weakened by insufficient analysis of the significant institutional constraints on implementing the proposed cartel style ivory market in an African context. This study was, however, only one of a number of factors that contributed to this highly political decision.

Studies B, C and F were relevant to policy-making at a national level and undertaken by local agencies (NGO projects, government departments and local consultants) with funding from the donor community. These studies were not, however, commissioned to address an impending policy decision and the extent to which they have influenced the policy arena is uncertain. As with the ivory market study, the recommendation of the studies B group, that culling and safari hunting of elephants be promoted, was weakened by its failure to address the managerial difficulties of controlling illegal use. Meanwhile, studies receiving World Bank support may influence work in other countries because they are promoted internationally (Bojo, 1994).

The policy impact of the remaining studies is even less certain. For example, although the valuation of elephant viewing by Brown and Henry (1993), category A (in our tables) formed one of the papers presented at the seventh CITES conference, along with the ivory market analysis, the research failed to address a specific policy question. It may have served a general purpose in highlighting the significance of the elephant's economic value and is often quoted in this regard. It may also have provided an additional justification for the substantial increase in the daily national park entrance fees for overseas visitors in the early 1990s in Kenya. There is, however, a danger of economic studies of this sort misguiding policy-makers because the values estimated are unlikely to be fully realized in financial terms and this is inadequately explained when the figures are quoted.

Most of the studies in category E were undertaken with donor funding in the course of evaluating a specific government project. As is the case with many project appraisals, they may have achieved little more than rubber stamping of the proposed initiative. The types of environmental values assigned a monetary figure vary across the studies. There are therefore considerable difficulties associated with using these studies as a basis for analysing the viability of investing in elephant conservation in different types of agro-economic and socio-economic conditions (Mendelssohn, 1996). Although relevant to current policy issues, the impact of the modelling work in categroy G may have been limited by its academic orientation. The approach in this case has been documented in academic journals but only indirectly linked to an imminent policy decision.

In general, in order to have a greater influence on policy making, these kinds of studies need to be directly related to specific policy questions and to include more thorough analysis of the political, institutional and cultural context.

7.4.3 Methodological Issues

In order to influence policies, economic analyses need to be theoretically sound and to complement the work of other disciplines. Section 7.2 has outlined the way in which economists are currently seeking to address environmental questions more efficiently by assigning monetary values to a range of preservation values and ecological service values. Amongst the studies reviewed, the research on elephant viewing is the only attempt to measure a specific element of the non-market value of elephants. Other studies attempt monetary evaluation of a range of environmental services, for example, soil erosion and the downstream effects of rainforest conservation on a watershed. Whether seeking to improve and develop these techniques with a view to measuring the total economic value is a fruitful exercise remains questionable.

In the analysis of a single species, there are problems associated with seeking to single out the costs and benefits of one species when these are closely linked with those for other species. In the comparison of alternative elephant use strategies, study B, elephants' contribution to tourism revenue was assumed to be 41 per cent, because this is elephants' contribution to total ecological biomass. In the study on the value of elephant viewing in Kenya, study A, visitors were asked to suggest the percentage of their enjoyment accounted for by elephants. Both these methods are unconvincing and may result in misleading conclusions about the value of wildlife viewing because they fail to capture fully the net benefits associated with elephants.

More appropriate tools for analysing policy questions related to a single species are available. One option is to estimate the marginal costs and benefits associated with maintaining or reintroducing a species. Vorhies and Vorhies (1993) examined whether to introduce lions into Pilansesberg National Park, South Africa by estimating the additional financial investment, management costs and income generation. They concluded that reintroduction would be worthwhile and this is likely to have influenced the decision to adopt the policy.

In contrast study A, on elephant viewing, sought to estimate the economic costs associated with a decline in elephants. The potential loss was estimated by asking visitors how their visitation patterns would be affected by a fall in elephant numbers. The results indicated a potentially significant drop in revenue as a result of a 25 per cent drop in elephant numbers. The analysis failed, however, to address adequately the relationship between elephant numbers and visitor enjoyment. The results conflict with experience in Kenya in the 1980s when there was a dramatic fall in elephant numbers but tourism areas were largely unaffected and tourism revenue continued to increase. An economic assessment needs to allow for the readiness of visitors to move to different locations and for the fact that relatively small numbers of elephants are required for elephant viewing. Although visitor surveys have a role in understanding the tourism attributes of most importance to visitors, they lack the precision required for assessing the economic loss associated with a decline in species numbers.

In order to have a richer picture of the economic value of elephant conservation a case might be made for assigning a monetary value to the ecological services provided by elephants. In theory this would be possible if the elephant's role can be specified. For example, elephant bush clearance maintains the option values associated with biodiversity and aids seed dispersal of species of economic value. However, the uncertainty regarding the ecological role of elephants would make such analysis infeasible for the foreseeable future. The issues surrounding this aspect of uncertainty are outlined in the textbox below. Despite this, some of the category E studies in Table 7.2 have sought to attach monetary values to ecological services but this required them to include highly questionable ecological assumptions which limit the usefulness of the results.

This review highlights the considerable theoretical and practical difficulties with seeking to isolate elephant specific costs and benefits, even in relatively straightforward financial terms. In some cases it will therefore be more appropriate to consider a range of use options that involve but are not restricted to elephants. For example, safari hunting can be compared with wildlife viewing rather than elephant hunting with elephant viewing. There are specific management questions that necessitate single species analysis. These include decisions related to: removing or reintroducing elephants on a particular piece of land; undertaking an elephant related investment such as fence construction or elephant translocation; and determining the most efficient ways of controlling elephant poaching. Further work on valuing elephants is likely to be influential if it focuses on the factors that can be readily assigned a monetary value. These include financial costs and benefits, and economic values such as opportunity costs and local consumptive use values. The costs associated with maintaining elephants need particular consideration because they tend to be overlooked in work seeking to justify elephant conservation. Uncertain ecological information, and the limitations of the contingent valuation method (see Spash and Hanley, 1995), suggest caution in seeking to undertake a comprehensive economic analysis.

7.4.4 Uncertainty and the Ecosystem Value of Elephants

While elephants are considered to be of significant conservation value, conclusive research on their role in savannah and forest ecosystems is surprisingly limited. Elephants have a significant impact on plant composition due to their large and varied diet, their physical impact on their surroundings and their ability to move large distances. They are valued as a keystone species. However, little research has been carried out on the effect of removing elephants from particular ecosystems and, although some species clearly benefit from the presence of elephants, it is likely that the removal of elephants would reduce species abundance rather than eliminate them entirely.

The conservation value of elephants is thought to be related to elephant density, with plant species richness and density being highest at moderate elephant density (Western, 1989). At high densities, there is considerable evidence that elephants can have a dramatic effect on their environment, particularly in savannah situations. Changes in vegetation composition, involving a reduction in woody cover, may even lead to the establishment of open grass land. While the prospect of these changes causing irreversible damage has served to justify the culling of elephants in some Parks in Southern Africa, there is also a concern that preventing natural fluctuations may affect species that regenerate following perturbations to herbivore numbers. Thus, although high elephant densities may have a negative effect on biodiversity in the short-term, allowing some fluctuations in time and space may benefit diversity in the longer-term. At low densities, there tends to be an increase in bush and tree cover and an associated decline in biodiversity. In terms of biodiversity, this suggests the conservation value of elephants is declining due to the current pattern of high elephant densities in PAs and low densities outside. This conclusion is tentative because of the paucity of research on the subject.

Regardless of their role in the ecosystem, elephants are considered of conservation value in their own right as the largest existing mammal on the African continent. In order to ensure their survival, conservationists are keen to conserve as many as possible. There is, however, a question regarding how many are needed to ensure the survival of the species and to what extent populations need to be maintained in wilderness areas where there is little disturbance from elephant use. The prospects for placing an economic value on elephant conservation are clearly limited by the lack of certainty regarding their ecological role and importance.

7.5 THE USE OF ECONOMIC VALUATION FOR PRIORITIZING ELEPHANT POPULATIONS

Due to the land-use and poaching pressure on elephants and the limited funds available for conservation, some attempt to allocate resources amongst elephant populations is considered important. This section examines the way in which a multiple criteria ranking system has been used to prioritize elephant conservation areas and outlines why such an approach may be preferable to a ranking based solely on economic valuation.

7.5.1 Prioritizing Using a MultiCriteria Ranking System

There have been a number of attempts to prioritize conservation areas using various measures of biodiversity without any reference to other socio-economic criteria (Weitzman, 1992; Williams et al., 1996). Recent work has also explored ways of developing indexes that incorporate cost-effectiveness and the probability of success (Moran et al., 1996). The African Elephant and Rhino Specialist Group (AERSG) has, in the context of elephant and rhino populations, developed a ranking system. AERSG comprises experts on management and conservation, and was established by the IUCN Species Survival Commission to advise IUCN member countries and organizations (see Cumming and Jackson, 1984; Cumming et al., 1990). The AERSG ranking system was based on the criteria summarized in Table 7.3.

The biological criteria highlight the features of elephant conservation considered to be of most importance. The population genetics of elephants has been given little research, but elephants in unique locations such as in the desert or in isolated forest locations are thought to be genetically distinct and thus of greater ecological importance. A population in a unique habitat is also considered of conservation value because it provides information about elephants' behaviour which is specific to that ecosystem. Large populations are considered to be of greater importance than small ones mainly because they are less vulnerable to extinction as a result of environmental catastrophes, such as droughts, and to a lesser extent due to their greater genetic diversity (Armbruster and Lande, 1993). The conservation factors also include the extent to which areas contain other species of special interest and the degree to which natural features confer protection. The ranking system incorporates the likelihood of success by including land pressures, the poaching threat and the stability of the political climate. The economic criteria include both income generating potential and an assessment of opportunity costs. The economic criteria are given slightly less weighting than the other factors.

Table 7.3 African elephant specialist group criteria for ranking elephant populations in Africa

Criteria	Scores Applied	Classification for Maximum Scores
Biological criteria		
Genetic rarity	1–3	A rare and isolated population in a continental context
Population size	1–10	Over 1000 elephants
Area's conservation significance	1–5	Rare ecosystem containing other species of special interest
Natural security of the area	0–3	Natural features accord good protection
Conservation status		
Administration and law enforcement	0–5	Full capacity to handle any poaching threat
Political climate	0–5	Political climate
Land pressures	1–5	Stable urban and rural population
Poaching threat	1–5	No poaching threat
Economic and national factors		
Economic values conflicting with wildlife use	1–5	Wildlife is the most suitable form of land-use
Natural conservation importance and investment	1–5	Nationally unique with high use and capital development
Economic potential of wildlife	1–5	High tourist and high cropping potential

Source: Cumming and Jackson, 1984

When the maximum scores are applied, the conservation criteria account for 38 per cent, the conservation status criteria 36 per cent and economic criteria 26 per cent.

This exercise by the AERSG represents an attempt to define criteria for establishing conservation priorities on a continental scale. Although undertaken by an IUCN specialist group, it appeared to have had relatively little influence on the international funding of elephant conservation. This was largely due to the general feeling of crisis at the time which resulted in most attention being paid to those populations under immediate poaching threat. Also the biological criteria were inadequately thought out; for example, why protection afforded by natural features and research investment qualify as criteria of biological importance is unclear and the term genetic rarity is loosely defined. In addition, the continental scope of the ranking exercise limited its relevance and acceptability at a national level. Some countries were opposed to the use of any scoring system, because they suspected that none of their elephant populations would be regarded as a priority if determined on this basis. The criteria have not been developed further or applied since 1987 (Cumming et al., 1990). In an ongoing review, the African Elephant Specialist Group (AESG), formerly part of the AERSG, is attempting to identify those elephant populations of highest conservation priority but without ranking them (Chris Thouless, pers. comm.).

Although scientifically unsophisticated, ranking systems allow biological factors to be combined with criteria reflecting the economic importance of the resource and conditions influencing the likelihood of success of conservation projects. The AERSG's experience highlights the importance of considering the political context when planning and conducting such analyses.

7.5.2   Prospects for Prioritizing based on Assessing Total Economic Value

An alternative ranking system based simply on financial or economic criteria would be inappropriate because this would fail to fully reflect conservation value. This is illustrated by the example in Table 7.4 which compares a ranking of elephant conservation areas in Kenya based on the AERSG criteria outlined above with a ranking based on strictly financial considerations. The results differ markedly. The biological criteria favour the forested areas (namely Aberdares, Meru and Mount Elgon) and Tsavo on account of its large size. The three highest priority areas from a financial perspective are Amboseli, Samburu and Mara, which are medium-sized savannah areas with large numbers of tourists. These are ranked relatively low on biological criteria, but somewhat higher when all the AERSG criteria are included, due to their economic importance.

While the financial ranking might be expanded to include economic values, such as option, existence and biodiversity values, it would still fail to capture many of the ecological concerns because of the underlying differences in analytical approach discussed earlier (Section 7.3). For conservationists the principal objective is the survival of the species which particularly requires a focus on large groups of elephants. Although economic use values depend upon the survival of the species, current economic methods are likely to place less emphasis on large populations. This is because the marginal benefits are likely to decline as more elephants are conserved and, due to the opportunity costs of land, may only be partially compensated for by the economies of scale of conserving large areas.

Similarly the priority ecologists attach to maintaining elephant populations in habitats where they are rarely found is unlikely to be fully reflected by an economic valuation. Economists will value these rare populations highly when there are significant direct use values, low opportunity costs and high preservation values. The latter depends on public perceptions of the importance of an area. Desert elephants which are particularly rare would expect to have high tourist and preservation values, and relatively low opportunity costs. However, other rare populations in, for example, isolated forest fragments of West Africa may have relatively low use values and less significant preservation values.

Table 7.4 Ranking of elephant conservation areas in Kenya

	Parks/reserves	Net revenue (US$ per Km²)[3]	AERSG ranking -all criteria	AERSG ranking -biological criteria
1	Amboseli	+2180	3	6
2	Samburu	+1194	5	6
3	Mara	+0612	3	5
4	Aberdares	+216	1	1
5	Shimba Hills	+470	9	8
6	Tsavo (East and West)	−22	8	3
7	Meru	−24	2	2
8	Marsabit	−340	6	8
9	Mt. Elgon	−415	6	3

Sources: Cumming and Jackson, (1984), Mendelssohn (1996)

Economic valuation also has difficulty in assigning a value to the potential but uncertain negative effects of consumptive elephant use and of high elephant densities. Economics is poorly equipped, for example, to capture the way in which elephant culling may damage the environment by preventing fluctuations in population size. The negative effects of high population densities would only be reflected in economic values if they were likely to result in reductions in tourist value. Less obvious changes of high densities, which might affect the resilience of the ecosystem and the diversity of species in the longer term, would be difficult to capture. Uncertainty regarding these issues makes them difficult to include in any economic analysis, although through sensitivity analysis a range of possible outcomes can be explored. For these various reasons, seeking to use monetary measures to assess conservation value is considered inappropriate.

7.6　CONCLUSIONS: WAYS OF STRENGTHENING THE INTERACTION BETWEEN ECONOMISTS AND ECOLOGISTS

The economics of the environment is in a very formative period and, in the conservation field, there is clearly a need for strengthening the links between ecology and economics. In view of the significant costs associated with multidisciplinary work, there is a need to determine the degree of integration that should be attempted. Three approaches are summarized in Table 7.5. The following suggestions are relevant to elephant conservation and are likely to be applicable to the conservation of other large and economically valuable endangered species.

These kind of analyses may be unnecessary for small animals and lower life forms because there is likely to be less controversy over protecting endangered species from these groups. This is because less land area is required, and the opportunity and management costs are therefore generally low (Hyde et al., 1994).

The strengthening of neoclassical environmental economics is the first item listed in Table 7.5. In applying existing valuation and CBA techniques, economists need to work more closely with ecologists so that their work reflects a better understanding of the ecological issues. In order for others to appreciate the significance of the results, economic analyses should explicitly state their value basis and the factors they exclude. Economics can make an important contribution by focusing on the readily measurable costs and benefits of projects and policies, by examining distributional issues and by advising on ways in which government policies can influence private decisions. Estimates of conservation value which are not based on marketed goods and services are considered less likely to influence policy because the methodologies are often unconvincing. They are therefore considered of low research priority.

Table 7.5 Analytical approaches for integrating ecology and economics

Type of Analysis	Approach	Level of Interaction	Comments
Strengthening Environmental Economics	Further development of existing techniques for valuing the environment, CBA and market analysis	Improving interdisciplinary understanding. Economics would clarify value basis and what is excluded.	Unable to address fully conservation concerns.
Ranking Systems	Develop ranking system to include conservation, economic and policy criteria	Pooling of concerns from a range of disciplinary backgrounds.	Theoretically weak basis for decision-making. Maybe helpful in order to draw together different types of values.
Ecological Economics Models	Developing fully integrated models drawing on ecological and economic principles, as they become relevant.	Combining analytical frameworks and developing new ones as appropriate	Long-term ideal. Likely to be difficult due to limitations of current ecological research. Relatively expensive. Unlikely to influence policy in near future.

In order to address conservation value, the concept of safe minimum standards has been proposed to allow traditional tools to be applied within some precautionary limits. SMS have been defined as 'those required to achieve a particular probability of survival of the targeted species for a specific period' (Hohl and Tisdell, 1993). Due to uncertainty regarding the ecological risk associated with reducing elephant numbers, a theoretically rigorous SMS would be impossible to determine in the foreseeable future. The work that the AESG is currently carrying out to identify the most important elephant populations in Africa could, however, be used as a guideline.

In order to have a significant impact on conservation decisions, a greater level of multidisciplinarity will probably be necessary. The second item in Table 7.5 refers to the use of ranking systems. While these are theoretically and scientifically unsophisticated, they do provide a practical way in which those from different backgrounds can pool their perspectives. They can incorporate a range of criteria reflecting both readily measurable economic considerations, such as management and opportunity costs, and more subjective assessment, for example biodiverisity importance and degrees of threat. The AESG's experience suggests that national level and local exercises are more likely to have an impact than work at the global or continental level because this is the level at which most land-use decisions are taken.

As an ideal for the future, joint modelling exercises referred to in the third row of Table 7.5 are an attractive option. They provide an opportunity to integrate an understanding of ecological systems with a study of the impact of market forces. There are a growing number of studies of this sort (Skonhoft, 1995, 1996). There is, however, need for caution in using these approaches in a policy context because of the difficulty of allowing for the political, institutional and cultural dimensions. This review of elephant conservation issues also suggests the ecological information may in many cases be inadequate. The complexity of these models may limit the ease with which the results can be readily conveyed to those working in the policy arena.

In practice future work is likely to include all three of these approaches. In each case there is need to focus on improving the interaction between economists and ecologists, and on ensuring that the broader institutional, political and cultural context is taken into account.

ACKNOWLEDGEMENTS

The author is indebted to a wide range of people who contributed to the study on the economics of elephant conservation on which this chapter draws. In particular Chris Thouless and Stephen Cobb helped with providing ecological perspectives. The EC is thanked for its financial support. The author would also like to thank Jane Corbett, David Duthie, Peter Evans, Keith Lindsay and Clive Spash for kindly commenting on drafts. Naturally, none of the above are responsible for the views expressed in the chapter or any remaining errors.

ENDNOTES

1. The term keystone species refers to species that play a particularly important role in an ecosystem and which other species depend on.
2. The title conservationist is used here to refer to a practitioner who is both applying ecological principles and playing an advocacy role to protect the environment.
3. Net revenue is calculated on the basis of entrance fee revenue in 1992/3 and includes an allowance for management costs. The later are estimates per kilometre according to the size of the area (Cumming et al., 1990).

REFERENCES

Armbruster, P. and R. Lande (1993), 'A population viability analysis for African elephant (*Loxodonta africana*): How big should reserves be?', *Conservation Biology*, 7, 602–10.

Barbier, E.B. (1989), *Economics, Natural-Resource Scarcity and Development: Conventional and alternative views*, London: Earthscan Publications Ltd.

Barbier, E.B., J.C. Burgess, T.M. Swanson and D.W. Pearce (1990), *Elephants, Economics and Ivory*, London: Earthscan Publications Ltd.

Barnes, J.I. (1990), 'Economics of different options of elephant management', in P. Hancock (ed.), *The Future of Botswana's Elephants*, Botswana: Department of Wildlife and National Parks, pp. 60–66.

Bojo, J. (1994), *The Economics of Wildlife*, Washington, DC: The World Bank.

Brown, G. and W. Henry (1993), 'The viewing value of elephants', in Edward B. Barbier (ed.), *Economics and Ecology: New frontiers and sustainable development*, London: Chapman and Hall, pp. 146–55.

Byrne, P.V., C. Staubo and J.G. Grootenhuis (1993), *The Economics of Living with Wildlife - The case for Kenya*, Report for the World Bank, Nairobi, Kenya, June 1993.

Clark, C.W. (1973), 'The economics of overexploitation', *Science*, 181, 630–34.

Cobb, S. (1989), *The Ivory Trade and the Future of the African Elephant*, Volume 1: Summary and Conclusions; Volume 2: Technical Reports. Oxford: Ivory Trade Review Group, Report for CITES.

Cumming, D.H.M. and P. Jackson (eds) (1984), *The Status and Conservation of Africa's Elephants and Rhinos*, Gland, Switzerland: IUCN.

Cumming, D.H.M., R.F. du Toit, and S.N. Stuart (1990), *African Elephants and Rhinos: Status survey and conservation action plan*, Gland, Switzerland: IUCN Species Survival Commission.

Davies, R.J. and T.J. Matebesi (1993), *Cost Benefit Analysis of Pilanesberg National Park*, Bophuthatswana National Parks Board, unpublished.

Douglas-Hamilton, I., F. Michelmore and A. Inamdar (1992), *African Elephant Database*, European Commission African Elephant Survey and Conservation Programme, February 1992.

Dublin, H.T., T. Milliken and R.F.W. Barnes (1995), *Four Years After the CITES Ban: Illegal killing of elephants, ivory trade and stockpiles*, IUCN/SSC African Elephant Specialist Group.

EIA (1994), *Living Proof - African Elephants: The success of the CITES Appendix I ban*, London : Environmental Investigation Agency.

Engelbrecht, W.G. and P.T. Van der Walt (1993), Notes on the economic use of the Kruger National Park, *Koedoe*, 36 (2), 113–19.

Hampicke, U. (1993), 'Ethics and economics of conservation', *Biological Conservation*, 67, 219–31.

Hanley, N. and C.L. Spash (1994), *Cost–Benefit Analysis and the Environment*, Aldershot, UK and Brookfield, US: Edward Elgar.

Hoare, R.E. (1992), *Fencing as a Management Tool in Zimbabwe's Wildlife Programmes*, Conference Proceedings. Harare: Department of National Parks and Wildlife.

Hoft, R. and M. Hoft (1995), 'The differential effects of elephants on rainforest communities in the Shimba Hills, Kenya', *Biological Conservation*, 73, 67–79.

Hohl, A. and C.A. Tisdell (1993), 'How useful are environmental safety standards in economics?: The example of safe minimum standards for protection of species', *Biodiversity and Conservation*, 2, 168–181.

Hyde, W.F., K.R. Kanal, and E.D. Misomali (1994), 'The marginal cost of endangered species management', in M. Munasinghe and J. McNeely (eds), *Protected Area Economics and Policy*, Washington: IUCN, pp. 171–80.

Jansen, D.J., I. Bond and B. Child (1992a), *Cattle, Wildlife, Both or Neither? A Summary of Survey Results for Commercial Ranches in Zimbabwe*, WWF Multispecies Project, Harare, October 1992. Multispecies Animal Production Systems Project Paper, 30.

Jansen, D.J., I. Bond and B. Child (1992b), *Cattle, Wildlife, Both or Neither? Results of a Financial and Economic Survey of Commercial Ranches in Southern Zimbabwe*, WWF Multispecies Project, Harare, Multispecies Animal Production Systems Project Paper, 27, Vol. 3, Annex 1–5.

Johansson, P.O. (1993), *Cost–Benefit Analysis of Environmental Change*, Cambridge: Cambridge University Press.

Mendelssohn, G. (1996), *Economics and the Conservation of the African Elephant*, report for the European Commission, Oxford.

Milner-Gulland, E.J. (1993), 'An econometric analysis of consumer demand for ivory and rhino horn', *Environmental and Resource Economics*, 3, 73–95.

Milner-Gulland, E.J. and J.R. Beddington (1993), 'The exploitation of elephants for the ivory trade: an historical perspective', *Proceedings Royal Society London*, 252, 29–37.

Milner-Gullard, E.J. and N. Leader-Williams (1992), 'A model of the incentives for illegal exploitation of rhinos and elephants: poaching pays in Luangwa Valley, Zambia', *Journal of Applied Ecology*, 29, 388–401.

Moran, D., D. Pearce and A. Wendelaar (1996), *Global Biodiversity Priorities: A cost-effectiveness index for investments*, CSERGE.

Munasinghe, M. (1992), *Environmental Economics and Valuation in Development Decision–making*, Washington DC: The World Bank.

Norton-Griffiths, M. (1994), 'Long term conservation of wildlife on the rangeland of the Serengeti ecosystem', in A.R.E. Sinclair and P. Arcese (eds), *Serengeti II: Research and Management for Ecosystem Conservation*, Chapters 29/30.

O'Riordan, T. (ed.) (1994), *Interpreting the Precautionary Principle*, London: Earthscan Publications Ltd.

ODA (1992), *Updated Economic and Financial Analysis for Mau Forest, Kenya*, Overseas Development Administration, Kenya Indigenous Forest Conservation Programme, unpublished.

Pearce, D., A. Markandya, and E.B. Barbier (1988), *Blueprint for a Green Economy*, London: Earthscan Publications.

Perrings, C., C. Folke, and K.-G. Maler (1992), 'The ecology and economics of biodiversity loss: the research agenda', *Ambio*, 21 (3), 201–11.

Randall, A. (1991), 'The value of biodiversity', *Ambio*, 20 (2), 64–8.

Ruitenbeek, J.H. (1990), *Tropical Forests — Economic Analysis of Conservation Initiatives: Examples from West Africa*, Godalming, UK: WWF.

Said, M.Y., R.N. Chunge, G.C. Craig, C.R. Thouless, R.F.W. Barnes and H.T. Dublin (1995), *African Elephant Database*, Gland, Switzerland: IUCN Species Survival Commission.

Sas-Rolfes, M. (1995), *Rhinos: Conservation, Economics and Trade-Offs*, London: The Institute of Economic Affairs.

Skonhoft, A. (1995), 'On the conflicts of wildlife management in Africa', *International Journal of Sustainable Development and World Ecology*, 2, 267–77.

Skonhoft, A. (1996), *Conservation vs. Exploitation of Transboundary Terrestrial Animal Species*, Inaugural Conference of the European Branch of the International Society for Ecological Economics, May 1996, Paris, Conference paper.

Spash, C.L. (1993), 'Economics, ethics and long-term environmental damages', *Environmental Ethics*, 15, 117–32.

Spash, C.L. and N. Hanley (1995), 'Preferences, information and biodiversity preservation', *Ecological Economics*, 12, 191–208.

Thresher, P. (1981a), 'The economics of a lion', *Unasylva*, 33 (134), 34–5.

Thresher, P. (1981b), 'The present value of an Amboseli lion', *World Animal Review*, 40, 31–3.

Vorhies, D. and F. Vorhies (1993), *Introducing Lion into Pilansesberg: An economic assessment*, Eco Plus (PTY), Ltd for Bophuthatswana National Parks and Wildlife Management Board, 4 July 1993.

Weitzman, M.L. (1992), 'On diversity', *Quarterly Journal of Economics*, 100, 363–405.

Western, D. (1989), The Ecological Value of Elephants: A keystone role in African ecosystems, in S. Cobb (ed.), Vol. 2. *The Ivory Trade and the Future of the African Elephant*, Oxford: Ivory Trade Review Group, Section 5.2.

Williams, P., D. Gibbons, C. Margules, A. Rebelo, C. Humphries and R. Pressey (1996), 'A comparison of richness hotspots, rarity hotspots and complementary areas for conserving diversity of British birds', *Conservation Biology*, 10 (1), 155–74.

WRI (1992), *World Resources Institute 1992–93: A guide to the global environment*, Washington: Oxford University Press.

8. Willingness to Pay, Willingness to Accept: A CVM Field Study of Environmental Commodities

Erkki Mäntymaa

8.1 INTRODUCTION

A persistent discrepancy between theoretical and empirical results within a branch of science is always a serious problem. In contingent valuation method (CVM) research the disparity between willingness to pay (WTP) to obtain something and willingness to accept (WTA) compensation for giving the same thing up has bothered scientists since the early days of the discipline. The conventional welfare theory developed for the case of price change by Willig (1976) and applied to quantity or quality change by Randall and Stoll, (1980) suggests that the two welfare measures should be almost equal so long as the income and welfare effects are small. Meanwhile, several empirical and experimental studies have shown frequent and substantial differences between WTP and WTA measures.

As a possible explanation for the contradiction Hanemann (1991) put forward a hypothesis that concurs with the conventional theory but interprets and expands its scope in a way more appropriate for environmental commodities. According to him the difference between WTP and WTA depends not only on an income effect but also on a substitution effect, that is, how easily a commodity can be replaced with another in order to maintain the welfare of the individual. Keeping the income effect constant, Hanemann showed analytically that low substitutability increases the difference between WTP and WTA, while high substitutability reduces the disparity. This paper tests Hanemann's proposition in a field study using environmental commodities.

The structure of the paper is as follows. Section 8.2 defines the problem (that is, how the difference between WTP and WTA is assumed to depend on the substitution effect), and presents a theoretical model for analysing the difference and develops the hypotheses to be tested. Section 8.3 explains the method used in the investigation and describes the essential features of the survey instrument, the data sets and the outlier analysis. The approach uses respondents' self-reported evaluations to indicate the degree of substitutability between two environmental commodities, the *Right of Common Access* (RCA) and the *Recreation Right*. Section 8.5 reports the empirical results, and conclusions are drawn in Section 8.6.

8.2   TESTING WTP VS. WTA

The Hicksian welfare measures include compensating variation (CV) and equivalent variation (EV) in the case of commodity price changes, and compensating surplus (CS) and equivalent surplus (ES) in the case of changes in amount or quality. In CVM studies, these correspond to individuals' maximum WTP and minimum WTA. According to general welfare theory, the values revealed by the WTP and WTA question formats should be of the same size given small income and welfare effects. One of the most important arguments supporting this viewpoint was presented by Willig (1976), who deduced exact upper and lower bounds for the differences between a consumer's surplus and CV and EV in cases where a commodity price change produces a welfare change. According to him, the ordinary Marshallian consumer's surplus is a good approximation to the theoretically correct but empirically cumbersome Hicksian welfare measures if the income elasticity of the commodity is proportionally low.

   Randall and Stoll, (1980) expanded the analysis of Willig (1976) from the case of a price change to a situation in which a change in the quantity or quality of a commodity creates welfare variation. Their main observations are as follows. First, that CV and EV are identical and equal to the Marshallian consumer's surplus if the commodities are fully divisible and tradable without transaction costs in an infinite market. Second, for fully indivisible commodities, CV is larger than EV in the case of welfare losses and smaller for welfare gains. Finally, the difference between CV and EV lies somewhere between these two cases if the commodity is divisible and its exchange entails transaction costs. As a practical guideline, Randall and Stoll, (1980) state that if the changing commodity is divisible, the market is fairly competitive, the transaction costs are low and the price elasticity is small, then use of the Marshallian consumer's surplus causes a small error by comparison with the inaccuracies of the estimation techniques. At the same time, CV and EV are so close that WTP and WTA should be almost equal. Thus these conclusions are comparable to those of Willig (1976).

   A number of researchers have subsequently tested the theoretical results of Randall and Stoll, (1980) empirically, but in most cases they have been unable to agree with them. WTA has usually exceeded WTP by a considerable margin. In a list of 15 studies reviewed by Cummings et al. (1986, p. 35), the average WTA was estimated to be 1.5–16.6 times larger than the corresponding WTP. Hanemann (1991) responded to these empirical findings in a paper where he claimed that Randall and Stoll, (1980) had 'misunderstood' their own results. According to him, the difference between WTP and WTA in the case of a change in quantity or quality depends not only on the income effect but also on a substitution effect, that is, how easily a commodity can be replaced with another in order to maintain the welfare of the individual.

Keeping the income effect constant, Hanemann (1991) showed that the smaller the substitutability of the commodity the larger is the difference between WTP and WTA, and the larger the substitutability the closer together WTP and WTA are in the case of a change in quantity or quality. If a commodity has practically no substitutes, WTP and WTA may differ greatly, for if the commodity is totally unique and essential, individuals may be ready to sacrifice everything they own for its maintenance or preservation. In this case the WTP is large but finite, but, since no amount of money can compensate for the loss of the commodity, WTA is infinite. Mäler (1985, p. 39) also referred to this possibility when criticizing the result reported by Willig (1976).

There have been two papers to date that have tested the argument of Hanemann (1991), those of Adamowicz et al. (1993) and Shogren et al. (1994). The former tested the difference between WTP and WTA in two experimental designs, varying substitutability among survey samples of undergraduate students. The first experiment, with an open-ended question format, used tickets to a film as an object of valuation and a possibility to watch the same film on a videocassette recorder, instead of at a cinema, as the substitute. The second experiment was a dichotomous choice survey valuing tickets to a hockey game and treating television and radio broadcasts of the game as substitutes. The results of the second experiment supported the argument of Hanemann (1991), indicating that the presence of a substitute for the hockey tickets reduced the gap between the expected values for WTP and WTA, while in the first one the authors did not find the potential substitute variables to be significant in explaining the difference between the welfare measures in regression analysis.

The article by Shogren et al. (1994) analysed the differences between WTP and WTA experimentally in a non-hypothetical auction market using an easily replaceable market commodity, a 'regular-size brand-name candy bar', and a non-market commodity, 'reduced risk from food-borne illness', which is difficult to replace. They perceived that WTP and WTA do not differ statistically significantly for market commodities with close substitutes but the difference is significant for a non-market commodity with no substitutes. Thus, their results lend support to the hypothesis of Hanemann (1991).

The purpose of this paper is also to test Hanemann's argument empirically, but employing a new set of tests developed on the basis of issues raised in the previous studies:

(1) The starting point for Shogren et al. was the substitutability of commodities with respect to money, approving Hanemann's (1991) interpretation,[1] whereas this work compares the substitutability of environmental commodities with respect to each other. In Adamowicz et al. (1993), the first substitute was a rentable videocassette, being an ordinary market commodity, and the second a radio or television broadcast, which was regarded as a public good or non-market commodity.

(2) Shogren et al. assume that the substitution effect for the same person varies between commodities, their purpose being to test how the difference between the WTP and WTA for an individual (that is, a representative consumer) changes if he or she is valuing a commodity with high or low substitutability by money. Like Adamowicz et al. this work assumes that the substitutability of a commodity can vary between consumers. For example, with respect to recreation in the countryside, some people are satisfied with a park in a city centre while for others nothing can replace hiking at will in a virgin wilderness area.

(3) The object of valuation considered here is the *Right of Common Access* as it exists in Finland, that is, the right to use undeveloped natural countryside relatively freely, and its hypothetical substitute is a *Recreation Right* in limited areas. Both are regarded as non-market environmental commodities.

(4) Here a CVM study is used to collect data from a random sample, as opposed to experimental data using 'convenience samples'.

(5) Both open-ended and dichotomous choice question formats are used here, while Shogren et al. used only open-ended questions. Adamowicz et al. used both formats but different commodities and different substitutes, making it difficult to separate the effects of the question formats from those of the definition of substitutability.

These considerations alter the new test arrangement considerably from the older ones and increase its relevance when discussing the adequacy of the CVM for the valuation of environmental commodities in a field situation.

A welfare loss involving a decrease in the quality or quantity of an environmental commodity can be measured with two Hicksian measures, ES and CS. Which one is chosen depends on the information demand, namely whether we wish to know the welfare change before or after the change in environmental quality. If we want to assess the welfare change relative to the original quality level here with RCA, and at a new, in this case lower, utility level, ES is an appropriate measure. ES can be defined by an indirect utility function as follows:

$$v(\boldsymbol{p}, RCA, y - ES) \equiv v(\boldsymbol{p}, R, y), \qquad (8.1)$$

where y is the income of a consumer and $\boldsymbol{p} = (p_1, ..., p_n)$ are the prices of ordinary market commodities. ES is an amount of the alteration income that leads to the same utility change as in the quality of a commodity. Correspondingly, CS is an income change that compensates for the utility loss caused by a decrease in recreation possibilities, namely

$$v(\boldsymbol{p}, RCA, y) \equiv v(\boldsymbol{p}, R, y + CS). \qquad (8.2)$$

The individual is thus on a new, poorer quality level but the original utility level. In a CVM study where there is a decrease in quantity or quality, ES corresponds to WTP and CS to WTA (Smith and Desvouges, 1986, p. 21, Mitchell and Carson, 1989, p. 25). Identities (8.1) and (8.2) can therefore be written in the forms

$$v(\boldsymbol{p}, RCA, y - WTP) \equiv v(\boldsymbol{p}, R, y) \qquad (8.3)$$

and

$$v(\boldsymbol{p}, RCA, y) \equiv v(\boldsymbol{p}, R, y + WTA). \qquad (8.4)$$

Identity (8.3) describes how much an individual is willing to pay for the existence of RCA so as to be on the same utility level as with R. Identity (8.4) tells us the minimum compensation that an individual would require to accept R while maintaining the same utility level as with RCA.

Let us now compare two extreme cases. In the first case, RCA and R are perfect substitutes, so that u(RCA) = u(R). Then $\boldsymbol{p} = \boldsymbol{p}$, $y = y$ and RCA = R on both sides of the equations in identities (8.3) and (8.4). In order for this to be valid, the WTP for the maintenance of RCA in (8.3) and the WTA for R replacing RCA in (8.4) have to be equal and both zero, that is, WTP = WTA = 0.

In the second extreme case R does not substitute for RCA at all. The magnitudes of WTP and WTA are now determined merely on the grounds of the value of RCA for a consumer, since R cannot be part of the compensation. The proportion (8.1) defines how much an individual's income should be reduced so that (8.1) is valid. If RCA is very valuable, the consumer's income can be reduced a great deal but only within his or her budget constraint, that is, WTP $\ll y$. Proportion (8.2) tells us how much an individual's income should be increased so that (8.2) is valid. If RCA is very valuable (and because R cannot even partially compensate for its loss), only a very large increase in WTA can make identity (8.2) valid. If RCA is infinitely valuable, then WTA $\rightarrow \infty$ since there is no budget constraint. Therefore, if the substitution effect is zero, the difference between WTP and WTA can be very large.

The hypothesis to be evaluated here is as follows: WTP and WTA should be larger and more distant from each other for those individuals whose substitution effect concerning an environmental commodity (here the *Right of Common Access*) *vis à vis* another environmental commodity (the *Recreation Right*) is low (subscript *L*) compared to individuals whose substitution effect between these commodities is high (subscript *H*), that is, $WTA_L - WTP_L > WTA_H - WTP_H$. If this hypothesis can be accepted in the light of the present empirical data, it will lend support to the argument of Hanemann (1991).

8.3 METHOD AND SURVEY INSTRUMENT

8.3.1 Commodities and Substitution in the Experiment

The empirical target of the valuation is environmental benefits existing under the *RCA* which is a traditional Scandinavian right that applies only in Finland, Sweden and Norway (see Ministry of the Environment, 1995 ; Vuolle and Oittinen, 1994 ; Hultkrantz, 1994 ; Hultkrantz and Mortazavi, 1992 and Bergfors, 1990). This right allows every person to use undeveloped land in the countryside without the permission of the landowner. One can usually walk, ski or ride a bicycle or horse in such countryside areas and swim or go boating on the watercourses, and access is likewise free when these are frozen in winter. Moreover one is allowed to pick unprotected plant species, wild berries and mushrooms freely, and to pitch a tent and camp for a short period, usually no more than one or two days. The *RCA* always includes the requirement that one must not do any damage or cause any disturbance. One is not allowed to chop down or damage growing trees on other people's land, nor to take possession of dead or fallen trees, lichen, moss and so on. One must not touch nests or disturb young birds or reindeer, or light a fire out of doors without compelling need, for example, in an emergency. One is also prohibited from driving off the road without permission from the landowner, and from hunting or fishing without appropriate licences.

The CVM questionnaire involved the construction of a hypothetical market in which the Finnish *RCA* was in danger of abolition and a hypothetical substitute, *R*, was proposed. The latter would allow people to walk and camp in natural surroundings for recreation, but only in certain delimited areas. It emulates the Central European system, in which landowners usually have the right to refuse an outsider access to their land and to forbid the gathering of wild produce. The public recreation areas concerned would be founded partly in existing recreation and nature conservation areas and would be classified as local, regional or national recreation areas according to their areal extent, distance from the main population centres and provision of services.

That the content and extent of both commodities can be changed marginally is important. The *RCA* was more comprehensive in earlier times, since most forests in Finland were collectively owned until the eighteenth century and even after their distribution into private ownership people still had the right to take timber for household use, for example, firewood from wherever they wished. Since then the content of the *RCA* has gradually been restricted. In the future some of the present rights, for example, the common right to camp, could be restricted. The inclusiveness of *R* can be varied by altering the extent and number of recreation areas and thereby marginally increasing or reducing people's recreation possibilities.

RCA and *R* have a clear difference in principle, however, which makes them quite distinct, so that *R* cannot be increased in order to reach *RCA* and *RCA* cannot be reduced to change it into *R*. The essential characteristic is the free access to nature permitted by *RCA*, while the recreation possibilities provided by *R* have been defined as within a restricted geographical area. This makes *RCA* much more valuable than *R* for most Finnish people, so that a change from the former to the latter would mean a substantial decrease in recreation possibilities and benefits.

Respondents were asked in the CVM survey how well in their opinion *R* would replace the present *RCA*. The alternatives were '*Would replace it completely*' (S_1), '*Would replace it well*' (S_2), '*Would replace it satisfactorily*' (S_3), '*Would replace it passably*' (S_4), '*Would not replace it at all*' (S_5) and '*Do not know*'. The dependence between the substitutability and WTP–WTA differences can be analysed with the help of Figure 8.1, where *RCA* is described on the horizontal axis, *R* on the left vertical axis and the individual's income (Y), budget constraint (Y^{max}), that is, income available for this purpose, compensations claimed (*WTA*) and willingness to pay (*WTP*) on the right vertical axis.

The first alternative, S_1, describes a situation where *RCA* and *R* are perfect substitutes. The respondents who chose this alternative were of the opinion that *R*, with the recreation areas, would completely satisfy their needs for an outdoor life close to nature. This implies that their willingness to pay for the maintenance of *RCA* and their claims for compensation for its loss would be equal and zero, or $WTP_1 = WTA_1 = 0$ provided that the recreation areas required for *R* were ready for use. This

154   *Valuation and the Environment*

case corresponds to the straight line indifference curve U_1 intersecting the R axis at R_1 in Figure 8.1. The indifference curve U_2, which is slightly convex and cuts the R axis at R_2, illustrates the alternative S_2 in which R almost completely replaces *RCA*. Consequently, in order to stay on the same old quality level, that is, with *RCA*, the persons with this choice are willing to pay a small sum of money (WTP_2) or in order to reach the same utility level as with RCA, the persons claim a small compensation (WTA_2) in spite of R. The payment and compensation are here, however, almost equal, that is, $WTP_2 \approx WTA_2$ assuming no income effect.

As the substitutability of respondents moves from S_2 to S_3 and to the indifference curve U_3 the shape of the curve becomes more convex and the influence of the individual's budget constraint (Y^{max}) on WTP increases. As a consequence the difference between WTP and WTA starts to grow. Alternative S_4 means that R is only a very poor substitute for *RCA*. In this situation the indifference curves U_4 and U_4' intersect the R axis at R_4 or even higher, and therefore both WTP and WTA should be very large. WTP is limited by Y^{max}, however, so that it is located at WTP_3 while the compensation claim increases to WTA_4.

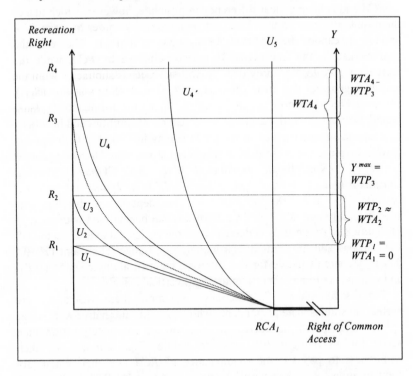

Figure 8.1 Substitutability and the difference between WTP and WTA

For those who chose alternative S_5, the substitution effect is zero, that is, the commodities are perfect complements and the indifference curve U_5 consists of a straight vertical line up from the point RCA_1 and a horizontal line from the same point connected to the horizontal axis to the right (that is, the emphasized part of the vertical axis in Figure 8.1). For these people R cannot compensate for the loss of RCA at all. Thus both WTP and WTA should approach infinity. Y^{max} does not allow WTP to grow, however, but forces it to stay at WTP_3. Therefore the difference between payments and compensation claims should be $WTA_4 - WTP_3$ or more.

The indifference curves in Figure 8.1 describe a situation in which both RCA and R are divisible goods, that is, their consumption can be varied marginally. The CVM survey, however, specifies that they constitute alternatives, that is, either RCA or R can exist alone, but not a combination of the two. In spite of this fact, the analysis of marginal changes helps us to see how substitutability affects the WTP–WTA difference in a non-marginal case.

The hypothesis is tested here by splitting each of the four data sets into two parts with regard to the substitution question (that is, the *Recreation Right* question). The differences in average values for WTA and WTP ($\overline{WTA}$, $\overline{WTP}$) between the groups were then calculated, for example, the average $\overline{WTP_L}$ value for the respondents in the low substitutability group who chose the alternatives '*Would replace it satisfactorily*', '*Would replace it passably*' or '*Would not replace it at all*' is subtracted from the $\overline{WTA_L}$ value for the same group, that is, $\overline{WTA_L}(S_{3,4,5}) - \overline{WTP_L}(S_{3,4,5})$. Correspondingly, $\overline{WTA_H}$ and $\overline{WTP_H}$ in the high substitutability groups are compared by $\overline{WTA_H}(S_{1,2}) - \overline{WTP_H}(S_{1,2})$. The final comparison is achieved by calculating the difference between the two differences obtained above. If this final difference is greater than zero, that is, $[\overline{WTA_L}(S_{3,4,5}) - \overline{WTP_L}(S_{3,4,5})] - [\overline{WTA_H}(S_{1,2}) - \overline{WTP_H}(S_{1,2})] > 0$, the result supports the argument of Hanemann (1991).

8.3.2 CVM Survey And Data

The data were collected by means of a postal questionnaire sent out in the summer of 1995 to a sample of 3000 persons selected at random from the national population register. This gave a sample of the Finnish-speaking population aged 18–75 years over the whole of Finland.[2] The sample was divided into four groups, in which the valuation question was asked as an open-ended question in a WTP format (*WTP~OE*), as an open-ended question in a WTA format (*WTA~OE*), as a dichotomous choice question in a WTP format (*WTP~DC*), and as a dichotomous choice question in a WTA format (*WTA~DC*), see Table 8.1. The bid vector in the *WTP~DC* subsurvey was FIM 20, 50, 75, 100, 150, 200, 300, 400, 500 and 1000 and that in the *WTA~DC* subsurvey FIM 100, 200, 300, 400, 500, 600, 800, 1000, 1500, 5000 and 10 000. A pilot survey carried out in the spring of 1995 with a sample of 500 individuals was used to determine these bid vectors (on the basis of an open-ended question).

Table 8.1 Questionnaire types used

Elicitation format	Question technique	
	Open-ended	Dichotomous choice
WTP	*WTP~OE*	*WTP~DC*
WTA	*WTA~OE*	*WTA~DC*

Before the valuation question itself, the questionnaire document contained a definition of citizens' rights and responsibilities under *RCA*, approximately one page of information for the respondents in all four groups as to the recreation behaviour allowed by the *RCA* in the countryside and the behaviour prohibited by it. This introduction ended as follows:

> Let us imagine that the *Right of Common Access* is in danger of being revoked in Finland and a *Recreation Right*, restricted to areas especially reserved for this function, were to be introduced instead.

The valuation question was then put to each group in a slightly different way. As shown in the Appendix, the payment for maintenance of the *RCA* or the compensation for its revocation being presented in the form of an annual increase in tax or tax reduction for each individual. The four sets of questionnaires sent out elicited 1622 replies, or 54.1 per cent (Table 8.2).

Table 8.2 Returning of the questionnaires

	Sample	Returned	Response rate
WTP~OE	500	273	54.6
WTA~OE	500	294	58.8
WTP~DC	1000	509	50.9
WTA~DC	1000	546	54.6
Total	3000	1622	54.1

8.3.3 Outlier Analysis

The use of different criteria in the subsamples had the effect of removing very influential, illogical or otherwise problematic observations from the data. In the case of the *WTP~DC* group, four respondents were omitted who had answered the substitution question in the form 'S_1' (*R* '*Would replace it completely*' *RCA*) but were nevertheless ready to pay the stated WTP bid, and also one case of strategic behaviour in which the respondent indicated a readiness to pay a bid exceeding 5 per cent of the net annual income per household.[3]

Correspondingly, the 13 respondents who answered the substitution question in the form 'S_1' although they would not have accepted the compensation offered were eliminated from the *WTA~DC* data. Their answers had to be interpreted as suggesting that they would not have claimed even this compensation but would have been satisfied with a smaller amount, perhaps zero compensation. The inclusion of these responses in the data would have distorted the expected value for *WTA~DC*.

The *WTP~OE* data include 74 respondents who announced their willingness to pay FIM 0. In order to separate the real zeros from the protest ones, a simple follow-up question was used, asking the respondent to give the reason for the zero. This procedure showed that the reasons for 59 zeros were something other than a worthless commodity, leading to elimination of these observations and indicating that the rest of the zeros, 15 responses, are real ones. As above, 7 respondents were removed for whom $R = S_1$ and *WTP~OE* > 0 and one *WTP~OE* / annual income > 5 per cent case.

Very large compensation claims in the *WTA~OE* subsample were analysed by reference to the *WTA~DC* data. Using the proportion of accepted WTA bids, an empirical survival curve was drawn to project the trend to the point where the proportion of 'Yes' answers reached 100 per cent. This limit at which all respondents accepted compensation was found at approximately FIM 55 000. The 14 instances of larger claims were thus removed from the analysis as indications of strategic behaviour. In addition, eight zeros out of the total of 41 were deleted as protest responses on the same basis as with the *WTP~OE* data set above. This subsample did not include any respondents for whom $R = S_1$ and *WTA* > 0.

8.4   EMPIRICAL RESULTS

The WTP and WTA means for the open-ended data and expected WTP and WTA values for the dichotomous choice data[4] in the substitution groups defined in Section 8.2 are shown in Tables 8.3 and 8.4. The groups are tabulated initially with those representing low substitutability, still including some cases of relatively high substitutability. The group $S_{2,3,4,5}$ on the first rows of the tables, for example, consists of those who have

Valuation and the Environment

estimated that R would replace RCA 'well', 'satisfactorily', 'passably' or 'not at all'. The observations are then removed from the list stage by stage starting from group S_2 (*'Would replace it well'*) and finally reaching group S_5, which contains only observations of respondents with the lowest substitutability, *'Would not replace it at all'*. Correspondingly, the high substitutability segment moves from highest substitutability (S_1) to data with lower substitutability as well ($S_{1,2,3,4}$).[5]

The mean values for all the data sets in Table 8.3 seem to satisfy the hypothesis that the lower the substitutability is, the larger the values become. The means of the data set $WTP_L\text{\textasciitilde}OE$, for example, increase consistently from group $S_{2,3,4,5}$ (FIM 273) to group S_5 (FIM 514).

Table 8.3 WTP and WTA means for the open-ended data by substitutability groups

		Mean	N
Low substitutability			
$WTP_L\text{\textasciitilde}OE$	$S_{2,3,4,5}$	273	166
	$S_{3,4,5}$	296	138
	$S_{4,5}$	337	97
	S_5	514	41
$WTA_L\text{\textasciitilde}OE$	$S_{2,3,4,5}$	7 182	150
	$S_{3,4,5}$	7 576	128
	$S_{4,5}$	8 905	82
	S_5	14 178	32
High substitutability			
$WTP_H\text{\textasciitilde}OE$	S_1	$-^a$	0
	$S_{1,2}$	158	28
	$S_{1,2,3}$	183	69
	$S_{1,2,3,4}$	194	125
$WTA_H\text{\textasciitilde}OE$	S_1	0	6
	$S_{1,2}$	3 843	28
	$S_{1,2,3}$	4 691	74
	$S_{1,2,3,4}$	5 029	124

Notes: [a] Cannot be calculated, since $WTP_H\text{\textasciitilde}OE$ has no observations with $R = S_1$.

Similarly the expected values in Table 8.4 behave in general fairly logically according to the hypothesis, especially in the $WTP_H\text{\textasciitilde}DC$ and $WTA_H\text{\textasciitilde}DC$ data sets. The two other data sets of Table 8.4 include some values which diverge from the hypothesis. The expected value for group S_5 in $WTP_L\text{\textasciitilde}DC$ (FIM 183) is not the largest in the data as it should be according to the hypothesis, and the figure for group $S_{4,5}$ in $WTA_L\text{\textasciitilde}DC$ (FIM 19 412) is, unexpectedly, the smallest in the whole data. At least in the former case, the illogic seems to follow from the low frequency of the group and an increase in the randomness of the results.

The results of the final comparisons between the substitution groups are presented in Tables 8.5 and 8.6. For this purpose the differences between the means and expected values for WTA and WTP in the corresponding low and high substitutability groups were calculated from Tables 8.3 and 8.4. The distances from the two ends of the substitution continuum were matched against each other in order to assess the variation in the position of the dividing line between low and high substitution. On the second row of Table 8.5, for example, the figure FIM 7 280 is the result of subtraction of FIM 296 on the second row $\overline{WTP_L} \sim OE(S_{3,4,5})$ in Table 8.3 from FIM 7576 on the sixth row $\overline{WTA_L} \sim OE(S_{3,4,5})$ in the same table. The last columns in Tables 8.5 and 8.6 describe the differences between the average WTA and WTP values in terms of how the people estimated the substitutability between the right of common access and the proposed right to recreation in their own judgement.

Table 8.4 Expected values of WTP and WTA for the dichotomous choice
data by substitutability groups

		β_1	β_0	Expected value	N
Low substitutability					
$WTP_L \sim DC$	$S_{2,3,4,5}$	−0.0022	0.8105	368	339
	$S_{3,4,5}$	−0.0023	0.9191	400	302
	$S_{4,5}$	−0.0018	0.8182	455	227
	S_5	−0.0006	0.1100	183	102
$WTA_L \sim DC$	$S_{2,3,4,5}$	0.0001	−2.2046	22 046	476
	$S_{3,4,5}$	0.0001	−2.5830	25 830	414
	$S_{4,5}$	0.0002	−3.8824	19 412	317
	S_5	3.60E–06	−3.9783	1 105 083	162
High substitutability					
$WTP_H \sim DC$	S_1	–	–	$-^a$	12
	$S_{1,2}$	−0.0010	−0.7168	−717	49
	$S_{1,2,3}$	−0.0034	0.6036	178	124
	$S_{1,2,3,4}$	−0.0029	0.9743	336	249
$WTA_H \sim DC$	S_1	–	–	$-^a$	13
	$S_{1,2}$	0.0002	−0.4085	2 043	75
	$S_{1,2,3}$	0.0001	−0.8328	8 328	172
	$S_{1,2,3,4}$	0.0001	−1.5764	15 764	327

Note : [a]If $R = S_1$ & WTP = 1 and $R = S_1$ & WTA = 0 the observations are deleted as outliers. Hence, no expected value can be calculated.

Valuation and the Environment

Table 8.5 Comparison of differences between mean values for WTA and WTP in the substitution groups, open-ended data

WTA_L~OE	WTP_L~OE	Difference	WTA_H~OE	WTP_H~OE	Difference	Difference of differences
$S_{2,3,4,5}$	$S_{2,3,4,5}$	6 909	S_1	S_1	_a	_a
$S_{3,4,5}$	$S_{3,4,5}$	7 280	$S_{1,2}$	$S_{1,2}$	3 684	3 595
$S_{4,5}$	$S_{4,5}$	8 568	$S_{1,2,3}$	$S_{1,2,3}$	4 508	4 060
S_5	S_5	13 664	$S_{1,2,3,4}$	$S_{1,2,3,4}$	4 508	9 156
S_5	S_5	13 664	S_1	S_1	_a	_a
$S_{4,5}$	$S_{4,5}$	8 568	$S_{1,2}$	$S_{1,2}$	3 684	4 884

Note : ^{a} Cannot be calculated, since WTP~OE has no observations with $R = S_1$.

Tables 8.5 and 8.6 point to substantial differences between the average WTA and WTP values in both the open-ended and dichotomous data, the ranges being from 3,595 to 9,156 FIM and from 10 807 to 1 089 472 FIM respectively. The smallest between the differences (FIM 3595) is given by the expression $[\overline{WTA}_L$ ~$OE(S_{3,4,5})$ $\overline{WTP}_L$ ~$OE(S_{3,4,5})]$ $[\overline{WTA}_H$ ~$OE(S_{1,2})$ $- \overline{WTP}_H$ ~$OE(S_{1,2})]$ in the open-ended data and the largest (FIM 1 089 472) by $[\overline{WTA}_L$ ~$DC(S_5) - \overline{WTP}_L$ ~$DC(S_5)] -[\overline{WTA}_H$ ~$DC(S_{1,2,3,4})$ $- \overline{WTP}_H$ ~$DC(S_{1,2,3,4})]$ in the dichotomous data. The tendency in all the differences is the same as proved theoretically by Hanemann (1991). The individuals for whom R cannot replace the loss of RCA have a predisposition to claim recognisably larger amounts of money in compensation than those for whom R can replace RCA are willing to pay.

Table 8.6 Comparison of differences between expected values for WTA and WTP in the substitution groups, dichotomous choice data

WTA_L~DC	WTP_L~DC	Difference	WTA_H~DC	WTP_H~DC	Difference	Difference of differences
$S_{2,3,4,5}$	$S_{2,3,4,5}$	21 678	S_1	S_1	_a	_a
$S_{3,4,5}$	$S_{3,4,5}$	25 430	$S_{1,2}$	$S_{1,2}$	2 759	22 671
$S_{4,5}$	$S_{4,5}$	18 957	$S_{1,2,3}$	$S_{1,2,3}$	8 150	10 807
S_5	S_5	1 104 900	$S_{1,2,3,4}$	$S_{1,2,3,4}$	15 428	1 089 472
S_5	S_5	1 104 900	S_1	S_1	_a	_a
$S_{4,5}$	$S_{4,5}$	18 957	$S_{1,2}$	$S_{1,2}$	2 759	16 198

Note : ^{a} $R = S_1$ & WTP = 1 and $R = S_1$ & WTA = 0 observations were deleted as outliers. Hence, no expected value can be calculated.

8.5   CONCLUSIONS

Numerous empirical studies have shown that WTP and WTA questions give different results, even though they should according to the conventional theory be equal. The theoretical reply given to such observations by Hanemann (1991) suggested that the closer the substitutes that a commodity has, the smaller is the disparity between its WTP and WTA, and the fewer substitutes it has, the greater the difference should be. The present result seems for the most part, at least, to support this argument.

This result leads to two remarks, however. First, although, as seen in the present survey, compensation claims can reach very large sums of money ($WTA_L \sim DC(S_5)$ = FIM 1 105 083), the corresponding willingness to pay is not very large. This is at variance with the opinion of Hanemann (1991), who states (pp. 635–6) that in some cases 'WTP could equal the individual's entire (finite) income, while WTA could be infinite'.

One explanation for this could be that although the Finns consider the *Right of Common Access* as a very important precondition for recreation and a fundamental part of their own culture and identity, it is not a *vital* commodity. Consequently, the WTA can be high but WTP is restricted by a very real budget constraint, the peoples' own incomes. Therefore no Finn would be ready to sell his or her dwelling for *RCA*, for instance, as he or she might do if there were a concrete threat to health or life.

Second, the experiment showed that despite very large differences between WTP and WTA with low substitutability, there also was substantial disparity at high substitutability, where the two measures should be equal or almost equal. Consequently, agreeing with Adamowicz et al. (1993, p. 425), substitutability seems to explain part of the disparity but it is not alone able to explain the whole phenomenon. Other explanations and more research are needed to reveal the entire picture.

ENDNOTES

1. Hanemann (1991, pp. 636, 637) compares the substitutability of his target commodity with respect to a private good. Since a private good is traded in a market, the analysis can also be interpreted as having money as its reference point, that is, it asks how easily the commodity can be replaced with money or with any other market commodity via the monetary medium.
2. Both Adamowicz et al. (1993) and Shogren et al. (1994) used student samples, which reduces the possibility for drawing general conclusions from their results.
3. This kind of threshold, that is, when WTP is so large that it is unlikely that the respondent would really pay the sum, is more or less arbitrary. The chosen

threshold is, however, almost the same as dropping a 5 per cent tail from the WTP/income distribution.

4. The expected values of the dichotomous data are calculated using a simple expression $E(WTP) = -\dfrac{\beta_0}{\beta_1}$, where β_0 and β_1 are parameters of a logarithmic regression model $\ln \dfrac{\pi(A)}{1 - \pi(A)} = \beta_0 + \beta_1 A$ (see for example, Nyquist 1995).

5. The grouping and comparison system conducted here may seem unnecessarily complicated. The reason for the arrangement is that by combining two or more groups it is possible to have more observations in the comparisons, avoid random variation and get more reliable results.

REFERENCES

Adamowicz, W.L., V. Bhardeaj and B. Macnab (1993), 'Experiments on the difference between willingness to pay and willingness to accept', *Land Economics*, 69 (4), 416–27.

Bergfors, U. (1990), Allemansrätten ur rättsekonomisk synpunkt, Arbetsrapport 155, Sveriges landbruksuniversitet, Institutionen för skogsekonomi, Umeå.

Cummings, R.G., D.S. Brookshire and W.D. Schulze (1986), *Valuing Environmental Goods: An assessment of the contingent valuation method*, New Jersey: Rowman & Allanheld Publishers.

Hanemann, W.M. (1991), 'Willingness to pay and willingness to accept: how much can they differ?', *The American Economic Review*, 81 (3), 635–47.

Hultkrantz, L. (1994), 'Allemansrätten – hur bör den förandras?', *Ekonomisk Debatt*, 22 (8), 759–71.

Hultkrantz, L. and R. Mortazavi (1992), 'Recreation, tourism and property rights to land: the economics of public access rights in Sweden', *Umeå Economic Studies*, no. 280, University of Umeå, Umeå.

Mäler, K.-G. (1985), 'Welfare economics and the environment', in A.V. Kneese and J.L. Sweeney (eds), *Handbook of Natural Resource and Energy Economics*, vol. I, *Handbooks in Economics* 6, Amsterdam: North-Holland, pp. 3–60.

Ministry of the Environment (1995), *Everyman's Right in Finland. Make the Most of the Countryside*, 1st edition, Brochure, Ministry of the Environment, Helsinki.

Mitchell, R.C. and R.T. Carson (1989), *Using Surveys to Value Public Goods: The contingent valuation method*, Washington, DC: Resources for the Future.

Nyquist, H. (1995), Lectures in an International Course on The Economics and Econometrics of Contingent Valuation Experiments organized by The Swedish University of Agricultural Sciences, Department of Forest Economics, in Umeå, Sweden, May 22–June 2, 1995.

Randall, A. and J.R. Stoll, (1980), 'Consumer's surplus in commodity space', *The American Economic Review*, 70 (3), 449–55.

Shogren, J.F., S.Y. Shin, D.J. Hayes and J.B. Kliebenstein (1994), 'Resolving differences in willingness to pay and willingness to accept', *The American Economic Review*, 84 (1), 255–70.

Smith, V.K. and W.H. Desvousges (1986), *Measuring Water Quality Benefits*, Boston: Kluwer-Nijhoff Publishing.

Willig, R.D. (1976), 'Consumer's surplus without apology', *The American Economic Review*, 66 (4), 589–97.

Vuolle, P. and A. Oittinen (1994), 'Jokamiehenoikeus: Perinteistä nykypäivää' (The Right of common access. In Finnish), Reports of Physical Culture and Health no. 92, Foundation for Promotion of Physical Culture and Health, Jyväskylä.

APPENDIX: FORMULATION OF THE VALUATION QUESTIONS

Willingness to pay format, open-ended question (WTP~OE subsample) :
Now, would you consider how valuable the *Right of Common Access* is for you **measured in monetary terms**, as compared with the *Recreation Right*, and would you like to estimate what amount of money you would be willing to pay **every year**, as a tax increase, for example, in order to maintain the *Right of Common Access* as it is in Finland at present. Let us assume that the corresponding sum would be collected from all taxpayers and that the resulting revenue would be used entirely for nature conservation. The money would prevent, repair and compensate for the problems and damage caused by the *Right of Common Access*. When considering your answer, keep clearly in mind what amount you can really afford.

- In order to maintain the *Right of Common Access*, I would be willing to pay at most_____**marks per year.**

Willingness to accept format, open-ended question (WTA~OE subsample) :

It is possible that the abolition of the *Right of Common Access* could cause a drop in your quality of life. Let us assume that the government would compensate people for this loss, by a tax reduction, for example. Would you now consider how valuable the *Right of Common Access* is for you **measured in monetary terms**, as compared with the *Recreation Right*, and would you like to estimate what would be the minimum amount of money that you would be willing to accept as compensation **on a yearly basis**.

- As compensation for the loss of the *Right of Common Access*, I would accept at least_____ **marks per year.**

Willingness to pay format, dichotomous choice question (WTP~DC subsample:

Would you consider whether you would be willing to pay an **amount of money every year**, as a tax increase, for example, in order to maintain the *Right of Common Access* as it is in Finland at present. Let us assume that the corresponding sum would be collected from all taxpayers and that the resulting revenue would be used entirely for nature conservation. The money would prevent, repair and compensate for the problems and damage caused by the *Right of Common Access*. When considering your answer, keep clearly in mind what amount you can really afford.

- Would you be willing to pay **A marks per year** in order to maintain the *Right of Common Access* in the future?
  Yes
  No
  Don't know

Willingness to accept format, dichotomous choice question (WTA~DC subsample) :

It is possible that the abolition of the *Right of Common Access* could cause a drop in your quality of life. Let us assume that the government would compensate people for this loss, by a tax reduction, for example. Assume that you would receive a certain **amount of money**. Would you consider whether this would be a sufficient **yearly** compensation for the loss of the *Right of Common Access* and its replacement with the *Recreation Right*.

- Would you accept that the *Right of Common Access* could be abolished and replaced by the *Recreation Right* if you were to receive **A marks per year** in compensation?
  Yes
  No
  Don't know

9. Assessing Public Preferences for the Conservation Quality of the British Coast[1]

Sandra Goodman, Shabbar Jaffry and Bill Seabrooke

9.1 INTRODUCTION

Economists concerned with estimating the value of non-marketed services provided by natural resources have made widespread use of the concept of non-use values. In Britain, this interest was stimulated by the government commissioned Pearce Report (Pearce et al., 1989) which recommended that the total economic value of natural resources be considered in project appraisals conducted by government agencies. This requires that policy-makers have a reliable method for integrating into cost–benefit analyses the public's total economic value for a wide range of natural resources.

An individual's total economic value of a resource can be thought of as their willingness to pay to preserve or maintain its present state (Freeman, 1993). Total economic value consists of use and non-use motives. While individuals might value a natural resource for many reasons unrelated to their use of it, option, bequest, and existence values have been widely discussed by environmental economists as the primary motives behind non-use values.

One of the difficulties with estimating non-use values is that there is no agreed theoretical basis for decomposing total value into use and non-use components. For this reason, non-use values are typically estimated by asking people who do not use a resource about their valuation of it. Non-use values are thereby represented through non-user values, and use values are attributed to users. This approach makes the implicit assumption that users have only use-related values, and only non-users have non-use values. However, there is no sound basis for interpreting user values as pure use values (Freeman, 1993; Cummings and Harrison,

1995). While it may be operationally simple to measure non-use values through the total economic value reported by non-users, relying on this method to estimate non-use values for widely used resources is likely to send misleading signals to policy-makers about the total benefits derived by the public from widely-used natural resources.

This paper presents the results of a contingent valuation method (CVM) study focusing on non-use values for the British coast. Recognizing that the British public uses the coast extensively, and values it for a myriad of reasons, our research agenda aimed to develop a reliable, cost-effective method that captures the public's total economic value of coastal resources. We also explore the use and non-use motivations lying behind individuals' valuation statements.

9.2   A CONSERVATIONIST FRAMEWORK

In an attempt to move closer toward uncovering non-use values, we identified coastal areas through the physical characteristics which give them conservation value. This does not imply that other service flows from the coastal environment are unimportant. However, in contrast to other potential measures of non-use benefit flows, such as aesthetics or landscape values, conservation values are more amenable to objective assessment and quantitative valuation.

Conservationists have clearly defined, highly structured evaluation frameworks which identify and evaluate the physical characteristics that give a natural resource conservation value. Across the range of coastal habitats, the criteria that are accepted as most significant in creating coastal conservation value are size, diversity, bird populations, and freedom from disturbance (Ratcliffe, 1977). Our consultation with environmental scientists identified the major landforms which characterize the British coast to be hard rock cliffs and headlands, soft earthy cliffs, sand and shingle spits and bars, sand dune systems, and estuaries. The key characteristics which give these landforms conservation value were determined to be diversity and rarity of habitats and species, ecological specialization, freedom from disturbance, size/lateral extent, and dynamism of geomorphological processes.

Our central hypothesis was that non-use values are linked to physical indicators of conservation quality. If this assumption was found to be valid, and if conservation and non-use values were directly related, a valuation model might be developed which uses levels of conservation quality to benchmark non-use values for coastal assets. The hypothetical nature of the contingent valuation method allowed us to explore individuals' preferences for different levels of conservation quality through the design and execution of a questionnaire.

9.3   THE CVM SURVEY DESIGN

The sample consisted of 806 personal interviews which were administered by trained interviewers in respondents' homes from November 1995 through January 1996. The process of evaluating respondents' preferences for different levels of conservation quality began by providing information about the characteristics which give the British coast conservation value. Respondents were told about a proposed programme designed to maintain current levels of conservation quality along the entire coast. They were told that, without the programme, coastal areas would experience what scientists considered to be a 'critical' level of loss, which was defined as a 75 per cent loss of plant and animal species and populations and an irreversible loss of coastal habitats over a 30 year period. The timespan of a human generation was chosen to be relevant for purposes of environmental policy-making in the UK,[2] and significant enough that people would notice the change.

The survey emphasized that the conservation programme would maintain current levels of conservation quality in coastal areas, but would not improve upon them. The clarification between maintaining current levels of conservation quality and increasing them has important implications for our welfare estimates. As discussed by Hanemann (1991), Tversky et al., (1990) and in Chapter 7 of this book, asking people how much they would be willing to pay to avoid a loss of environmental services can produce very different results from asking them what they would be willing to pay to gain an improvement in these services. In order to estimate accurately the public benefits of the conservation quality of the British coast, it was important that respondents understood that the benefits to be gained from the conservation programme would result from avoiding a loss of conservation quality levels, rather than from increasing them.

Respondents were asked if, in principle, they would be willing to pay additional taxes for the coastal conservation programme. Individuals who responded positively to this 'payment principle' question were asked to state how much additional tax they would be willing to pay for a conservation programme for the entire coast. This identified the relevant budget from which respondents' stated expenditures on coastal protection would be drawn. This 'mental accounting' technique has been developed (Deaton and Muellbauer, 1980; Kemp and Maxwell, 1992) to address the problem of part-whole bias, also known as 'the embedding problem', which occurs when respondents are insensitive to the size or scope of the environmental amenity they are asked to value (Arrow et al., 1993).

Respondents who stated a positive tax amount for the coastal conservation programme were asked how much of this additional tax they would like to see spent in a specific group of areas. This question formed the core of the valuation scenario. It evaluated whether respondents held distinct values for different levels of conservation quality, and whether these values could be expressed in monetary terms. Willingness to pay (WTP) responses to this question were limited by the respondent's budget for the entire coastal conservation programme. Thus, WTP for a conservation programme in a specific group of sites was constrained by income and substitution effects. From the public's perspective, coastal areas with different levels of conservation quality are substitute goods (however imperfect). This was deemed appropriate on the basis that was the relevant policy question how best to use limited resources to protect the conservation quality of the British coast.

At this point in the questionnaire, the sample was split and respondents were asked only to value one of two groups of coastal areas. This technique of splitting the sample and valuing a single good is another procedure recommended to reduce embedding problems, especially when complex environmental goods are being evaluated (Carson and Mitchell, 1995; Mitchell and Carson, 1989). Each group of coastal areas was described in terms of the five coastal landforms and their key conservation characteristics.[3] One group represented areas with a relatively high level of conservation quality, and the other group characterized areas with a lower level of conservation quality. Respondents were told that each group represented about 10 per cent of the coastline around England and Wales. Pretesting had indicated that this amount was large enough to be significant to respondents and small enough to be accurate in an ecological sense. The conservation value of the remaining 90 per cent of the coast was described to respondents in relation to the areas comprising 10 per cent of the coast. This reminded respondents about other areas that might be included in their budget for a coastal conservation programme, and expressly addressed the need for CVM studies to remind respondents of potential substitutes when asking the valuation question (Arrow et al., 1993).

We did not expect that all respondents would express a positive monetary value for the coastal conservation programme. Some people would truly hold no value for the programme. Others might object to the notion of exchanging environmental quality for income (Stevens, et al., 1991; Spash and Hanley, 1995), or some aspect of the valuation scenario (for example, the payment vehicle). Other people might find it difficult to express in monetary terms their value for an environmental amenity as complex as conservation quality (Gregory et al., 1992; Payne et al., 1993).

Therefore, we evaluated the reasons individuals gave for being unwilling to support a tax-financed coastal conservation programme, and explored their perceptions of conservation quality. People who responded negatively to the payment principle question were told that, without additional taxes, a conservation programme could be started in selected areas only. The conservation qualities of two groups of coastal areas, each comprising 10 per cent of the total coast, were described to this sample subset. To remind people of other coastal areas, conservation quality levels were described in relation to the remaining coastline. Respondents were asked to select the group of sites in which they would like to see a conservation programme started first. The results of this investigation are discussed below.

9.4 WTP RESULTS

9.4.1 Relationship between Conservation and Non-Use Values

In total, 98 per cent of all respondents had visited the British coast, and most (62.8 per cent) had visited it within the past six months. This confirmed our expectation that we would be unable to estimate distinct non-use values for the coast by reporting non-user values.

While we were unable to quantify use and non-use components of respondents' value estimates, our qualitative findings suggest that a substantial portion of the total value for coastal conservation quality derives from non-use motivations. This observation is based on respondents' comments about what makes the British coast valuable.[4] Over half of these comments related to the coast's natural and cultural features.

Respondents' reasons for wanting to protect natural resources indicate the significance of non-use motivations. Just over 67 per cent of respondents said that it was extremely or very important to protect natural resources for reasons related to their use; whereas 88.7 per cent said that reasons unrelated to their current use were important grounds for protecting them. A closer look at specific non-use motivations reveals that 86 per cent of the sample said that maintaining the option to use resources in the future is an extremely or very important reason for protecting them (option value), 92 per cent said that it is extremely or very important to protect natural resources for the benefit of future generations (bequest value), and 88 per cent considered conserving plants and wildlife (existence value) to be an extremely or very important justification for resource protection.

9.4.2   Refusals to Pay

Nearly 74 per cent of respondents said that, in principle, they would be willing to pay additional taxes for a coastal conservation programme. Just under 21 per cent responded negatively to the 'payment principle' question, and 5.9 per cent were not sure if they would be willing to pay additional taxes for this programme. Seventeen respondents who initially stated 'don't know' later stated a positive WTP amount. Twenty-seven respondents remained unsure of what they would be willing to pay for the programme throughout the valuation scenario, and failed to state a WTP amount. Another 27 people who had responded positively to this question later stated a maximum WTP of zero for the programme. This was interpreted to mean that these individuals had reconsidered their earlier response, and did not support a tax-sponsored coastal conservation programme. In total, 70 per cent of respondents stated a positive amount of additional tax that they would be willing to pay for a coastal conservation programme.

Because the estimation of welfare benefits through the CVM can be affected by respondents' rejection of the valuation scenario or by strategic behaviour which leads to their overstating or understating their 'true' value, we analysed the reasons people gave for their unwillingness to pay additional taxes for the coastal conservation programme. The reasons behind respondents' unwillingness to pay additional taxes for this programme are given in Table 9.1.

Only 23.7 per cent (50) of these reasons suggest that the respondent's true valuation of the coastal conservation programme was zero. This includes individuals who said that they could not afford to pay for the programme, or that they would not benefit from it. However, 76.3 per cent (161) of respondents objected to some aspect of the valuation scenario when they stated a refusal to pay additional taxes. The majority of these protest votes (51.2 per cent) were due to respondents' objection to the notion of paying additional taxes.

9.4.3   Reasons for Positive Bids

The selection of mean or median WTP as an appropriate welfare estimate is determined, in part, by sample characteristics, and is an especially important decision when aggregating survey results across a population. As the goal of this study was to explore individuals' preferences for different levels of conservation quality, and to evaluate whether these preferences could be expressed monetarily, rather than produce an aggregated benefit estimate, we report both mean and median WTP estimates. The results of all hypothesis tests were similar for both estimators.

Table 9.1   Reasons for not wanting to pay additional taxes for a coastal conservation programme

	Number of respondents	Percentage of respondents	Valid or invalid bid
• I cannot at present afford to pay, but would do so if I could.	39	16.4	Valid
• I would not derive any benefits from a coastal conservation programme, so do not want to pay for it.	6	2.5	Valid
• I do value the conservation quality of the coast but feel I pay too much tax already.	73	30.7	Invalid
• I need more information to answer this question.	27	11.3	Invalid
• I do not think maintaining coastal conservation quality should be the taxpayer's responsibility.	24	10.1	Invalid
• I would not pay any more tax to create a coastal conservation programme, but would be prepared to pay for the protection of coastal conservation values in some other fashion.	11	4.6	Invalid
• I would rather someone else paid instead of me.			
• I do not feel that this sort of questioning is appropriate.	9	3.8	Invalid
• I do not wish to answer the question.	9	3.8	Invalid
• I don't know.	3	1.3	Invalid
• Other	10	4.2	32 invalid bids
	27	11.3	*5 valid bids
	N=238	100	

Note :   Respondents who answered 'I don't know' or 'Other' were asked follow-up questions about their uncertainty or other reasons. Bids were validated on these open-ended questions and validation protocols.

Mean WTP for a coastal conservation programme for the entire British coast was £48.36, and median WTP was £25.00. Mean WTP for a conservation programme at a limited group of coastal areas (regardless of the level of conservation quality) was £20.82, and the median WTP was

£10. This reflects the skewed pattern of WTP bids, which included several low bids and a few high ones.

Based on an analysis of follow-up questions, nearly 83 per cent of all WTP bids offered for a conservation programme in a limited group of coastal areas were considered to be valid estimates of respondents' true WTP. Table 9.2 lists the reasons behind respondents' stated WTP.

Table 9.2 Reasons for WTP for a coastal conservation programme in a group of sites representing 10 per cent of the coast

	Number of respondents	Percentage of respondents	Valid or invalid bid
I'm in favour of preserving the natural coastal environment	274	55.1	Valid
It seems like a reasonable amount of money to pay for this programme in these areas	103	20.7	Valid
I wish to show my support for environmental issues in general	80	15.5	Invalid
I really feel that I would pay this amount for a coastal conservation programme in these areas	35	7.0	Valid
I'm not sure	3	0.6	* 3 valid bids
			2 invalid bid
Other	2	0.4	
Total	497	100	

Note : * Respondents who answered 'I'm not sure' or 'Other' were asked follow-up questions about their uncertainty or other reasons. Bids were validated on these open-ended questions and validation protocols.

We considered eight bids exceeding £150 to be extremely high. Three of these high bids were determined to be valid estimates of respondents' WTP for the programme, in that these respondents stated that they genuinely felt that they would pay this amount for a coastal conservation programme, and could afford to do so. Three of the remaining five invalid bids suggested protest behaviour, as these respondents stated that they had named a large sum in order to signal their support for protecting the conservation value of all coastal areas. Analysis of reasons respondents gave for supporting a coastal conservation programme through additional taxes, and their reasons for not supporting this tax-financed programme, indicate that, overall, protest behaviour in the form of strategic and free-riding bids was not a major phenomenon in this study. A *t*-test comparison was used to determine the significance of the difference between respondents' value for a conservation programme for the entire coast and this programme at 10 per cent of coastal areas. The difference between both mean and median WTP amounts was significant at the 0.05 level. This indicates that our results do not suffer from part–whole bias at the univariate level of analysis.

9.4.4 Conservation Quality

Mean WTP for a conservation programme in areas described as having a relatively high level of conservation quality was £24.75 (median WTP = £10). This compares to a mean WTP of £17.87 for this programme in areas which were described as having a relatively low level of conservation quality (median WTP = £10). A univariate *t*-test indicated that the difference between the two means was significant at the 0.10 level, but not at the 0.05 level. Multivariate analysis of the difference in WTP amounts was also conducted. A dummy variable representing *area category* was included as an independent variable in a multiple regression model of WTP. This considers the effects of other variables affecting WTP, as well as an area's level of conservation quality. *Area category* was insignificant at the 0.05 level.

Overall, respondents accurately perceived differences in conservation quality levels. This was made clear by observing the reasons offered for wanting to start a conservation programme in a particular group of coastal areas. Respondents' comments indicate that they recognized characteristics imparting high and low conservation quality levels. Some reasons for wanting part of their coastal conservation budget to be spent in a specific group of areas were similar, regardless of the described level of conservation quality. Importantly, other comments suggest that respondents used different criteria to evaluate the benefits of a conservation programme in different areas, depending on the information described to them. Respondents who were given information about areas with a high level of conservation quality generally wanted to start a conservation programme here to protect the high levels of conservation value. Alternatively, respondents who saw information about areas with low conservation qualities perceived these sites as being more vulnerable to external threats, and wanted to start a conservation programme here to prevent further losses of conservation value.

These findings indicate that, overall, our sample failed to express an economic preference for higher, rather than lower, levels of conservation quality. This could be explained in several ways: either respondents did not hold such a preference; they were unable to express their preferences in monetary terms; or their preference statements were constructed according to the information presented to them during the interview. These latter two interpretations are supported by other survey findings. Just over 54 per cent of the individuals who were unwilling to pay additional taxes for a coastal conservation programme, and had been asked to select one of two coastal groups for this programme, chose the group described as possessing a higher level of conservation quality. Only 24.5 per cent selected the group of lower quality areas. While inconclusive, this suggests that individuals hold preferences for higher levels of conservation quality, but that it is difficult to capture these preferences through monetary expressions of value.

9.4.5 Valuation Functions

Valuation functions were modelled to assess the theoretical validity of our WTP estimates. These valuation functions were specified according to four 'core' variable sets, which economic and behavioural theory and common sense suggest should be positively related to an individual's willingness to pay for a coastal conservation programme.

The first variable set measured respondents' environmental attitudes and behaviour. Environmental attitudes were evaluated through several statements, including the respondent's feelings of responsibility for environmental protection; perceived conflicts between environmental protection and economic growth; and perceptions of environmental threats. Environmental behaviour was evaluated through membership of environmental or conservation organizations and recycling behaviour. Because an individual's valuation of a good is often related to their use of it, a second set of questions measured respondents' use of the British coast. These questions asked how often and how recently the respondent had visited the coast, the primary location(s) of coastal visits, and the activities participated in when visiting the coast. The third set measured socio-economic status, and included information about the respondent's occupational status, household income level and household size. A final set of questions evaluated respondents' familiarity with coastal conservation characteristics, and their understanding of the CVM scenario. This set of variables included questions asked directly to respondents, as well as to interviewers, asking for their assessment of the respondent's level of comprehension.

The validity of our value estimates was assessed through the specification of three valuation functions: (i) a sample selection model;

(ii) a model of WTP for the entire coast ; and (iii) a model of WTP for selected areas of coast. First, a sample selection univariate probit model was specified to predict the probability of a yes/no response to the 'payment principle' question.[5] This model was used as we had no a priori reason to assume that individuals who were willing to pay additional taxes were randomly distributed throughout the sample (indicating sample selection bias). This model generated a variable (λ) which was included as an explanatory variable to test for sample selection bias in the remaining two valuation functions. This model coherently accounted for over 90 per cent of responses to the payment principle question.

With the exception of socio-demographic variables, questions within each variable set were significant at the 0.10 level. All estimated relationships were consistent with our expectations. Table 9.3 reports all statistically significant relationships. Factors which had a significant effect on the probability of a positive response included respondents' belief that environmental protection was more important than economic growth, and that the government should do more to protect the environment, even at the cost of higher taxes; a recent coastal visit (within the last six months); and any degree of familiarity with coastal conservation qualities. Respondents who had difficulty understanding the questionnaire had a greater probability of stating a negative response. As indicated by the quasi-elasticity coefficients in Table 9.3, respondents' familiarity with conservation characteristics had the strongest effect on the probability of an affirmative response to the payment principle question.

Valuation functions were estimated to explain WTP for a conservation programme for the entire British coast and for a specific group of coastal areas. Both models were specified in semi-loglinear format. Core variables and additional factors were included in the valuation function for the entire coast model. Parameter estimates and *t*-statistics for significant variables are given in Table 9.4. All parameters have the expected sign and are significant at the 0.10 level, with many being significant at the 0.05 level. Variables having a significant positive effect on WTP included respondents' agreement with the statement that the government should spend more money protecting the environment, even at the risk of restricting economic growth or increasing taxes; their membership in an environmental organization or recycling behaviour; a visit to the coast within the past six months; profession; and household income. As expected, the sign of the coefficient increased as the level of income increased. While the respondent's degree of familiarity with coastal conservation characteristics had an insignificant effect on WTP, the interviewer's assessments that a respondent had been somewhat (as opposed to very or not at all) cooperative at the end of the interview, and that a respondent appeared to have given superficial consideration to the valuation questions had significant negative impacts on WTP. This suggests that some individuals may have found aspects of the interview difficult or unpleasant, and that this influenced their value statements.

Table 9.3 Results of a sample selection univariate probit model (i) of factors influencing responses to the Payment–Principle question

Cluster	Variable name	Coefficient	*t* statistic	p/Xi**
Attitude	• Respondent stated that protecting the environment should be given priority, even at the risk of holding back economic growth.	0.64	1.91*	11.0
	• Respondent stated that as a nation, it is possible to protect the environment and have a growing economy at the same time.	0.69	2.69*	12.0
	• Respondent stated that governments should do more to protect the environment, even if this sometimes leads to higher taxes for everyone.	1.03	4.96*	17.9
Coastal use familiarity & understanding	• Respondent visited the coast within the last 6 months.	0.41	2.69*	7.14
	• Respondent seemed very familiar with coastal nature conservation.	1.49	3.52*	25.89
	• Respondent seemed somewhat familiar with coastal nature conservation.	1.66	4.14*	25.89
	• Respondent seemed slightly familiar with coastal nature conservation.	1.00	2.45*	17.43
	• Respondent had difficulty understanding the payment questions.	−0.05	−3.47*	−18.34
	• Constant.	−1.41	−2.03*	−24.47

Notes : * Significant at the 0.10 level N = 605 log-likelihood = −182.0735
 ** This quasi-elasticity coefficient measures the percentage change in the probability of a positive response with respect to a one unit change in the explanatory variable

The estimated variable λ was significantly different from zero at the 0.10 level. This indicates the presence of sample selection bias, which was corrected using the sample-selection univariate probit model.

Additionally, the constant was shown to be significant. This suggests that variables omitted from our valuation function may influence WTP for a coastal conservation programme.

Table 9.4 Results of a two-stage least-squares for model (ii)

Cluster	Variable name	Coefficient	*t*-statistic
Attitude	• Respondent stated that the government should spend more protecting the natural environment.	0.343	1.947*
	• Respondent stated that protecting the environment should be given priority, even at the risk of holding back economic growth.	0.271	1.710**
	• Respondent stated that governments should do more to protect the environment, even if this leads to higher taxes.	0.414	1.977*
	• Member of an environmental or conservation organization or regularly recycled newspapers and used items.	0.262	1.986*
Coastal Use	• Respondent visited the coast within the last 6 months.	0.404	3.557*
	• Respondent participated in fishing when visiting the coast.	0.479	2.587*
Socio-economic characteristics	• Professional occupational status.	0.519	4.357
	• Annual household income category £30,000–£39,000.	0.570	3.143*
	• Annual household income category £40,000–£49,000.	0.860	3.427*
	• Annual household income category £50,000–£59,000.	1.258	4.075*
Familiarity and understanding	• Respondent was somewhat cooperative at end of interview.	−0.422	−2.207*
	• Respondent gave somewhat serious consideration to WTP questions.	−0.409	−3.248*
	• Lambda (λ)	0.626	1.708**
	• Constant	1.414	2.892*

Notes : * Statistically significant at 5 per cent level of significance.
 ** Statistically significant at 10 per cent level of significance.
 Adjust $R^2 = 0.19 F[18,483] = 7.61(0.0000)$ N=502

Core and other variables were also included in the valuation function for a conservation programme covering only 10 per cent of all coastal areas. Parameter estimates and *t*-statistics for significant variables are given in Table 9.5. Again, all parameters have the expected sign and are significant at the 0.10 level, or higher.

Respondents' use of the coast exerted conflicting effects on WTP. Recent visits to the coast (within the past six months) had a significant positive impact on WTP, whilst frequent coastal visits (at least once every two months) had a negative impact. The reasons for this negative relationship between frequent visits to the coast and WTP are unclear. Perhaps individuals who visit the coast frequently wanted to see a conservation programme started in the areas with which they were most familiar. Alternatively, some people who visit coastal areas frequently may do so for reasons unrelated to their interest in the coastal environment *per se* (for example, business trips or visiting friends and family).

Table 9.5 Results of a two-stage least-squares for model (iii)

Cluster	Variable name	Coefficient	t-statistic
Attitude	• Respondent stated that the government should spend more protecting the natural environment.	0.38	1.62**
	• Respondent stated that protecting the environment should be given priority, even at the risk of holding back economic growth.	0.34	1.74**
Coastal Use	• Respondent visited the coast within the last 6 months.	0.38	2.63*
	• Frequent trips to the British coast.	−0.56	−1.63**
Socio-economic characteristics	• Professional occupational status.	0.38	2.50*
	• Annual household income category £30,000–£39,000.	0.57	2.63*
	• Annual household income category £40,000–£49,000.	0.84	2.73*
	• Annual household income category £50,000–£59,000.	0.75	1.92*
Familiarity and understanding	• Respondent was somewhat cooperative at end of interview.	−0.93	−2.01*
	• Respondent gave somewhat serious consideration to WTP questions.	−0.42	−2.74*
	• Lambda (λ)	0.77	1.70**

Notes: * Statistically significant at 5 per cent level of significance.
       ** Statistically significant at 10 per cent level of significance.
       Adjust $R^2 = 0.11 F[18,371] = 3.77(0.00000)$ N=502

This valuation function included a dummy variable that enabled us to test the hypothesis that respondents held a higher valuation for the group of sites with a higher level of conservation quality. The estimated coefficient for this variable was positive, yet insignificant at the 0.10 level.

This indicates that the described level of conservation quality did not have a significant effect on WTP. The variable was also significantly different from zero at the 0.10 level in this model.

As indicators of environmentally-supportive attitudes, respondents' opinions that the government should spend more money protecting the environment, and that environmental protection should be a priority over economic growth had significant positive effects on WTP. However, environmentally-supportive behaviour, either through membership in an environmental organization or recycling, was insignificant.

Explanatory variables from each set of core variables explained 19 per cent and 11 per cent of the variation in WTP for a conservation programme for the entire coast and a limited group of coastal areas, respectively. These results are similar to those of other CV studies conducted in the UK and US (Bateman et al., 1992; Willis et al., 1993; Mitchell and Carson, 1989). More importantly, from the standpoint of assessing the theoretical validity of our WTP estimates, all three valuation functions were consistent with our theoretical and a priori expectations, as well as with one another.

9.5   CONCLUSIONS

Because this investigation of the relationship between non-use values and conservation quality levels was exploratory, it is difficult to draw firm conclusions about the nature of this relationship. However, useful observations can be made. Our results suggest that individuals value the natural coastal environment for reasons that are related to its conservation value. Whilst defining coastal areas according to their conservation characteristics led people to consider the coast in ways unrelated to their own use of it, expressions of value for coastal areas were related to use, as well as non-use motivations. This leads us to believe that conservation and non-use values are linked, however loosely, and that further work needs to be done before this relationship can be meaningfully measured.

Our second finding was that, based on the information in our questionnaire, respondents perceived differences in conservation quality levels in ways that were generally consistent with environmental scientists' perceptions. However, when considering specific attributes of conservation quality, public and scientific assessments sometimes differed concerning what is desirable. This suggests that, while there may be a reasonable degree of congruence between scientific and public perceptions of conservation value, what the public values as a desirable environment may conflict with the ecologically preferable management strategy for that habitat.

Third, we found that while respondents in our study did not express a preference for higher levels of conservation quality in monetary terms, often they did so in non-monetary terms. Furthermore, respondents' preference statements appear to have been influenced by information presented to them during the interview. This is consistent with other studies which have found that respondents' value statements are highly dependent on the information contained in a CVM questionnaire (Fischhoff and Furby, 1988; Mazzotta and Opaluch, 1995; Ajzen et al., 1996). This has important implications for measuring the social value of environmental quality through CVM surveys. It suggests that respondents constructed their value statements during the CVM interview, rather than retrieving some pre-existing value for coastal conservation quality. It also implies that individuals used different decision-making criteria to formulate their valuation responses. The criteria they selected depended largely upon the information contained in the questionnaire and their prior conceptions of coastal processes. As Mazzotta and Opaluch, (1995) found, when there are no established or widely accepted guidelines to provide a frame of reference for decision-making, it becomes difficult to predict individuals' choice statements, as it is difficult to predict which heuristic they will use in their decision-making process.

The real issue in integrating environmental values into public policy is how well the methods we use to estimate the total social value of environmental resources relate to the ways in which people — scientists and lay persons alike — perceive and value these assets. Our study suggests that individuals' preferences for conservation quality levels are multidimensional and difficult to assess monetarily. Rational policy decisions affecting environmental resources should include elements of scientific analysis and public values. Such policies require greater understanding of the differences in value systems between the public and scientists. Only then can a framework synthesizing these values be developed.

ENDNOTES

1. The research on which this chapter is based was commissioned by the Flood and Coastal Defence Division of the Ministry of Agriculture, Fisheries and Food, whose support we gratefully acknowledge.
2. Our study described an irreversible loss in coastal conservation quality that would occur over the span of a human generation because this is the timeframe which 'This Common Inheritance' (HMSO, 1990) suggests to be appropriate for evaluating environmental sustainability. English Nature, in turn, has suggested that the theory of environmental sustainability be operationalized by 'identifying elements of the natural environment whose loss would be serious,

or which would be irreplaceable, or which would be too difficult or expensive to replace in human timescales' (*English Nature*, 1992).

3. Hypothetical, rather than actual, areas were described as part of our attempt to come closer to capturing non-use values by directing respondents' thoughts away from their experiences with a specific area and toward the conservation characteristics of coastal areas.

4. In order not to bias their responses, respondents were asked an open-ended question, 'In your opinion, what, if anything, makes the British coast valuable' before they were given any information about the conservation quality of the coast or a coastal conservation programme.

5. Our analysis utilized the sample selection univariate probit model provided through LIMDEP (Version 7). This model was used in order to consider sample selection bias, which occurs if the probability of obtaining a valid WTP response among respondents having a particular set of characteristics is related to their value for the good. The alternative of using weighting and imputation procedures to separately estimate a probit model for the payment principle question and two ordinary least-squares models for the two WTP questions does not address sample selection bias, and would produce biased results (Greene, 1995).

6. The SITE dummy variable included in the model only captured the shift in the demand curve. Dummy variables capturing any change in the slope of the demand curves for the two groups of sites were also found not to be significant.

REFERENCES

Ajzen, Icek, Thomas C. Brown and Lori H. Rosenthal (1996), 'Information Bias in Contingent Valuation: Effects of Personal Relevance, Quality of Information, and Motivational Orientation', *Journal of Environmental Economics and Management*, 30, pp. 43–57.

Arrow, K.R. Solow, P.R. Portney, E.E. Leamer, R. Radner and E.H. Schuman (1993), Report of the NOAA Panel on Contingent Valuation. Report to the General Counsel of the US National Oceanic and Atmospheric Administration. US Department of Commerce. Natural resource damage assessments under the Oil Pollution Act of 1990, 58 Federal Register, pp. 4602–4614.

Bateman, I., K.G. Willis, G.D. Garrod, P. Doktor, I. Langford and R.K. Turner (1992), *Recreation and Environmental Preservation Value of the Norfolk Broads: A Contingent Valuation Study,* report to the National Rivers Authority, Environmental Appraisal Group, University of East Anglia, Norwich.

Carson, T. Richard and Robert Cameron Mitchell (1995), 'Sequencing and nesting in contingent valuation surveys', *Journal of Environmental Economics and Management*, 28, 155–73.

Cummings, G. Ronald and Glenn W. Harrison (1995), 'The measurement and decomposition of non-use values: a critical review', *Environmental and Resource Economics*, 5, 225–47.

Deaton, A. and J. Muellbauer (1980), *Economics and Consumer Behaviour,* Cambridge: Cambridge University Press.

Fischhoff, Baruch and Lita Furby (1988), 'Measuring values: a conceptual framework for interpreting transactions with special reference to contingent valuation of visibility', *Journal of Risk and Uncertainty*, 1, 147–84.

Freeman, A. Myrick, III (1993), *The Measurement of Environmental and Resource Values. Theory and Methods*, Washington, DC: Resources for the Future.

Greene, William H. (1995), *Econometric Analysis*, 2nd edition, Oxford: Macmillan.

Gregory, Robin, Donald MacGregor and Sarah Lichtenstein (1992), 'Assessing the quality of expressed preference measures of value', *Journal of Economic Behaviour and Organization*, 17, 277–92.

Hanemann, W. Michael (1991), 'Willingness to pay and willingness to accept: how much can they differ?' *American Economic Review*, 635–47.

Kemp, Michael A. and Christopher Maxwell (1992), 'Exploring a budget context for contingent valuation estimates', in Jerry A. Hausman (ed.), *Contingent Valuation: A Critical Assessment*, Amsterdam: North Holland.

Mazzotta, Marisa J. and James J. Opaluch (1995), 'Decision-making when choices are complex: a test of heiner's hypothesis', *Land Economics*, 4 (71), 500–515.

Mitchell, Robert C. and Richard T. Carson (1989), *Using Surveys to Value Public Goods: The Contingent Valuation Method*, Washington, DC: Resources for the Future.

Payne, John W., James R. Bettman and Eric J. Johnson (1993), 'Behavioural decision research: a constructive processing perspective', *Annual Review of Psychology*, 43, 87–132.

Pearce, D., A. Markandya and E. Barbier (1989), *Blueprint for a Green Economy*, London: Earthscan.

Ratcliffe, D.A. (ed.) (1977), *A Nature Conservation Review: The Selection of Biological Sites of National Importance to Nature Conservation in Britain*, vol.1, Cambridge: Cambridge University Press.

Spash, C.L. and N. Hanley (1995), 'Preferences, Information and Biodiversity Preservation', *Ecological Economics*, 12, 191–208.

Stevens, T.H., J. Echeverria, R.J. Glass, T. Hager and T.A. More (1991), 'Measuring the existence value of wildlife: what do cvm estimates really show?' *Land Economics*, 4 (67), 390–400.

Tversky, A., P. Slovic and D. Kahneman (1990), 'The causes of preference reversal', *American Economic Review*, 80, 204–17.

Willis, K.G., G.D. Garrod and C.M. Saunders (1993), *Valuation of the South Downs and Somerset Levels and Moors Environmentally Sensitive Area Landscapes by the General Public*, Research Report to the Ministry of Agriculture, Fisheries and Food, Centre for Rural Economy, University of Newcastle upon Tyne.

10. On Behavioural Intentions in the Case of the Saimaa Seal. Comparing the Contingent Valuation Approach and Attitude–Behaviour Research

Eija Moisseinen

10.1 INTRODUCTION

Revealing the individuals' willingness (or intention) to pay has been the main objective of contingent valuation surveys. Attitudes, on the other hand, have been more or less ignored for they are considered to belong outside of the economic analysis. But at present economists feel uncomfortable with the fact that they do not know enough about the respondents' behaviour when applying the contingent valuation method (CVM), for example Navrud (1992). Discussions of the intersecting points between the fields of psychology and economics are relevant. The purpose of this paper is to compare the CVM approach and attitude–behaviour research and illustrate, via the case of the Saimaa seal, a possible way to connect these approaches with each other. Also a broader framework enables one to consider implications for policy, too.

To date, the Saimaa seal *(Phoca Hispida Saimensis)* is one of the most endangered seals in the world.[1] House building, fishing with strong nets, and artificial lowering of the water level in the Saimaa Lake in the winter, and effects of environmental pollutants (including diseases) are among the factors that are threatening the future of the population, which at present numbers only about 200. When it became obvious that the most efficient means of protection were needed to save the seal population, the State decided to take care of the problem. The proposal for protection of breeding areas of the Saimaa seal was introduced in 1991, and in 1992 the Ministry of the Environment appointed a committee to work out a program of conservation for the Saimaa seal.

However, due to the 1992–93 economic recession the question in the case of the Saimaa seal became 'What kind of conservation program can we afford?' instead of 'What kind of conservation program do we need?'. This was reflected in an interim report of the committee (published in 1993) which suggested that only some of the proposed protected areas should be established in the Pihlajavesi part of Saimaa lake. A list of voluntary restrictive directives as to use of those areas without proposed protection was introduced (see Appendix, question 10).

A contingent valuation mail survey was conducted before the interim Pihlajavesi report was published. According to the results of this national survey, the majority of respondents are both willing to save the seal population and approve the suggested costs of the planned program of conservation.[2] But the observed gap between the high willingness to save the seals and low willingness to accept the costs of the program of conservation was disturbing: Some 97 per cent of the respondents considered that the Saimaa seal should be protected, but only 51 per cent of them were willing to pay the suggested bid.

A possible explanation within the contingent valuation framework with a discrete choice elicitation method is that in some cases the willingness to pay (WTP) can be positive but distinctly lower than the offered bid in question. If so, a relevant solution would be to offer the respondent also an open-ended alternative to state their WTP amount. Another explanation for the difference is that the CVM ignores some factors that could provide new information if included in the analysis. Therefore, a more fundamental attempt to explain the gap is to choose a broader perspective to investigate the problem. This would mean, first, that the survey sample consists of local people since from the ecological point of view conservation activities at their best require local participation (see Haila and Levins, 1992). Second, in light of the interim Pihlajavesi report, it is relevant to consider both collective provision (willingness to pay for collective action) and private provision (willingness to protect by private actions). From the individual's viewpoint, these can be substitutes.

To consider these possible explanations another survey was conducted. The standard CVM approach was supplemented by Fishbein and Ajzen's (1975) theory of reasoned action. See also, Mitchell and Carson, (1989) for a discussion of the broader behavioural model underlying the contingent valuation method.

10.2 THEORY OF REASONED ACTION

Some people support social policies such as welfare assistance for the poor or establishing protected areas for an endangered species and others do not. Understanding individual differences such as these is an interest of social psychologists, who use the concept of attitude to describe them. A person who favours, for example, establishing protected areas is viewed as holding a positive attitude towards this policy, whereas a person who is against establishing protected areas is viewed as holding a negative attitude toward this policy.

The theory of reasoned action deals with attitudes toward behaviour.[3] The theory assumes that an individual assesses the goodness or badness of the behaviour in question by personal attitudes either for or against it. 'Subjective norms' aim to understand the social pressure connected with the behaviour. In general, individuals intend to behave in a certain way, if they think that the behaviour in question is good, as defined below, and if they believe that their 'important others' (like family and friends) approve of this behaviour. The model is

$$B \approx BI = w_1 AB + w_2 SN \qquad (10.1)$$

where B is behaviour, BI are behavioural intentions, AB attitude toward behaviour, SN subjective norm and w_1 and w_2 are empirical weights indicating the relative importance of the first and the second term. Following Eagly and Chaiken, (1993 p. 169), the attitude toward the behaviour is a probability weighted sum over the values of important consequences, algebraically as

$$AB = \Sigma_i \, b_i \, e_i, \, i = 1,2,...,n, \qquad (10.2)$$

where b_i is a subjective probability that the behaviour in question has a consequence i ; e_i is an evaluation of the consequence, and n is the number of important consequences. Similarly, the relation between the subjective norm and normative beliefs can be expressed as a sum

$$SN = \Sigma_j \, b_j \, c_j, j = 1,2,...,r, \qquad (10.3)$$

where b_j is a normative belief (that is, subjective probability) that the referred individual j thinks that the action should be taken; c_j is motivation to comply as j thinks, and r is the number of relevant individuals. The theory is restricted to the class of behaviours that can be termed 'volitional' or 'voluntary', that is, behaviours that people perform because they decide to perform them. But while the relations specified above are always assumed to hold if appropriate measures are obtained, 'external' variables, such as demographic variables, personality traits, and attitudes toward people or institutions are not assumed to have such consistent effect. These can affect behaviour only indirectly. Measures of attitudes toward the behaviour and the subjective norms provide all the information needed to predict the intention see Ajzen and Fishbein, (1980 p. 90).

According to Ajzen and Fishbein, (1980) there are likely to be some human behaviours that cannot be explained by the theory of reasoned action, such as emotional outbursts and performance of well learned skills.

There can also be individuals for whom the theory does not apply; some people may arrive at their decisions in different ways. In general, however, they consider the reasoned action model as useful for most individuals and with respect to most social behaviour. But in the light of the recent literature this view is too optimistic, a review of literature can be found in Eagly and Chaiken, (1993). In the following, the Fishbein and Ajzen's theory (1975) is assessed and compared with non-market valuation using the CVM.

10.3 ATTITUDE–BEHAVIOUR RESEARCH AND THE CONTINGENT VALUATION APPROACH

Theoretical measures of attitude–behaviour research and non-market valuation, mediating frameworks, and types of model for empirical questions are presented in Table 10.1. Theoretical measures are considered first. Within attitude–behaviour research, a tripartite distinction (cognitive, affective, and behavioural categories) provides an important conceptual framework, which allows psychologists to express the fact that evaluation can be manifested through responses of all three types.[4] However, attitudes need not have all these aspects, neither at the point of attitude formation nor at the point of attitudinal response (see Eagly and Chaiken, 1993, p. 16).

Table 10.1   Attitude–behaviour research and the contingent valuation approach

	Attitude–behaviour research	Contingent valuation approach
Theoretical measure	Cognitive and/or affective and/or behavioural measure of attitudes	Monetary measure
Mediating framework	Theory of reasoned action	Discrete choice (open-ended)/ utilitarian framework
Type of model	Reasoned action	Contingent valuation

As to non-market valuation, the cognitive category of attitudes matters. A distinction to be made here is that between certainty (the ex post perspective) and uncertainty (the ex ante perspective). If certainty is assumed within the neo-classical, utilitarian framework, individuals know how much utility they would get from the availability of a public good. Under this condition, the objects of choice are bundles of commodities and no distinction is made between the act of choice, on one hand, and its consequence on the other. Only a trivial distinction is possible, since the act is the choice of a commodity bundle and the consequence its receipt. When certainty is assumed the Hicksian welfare measures are appropriate. For example, responses to open-ended questions about willingness to pay can be interpreted as estimates of each individual's compensating surplus or equivalent surplus, depending upon the format of the question. Alternatively, discrete choice models can be used for converting data on 'yes' or 'no' responses to a survey question into a monetary measure. Discrete choice models have been developed to predict individuals' behaviour in a choice context and to draw inferences about welfare change on the basis of observed choices. A problem can be viewed as involving the choice of one option from a range of discrete alternatives. The outcome is a corner solution; there are no tangencies from which a marginal rate of substitution can be inferred.

If uncertainty is assumed, the concequences of any act will vary according to the outcome of events beyond the control of the individual. Uncertainty is characterized as an aspect of nature external to individuals. The terms 'states of nature' or 'states of the world' have been used to refer to these outside events determining the consequences of actions. The standard model of individual preferences is based on the hypothesis that individuals maximize their expected utility and new welfare measures, such as 'option price',[5] are required. Expected utility models assume that each behavioural alternative has a value or utility and that each such value is the sum of the products of the likelihoods and values of the various outcomes associated with each behavioural alternative. Although criticized, these models represent an important tradition in the study of decision-making.

The mediating framework on the attitude side is the theory of reasoned action, probably the most discussed and criticized theory in attitude–behaviour research. In the reasoned action framework, causal pretensions place attitude in a sequence of psychological processes that determine behaviour. Fishbein and Ajzen, (1975) attempt to identify interrelations between their conceptual framework and some contemporary theories of attitude, such as learning theories, expectancy-value theories, consistency theories and attribution theories, but the theory of reasoned action cannot be considered as a general theory of behaviour.[6] Major restrictions in that respect are its difficulties in predicting behaviours that require skills, abilities, opportunities and the cooperation of others. Also the volitional restriction limits the model to behaviours that 'require only motivation' on the part of the individual. Within these limits, for example Eagly and Chaiken, (1993 p. 168) agree that attitudes toward behaviours are better predictors of single behaviours than are attitudes toward targets. Ajzen and Fishbein's approach thus appears viable for relatively simple and easily executed behaviours that are under one's own control.[7]

But if implemented with respect to the choices between alternatives the theory of reasoned action becomes somewhat similar to expected utility models. Because attitude toward behaviour in the theory of reasoned action is a function of the perceived likelihoods of outcomes and their perceived value, it is the attitude aspect of the theory of reasoned action that resembles these models or the standard economic approach.

Recall that the reasoned action model uses measures of attitudes toward behaviour and subjective norms to predict behaviour, but the economic approach relies on 'external variables'. Therefore, via connecting these approaches one is able to investigate if the standard economic approach really matters as to intentions to behave in a certain way. To illustrate, if external variables such as age, education, and income appear to be significant in the case of the Saimaa seal, a broader behavioural model is of the form:

$$WTP_{ca} = f(\text{Attitude, Norm}) + g(\text{Age, Education, Income}) \qquad (10.4)$$

where WTP_{ca} are behavioural intentions for collective action, $f(\cdot)$ represents the theory of reasoned action and $g(\cdot)$ represents the standard economic approach. Intentions to follow the planned directives can be modeled in the same way. The model is:

$$BI_{pa} = f(\text{Attitude, Norm}) + g(\text{Age, Education, Income}) \qquad (10.5)$$

where BI_{pa} denotes behavioural intentions to protect by private actions.

The first model (10.4) belongs to the 'direct hypothetical' approach and the second (10.5) belongs to the 'indirect hypothetical' approach.[8] The difference between these approaches is that the first yields monetary values directly but the second requires that possible monetary values must be inferred through an indirect technique based on a model of individual behaviour and choice. Both models are considered further in the next section, but monetary values connected with the indirect hypothetical approach do not become apparent until implications for policy are introduced.

10.4 EMPIRICAL STUDY

A local mail survey was conducted in September 1993. By then it had become clear that funds were inadequate for a large scale programme, because the public sector was rapidly cutting down its expenditure. Prices were set on many social services that had been 'free' for individuals to that point, or subsidized prices were raised (for example health care and library services). Thus, the context was provided to request that citizens also needed to pay for the conservation of the Saimaa seal. The discrete valuation question was: 'Would your household be willing to pay 150 FIM as a single payment to cover the costs of the program of conservation of the Saimaa seal?' (see Appendix).[9] In addition, an open-ended valuation question was asked.

The survey consisted of two parts, a contingent valuation survey and a survey dealing with respondents' behavioural intentions to protect the Saimaa seal.[10] The response rate was moderate, 56 per cent. However, of those who completed the first part of the survey questionnaire (the CVM survey) some respondents failed to complete the second part (the attitude survey). Consequently, only 215 observations (54 per cent) could be used in the analysis of behavioural intentions.

10.4.1   Main Results of the CVM Approach

The descriptive statistics for the open-ended valuation question are presented in Table 10.2. The mean WTP is 71.19 FIM and the median 50 FIM. Less than one third (26 per cent) of the local people were willing to pay the suggested bid 150 FIM. In terms of a referendum this means that the protection programme should be rejected. However, some 96 per cent of the respondents considered that the Saimaa seal should be protected and the majority of the respondents were willing to pay some small positive amount of money (56 per cent at least 50 FIM) for collective action.

Table 10.2   Summary statistics for the valuation question in the local survey

Mean	Median	Std. dev.	Min	Max	N
71.19	50	103.44	0	1000	219

In Table 10.2 the maximum offer is 1000 FIM and the minimum offer zero FIM.[11] But in one case the reported willingness to pay was in fact negative since the future use of one household's summer cottage (located at the area to be protected) was uncertain.

To illustrate the difference between the results of the two surveys made, the median value can be aggregated to the national level.[12] Based on the local survey, an estimate of the total costs of the project approved by the majority of Finnish people would be around 100 million FIM, a third of the conservative estimate of the national survey, which was 300–350 million FIM.

10.4.2   Analysis of Behavioural Intentions

As to intentions to protect by private actions, for example, the respondents were asked to indicate their subjective probability that they will follow the planned voluntary government regulations, as follows:

1. Intention
   I am going to follow the directions likely ___:___:___:___:___
   unlikely

2. Attitude toward the behaviour
   Following the directions would be sensible ___:___:___:___:___ be
   unnecessary in my opinion

3. Subjective norm
   My family think that one should ___:___:___:___:___ need not follow
   the planned directions

Although responses to these three questions should provide all relevant information from the standpoint of the theory of reasoned action, consideration of the standard economic approach requires a broader model see Ajzen and Fishbein, (1980 p. 90).[13] A more general form of the models (4) and (5) is:

$$BI = \alpha_0 + \beta_1 A_B + \beta_2 SN + \beta_3 E_1 + \ldots + \beta_{n+2} E_n, \tag{10.6}$$

where A_B is the attitude toward behaviour, SN is the subjective norm, and $E_1, \ldots, E_n$ are the external variables. To investigate if the regression as a whole matters the F test for the hypothesis H_0: $\beta_i = 0$, for all i, and H_0: $\beta_i \neq 0$ for some i, is used.[14] To test nonnested hypotheses of attitude and external variables, Davidson and MacKinnon's J test and the Cox test were applied see Greene (1993, pp. 222–5). The tests appeared to be inconclusive: in every case the J test and Cox test suggest that neither the attitude variables nor the external variables in question are preferable.

10.4.2.1   Intentions to pay for collective action
Table 10.3 reports the results from the regression analysis without external variables. Both attitudes toward payment behaviour and subjective norm are significant. The model explains 27 per cent of the variation of WTP. The F-statistics show that the model is significant at the 1 per cent level (the critical level is 4.61). The results can be interpreted such that one step to the positive direction within the five step attitude scale increases the expected WTP by 22 FIM. Similarly, a step to the positive direction within the five step norm scale increases the expected WTP by 29 FIM.

A broader model includes attitudes toward behaviour, subjective norms, and the significant external variables found via estimating the 'bid function'.[15] Table 10.4 reports the results from the regression analysis of this combined model. R^2 of 45 per cent is now much higher than it is in the attitude–norm model above. The F-statistics show that the model is significant at the 1 per cent level (the critical level is around 2.6). Since all external variables are significant (the significance level does not exceed 0.05), the hypothesis H_0 is rejected as to willingness to pay for collective action, external variables matter.

Table 10.3   Collective provision: OLS estimates of an attitude–norm model, full sample

| Dependent variable: WTP | | | | | |
Variable	DF	Coefficient	Std error	T-ratio	$P[\,|T| \geq t\,]$
Constant	1	−57.1	16.1	−3.5	0.0005
Attitude	1	22.4	6.3	3.6	0.0005
Norm	1	28.9	7.8	3.7	0.0003

Note : $R^2 = 0.27$ Adjusted $R^2 = 0.26$ $F(2,208) = 38.9$

Table 10.4 Collective provision: OLS estimates of a combined model, full sample

| Dependent variable: WTP | | | | | |
Variable	DF	Coefficient	Std error	T-ratio	$P[\,|T| \geq t\,]$
Constant	1	57.7	29.4	2.0	0.0513
Attitude	1	13.7	6.2	2.2	0.0277
Norm	1	26.1	7.1	3.7	0.0003
Education	1	130.7	22.3	5.9	0.0000
Household	1	−10.8	4.2	−2.6	0.0112
Sex	1	−30.3	11.1	−2.7	0.0068
Age	1	−1.4	0.4	−3.4	0.0009
Fund	1	53.1	14.8	3.6	0.0004

Note : $R^2 = 0.45$ Adjusted $R^2 = 0.43$ $F(7,200) = 23.4$

The results can be interpreted such that a person with an academic degree is expected to pay some 130 FIM more than a person without one. Positive attitudes toward establishing a 'coast fund' also have a positive effect on willingness to pay.[16] A two person household is expected to have about 10 FIM lower WTP than a single person household. A 30 year old person is expected to pay 1.4 FIM less than a 20 year old person. A woman is expected to pay some 30 FIM less than a man.

In comparing the results we find that one step in the positive direction on the norm scale increases the expected WTP by 29 FIM in the attitude–

norm model, and by 26 FIM in the combined model. Similarly, one step in the positive direction on the attitude scale increases the expected WTP by 22 FIM in the attitude–norm model and 14 FIM in the combined model. However, when a new set of demographic variables is added to the model the marginal effect of attitude on WTP decreases three times more than the marginal effect of norm on WTP. This suggests the attitude aspect of the reasoned action model resembles the standard economic approach.

10.4.2.2   Intentions to protect by private action

Two questions were asked concerning the respondents' intentions to protect by private actions. First, the respondents were asked to indicate their subjective probability that they will follow the planned voluntary directions, as follows: 'What are your intentions as to following the previously listed voluntary based directives? (I am going to follow the directives, likely — unlikely.)'

Second, the respondents were asked to indicate their subjective probability that they would follow the planned voluntary directives, as follows: 'What would be your intentions as to following the directives on conservation of the Saimaa seal if the State would, for example, go strongly to the monetary support of nature tourism[17] in your home municipality, to compensate the residents that the directives will be followed? (I would follow the directives, likely — unlikely.)'

Tables 10.5   Private provision: OLS estimates of two attitude–models, full sample

Attitude–norm model 'without economic incentives'

Dependent variable: Intention to follow new directions					
Variable	DF	Coefficient	Std error	*T*-ratio	$P[\,|T|\geq t\,]$
Constant	1	0.9	0.2	3.8	0.0002
Attitude	1	0.6	0.1	9.5	0.0000
Norm	1	0.2	0.1	2.5	0.0124

Note : $R^2 = 0.54$ Adjusted $R^2 = 0.53$ $F(2,201) = 118.34$

Attitude–norm model 'with economic incentives'

Dependent variable: Intention to follow new directions					
Variable	DF	Coefficient	Std error	*T*-ratio	$P[\,|T|\geq t\,]$
Constant	1	0.7	0.2	2.9	0.00428
Attitude	1	0.7	0.1	13.5	0.00000
Norm	1	0.2	0.04	4.6	0.00001

Note : $R^2 = 0.55$ Adjusted $R^2 = 0.54$ $F(2,209) = 125.6$

Results of the two attitude–norm models based on these questions are reported in Table 10.5. The regression is considered as a linear probability

model where answer 'unlikely' refers to Prob(follows the directives) = 0
and answer 'likely' refers to Prob(follows the directives) = 1. Thus the
answer scale from 1 to 5 refers to equal-sized probability steps. The
problem in a linear probability model is that the predicted probabilities are
unlikely to be within the range from 0 to 1. However, in this case we are
interested in only the prediction power of the explanatory variables and
their marginal effects. A unity parameter value for attitude–norm variables
would mean equal change in probability. The further a parameter is below
unity, the less is the variable's impact on probability.

Both models in Table 10.5 are statistically significant and explain more
than half of the variation of intentions to protect by private actions. In
addition, the latter model which includes economic incentives to protect
by private actions is slightly better in terms of R^2 and F value: $R^2 = 0.55$
and $F(2,209) = 125.6$ are higher than $R^2 = 0.54$ and $F(2,201) = 118.3$.

Two combined models of private provision were formed via connecting
the attitude and norm variables and the significant external variables. In
both cases (that is, the models 'without' and 'with' economic incentives)
one significant external variable was found. These were 'education' and
'sex', respectively. These external variables were included in the final
combined models, reported in Table 10.6.

*Table 10.6 Private provision: OLS estimates of two combined models, full
    sample*

Combined model 1 'without economic incentives'

Dependent variable: Intention to follow new directives					
Variable	DF	Coefficient	Std error	T-ratio	$P[\,|T|\ge t\,]$
Constant	1	0.9	0.2	3.9	0.0001
Attitude	1	0.6	0.1	9.4	0.0000
Norm	1	0.1	0.1	2.1	0.0133
Education	1	0.3	0.2	1.9	0.0633

Note : $R^2 = 0.55$ Adjusted $R^2 = 0.54$ $F(3,200) = 81.0$

Combined model 2 'with economic incentives'

Dependent variable: Intention to follow new directives					
Variable	DF	Coefficient	Std error	T-ratio	$P[\,|T|\ge t\,]$
Constant	1	0.6	0.2	2.5	0.0133
Attitude	1	0.7	0.1	13.5	0.0000
Norm	1	0.2	0.04	4.8	0.0000
Sex	1	0.2	0.1	2.2	0.0304

Note : $R^2 = 0.56$ Adjusted $R^2 = 0.55$ $F(3,208) = 86.3$

As to these final models, the R^2 of 55 per cent and 56 per cent suggest rather good model performance. The models explain more than half of the variation of willingness to protect by private actions. The F-statistics show that the models are significant at the 1 per cent level (the critical level is 3.87). The increase of the adjusted R^2 (compared to the attitude–norm models) indicates that the added external variables improve these models. Moreover, since both external variables are significant (the significance level does not exceed 0.1 or 0.05), the hypothesis H_0 is rejected with regard to intentions to protect by private actions.

According to the results of model [1] in Table 10.6, an academic degree has a positive effect on willingness to protect by private actions. This result parallels the result found in Table 10.4. When intentions to pay for collective action are analysed, the results suggest that a person with an academic degree is willing to pay some 130 FIM more than a person without one. But in fact, the context of this first model is not quite correct. Economic incentives are needed to compensate those who will lose something because of the planned program. The second model [2] in Table 10.6 'includes' such incentives.

According to the results of model [2], the external variable 'sex' is significant. In addition, the variable 'sex' appears to be the key or 'the missing link' between the analysed intentions: while a woman is expected to pay around 30 FIM less for collective action compared to a man (Table 10.4), she is expected to prefer protecting by private actions compared to a man. This result is in accordance with the suggestion that willingness to pay for collective action and willingness to protect by private actions can be substitutes.[18]

In all, the gap between the willingness to protect and willingness to behave in a certain way to protect the seal population can now be explained much better than within the standard CVM framework. Of the respondents in the local survey, some 96 per cent consider that the Saimaa seal should be protected, 56 per cent are willing to pay at least 50 FIM for the program of conservation and some 87 per cent are willing to protect by private actions. The majority of respondents thus support both collective provision and private provision.

10.5 FRAMEWORK FOR USING THE CONTINGENT VALUATION METHOD

There are three kinds of variables in the economic system: those endogenous to individuals, exogenous to individuals but endogenous to the economic system, and exogenous to both individuals and the economic system. Economists tend to value the reduction of risk through some form of collective action or government intervention. From the individual's point of view the risk is then exogenous, outside their control. By intuition and evidence this is not true. Individuals are able to make choices that alter risk. Crocker and Shogren, (1992) define this ability to alter the likelihood and severity of a harmful event as endogenous risk.

In their innovative article, Ehrlich and Becker, (1972) deal with self-protection, as a reduction in the probability of a loss, and self-insurance, as a reduction in the size of a loss. Crocker and Shogren, (1992) suggest that with ex ante efforts to reduce probability, s, and ex ante efforts to reduce prospective severity, x, the individual's economic problem becomes selecting s and x to maximize her von Neumann-Morgenstern expected utility index, EU, as follows:

$$Max_{s,x}\, EU = [p(s)\ U(m - s - x) + (1 - p(s))\ U(m - L(x) - s - x)] (10.7)$$

where p is probability, m is wealth, L is the money equivalent of realized severity, and s and x are expenditures on self-protection and self-insurance against the realization of an undesirable state, derivatives are $p' > 0$, $p'' < 0$, $L' < 0$, $L'' > 0$.

The necessary conditions for the individual's optimal levels of self protection and self-insurance are

$$s: p(s)\,'\, V - p(s)\ U'\ (m - s - x) - [1 - p(s)] U'[m - L(x) - s - x] = 0 \quad (10.8)$$

$$x: -p(s)\ U'(m - s - x) + [1 - p(s)] U'[m - L(x) - x - s](-1 - L') = 0 \quad (10.9)$$

where

$$V = U(m - s - x) - U(m - L(x) - s - x) > 0,\ U' > 0,\ \text{and } |L'| > 1. \quad (10.10)$$

Equations (10.8) and (10.9) state that the individual maximizes expected utility by equating the marginal cost of influencing probability or severity to the marginal wealth aquired. Self-protection or self-insurance activities are avoided if doing so is not expected to increase net wealth.

Within this framework it is possible to consider self-protection at the individual level or at the governmental level. However, risk assessment and risk management are usually considered to be separate issues. The former quantifies environmental risk and the latter regulates it. Both require experts of their own in the process of dealing with risks. But if individuals privately self-protect, risk assessment and risk management become inseparable. Moreover, from the individual's viewpoint private and collective provision can be substitutes. Relative productivities and prices affect individual's willingness to substitute one for another. A low or zero price for collective provision will lessen the efforts to self-protect. If the price for collective provision is high, individuals prefer self-protection. In that respect, the introduced theoretical framework sheds new light on risk management, usually interpreted as the collective provision of a more desirable state.

Now let us consider the relevance of risk to the two contingent valuation surveys conducted to reveal the Finnish people's willingness to pay for a program to conserve the Saimaa seal. The money estimates of these surveys can be used to illustrate actual use of the CVM survey results. From the standpoint of endogenous risk it is necessary that the government selects s and x to maximize its von Neumann-Morgenstern expected utility index in equation 10.7.

According to the national survey the majority of Finnish people accept that the government use some 300–350 million FIM as expenditures for collective risk reduction. Let this money amount represent the money available for the program to conserve the Saimaa seal. If only exogenous risk is considered all this money will be spent on collective risk reduction. But it is relevant to consider also endogenous risk reduction strategies since the local residents of the Pihlajavesi area are expected to protect by private actions. In doing so, the government reduces s in favour of x. The local CVM survey results suggest that the government could use about 100 million FIM on collective risk reduction. That would leave some 200–250 million FIM to create and manage economic incentives for private risk reduction locally. Some part of this money could be saved also for other relevant purposes.

10.6 CONCLUSIONS

That attitudes cause behaviour is one possible reason why attitudes are often correlated with behaviour. Non-market valuation focuses upon the cognitive category of attitudes where preferences or beliefs represent benefits or costs. But the tripartite distinction of attitudes implies that the pure cognitive component may be unimportant while other attitudinal categories are at present simultaneously.

In the case of the Saimaa seal, the observed gap between high willingness to save the seal and low willingness to pay could not be explained by using the standard approach to contingent valuation. Therefore, the standard approach was connected with the theory of reasoned action, developed to predict and understand individuals' behaviour. The results of this analysis are in accordance with the suggestions of recent attitude–behaviour research. External variables may be relevant in an analysis of behavioural intentions and therefore should be included in CVM surveys using questions about attitudes toward behaviour and subjective norms.

The 'State takes care of the problem' as a general principle of environmental policy has been applied to programs of conservation in Finland. A well-known problem connected with this principle is that it does not change the way people behave. If the policy-makers treat risk as exogenous, the risk is outside the individuals' control. But individuals can alter risk. Recognition of endogenous risk leaves space also for the 'cooperation principle' which is expected to change the individuals' behaviour, particularly if relevant economic incentives are provided.

ENDNOTES

1. It was the first subspecies to be included in the Red Data Book, published by the Survival Service Commission of the International Union for Conservation of the Nature and Natural Resources. This subspecies, found only in Finland, was protected by law in 1955.
2. The survey sample consisted of three subsamples: 700 recreational fishermen (the reference group) and 1000 'ordinary' Finnish people, half of them living in cities more than 100 000 residents and the other half living in smaller cities and the countryside. Random sampling of the research groups was based on the 'one person per household' principle. People from the age of 20 to the age of 69 years were included in the sample. The data was extracted from the official files on the Finnish population. The response rate was moderate, 60 per cent. The discrete choice elicitation method was applied. According to the survey results, a conservative estimate of the total costs of the program of conservation of the Saimaa seal, approved by the majority of Finnish people would be some 300–350 million FIM.
3. A distinction to be made here is the one between attitudes toward targets and attitudes toward behaviours. The target is the entity (for example, thing, person) toward whch a particular behaviour is directed. See Eagly and Chaiken, (1993, p. 163).
4. Different responses are classified into three categories: cognitive (perceptual responses and verbal statements of belief), affective (sympathetic nervous responses and verbal statements of affect), and behavioural (overt actions and verbal statements of behaviour). See Ajzen and Fishbein, (1980), p. 20.
5. Mitchell and Carson, (1989), p. 71, define option price as 'the ex ante state independent willingness to pay for a specified change in the level of the public good in question'. It may thus be viewed as what a consumer will pay now in order to obtain a good.
6. In fact, there are no 'general models' in attitude–behaviour research to this point. Much research is still needed for more general theories of how behaviour is affected by attitudes toward targets and toward behaviours. Development in that direction requires coodinating attitudes towards targets and attitudes toward behaviour with other psychological tendencies that regulate behaviour (such as habits, self-identity, or norms). See Eagly and Chaiken, (1993), pp. 670–71.

7. The majority of the studies supporting the theory of reasoned action have concerned relatively simple behaviours, such as voting, church attendance, and choice of strategies in Prisoner's Dilemma games.
8. A classification of behaviour-based methods of valuing public goods can be found in Mitchell and Carson, (1989), p. 75.
9. The suggested bid was based on the results of the national survey.
10. In the Pihlajavesi area (municipalities Savonlinna, Punkaharju, and Sulkava) there are about 14 000 households and 400 of them were sampled. Random sampling was based on the 'one person per household' principle. People from the age of 20 to the age of 69 years were included in the sample. The data was extracted from the official files on the Finnish population.
11. In censoring troublesome responses Lindsey's (1994) framework was followed. Lindsey suggests that decisions concerning analysis of troublesome responses should be consistent with the choice of the 'conceptual market model' for the application. Fewer bids need to be censored under the conceptual model of political markets. As a result, three possible protest zeros were censored from the data. This had no effect on the main result of the survey.
12. For example Arrow et al. (1993) recommend the referendum interpretation of survey results, that is, use the median.
13. To assess the relative importance of attitude and subjective norm the answers were scaled as (5, 4, 3, 2, 1).
14. All calculations are performed by using LIMDEP statistical software (Greene, 1995).
15. A simple linear model can be viewed as a way of extrapolating characteristics of sample behaviour. Such models, bid functions, are commonly used in CVM studies with open-ended valuation questions.
16. The WWF of Finland has suggested that one possibility to collect funds for future programs of conservation is to establish a particular 'coast fund'. If someone builds a house on a coastal area or sells land for this kind of purpose, she should invest some share of the price of the land to this coast fund.
17. The term nature tourism refers to a sustainable form of tourism.
18. Estimation of a multinomial probit model with ordered responses provided similar results, see Moisseinen (1997).

REFERENCES

Ajzen, I. and M. Fishbein (1980), *Understanding Attitudes and Predicting Social Behaviour*, Englewood Cliffs, NJ: Prentice-Hall.
Arrow, K., R. Solow, P.R. Portney, E.E. Leamer, R. Radner and H. Schuman (1993), report from the NOAA Panel on Contingent Valuation, Federal Register 58 (10), 4601–14.

Crocker, T.D. and J.F. Shogren (1992), 'Endogenous risk and program evaluation', paper presented at the *U.S. Army Environmental Policy Institute Conference in Environmental Program Evaluation*, San Francisco, CA.

Eagly, A.H. and S. Chaiken (1993), *The Psychology of Attitudes*, Orlando, FL: Harcourt Brace Jovanovich, Inc.

Ehrlich, I. and G.S. Becker (1972), 'Market insurance, self-insurance and self-protection', *Journal of Political Economy*, 80 (4), 623–48.

Fishbein, M. and I. Ajzen (1975), *Belief, Attitude, Intention and Behaviour: An Introduction to Theory and Research*, Reading, Mass: Addison Wesley.

Greene, W.H. (1993), *Econometric Analysis*, Englewood Cliffs, NJ: Prentice Hall, Inc.

Greene, W.H. (1995), *Limdep version 7.0*, Australia: Econometric Software, Inc.

Haila, Y. and R. Levins (1992), 'Humanity and nature', *Ecology, Science and Society*, London: Pluto Press.

Lindsey, G. (1994), 'Market models, protest bids, and outliers in contingent valuation', *Journal of Water Resources Planning and Management*, 120 (1), 121–9.

Mitchell, R.C. and R.T. Carson (1989), *Using Surveys to Value Public Goods. The Contingent Valuation Method*, Washington DC: Resources for the Future.

Moisseinen, E. (forthcoming 1997), *Contingent Valuation. The Case of the Saimaa Seal*, Academic Dissertation. University of Joensuu, Publications in Social Sciences.

Navrud, S. (ed.) (1992), *Pricing the European Environment*, Oslo: Scandinavian University Press.

APPENDIX

CONSERVATION OF THE SAIMAA SEAL ON THE PIHLAJAVESI AREA OF LAKE SAIMAA. University of Joensuu/Karelian Institute, Survey research 3.9.1993

1. Do you find environmental issues important? Mark with a cross the alternative you consider as relevant.

   Yes, very important
   Yes, rather important
   No, not very important
   No, not important at all

2. What outdoor recreation have you and the members of your household participated in the Pihlajavesi area during the past 12 months. Mark with a circle.

	Yes	No
Rowing	1	2
Boating	1	2
Surfing	1	2
Swimming, sun bathing	1	2
Fishing	1	2

Living in a summer cottage	1	2
Camping in a tent, camping	1	2
Watching animals, photographing	1	2
Picking berries, mushrooms	1	2
Picknic, watching scenic views	1	2
Walking, jogging	1	2
Walking pets	1	2
Hunting	1	2
Something else, what?_____	1	2

3. How often do you spend time at these outdoor recreations

☐ Very often
☐ Rather often
☐ Seldom
☐ Never

Preservation is based on the assumption that we are able to prevent risk of worldwide degradation of the environment. Research on the Saimaa seal, for example, provides much information about the changes in states of our environment, e.g. showing seals gather slowly dissoluble environmental pollutants.

4. Have you ever donated money for conservation of the Saimaa seal

☐ Yes, in which collection or a similar donation have you participated?
_____
☐ No

Currently the Saimaa seal population numbers about 180. House building, human activities which disturb seals, fishing with strong nets and effects of environmental pollutants are the factors whose impact decreases the seal population most. According to researchers the Saimaa seal is going to become extinct if we do not protect its breeding areas. In March 1992 the Ministry of the Environment appointed a committee to work out a programme for conservation of the Saimaa seal. An official decision, positive or negative, will be made after this proposal is completed.

5. In your opinion should the Saimaa seal be protected?

☐ Yes, why? Mark two most important reasons for preservation:
☐ We have no right to destroy
☐ People get knowledge about the quality of the environment
☐ Other plants and animals and also clean nature of the
area will be protected at the same time
☐ The Saimaa seal has the right to live and the right to a future
☐ Some other reason, please explain?_____
☐ No, why?_____
☐ I don't know

At the meeting of the United Nations held in June 1992 at Rio de Janeiro, Finland signed a biodiversity contract. It obliges Finland to protect endangered species, which means that the government has to pay for the establishment of protected areas. Conservation programmes affect our government's budget so that, for example, in 1993 charges for about 1000 hectares for the protection of the white-backed woodpecker will begin. In all there are about one hundred proposals for endangered species protection under discussion in Finland. Therefore, extra money from households is needed to ascertain the extent of the programme of conservation for the Saimaa seal.

6.   Is your household willing to pay as a single payment the amount of 150 FIM for protecting the Saimaa seal?

     ☐   Yes, why? (Move to question 9.)
     ☐   I don't know
     ☐   No

7.   If your answer was 'I don't know' or 'no', mark with a cross the correct alternative

     ☐   We would pay less, at most _____ FIM
     ☐   We would pay zero FIM
     ☐   We ought to be compensated
     ☐   As to our welfare it makes no difference to use money for the seals or other consumption

8.   our answer was 'I don't know' or 'no', mark with a cross the correct alternative

     ☐   Economic reasons
     ☐   Too much to protect only one species
     ☐   Polluters (industry) should pay
     ☐   The Saimaa seal is already predetermined to extinction
     ☐   Other reason, what?_____

9.   Would you pay more than 150 FIM for protection?

     ☐   Yes, ...FIM
     ☐   No
     ☐   I don't know

In addition to the buying of land, other means of protection are planned. For example the interim report of the committee of the conservation for the Saimaa seal includes detailed suggestions to protect the species. Protected areas will be established to the most important breeding areas. These areas include 1) Hirvolanselkä-Porkalanselkä, 2) Kongonselkä, 3) Paattisenselkä-Kaukiinvesi, 4) Iso Kankaisselkä, 5) Tuohiselkä and 6) South Kokonselkä and 7) North Kokonselkä. The plan includes also voluntary based measures.

10. Do the following planned restrictions cause you any harm?	Yes	No	I don't know
Establishing protected areas	1	2	3
Voluntary based regulations:			
– Restrict use of certain areas in winter	1	2	3
– Restrict fishing with nets in spring	1	2	3
– Prohibit strong nets within the most important breeding areas	1	2	3
– Place routes for snowmobiles and cars away from coasts and islets	1	2	3

– Restrict forestry in close proximity, 100 meters, of the coast in wintertime	1	2	3
– Prohibit use of small islets under 2 hectares from beginning of December to the end of April	1	2	3
– Restrict shipping in wintertime (From the beginning of December to the end of April only the 4.2 metres deep route should be used and routes to regularly populated islands. Only official use of all-weather crafts allowed.)	1	2	3

To the following 5 step scale questions, we would like you to cross the alternative describing your opinion best.

An example:

'The quality of the water in Lake Saimaa is'
good ____:____:____:____:____ bad
      very rather neither rather very

If you consider the quality of water as rather good, cross the following alternative:

'The quality of the water in Lake Saimaa is'
good ____:___:____:____:___ bad
      very rather neither rather very

10.   What is your attitude towards the extra payment to protect the Saimaa seal?
      The idea of collecting money from the households
      good ___:___:___:___:___ bad

Majority of the people I know would participate by paying the asked amount

      likely ___:____:_____:____:___ unlikely
         very rather neither rather very

12. What is your attitude toward the previously listed voluntary directives?
      I will follow the directives

      likely ___:____:_____:____:___ unlikely
         very rather neither rather very

      I consider following the directives as

      reasonable ___:____:_____:____:___ unreasonable
         very rather neither rather very

      My family thinks that it is

      reasonable ___:____:_____:____:___ unreasonable
to follow the directives

13. In question 9 we asked about harm caused by the directives. If you would follow the directives, what would be the benefits for you ?

_____

14. Who would agree with you in this issue? (For example family, relatives, fellow employees)_____

15. Who would not necessarily accept your opinion?_____

16. The voluntary based restrictions aim to save the Saimaa seal. What is your opinion about this target?   Following the directives helps to save the Saimaa seal

likely ___:___:_____:___:___ unlikely
very rather neither rather very

Saving the seal population
matters ___:___:_____:___:___ does not matter

17. Every man's rights means that citizens' use of nature is independent of the ownership of some areas. One cannot however use these rights such that harm will be caused. Have you yourself followed this last requirement when using the environment?

Almost always___:___:_____:___:___ never

18. What would be your attitude toward the voluntary directives if the state would strongly support for example nature tourism in your home municipality to compensate following the directions?

I would follow the directives
likely ___:___:_____:___:___ unlikely
very rather neither rather very

I would consider following the directives as
reasonable ___:___:_____:___:___ unreasonable
very rather neither rather very

Most of the local people would follow the directives
likely ___:___:_____:___:___ unlikely
very rather neither rather very

19. One possibility to finance protection programmes in the future is to establish a particular coast fund proposed by environmental organizations. Everyone who builds near coast or sells land for that purpose should invest some of the price to the coast fund. The money would be used for programmes of conservation. What is your opinion about the coast fund?

The idea about the coast fund is
good ___:___:_____:___:___ bad
very rather neither rather very

20. If the fund will be established should all owners of coastal sites be obliged to invest in the fund?

☐ Yes   ☐ No   ☐ I don't know

Why?_____

21. Should industrial plants located near watercourse also be obliged to invest in the fund?

☐ Yes   ☐ No   ☐ I don't know

Why?_____

22. How many persons are there in your household?
_____ persons

23. What is your education? Mark the highest degree you have (If you don't find the right alternative from the following classes, please write your *education* in the empty row of alternative 6.)

☐ 1. Elementary school and/or junior high school
☐ 2. Vocational school
☐ 3. Graduate from high school
☐ 4. Graduate from college
☐ 5. University degree
☐ 6. Other which?_____
☐ 7. No education
☐

24. Which on of the following definitions describing employment or other activity tells most about your current situation? (If you find it difficult to put yourself into any of the following classifications, please write your occupation on the empty rows at the end of the page.)

☐ 1. Employer or own account worker
☐ 2. Farmer
☐ 3. Upper-level white-collar worker
☐ 4. Lower level white-collar worker
☐ 5. Blue collar worker
☐ 6. Unemployed
☐ 7. Pensioner
☐ 8. Family mother or -father
☐ 9 Student
☐ 10. Other, which?_____

25. Finally a question about your household's income. We remind you that only average values of big groups will be seen in the research report.
About what size is your household's current net income per a month ? (Mark with a cross.)

☐ 0 – 3000 FIM
☐ 3001 – 5000 FIM
☐ 5001 – 7000 FIM
☐ 7001 – 9000 FIM
☐ 9001 – 11 000 FIM
☐ 11 001 – 13 000 FIM
☐ 13 001 – 15 000 FIM
☐ 15 001 – 17 000 FIM
☐ more than 17 000 FIM

If you want, on the following lines you may describe your own experiences about the Saimaa seal and/or tell your opinions about how this protection issue affects your life and lives of other residents of the area…

11. Sustainable Development and Appraisal Methodology: Reconciling Legislation and Principles for the Environment Agency in the UK

Andrew Gibbons

11.1 INTRODUCTION

This paper looks at option appraisal methodology in the new environmental regulatory body for England and Wales, the Environment Agency. It considers current achievements and the way ahead in developing an approach to appraisal which can be consistently applied across a range of decisions and circumstances. The new approach must be based on accepted principles of social cost–benefit analysis and of environmental assessment, but must also comply with the legislative and other requirements for the Environment Agency.

The Agency is managing the transition from a range of appraisal and assessment traditions held by different institutions to a unified system of environmental decision-making grounded in scientific and social cost–benefit considerations. It has to reconcile areas of potential conflict between sustainable development perspectives emerging from scientific/environmental viewpoints, the government's perspective on sustainable development and the social cost–benefit approach of neoclassical welfare economics. The challenge is to find solutions which are intellectually sound, publicly defensible and workable in practice. The final outcome will depend on the interplay between three influences discussed below, namely, the legislation, the government's guidance to the Agency on 'sustainable development', and existing option appraisal practices in the constituent organizations. The timing for the work is urgent. With the statutory obligations in place, rapid progress is needed both to deliver the high quality of environmental regulation which the Agency intends should be its hallmark and to minimize the scope for legal challenges to regulatory decisions.

11.2 AIMS AND ACTIVITIES

On 1 April 1996 the UK's two new environment bodies started operations: the Environment Agency covering England and Wales, and its northern counterpart the Scottish Environment Protection Agency (SEPA). The Environment Agency has, as its principal aim, the duty to play its part in achieving the objective of sustainable development. Sustainable development is, nevertheless, a continually developing concept and thus liable to change. The principle aim requires the Environment Agency 'to protect and enhance the environment, taken as a whole'. It is responsible for a range of environmental regulatory functions previously carried out by other bodies, and some new duties are imposed on it. The pre-existing functions include: protecting the inland and coastal water environment, managing water resources, providing river and sea flood defence, applying integrated pollution control to the most polluting industrial processes, regulating the use of radioactive material, and the disposal of solid waste. Effective management of these functions will require the use of appropriate forms of option appraisal to reflect the obligations imposed on the Agency.

The new organization was created from three groups of constituent organizations, being the National Rivers Authority (NRA), Her Majesty's Inspectorate of Pollution (HMIP), and more than 80 local Waste Regulation Authorities (WRAs). Some staff from the Department of the Environment were also included, giving an initial staff of some 9000.

A wide range of functions were carried over from the constituent organizations, and cover the regulation and control of industry, waste and the water environment. They can be grouped as follows:

- regulation of prescribed industrial processes
- control of sites producing radioactive waste
- consent for discharges to controlled waters
- consent for abstractions from controlled waters
- setting statutory water quality objectives
- establishing catchment management plans
- river low flow alleviation schemes
- flood defence capital and maintenance work
- development planning and control
- water resources planning
- fisheries, recreation and conservation projects and services
- providing navigation projects and services
- treatment and disposal of controlled waste.

When the Agency is considering actions, a range of duties applies. It must have regard to the desirability of protecting items of historic, archaeological, architectural or engineering interest; take into account effects on the beauty or amenity of any rural or urban area or on any such flora, fauna, features, buildings, sites or objects; and have regard to any effect which the proposals would have on the economic and social well-being of local communities in rural areas. When carrying out its functions, the Agency must have regard to the desirability of conserving and enhancing natural beauty and of conserving flora, fauna and geological or physiographical features of special interest.

11.3 LEGISLATION AND GUIDANCE ON SUSTAINABILITY

Created under the Environment Act 1995 (EA95), the Environment Agency is charged with a range of tasks, duties and obligations. As well as the role of continuing the environmental functions of the constituent bodies, new and broader obligations are specified. For the first time, a 'principal aim' is given. It is the only aim in the legislation.

Section 4 of the Act covers the principal aim and objectives of the Agency.

(1) It shall be the principal aim of the Agency (... taking into account any likely costs) in discharging its functions so to protect or enhance the environment, taken as a whole, as to make the contribution towards attaining the objective of achieving sustainable development mentioned in subsection (3) below.
(2) The Ministers shall from time to time give guidance to the Agency with respect to objectives which they consider it appropriate for the Agency to pursue in the discharge of its functions.
(3) The guidance given under subsection (2) above must include guidance with respect to the contribution which, having regard to the Agency's responsibilities and resources, the Ministers consider it appropriate for the Agency to make, by the discharge of its functions towards attaining the objective of achieving sustainable development.
(4) The Agency shall have regard to guidance given.

This principal aim recognizes that the Agency has an important role to play in the delivery of sustainable development, which itself is as much a matter for political judgement as for scientific and technical analysis. The costs to be taken into account are those to industry and to the environment.

Statutory guidance, including advice on the contribution towards the objective of achieving sustainable development was issued to the Agency by ministers (Department of the Environment, Ministry of Agriculture, Fisheries and Food, and Welsh Office, 1996). With regard to the national objective of attaining sustainable development, the ministerial guidance says that the appropriate contribution of the Agency should be as follows:

- To take an integrated, holistic approach to the protection and enhancement of the environment, for example by exercising its functions in combination where possible;
- To take a long-term perspective, especially for irreversible impacts or those affecting intergenerational equity;
- To maintain biodiversity;
- To maximize the scope for cost-effective investment by business in improved technologies and management techniques;
- To develop close working relationships with the public, local authorities, and other representatives of local communities working towards Local Agenda 21; and
- To become a source of high quality information and advice on the environment.

The UK government's broader aims for sustainable development are set out in a series of publications covering sustainable development strategy, climate change, biodiversity, and other issues (British Government Panel on Sustainable Development, 1996; Department of the Environment 1994, 1994a, 1994b, 1996, House of Lords Select Committee, 1995). The principles contained in these documents are supposedly embodied in the ministerial guidance.

Guidance on the practical application of the sustainable development strategy is contained in parts of a number of documents. For example, the requirement for integration is a key element of the guidance on best practicable environmental option (BPEO). Planning policy guidance notes address among other themes, transport and the influence of pollution control on planning. In addition there are various documents that provide advice to government on sustainable development and which contain information helpful to the Agency in specific areas (Department of the Environment, 1995; Department of the Environment, The Scottish Office, Welsh Office, 1997; Department of the Environment and Welsh Office, 1995, 1996a ; Royal Commission on Environmental Pollution, 1996).

Thus the objectives of the Agency are subject to definition by ministers by means of the guidance on sustainable development. This allows the Agency's objectives and powers to be reduced or extended without resort to further legislation.

11.4 LEGISLATION AND GUIDANCE ON COSTS AND BENEFITS

The legislation requires that while protecting or enhancing the environment, taken as a whole, the Agency must take into account any likely costs, as well as contributing towards attaining the objective of achieving sustainable development. Further, the Agency must 'take into account the likely costs and benefits' when deciding how to exercise any of its powers. Costs are defined as those to any person or organization, and to the environment. The Agency regards this duty as implying a form of appraisal in the spirit of cost–benefit analysis which potentially examines all aspects of the available options, including environmental, economic and relevant social impacts. The legislation has no explicit requirement about the weight to be given to any kind of impact. The duty to consider costs and benefits recognizes that sustainable development involves reconciling the need for economic development with that for protecting and enhancing the environment.

The Agency's principal aim (Section 4, EA95) is to discharge its functions in such a manner as to attain the objective of achieving sustainable development, as guided from time to time by ministers, under the provisions of the Act and taking into account any likely costs. More specifically (Section 39, EA95), the Agency has a duty in considering whether or not to exercise its statutory powers, or in deciding the manner in which to exercise its powers, to take into account the likely costs and benefits, unless and to the extent that it is unreasonable for it to do so in view of the nature or purpose of the power, or the circumstances of the particular case. The Act makes clear that this does not affect the Agency's obligation to discharge any of its other duties such as furthering and promoting conservation.

From the parliamentary debates on the Environment Bill it appears that the specific legislative form of the duty arises from the view that, because sustainable development itself requires a reconciliation of the pursuit of economic development and environmental protection, the Agency's role of protecting or enhancing the environment has to be balanced by a need for it also to take account of the costs. Within a sustainable development context, the duty relating to likely costs and benefits is only one among several which apply to the exercise of the Agency's functions.

What are the relevant costs and benefits? Section 56 of EA95 defines costs as including costs to any person and costs to the environment, so the definition is not restricted to financial costs. Benefits are not defined. In some cases the benefits are effectively set by statute in terms of the need to meet statutory environmental standards or to meet nationally-set targets or goals. In other cases the physical benefits may be equally obvious — as in the stopping of pollution, or in upholding the law. Benefits also include fulfilment of the Agency's duties: for example, that of exercising all of its pollution control powers for the purposes of preventing, or minimizing, or remedying or mitigating the effects of, pollution of the environment.

The Agency can only take into account those likely costs for which information is available, or those which it considers feasible to assess. There is no duty to demonstrate that likely benefits however defined should exceed likely costs however defined before any action is taken. Indeed the legal duty requires that costs and benefits be considered, but effectively specifies no further details. This leaves the Agency with the freedom, and the necessity, to address many of the key areas of debate in cost–benefit analysis in order to determine its own approach. Inevitably the questions of monetization and distribution of impacts are central.

Official guidance on the use of cost–benefit analysis recognizes that in many contexts prices will be absent (HM Treasury, 1997). Rarely in environmental regulation are the costs and benefits of options fully available in money value terms as envisaged in formal cost–benefit analysis. Observable price data is normally lacking because of the general absence of markets in environmental goods and services. The need to combine monetary and direct measures of impacts and their distributional implications in a consistent and rigorous manner is particularly challenging. Further, balancing costs and benefits in terms of an intertemporal distribution of entitlements to environmental services involves addressing by discounting or otherwise the impacts on future generations. Discussion of sustainability criteria inevitably raises such distributional issues, and these are difficult to resolve by a rigorous, formulaic approach. Precision with regard to welfare maximizing efficiency questions may be a second order consideration. The principal need is for the Agency to be able to justify its actions in a reasonable way by demonstrating that account was taken of all those duties required of it.

A simple model of government regulation could see environmental regulation as offering a means for increasing social welfare by redressing the market failures which arise particularly from the uncompensated side effects (externalities) of human activities. To stand a good chance of achieving this, regulators' decisions need to be based on a systematic appraisal methodology which reflects the values society places on those environmental and other goods and services now and for future generations between which choices have to be made.

In many respects the environment is an essential resource for the development process, and excessive degradation of the environment and consequent reduction in the services which it provides would be counterproductive in terms of human welfare. Clearly a flow of environmental services needs to be sustained over time for development to continue, while at the same time development must not compromise the present or future ability of the environment to deliver. 'Sustainable development' can be taken to require the sustaining of both the environment and the development process, so the Agency is likely to seek 'win–win' policy solutions with both economic efficiency and environmental benefits. This could maximize some intertemporal distribution of human welfare subject to the constraints of available resources defined in the broadest sense to include all environmental services. In this form the objective function is fully consistent, and there is no conflict between 'economic' and 'environmental' frames of reference: they are both geared towards welfare maximization given collective preferences and available resources.

Although option appraisal can be approached on environmental grounds, environmental considerations alone are unlikely to provide a sufficient basis for taking decisions which may affect the welfare of individuals. Hence environmental impact assessment for the Agency or any other decision-maker should be supplemented by a methodology based on a broader decision tool reflecting the principles of cost–benefit analysis.

11.5 THE INHERITED METHODOLOGIES

The constituent organizations of the Agency have progressed differently in implementing option appraisal strategies. This section catalogues their past approaches.

11.5.1 Integrated Pollution Control (IPC) for Industry and the BPEO Methodology

IPC applies to the most seriously polluting industries. Best practicable environmental option (BPEO) appraisal was developed by HMIP and is an intermediate form between cost–benefit analysis and financial analysis. It goes beyond the scope of financial appraisal but not to the full extent of cost–benefit analysis. Externalities are considered in terms of the environmental impacts of each option, but comparisons are made directly rather than through the medium of money valuation of such impacts. The method is not directly standards-based, but uses a comparison of the relative costs and relative environmental effects of a number of alternative options in order to identify the most appropriate option, effectively that for which the marginal cost of abatement (to the operator of an industrial plant) is judged broadly equivalent to the marginal social benefit of the environmental protection. This methodology has been devised in the general absence of robust and explicit valuations of environmental benefits, in an attempt to provide for consistent and transparent decision-making (Environment Agency, 1997).

Clearly, balanced judgement on the control of releases needs to include consideration of the costs of abatement as well as the environmental impacts. From a cost–benefit 'optimizing' point of view, it is only worth devoting further resources to reducing environmental harm as long as the social benefits exceed the costs. Complete information is rarely available, but in principle the optimum level of releases from a process would be where the marginal cost of abatement (to the operator) was equal to the money value of the marginal benefit of that abatement to society as a whole.

11.5.1.1   BPEO and BATNEEC

Part I of the Environmental Protection Act 1990 introduced a system of integrated pollution control (IPC) and provided the framework for controlling releases from certain prescribed industrial processes.

Under the Act no process prescribed for control by the central authority in England and Wales (now the Environment Agency) may be operated without an authorization. In carrying out a prescribed process the best available techniques not entailing excessive cost (BATNEEC) must be used:

- for preventing the release of substances prescribed for any environmental medium into that medium, or where that is not practicable by such means, for reducing the releases of such substances to a minimum and for rendering harmless any substances which are so released; and
- for rendering harmless any other substances which might cause harm if released into any environmental medium.

Furthermore, where the process is designated for control by the Agency and is likely to involve the release of substances into more than one environmental medium, section 7(7) of the Act requires that BATNEEC will be used:

- for minimizing the pollution to the environment as a whole having regard to the best practicable environmental option (BPEO) available as respects the substances which may be released.

Where a process involves the release of substances to more than one environmental medium, the Agency will need to determine whether the proposed operation represents the best practicable environmental option for the pollutants concerned. As the Act does not define the BPEO, the definition given by the Royal Commission on Environmental Pollution in their Twelfth Report has been adapted to the requirements of IPC. Thus the IPC BPEO is regarded as the option which in the context of releases from a prescribed process provides the most benefit or least damage to the environment as a whole, at acceptable cost, in the long-term as well as the short term. In considering the release of substances to more than one environmental medium, several different dimensions of impact need to be addressed. The ensuing judgement may thus involve multicriteria tradeoffs between different impacts.

Because section 7(7) of the 1990 Act refers specifically to 'the substances which may be released', this definition of the IPC BPEO is restricted to the releases from the prescribed process and therefore excludes other environmental effects such as those arising from the production and delivery of raw materials for the process. Although IPC is responsible for regulating all releases from the process including in particular solid and liquid waste streams, it is not responsible for regulating the method of disposal of these waste streams, and it cannot therefore control the ultimate releases from the waste streams to air or water. The IPC BPEO therefore excludes the environmental effects arising from the disposal of these waste arisings. That said, the operator must be aware of the final disposal options. This area represents one of the potential synergies from combining various previously-separate functions into one organization.

11.5.1.2 Costs and environmental effects
The costs of abatement options need to be presented on a basis which is comparable between different projects which may have different timescales. As with financial appraisal, this requires that capital and operating costs are reduced to a comparable basis by means of discounted cash flow techniques. Abatement costs are converted to equivalent annual values, so that comparisons can be made between potential process/abatement options even if they have different economic lives (Environment Agency, 1997, Vol. I, ch. 7).

In the BPEO methodology, environmental impacts are expressed in terms of an Integrated Environmental Index (IEI). This is created by normalizing and summing all the release levels associated with a technique/option as fractions of comparator ('limit') values for each substance in each environmental medium. This approach is open to several criticisms, including the use of an implicit weighting between substances and the assumptions of linearity in dose/response relationships, which arise from using environmental quality standards as reference levels. In defence, the existence of quality standards for substance concentrations may be assumed in some way to reflect a social view of what levels are unacceptable.

Comparing the IEI against operators' costs allows a tradeoff to be made between options at a site, and a balance to be sought between environmental impacts as implied by the IEI and the costs of avoiding this harm. The preferred process/abatement option is the one for which the incremental environmental benefits (the change in the IEI) are judged as broadly equivalent to the incremental cost. Comparison of each option with the next allows the costs of achieving more stringent levels of pollution control to be shown. Similarly, comparison of each option with the base case allows the magnitude of the incremental costs and environmental effects between the options and the base case to be established.

11.5.1.3   The BPEO decision
In theory, an economic optimum would be where the marginal cost of an improvement just equals the value of its marginal benefit. Even if the paradigm of neoclassical economics is accepted, in the absence of robust money valuations for the environmental impacts of the releases under discusssion, there is little prospect of identifying such a point with any precision (Pearce and Brisson, 1995).

In comparing costs and environmental impacts, a useful comparator may be the cost per unit of substance abated at relevant levels of plant operation. This is an information intensive approach but is still only an intermediate stage in comparison with the cost of reducing harm to the environment. It has the potential to give some information about the techniques most likely to be worthwhile.

In practice, the option likely to be identified as preferable using the current BPEO methodology will be either the most cost-effective option (that is, the least cost per IEI unit of environmental benefit) or the option closest to any sharp increase in the slope of the marginal private cost of abatement curve or, more accurately, step function. Neither of these are necessarily where marginal social cost of abatement equals marginal social benefit, although given the practical difficulties, this approximation may be appropriate for regulatory purposes. The BPEO methodology may be seen as a secondbest approach in economic terms, but it has the merit of being both broadly practicable and acceptable to industry. Part of this acceptability has been achieved by ensuring that 'those responsible for a BPEO decision needed to make a clear distinction between facts, scientific deductions, and conclusions which depended on value judgements' (Silberston, 1993).

In sum, to replace the BPEO methodology with full cost–benefit analysis, if that were feasible, may seem attractive, but at present there are a number of difficulties:

- The need to superimpose inexact economic analysis (valuations) on inexact scientific analysis (for example, unclear dose/response functions) compounds the information problems of both.
- Much of the more widely publicized and successful contingent valuation work is based on relatively tangible, easily observable impacts to amenities, whereas the impacts which IPC has to consider are often much more subtle.
- The choice of abatement options for a typical IPC case tends to cover only a relatively small change in releases relative to the ambient level, and it is hard to derive money values for these modest incremental changes, given the significant noise intrinsic to the valuation methodology.
- IPC decisions often involve baskets of releases, with effects that are difficult to identify separately.

One issue encountered in the application of integrated pollution control is the tension between the cost of compliance with environmental requirements and the financial performance of regulated plants. In most cases it is existing plants which are being regulated, rather than proposed ones. Cleaner production may sometimes produce synergies in terms of lower cost, for example through lower energy, materials or waste dispossal costs, but in many cases the opposite is true, and cleaner production entails higher costs.

The requirements of IPC are that site-specific BATNEEC will be used for minimizing pollution, having regard to the BPEO. In this context a technique is regarded as 'not entailing excessive cost' if the benefits, defined as all the relevant environmental impacts avoided (regardless of whether they can be valued in money terms) are judged by the regulator to outweigh the costs to the operator.

BATNEEC requires as objective a consideration as possible of what costs for a sector *in general* are excessive; the lack of profitability of a particular business should not affect the determination (Department of the Environment and Welsh Office, 1996). Where a firm cannot finance investment which is necessary to achieve an acceptable level of protection for the environment, the fact that a firm may be unable to afford to reduce emissions to the required level should be disregarded in setting the conditions in the authorization.

These considerations apply equally to the determination of what is not 'entailing excessive cost' for existing plant as for new plant. However, in the case of existing plant there are additional factors to take into account in the assessment:

- the configuration of the existing plant, which may make it excessively costly (in relation to the harm which would be avoided) to fit particular types of abatement technology; and
- the disruption to existing operations which could arise were upgrading of the plant standards to be required immediately. Again, the harm which would result from delaying the achievement of new plant standards should be weighed against the benefit (to the operator, his employees and so on) of allowing such a delay.

In practical terms, frequent resort is made to phasing of improvements. Costs may not be excessive if they can be spread over a greater time period, or programmed to coincide with major plant capital works such as mid-life refurbishment, improvement or rationalization. In the light of the operator's plans and proposals, the Agency must decide what is BATNEEC in relation to each application, and translate that decision into conditions to be included in the authorization. There must be broad consistency in these decisions, especially between processes of the same kind. To aid consistency, IPC guidance notes are published for all processes coming within IPC. These represent guidance to inspectors, and provide information on the best available techniques for new plant, their application to existing plant and the financial strength of the sector. The notes also set out the release levels which the Agency believes can be achieved by their use.

11.5.2   Water and the CBA-Based Approach to Appraisal

The Environment Agency's predecessor body responsible for the water environment was the National Rivers Authority (NRA), which had an awareness of the role that environmental economics and cost–benefit analysis could play in ensuring the effectiveness of its functional activities. Its responsibilities broadly covered the areas of Water Resources, Water Quality, Flood Defence, and activities to support use of the water environment for Fisheries, Recreation, Conservation and Navigation.

Economic analysis had been an integral part of the assessment of flood and coastal defence schemes for a number of years, with an appraisal methodology based on cost–benefit analysis and the estimation of the private benefits of avoiding flood damage. Such an approach became increasingly important for other activities, such as water quality and resource management, driven partly by the need to deliver good 'value for money'.

Given the appreciation that economic appraisal techniques appeared to offer practical contributions to a consistent process of decision-making, the NRA produced an *Economic Appraisal Manual*. It also undertook a series of strategic investigations into the practicability of using cost–benefit analysis at all levels of the organization and in all its fields of activity. This work included research on the economic value of changes to the water environment, and an ex ante evaluation of the costs and benefits of low flow alleviation.

Cost–benefit analysis and economic instruments (especially charging regimes for discharges and abstractions) were examined for their broader potential to assist decision-making. The question of valuation of environmental impacts emerged as central to many applications of economic techniques to environmental issues. With a commitment in principle to the use of cost–benefit analysis in a context of sustainable development, recent work has addressed surface water quality benefit assessment.

In terms of water-related issues, the Environment Agency has started life with a number of guidance manuals completed, and with further developments currently under way. Much of the analytical groundwork has been done, providing great scope to implement rigorous and transparent decision techniques at the functional level of managing and regulating the environment. The scope for market-based approaches to trading permits for discharges to and abstractions from controlled waters is on the agenda. What may not necessarily be readily available is adequate information on the valuation of environmental impacts, for example by using techniques of benefits transfer between different appraisals. Nor are resources likely to be sufficient to carry out project-specific valuation studies if the use of highly resource intensive techniques is required.

11.6 THE WAY FORWARD

This section reports the institutional and managerial arrangements set up to achieve the required synthesis. How the managerial objectives are specified will be a focus of interest, as the end product must be a system of appraisal which is suitable for applying to several kinds of environmental regulatory decisions.

In October 1996 the Environment Agency published an external consultation paper *Our Strategy for the Environment: an Integrated Approach to Management of the Environment*. This set out the Agency's thinking on an overall strategic plan to fulfil its vision of 'a better environment in England and Wales for present and future generations'. It contained outline strategies for the three policy directorates: Environmental Strategy, Pollution Prevention and Control (since renamed Environmental Protection) and Water Management.

This work has been taken a stage further by a document currently in draft with the working title *An Environmental Strategy for the Millenium and Beyond*. This is likely to contain proposals for dealing with the nine main areas of environmental problems, namely climate change, air quality, water resources, biodiversity, freshwater fisheries, integrated river basin management, land conservation, waste management and regulating major industries. The document will contain the Agency's undertaking to develop and use methods to assess likely costs and benefits when the choices can be clearly costed, to use multicriteria techniques when not all impacts can be costed and, where matters are complicated and views may be varied and extreme, to seek conflict resolution through consensus building. This strategic view is to be translated into the Agency's annual corporate plan.

New approaches will be considered to establish forms of option appraisal which enable the Agency to fulfil its legal and social obligations effectively, possibly combining conventional methods with other techniques such as least-cost planning or decision analysis.

A development of potentially major significance for the appraisal of environmental regulatory options is the European Council's Directive 96/61/EC of 24 September 1996 concerning Integrated Pollution Prevention and Control. Member states have until 30 October 1999 to transpose its requirements into national legislation. Some of the ways this may affect regulatory decisions are being canvassed as part of the consultation process in the UK prior to implementation, especially questions of performance standards and how they should be determined, and the basis for decisions in view of the inevitable uncertainties in comparisons of environmental costs and benefits (Department of the Environment, Transport and the Regions, The Scottish Office, Welsh Office, 1997).

Attempts at environmental valuation can potentially entail extremely large costs for operators or regulators. IPC requires that the costs of environmental analysis and appraisal are borne by the firms applying for authorizations. Such are the potential complexities of establishing substance impacts that in some cases the scientific and economic valuation costs could be completely disproportionate to the ability of regulated firms to bear them. Appraisal costs might also be judged disproportionate to the level of environmental harm, once that level and its causes were fully understood. Realism requires guarding against both excessive appraisal costs, and against operators proposing decisions on a basis of inadequate environmental information which might jeopardize urgent environmental improvements.

Two potential solutions may be explored. Firstly the Agency will have to consider providing guidelines on a hierarchy of analysis required for decisions, tailoring the requirements to the levels of concern. This approach is common in many contexts, and experience from engineering or other projects may be relevant. The issue is wider than that of organizations taking their own investment decisions, as the regulator is able to impose appraisal costs on regulated enterprises. Clearly, 'proportionality' is likely to figure in any regime. The aim will once more be to balance the safeguarding of the environment against the financial positions of regulated operators.

Where external costs are involved, any proportionality rubric would be more challenging to specify. For example, a small but highly polluting firm might *a priori* be a candidate for being required to assess further abatement options, but the appraisal costs might exceed the total value added in production, or even its turnover. Nevertheless, assessing the environmental harm could be essential to decide whether the socially preferable solution was to insist on costly abatement (which might be equivalent to closing down the plant/firm) or to allow continuing pollution. In principle we need to know the expected return on performing the appraisal, which may often be almost impossible to estimate. This suggests the need for a system which provides for professional but transparent judgements to be made about tradeoffs between resource costs and environmental impacts.

The second area may involve developing a strategic approach to project decisions. Since abatement costs are often relatively well determined, the further information needed may only be an order of magnitude valuation of the environmental benefits for comparison. If a potential abatement option is being considered, and it could be shown both that all likely environmental impacts were being assessed, and yet that no feasible contingent valuation study was likely to show environmental benefits of comparable value, then there would be a *prima facie* case for not requiring the abatement. Conversely, if preliminary information suggested that the social costs of environmental pollution were likely significantly to exceed the costs of abatement, then it might well be unnecessary to incur the costs of precise money valuation of environmental impacts in order to make a robust and consistent decision. It follows that there may be little point in undertaking costly exercises to obtain money valuations for a limited set of the environmental impacts of an option unless the information gained is really likely to facilitate a conclusive decision.

REFERENCES

British Government Panel on Sustainable Development (1996), Second Report, London.

Department of the Environment (1990) *Environmental Protection Act*, London: HMSO.

Department of the Environment (1995) *Environment Act*, London: HMSO.

Department of the Environment (1995), *Guide to Risk Assessment and Risk Management for Environmental Protection*, London: HMSO.

Department of the Environment (1996), *Indicators of Sustainable Development for the United Kingdom*, London: HMSO.

Department of the Environment, (1994), *Sustainable Development: the UK Strategy*, Cm 2426, London: HMSO.

Department of the Environment, (1994a), *Climate Change: the UK Programme*, Cm 2427, London: HMSO.

Department of the Environment, (1994b), *Biodiversity: the UK Action Plan*, Cm 2428, London: HMSO.

Department of the Environment, Ministry of Agriculture Fisheries and Food, Welsh Office (1996), *The Environment Agency and Sustainable Development*, London.

Department of the Environment, The Scottish Office, Welsh Office (1997), *The United Kingdom National Air Quality Strategy*, London: The Stationery Office.

Department of the Environment and Welsh Office (1995), *Making Waste Work: A Strategy for Sustainable Waste Management in England and Wales*, London: HMSO.

Department of the Environment and Welsh Office (1996), *Integrated Pollution Control: A Practical Guide*, London.

Department of the Environment and Welsh Office (1996a), *Water Resources and Supply: Agenda for Action*, London: HMSO.

Department of the Environment, Transport and the Regions, The Scottish Office, Welsh Office (1997), *UK Implementation of EC Directive 96/61 on Integrated Pollution Prevention and Control: Consultation Paper*, London.

Environment Agency (1996), *Our Strategy for the Environment: an Integrated Approach to Management of the Environment*, Bristol.

Environment Agency (1997), *Best Practicable Environmental Option Assessments for Integrated Pollution Control*, London: The Stationery Office.

Government Response to the Lords Select Committee *Report on Sustainable Development*, (1995), Cm 3018, London : HMSO.

HM Treasury (1997), *Appraisal and Evaluation in Central Government: Treasury Guidance*, London : The Stationery Office.

House of Lords Select Committee (1995), *Report on Sustainable Development*. HL Paper 72, London: HMSO.

National Rivers Authority (1993), *Economic Appraisal Manual*, Bristol.

Pearce, D. and I. Brisson (1995), 'BATNEEC: the Economics of Technology-Based Environmental Standards, with a UK Case Illustration', *Oxford Review of Economic Policy*, 9, (4).

Royal Commission on Environmental Pollution (1988), Twelfth Report: *Best Practicable Environmental Option*, London: HMSO.

Royal Commission on Environmental Pollution (1996), Nineteenth Report: *Sustainable Use of Soil*, Cm 3165, London: HMSO.

Silberston A. (1993), 'Economics and the Royal Commission on Environmental Pollution', February, *National Westminster Bank Quarterly Review*.

12. Combining Economics, Ecology and Philosophy: Safe Minimum Standards of Environmental Protection

Tom M. Crowards

12.1 INTRODUCTION

As the cumulative effect of human impacts on the environment increases, the likelihood that thresholds of irreversible environmental damage will be crossed becomes ever greater. In addition to difficulties involved in identifying the existence of ecological thresholds, it may be impossible to predict the exact effects of discontinuous change resulting from crossing a threshold. Perturbations to highly complex ecological systems can be associated with any number of possible outcomes. Further uncertainty derives from the possible future benefits which might be derived from environmental assets; an issue of critical importance with regard to intergenerational equity and our commitment to the well-being of future generations. Uncertainty surrounding current damage to the environment means the possibility of huge losses being imposed on future generations, either in terms of catastrophes yet to occur or by removing potentially beneficial resources. When environmental damage is irreversible we should proceed with caution.

One way of operationalizing this caution is by introducing the concept of safe minimum standards (SMS) into decision-making. This is fundamentally based on the assumption that there is absolute uncertainty surrounding the future effects of current irreversible damage to the environment. Such uncertainty is amenable neither to quantification nor to being assigned meaningful probabilities. This suggests that a quantitative economic approach, relying upon the assignment of probabilities to alternative future outcomes, is insufficient for evaluating projects which threaten to degrade the environment beyond critical threshold levels. The SMS decision rule, as envisioned by Bishop (1978) and advocated here, acts as a constraint to purely economic concerns by requiring that maximum possible future losses be kept low, unless the present costs of avoiding these possible future losses are regarded as unacceptable. Since irreversible damage is associated with absolute uncertainty, any option which threatens to push the integrity of ecological systems beyond threshold levels, will necessarily be associated with the maximum *possible* loss. The recommendation, then, is that preservation be the preferred option unless forgoing the benefits expected to derive from a development project is regarded as 'unacceptable'.

Three important issues arise with regard to implementing SMS as an aid to decision-making. First, what is meant by the 'social costs' of applying minimum standards? Second, how can a society determine when these costs represent an 'unacceptable' sacrifice for the sake of avoiding possibly huge future losses? And, third, what minimum standard can be regarded as 'safe' when confronted with such absolute uncertainty?

In analysing these issues, features of the SMS decision-making framework which make it a suitable vehicle for addressing an array of economic, ethical and ecological imperatives are highlighted. Deriving the 'social costs' of imposing a minimum standard is based on an economic efficiency criterion of comparing costs and benefits, including the benefits expected to derive from preservation of the environment. Extending the decision-making process to consider whether society regards the forfeiting of current benefits as 'unacceptable' provides an opportunity for moral and ethical concerns to be expressed and considered. And setting some 'safe' limit will be influenced by a society's attitude to risk, in assessing the likelihood that impacts will indeed be irreversible, allowing the incorporation of the precautionary principle within a systematic decision-making process.

12.2 OUTLINE OF SMS

The 'safe minimum standard of conservation' was originally introduced by Ciriacy-Wantrup (1952) as a means of explicitly incorporating uncertainty and irreversibility into the appraisal of natural resource utilization. The concept was modified by Bishop (1978) who derived a normative framework for public decision-making based on a 'minimax' strategy of minimizing maximum possible losses.

This minimax strategy is modelled in a games theory approach by Ready and Bishop, (1991). The two person game depicts society's choice either to develop or to preserve by maintaining SMS. Uncertainty derives from the future state of nature: whether events will occur, such as the outbreak of a disease, for which the preserved resource can be of use, for instance in providing a cure. A loss matrix is presented as in Table 12.1.

Table 12.1 Matrix of losses

Current Policy	Future outbreak DOES occur, for which resource is of use	Future outbreak does NOT occur	Maximum Loss
SMS	0	0	0
Develop	L – Bd	–Bd	L – Bd

Source : Ready and Bishop, 1991

In this game, the baseline (zero-loss case) outcome is taken to be where the SMS option is chosen, which is the same for both possible states of nature; whether or not a disease outbreak occurs, no loss is incurred since a cure has been retained. In comparison to this baseline case, if the development option is chosen then society would gain the benefits from that development, which represents a negative 'loss' (–Bd). However, if development is chosen and a future outbreak *does* occur, society will suffer considerable (though unpredictable) losses (L) in the absence of a cure. In order to minimize the maximum possible loss (as presented in the final column of Table 12.1), the preferred strategy will be to adopt SMS so long as the large future losses could exceed the benefits of development; that is, $L - Bd > 0$. Since the extent of the potential large future losses is by definition unknown, their maximum possible value must exceed the expected benefits of development. A rigorous minimax strategy (based on the 'insurance game', as above, but not necessarily with other formulations of the 'game'; Ready and Bishop, 1991) would therefore call for development to be rejected wherever it threatened irreversible environmental damage.

The costs of maintaining minimum standards were regarded by Ciriacy-Wantrup (1952, p. 255) as 'small absolutely and very small relatively', so the sacrifice involved in ensuring that these standards are upheld would be insignificant. On the other hand, Bishop regarded such a strict minimax criterion as overly conservative, which led him to propose a 'modified minimax principle', which recommends that SMS be adopted 'unless the social costs are unacceptably large' (Bishop, 1978, p. 13). According to this modified rule, preservation is treated as a first priority wherever irreversible damage is threatened, only to be abandoned if the benefits of development are judged sufficient to justify exposing the future to unknown but possibly substantial losses.

The 'social costs' of adopting the SMS strategy constitute the gross benefits to be derived from a development project net of the benefits of preservation expected to be lost due to environmental degradation. Whilst there is some question in the literature as to whether these social costs refer simply to the gross benefits of development forgone, it is argued in Crowards (1997a) and assumed here that they necessarily include an allowance for the quantifiable environmental benefits lost as a result of such development. The rationale for including in the analysis the loss figure, 'L', in addition to the loss of *expected* benefits of preservation, is that it represents *unquantifiable* potential losses resulting from irreversible environmental damage. These losses are unquantifiable due to the absolute uncertainty which surrounds unknown future benefits deriving from unpredictable future outcomes. They may therefore be considered as an additional category to the quantifiable benefits of preservation which can include both use and non-use values.

12.3 UNACCEPTABLE COSTS AND ETHICAL CONCERNS

Given that the social costs of imposing minimum standards of preservation could be considerable, a *modified* minimax criterion might be deemed reasonable if excessive burdens for the current generation are to be avoided. This introduces the issue of identifying what level of sacrifice for the sake of future generations is regarded by a society as 'unacceptable'. This is a socio-political decision beyond the realm of narrow economic criteria, although economic analysis may inform the process. The question is whether a society is prepared to accept current costs for the sake of avoiding potentially massive, but wholly uncertain future losses. This will depend on the ethical stance society takes towards intergenerational equity and our obligations to the future, in particular the imposition of hazards or possible irreversible losses. Thus, SMS can provide a mechanism for incorporating broader moral or ethical concerns into a decision-making process which stems from initial economic criteria.

Such an approach, applying SMS as a constraint to otherwise market-based cost–benefit analysis, is consistent with Page's (1991) two-tiered approach to achieving wider social goals such as sustainable development. Safe minimum standards form part of the first tier, which represents generalized social-interests within which the second tier can function. The second tier is based on a liberal state which allows individual preference satisfaction and the price mechanism to determine efficient allocation of resources. Hence, cost–benefit analysis and economic valuation are based on second tier conditions, the results of which are to be established and assessed within the bounds set by other social priorities in the first tier. This approach endorses economic valuation of resources to determine their relative worth to society in terms of self-interested motivations and utility maximization (perhaps including non-use benefits deriving from 'selfish altruism'; Crowards, 1997b), but provides a mechanism by which non-commensurate motivations which cannot be reduced to a substantive principle of self-interest can be formally considered within project appraisal.

There is a considerable literature critiquing neo-classical economics and in particular its reliance upon individuals acting solely as 'rational', self-interested agents. For instance, Sen (1977) has suggested that some human choices may be guided by moral commitment rather than self satisfaction, making them in some situations 'counterpreferential'. In a similar vein, Sagoff (1988) argues that individuals, as well as acting as 'consumers' as depicted by economic theory, make choices consistent with their role as 'citizens'. Thus, especially with regard to preserving attributes of the environment, individuals may exhibit truly self-less behaviour in considering a wider conception of the good of society, even if this violates personal welfare. Such motivations are derived from 'social-interest', as opposed to self-interest, and could be instilled via social norms as to what is right or wrong (Elster, 1989; Mohr, 1994). Choices associated with social-interest, based on truly self-less motivations and a greater pluralism of values, are incompatible with standard cost–benefit analysis and economic theory based ultimately on utility maximization.

SMS, based on a two-tiered system of values, represents one possible means of integrating these two apparently divergent approaches within a decision-making framework. Randall (1994) suggests such a combined decision rule may be compatible with alternative approaches to moral reasoning, including those which are consequentialist, duty-based and contractarian. The idea of a bounded efficiency criterion is illustrated in Figure 12.1, where a second tier based on underlying self-interest, satisfaction of personal preferences and maximization of utility is constrained within a first tier representing a broader range of concerns associated with social-interest. These incorporate ethical judgements such as our commitment to intergenerational equity, reflecting motivations beyond pure self-interest (perhaps in our role as 'citizens') which may derive from social or cultural norms which dictate whether or not particular actions are regarded as acceptable.

A somewhat different two-tiered system, envisioned by Norton (1995), splits decisions into those that are essentially economic, in the sense of efficiency in resource allocation, and those that deal with other considerations, such as intergenerational equity. This approach attempts to integrate economic efficiency and ethical considerations into a single decision framework. This assumes that, initially, all decisions can be boiled down into commensurate costs and benefits which can be aggregated and compared so as to guide efficient allocation of scarce resources. However, it calls for such decisions to be subject to overarching constraints based on wider social concerns such as sustainability, prudence and intergenerational equity. Rather than 'abandoning' the reduction of intertemporal environmental values to present values, such reduction is made subject to an ethical examination of the current generation's obligations to the future. In particular, when minimum standards and the integrity of ecosystems are threatened, a socio-political process needs to be initiated to consider the implications of imposing potentially huge costs upon future generations, in the context of the current benefits to be derived from these actions.

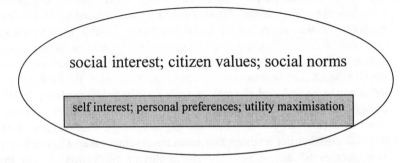

Figure 12.1 Two-tiered approach to achieving broad social goals

However, investing in intergenerational equity may require a considerable sacrifice by the current generation, in terms of losses 'in other domains of human concern' (Randall, 1988, p. 221). When poverty, disease and malnutrition (among other concerns) are still prevalent within the current generation, and often the least well-off in society bear the costs of forgone development (Holdgate, 1995; Turner and Pearce, 1990), ethical claims on behalf of as yet intangible populations and problems, should be weighed against the associated costs. Moreover, as Söderbaum (1992, p. 128) notes, with regard to the natural resource base, 'irreversible impacts are the common case rather than the exception'. Were all such impacts to be ruled out *a priori* the cost to current generations could well be enormous. Instead, a modified SMS approach accepts that economic considerations are fundamental to decision-making when resources are scarce, but acknowledges that ethical considerations beyond the realm of economics are important when considering irreversible impacts to ecological systems which provide life-support functions and maintain the economic processes.

Determining whether forgoing the current benefits of development represents an 'unacceptable' sacrifice for society represents a considerable hurdle in itself, and will be specific to project specifications, local circumstances and social priorities. As Pearce and Turner, (1990, p. 317) emphasize, the SMS approach is deliberately 'fuzzy' because it does not rely on a single criterion for making discrete choices. Assessing social (as opposed to individual) priorities might involve local community participation in the decision-making process, stakeholder groups, central government edict, international collaboration, or some combination of measures. This could require a process of public enquiry or public forum (Hodge, 1995; Perrings et al., 1995; Jacobs, 1997), explicitly considering ethical connotations and possibly promoting 'discursive ethics' to 'reach agreement on moral aspects of practical issues' (O'Hara, 1996, p. 97). There may also be social rules, expressing community or social-interest, embedded within legal or political institutions, which enable policy-makers to reflect ethical judgements on behalf of the public (Perrings et al., 1995; Toman, 1994). Any decisions will still need to consider the economic ramifications of a policy choice, but would be beyond the realm of narrow economic cost–benefit concerns. The final outcome hinges in part on perceptions of intergenerational equity, requiring an explicit assessment of the extent to which the current generation should be prepared to sacrifice present consumption for the sake of maintaining opportunities for future generations. Employing SMS would allow the second tier to determine the best use of scarce resources according to economic criteria, subject to other social imperatives enshrined within the first tier.

12.4 SAFETY AND PRECAUTION

Applying SMS as a constraint to project evaluation is a way of applying a more precautionary approach to development without stifling opportunities for economic progress and welfare enhancement. It urges an avoidance of the risks associated with irreversible losses, encouraging wherever possible the adoption of development options whose impacts upon the environment may be less permanently damaging and which remain within safe ecological limits. The SMS concept has most frequently been considered in relation to species extinction, which represents perhaps the most truly irreversible consequence of environmental degradation. However, as Hohl and Tisdell, (1993, p. 177) point out, 'there appears to be no definite ecological-biological Safe Minimum Standard for the conservation of any species either in terms of its population-size or its supply of habitat'.

Whilst policy-makers may reasonably request some estimate of the 'bottom line', as to what constitutes a viable or 'safe' minimum population to ensure species survival, 'biologists have the right and sometimes the obligation not to give an oversimplified, misleading answer to such a question' (Soule, 1987, p. 175). The complexity of ecosystems makes it impossible to predict with certainty the long-term outcome of a particular impact. Regardless of any 'added risk' due to anthropogenic disturbance, there are natural processes driven by population and environmental dynamics which provide a continuous 'background risk' of extinction (Gilpin and Soule, 1986; Burgman et al., 1993). So, while there is clearly information to be gained from implementing population viability analysis and estimating 'minimum viable populations' for species (Shaffer, 1990), in relation to ecological criteria which explicitly consider the threats to these populations (Harcourt, 1996), no minimum level of population and associated habitat can be guaranteed to remain viable in the indefinite future. Tisdell (1995, p. 222) points out, 'the SMS criterion needs further development because there may be no standard which ensures the survival of any species'. Burgman et al., (1993, p. 12) emphasize, 'we can never, whatever we do, guarantee the survival of a species for any period of time'.

As well as being unable to predict exactly (or perhaps even approximately) what the risks are of a particular species becoming extinct, there is considerable uncertainty surrounding the impacts that any such extinction might have on overall ecosystem functioning. Orians and Kunin, (1990) talk of 'ecosystem uniqueness' and the sensitivity of ecosystems to the loss, or 'deletion', of a particular species. They suggest that the removal of highly unique species may result in major population shifts and possibly extinctions in other species. This is related to the concept of 'keystone species' (Paine, 1969), although Mills et al., (1993) question this approach and advocate instead studying 'interaction strengths' to more accurately address the complexity of natural systems. Some of these ideas are reflected in what Barbier et al., (1994) term 'keystone process species' which are cornerstones of continued ecosystem functioning, and they suggest that ecosystem resilience and long-run sustainability may depend upon maintaining a wide array of species diversity. On the other hand, Moffat (1996) reports that whilst increased diversity might enhance ecosystem functioning and sustainability, it can lead to increased fluctuations in individual species populations, thereby increasing their risk of extinction.

Clearly, in addition to being faced with absolute uncertainty as to the future benefits of any given species (hence the fundamental rationale for imposing SMS), we are also confronted with the problem of predicting the effects of perturbations on highly variable and complex natural systems.

The question, then, is what degree of assurance of species or ecosystem preservation — or, conversely, what degree of risk of loss — is society prepared to accept? Or, in other words, how 'safe' should a minimum standard of preservation be?

In this regard the precautionary principle (O'Riordan and Cameron, 1994a), can be usefully incorporated. A common interpretation of the precautionary principle is clearly outlined by O'Riordan and Jordan, (1995):

> At the core of the precautionary principle is the intuitively simple idea that decision makers should act in advance of scientific certainty to protect the environment (and with it the well-being interests of future generations) from incurring harm.

On this basis, SMS criteria giving the benefit of the doubt to the preservation option (based on the interests of future generations) could be introduced without firm evidence that irreversible environmental damage will in fact ensue from a proposed development. The extent to which such precaution is applied is inevitably an 'administrative and legislative matter' (Gray, 1990, p. 174), which will reflect to some extent the degree of risk aversion present in social decision-making.

Here the difference (noted in the 1920s and 1930s) between 'risk' based on estimable probabilities, and 'uncertainty' where probabilities cannot meaningfully be applied, is relevant. Whilst natural systems might be highly complex, the physical effects of perturbations *can* be predicted. The call for a precautionary approach when assessing whether these effects will be irreversible stems partly from the fact that scientific predictions are far from infallible, but more fundamentally from whether, given an estimated probability of irreversible damage, society is willing to take such a (quantified) risk. This issue is distinct from the next stage in applying SMS which assesses whether the sacrifice required of the current generation in forgoing development is tolerable, for the sake of wholly *uncertain*, but potentially huge, future losses.

Even though thresholds which threaten species existence (or ecosystem functioning) might be accurately predicted, unconstrained market forces would inevitably push the level of impact dangerously close to such thresholds, or beyond, as Perrings and Pearce, (1994) illustrate. There is therefore a rationale for applying precaution in setting minimum standards in order to reduce the danger that anthropogenic disturbances based on private decision-making will jeopardize predicted thresholds in ecosystem attributes. A further argument for setting minimum standards with a margin of safety is to allow not only for species survival, but also for satisfying minimum future human requirements (Randall and Farmer,

1995). What is regarded as an appropriate safety margin will vary with any number of issues specific to each case, although political processes will inevitably be highly influential (Maguire et al., 1987).

Whilst we cannot ensure that any minimum standard is indeed 'safe', the precautionary principle can be applied to determine when a society regards the threat of irreversible environmental damage as sufficient to warrant explicit consideration of the potentially huge but unquantifiable future losses which could result. On the one hand, this broadens the extent to which the decision-making process based on SMS can incorporate a range of social priorities and norms. On the other hand, it provides a decision-making framework within which the precautionary principle may be operationalized. Such an approach is illustrated in the risk-benefit box of Figure 12.2.

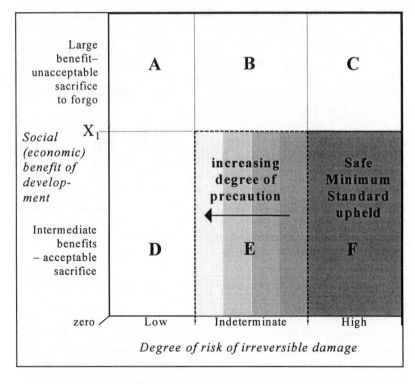

Figure 12.2 Irreversible damage, sacrifice and risk

The vertical axis of Figure 12.2 represents the net benefits that a development project is expected to generate, and since only projects that derive positive net benefits are considered, all projects in this risk–benefit box would be accepted on economic cost–benefit grounds. The horizontal axis illustrates increasing degrees of risk of irreversible environmental damage, as perceived by society, leading to the imposition of the SMS framework.

Let us suppose that, in this instance, society was willing to forgo benefits of development of up to X_1 in order to uphold ethical principles of intergenerational equity when confronted with the prospect of irreversible loss of specific environmental attributes. In this case, a society which regarded anything below a 'high' risk of irreversible damage as 'safe', would choose to reject any proposed projects falling within area F. All other projects would be accepted, either on the basis that they provide positive net benefits and a sufficiently low risk of irreversible damage, or because the benefits they provide are regarded as sufficiently high as to represent an unacceptable sacrifice for the sake of avoiding *possible* future losses following irreversible damage. A more precautionary society — one less willing to risk breaching irreversible thresholds of environmental change — might, in addition, choose to reject projects falling within area E, where an indeterminate risk of irreversible damage is judged sufficient to justify employing SMS with an initial presumption in favour of preservation.

Decisions made on the basis of a strict interpretation of the precautionary principle, perhaps according to other first-tier social priorities, might only consider the risks of damage regardless of economic concerns. Such a strict precautionary approach is likely to reject any projects falling in areas C or F, where the risk of damage is judged to be high. As increasingly risk-averse definitions of the precautionary principle are incorporated, perhaps requiring preservation unless it can be *shown* that environmental damage is limited (Johnston and Simmonds, 1990), fewer and fewer projects will be accepted (perhaps rejecting those falling within areas B, C, E and F). At the extreme, an interpretation of the precautionary principle requiring 'zero impact', would clearly reject all projects where serious environmental damage is recognised as possible.

A rather less rigid interpretation is presented in Figure 12.3. This allows for the fact that greater sacrifices might be regarded as acceptable when the risks of irreversible damage are judged to be high. Different societies will have different attitudes towards the risk of environmental damage and their obligations to future generations, which will vary also according to the particulars of projects under consideration. The shading in Figure 12.3 illustrates the case of a society which is relatively risk averse — accepting some economic sacrifice even at a 'low risk' of irreversible damage — but which is prepared to make only limited sacrifices for the sake of future generations, even where there appears to be a high likelihood of irreversible damage. The dashed line illustrates, by contrast, a society which is less risk averse, choosing to preserve only at a 'high risk' of irreversible damage, but which is prepared to make greater sacrifices of forgone development benefits for such apparently high levels of risk.

Project evaluations need to incorporate this social dimension of decision-making, acknowledging the importance of a broad range of issues, such as the benefits to be derived from development, attitudes to risk avoidance and precaution, and commitment to the well-being of future generations. In this way, policy choices can be informed by scientific evidence and best estimates of potential physical impacts, by fundamental economic considerations of personal preferences expressed through prices and markets, and by more general social concerns regarding our commitment to future generations and the degree of risk to be tolerated with respect to irreversible environmental damage.

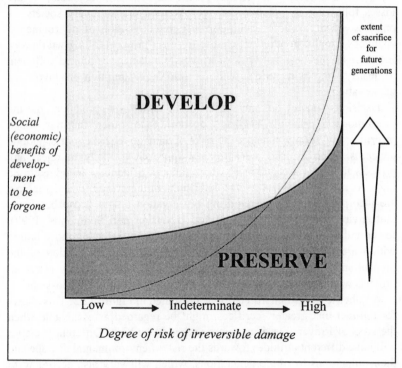

Figure 12.3   Project selection and irreversibility: combining precaution and economic sacrifice

12.5 CONCLUSIONS

The terms 'safe minimum standards' and, to a lesser extent, the 'Precautionary Principle', are being increasingly cited in the ecological and environmental economics literature as mechanisms for addressing concerns which extend beyond the realm of economic consideration. They have been related to issues such as the complex dynamics and interactions between ecological and economic systems (Perrings, 1995) and to maintaining critical natural capital (Folke et al., 1994). They are also intimately associated with moral and ethical concerns that go beyond sovereignty utilitarian values and consumer (Attfield, 1994; Bishop, 1993), where future generations, are given more weight than a mere aggregation of individual preferences of the current generation would allocate them.

In terms of the 'social costs' associated with avoiding irreversible damage, the progenitor of the concept of the 'safe minimum standard of conservation', Ciriacy-Wantrup, considered that these costs would be insubstantial. However, he explicitly examined a range of costs and benefits to justify the preservation option in a study of Elk conservation (Ciriacy-Wantrup and Phillips, 1970). Clearly, Bishop considered that there may be occasions where significant costs will be associated with avoiding irreversible environmental damage, and proposed the modification that the social costs should not be so high as to be 'unacceptable'. By incorporating an economic assessment of the forgone benefits within a framework of minimum standards, as advocated in this paper, SMS and cost–benefit analysis, rather than representing 'competing guidelines' (Wilson, 1993), can be regarded as part of a combined process which moderates recommendations formulated on economic efficiency criteria, according to other, perhaps incommensurate or directly conflicting, social priorities. In particular, the SMS approach highlights the issue of intergenerational equity in the context of uncertainty surrounding irreversible damage to the environment. The next stage is therefore to determine how such a supraeconomic decision-making process could be conducted, which, depending on the details of particular projects and their potential for environmental damage, will need to address issues ranging in scale from immediate localities to the truly global. Those involved in mediation, discussion and participation might therefore include local communities, various stakeholder groups, government bodies and international agencies or networks.

The extent to which potential impacts are to be subjected to such a two-tiered evaluation procedure depends in part upon a society's attitude towards risk, and the premium attached to 'playing safe' (O'Riordan and Cameron, 1994b). Where a more pro-active stance is taken, reflecting a greater aversion to risks of environmental damage, the threat of critical ecological thresholds being crossed will be regarded more seriously and a more generous margin of safety applied in setting minimum standards. Once again, this is a socio-political decision beyond the realm of quantitative economic analysis, resting heavily on the ability of the physical and life sciences to accurately predict the possibilities of 'non-linear phase changes' in ecological systems, and on the structure of social institutions which will interpret those predictions.

Complexity and uncertainty are inherent in the economic and ecological system with which we interact and within which decisions have to be made. We can never know for sure what might be of value in the future, nor can we predict the exact future state of complex and dynamic ecosystems. The SMS concept as developed in this paper acknowledges such uncertainty and its ethical implications in terms of our bequest to future generations. It formulates a decision rule which can address these issues as well as considering economic efficiency criteria and the trade-offs involved in realising concern for the future. By incorporating the competing claims of economic, ecological, political and ethical imperatives, it represents a practical, 'ecological economics' approach to decision-making. However, the dimensions of judgement required in an operational formulation of such an approach need to be clearly understood, and a good deal of both empirical and theoretical research is required to determine how the essential 'socio-political' processes are to be conducted.

REFERENCES

Attfield, R. (1994), 'The precautionary principle and moral values', in T. O'Riordan and J. Cameron (eds), *Interpreting the Precautionary Principle*, London: Earthscan, pp. 152–64.

Barbier, E.B., J.C. Burgess and C. Folke (1994), *Paradise Lost? The Ecological Economics of Biodiversity*, London: Earthscan.

Bishop, R.C. (1978), 'Endangered species and uncertainty. The economics of a safe minimum standard', *American Journal of Agricultural Economics*, 60, 10–18.

Bishop, R.C. (1993), 'Economic efficiency, sustainability, and biodiversity', *Ambio*, 22 (2–3), 69–73.

Burgman, M.A., S. Ferson and H.R. Akcakaya (1993), *Risk Assessment in Conservation Biology*, London: Chapman & Hall.

Ciriacy-Wantrup, S.V. (1952), *Resource Conservation: Economics and Policies*, Berkeley: University of California Press.

Ciriacy-Wantrup, S.V. and W.E. Phillips (1970), 'Conservation of the California Tule Elk: A Socioeconomic Study of a Survival Problem', *Biological Conservation*, 3 (1), 23–32.

Crowards, T.M. (forthcoming 1997a), 'Safe minimum standards: costs and opportunities', *Ecological Economics*.

Crowards, T.M. (forthcoming 1997b), 'Nonuse values and the environment: economic and ethical motivations', *Environmental Values*.

Elster, J. (1989), 'Social norms and economic theory', *Journal of Economic Perspectives*, 3 (4), 99–117.

Folke, C., M. Hammer, R. Costanza and A.-M. Jansson (1994), 'Investigating natural capital — why, what, and how?', in A.-M. Jansson, M. Hammer, C. Folke and R. Costanza (eds), *Investing in Natural Capital: The Ecological Economics Approach to Sustainability*, Washington, DC: Island Press, pp. 1–20.

Gilpin, M.E. and M.E. Soule (1986), 'Minimum viable populations: processes of species extinction', in M.E. Soule (ed.), *Conservation Biology: The Science of Scarcity and Diversity*, Sunderland: Sinauer Associates Inc., pp. 19–34.

Gray, J.S. (1990), 'Statistics and the precautionary principle', *Marine Pollution Bulletin*, 21 (4), 174–6.

Harcourt, A.H. (1996), 'Is the gorilla a threatened species? how should we judge?', *Biological Conservation*, 75 (2), 165–76.

Hodge, I. (1995), *Environmental Economics: Individual Incentives and Public Choices*, London: Macmillan Press.

Hohl, A. and C.A. Tisdell (1993), 'How useful are environmental safety standards in economics? — The example of safe minimum standards for protection of species', *Biodiversity and Conservation*, 2, 168–81.

Holdgate, M. (1995), 'How can development be sustainable?', *RSA Journal*, CXLIII (5464), 15–26.

Jacobs, M. (forthcoming 1997), 'Environmental value, deliberative democracy and public decision-making institutions', in J. Foster (ed.), *Valuing Nature? Economics, Ethics and the Environment*, London: Routledge.

Johnston, P. and M. Simmonds (1990), 'Precautionary principle', *Marine Pollution Bulletin*, 21 (4), 402.

Maguire, L.A., U.S. Seal and P.F. Brussard (1987), 'Managing critically endangered species: the sumatran rhino as a case study', in M.E. Soule (ed.), *Viable Populations for Conservation*, Cambridge: Cambridge University Press, pp. 141–58.

Mills, L.S., M.E. Soule and D.F. Doak (1993), 'The keystone-species concept in ecology and conservation', *BioScience*, 43 (4), 219–24.

Moffat, A.S. (1996), 'Biodiversity is a Boon to Ecosystems, not Species', *Science*, 271, 1497.

Mohr, E. (1994), 'Environmental norms, society, and economics', *Ecological Economics*, 9 (3), 229–39.

Norton, B.G. (1995), 'Evaluating ecosystem states: two competing paradigms', *Ecological Economics*, 14 (2), 113–27.

O'Hara, S.U. (1996), 'Discursive ethics in ecosystems valuation and environmental policy', *Ecological Economics*, 16 (2), 95–107.

O'Riordan, T. and J. Cameron (eds) (1994a), *Interpreting the Precautionary Principle*, London: Earthscan.

O'Riordan, T. and J. Cameron (1994b), 'The history and contemporary significance of the precautionary principle', in T. O'Riordan and J. Cameron (eds), *Interpreting the Precautionary Principle*, London: Earthscan, pp. 12–30.

O'Riordan, T. and A. Jordan (1995), 'The precautionary principle in contemporary environmental politics', *Environmental Values*, 4, 191–212.

Orians, G.H. and W.E. Kunin (1990), 'Ecological uniqueness and loss of species', in G.H. Orians, G.M. Brown, W.E. Kunin and J.E. Swierzbinski (eds), *The Preservation and Valuation of Biological Resources*, Seattle: University of Washington Press, pp. 146–84.

Page, T. (1991), 'Sustainability and the problem of valuation', in R. Costanza (ed.), *Ecological Economics: The Science and Management of Sustainability*, New York: Columbia University Press, pp. 58–74.

Paine, R.T. (1969), 'A note on trophic complexity and species diversity', *American Naturalist*, 103, 91–93.

Pearce, D.W. and R.K. Turner (1990), *Economics of Natural Resources and the Environment*, London: Harvester Wheatsheaf.

Perrings, C. and D.W. Pearce (1994), 'Threshold effects and incentives for the conservation of biodiversity', *Environmental and Resource Economics*, 4, 13–28.

Perrings, C. (1995), 'Ecology, economics and ecological economics', *Ambio*, 24 (1), 60–64.

Perrings et al., (1995), 'The Economic value of biodiversity', in V. H. Heywood (ed.), *Global Biodiversity Assessment*, Cambridge: Cambridge University Press for UNEP, pp. 825–914.

Randall, A. (1988), 'What mainstream economists have to say about the value of biodiversity', in E.O. Wilson (ed.), *Biodiversity*, Washington, DC: National Academy Press, pp. 217–23.

Randall, A. (1994), 'Thinking about the value of biodiversity', in K.C. Kim and R.D. Weaver (eds), *Biodiversity and Landscapes*, Cambridge: Cambridge University Press, pp. 271–285.

Randall, A. and M.C. Farmer (1995), 'Benefits, costs, and the safe minimum standard of conservation', in D.W. Bromley (ed.), *The Handbook of Environmental Economics*, Oxford: Blackwell, pp. 26–44.

Ready, R.C. and R.C. Bishop (1991), 'Endangered Species and the Safe Minimum Standard', *American Journal of Agricultural Economics*, 73, 309–311.

Sagoff, M. (1988), *The Economy of the Earth*, Cambridge: Cambridge University Press.

Sen, W.K. (1977), 'Rational fools: a critique of the behavioural foundations of economic theory', *Philosophy and Public Affairs*, 6 (4), 317–44.

Shaffer, M. (1990), 'Population Viability Analysis', *Conservation Biology*, 4, 39–40.

Söderbaum, P. (1992), 'Neoclassical and institutional approaches to development and the environment', *Ecological Economics*, 5 (2), 127–144.

Soule, M.E. (1987), 'Where do we go from here?', in M.E. Soule (ed.), *Viable Populations for Conservation*, Cambridge: Cambridge University Press, pp. 175–84.

Tisdell, C.A. (1995), 'Issues in biodiversity conservation including the role of local communities', *Environmental Conservation*, 22 (3), 216–222.

Toman, M.A. (1994), 'Economics and "sustainability": balancing trade-offs and imperatives', *Land Economics*, 70 (4), 399–413.

Turner, R.K. and D.W. Pearce (1990), *The Ethical Foundations of Sustainable Economic Development*, LEEC Paper 90–01, London: London Environmental Economics Centre.

Wilson, E.O. (1993), *The Diversity of Life*, London: Penguin.

13. Taking Non-Monetizable Impacts (NMIs) into Account in an Eco-Development Strategy

Hélène Connor

As long as the sustainability of economic development remained unquestioned, neoclassical economic theory seemed to offer a reasonably useful representation of the world for economists. When, however, it became obvious that what this traditional outlook on the world considered as 'external' was in fact 'essential' to the production of wealth and to human existence, a new model of the world and of its economic processes was required. So far, unquantifiable and therefore unmonetizable elements have been considered as too difficult or of too little significance to be studied and integrated. This paper shows that this is not true, and in this spirit it attempts a typology of these elements and identifies ways of dealing with them, using the energy sector as an example.

13.1 INTRODUCTION: WHY WE NEED TO DEAL WITH NON-MONETIZABLE IMPACTS

The acknowledgement of the need for a new style of economic development, for an 'eco-development' as defined by Ignacy Sachs, dates back to the late 1960s, but the economic profession has been slow in reacting and in operationalizing the new concept. Various attempts to better represent the world in economic analyses and methods to internalize externalities have thus appeared only lately in the mainstream of economics.

Efforts to implement Pareto efficiency in resource allocation, what O'Connor refers to as 'narrow internalization', can have only limited results as social and environmental externalities mostly defy monetization, quantification and even sometimes identification. A second set of problems is inherent to the fact that the market is not apt to lead to the enforcement of the polluter pays principle,[1] when it, itself, harbours distorsions of all kinds, only allows one signal — production prices — and therefore ignores non-monetizable goods and bads, even when a life-cycle approach is adopted.

Thirdly, internalization procedures have been confronted in the past decade with the emergence of global threats to the environment and to human survival which are fully in the realm of hence unknown impacts which would require implementation of the precautionary principle as reiterated at the 1992 Rio Earth Summit — and a different approach altogether. Over the last half of the twentieth century, human activity has come to cover the whole earth: there are more and more people everywhere and no real frontier left. Humankind seemingly has all it will ever have to play with and hoping for possible technological or resources discoveries is just that: a hope. As Herman Daly (Goodland et al., 1992) puts it: 'From empty-world economics to full-world economics: Recognizing an historical turning point in economic development'.

All the social, economic or environmental costs and benefits of development, should be considered at some point in the decision-making process. Private costs are born by the promoter, but external costs have to be taken into account, 'internalized' somehow, instead of remaining as 'externalities' imposed on parties alien to the decision, or to society at large.

So far two main approaches coexist for the valuation of external costs. The first, the avoidance method, takes into consideration the cost of pollution prevention and control, that is, antipollution devices and services (an ex ante view). The other approach, sometimes called the resources method, counts the actual cost of damages to people and to the environment (an ex post view).

The avoidance method has the advantage of showing what it costs to avoid the pollution, but the disadvantage that this amount may be more than what society thinks it is worth. The resource method has the exact opposite advantage and disadvantage; it shows what society is prepared to pay, but this may be less than the pollution costs.

These measurement procedures are also fraught with various difficulties, even for damages which are easy to identify, as they are submitted to subjective evaluation and to space and time constraints which do not fit into traditional accounting books, nor in official national statistics. Some quantification, monetization and standardization efforts are nevertheless being attempted, in particular for the external costs of the energy sector by the European Union's large Externe Project (EC 1994).

The search for life-cycle costs of various products or technologies and the gradual enforcement of the polluter pays principle (PPP) has led to the identification of externalities and to the evaluation of those costs which are the most readily quantifiable and monetizable. Such knowledge has already contributed to more enlightened policies and investments. Furthermore, some countries have established various eco-taxes[5] and charges, in particular on effluents and wastes, with the goal of raising revenues. This will contribute to changing attitudes towards the environment. There remain, however, a number of methodological and measurement difficulties to overcome before arriving at accurate and widely accepted estimates.

In the present paper, we propose to push further the investigation of damage costs through suggesting ways of taking non-monetizable impacts (NMIs) into account. Our thesis is that NMIs are more important and pervasive than many economists had supposed them to be, that their specificity deserves specific attention, and that over time they will increase in number and importance.

Before suggesting how to deal with NMIs, we will identify and define some NMIs, distinguishing between several categories, according to their degree of knowledgeability, that is, to our ability to identify and quantify them with some precision.

Then, in a second step, we will focus on the methodologies, both conventional and new, that could be used to evaluate NMIs. This effort would reinforce the application of the PP and of the PPP and, therefore, the sustainability of development.

Thirdly, we will see how the study of NMIs can help us to select energy sources and technologies appropriate for sustainable development.

13.2 WHAT ARE NON-MONETIZABLE IMPACTS (NMIS)?

NMIs are social, economic, environmental and other impacts which are theoretically identifiable at some point, now or in the future, but are neither readily quantifiable (or even apparent), nor accurately monetizable (even if an attempt to do so arbitrarily is sometimes made). The distinctions illustrated in Figure 13.1 show that amongst all externalities, some are monetized even though they are, under our definition, deemed non-monetizable (for example, human life). Once quantified, however, these externalities are considered 'internalizable', contrary to NMIs or here 'remaining external impacts'.

These NMIs are not monetizable for a variety of reasons. Some are too complex to be evaluated as there is too much uncertainty surrounding the occurrence and/or the point of impact. We still lack information and the existing data are often of dubious quality, or not consistent enough to allow comparisons.

Contrary to monetizable externalities which exhibit a fair degree of certainty and predictability and can be made to fit into a legitimate market or semi-market setting, NMIs exist because the very logic of nature is at odds with the logic of the market which, comparatively, operates in a simplistic, mechanistic and materialistic manner. Hence we contend here that NMIs are not just an extreme case of externalities, they are a separate category altogether.

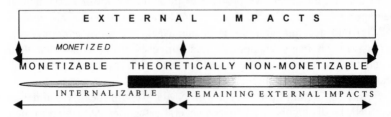

Figure 13.1 Categories of externalities

Indeed, in trying to assess these types of non-marketable impacts, we meet some irreducible obstacles to their identification and quantification as René Passet has stressed (Passet 1979; Funtowicz and Rowetz, 1994):

- the irreversibility of some damage makes it impossible for the original equilibrium to be restored even in the long term (dam reservoirs, for instance, change ecosystems and can modify local ways of life indefinitely). There is no way to assess an adequate compensation valid for all times for such costs.
- the effect of synergies between pollutants is still generally ignored and variable in different environments. Data are almost nonexistent.
- the existence of thresholds, ill-defined or totally unpredictible, can condemn entire ecosystems. Thresholds which can be defined are not transposable as every milieu has different levels of resistance and resilience. Often thresholds have a way of revealing themselves only when it is too late to preserve even the status quo.
- the phenomenon of amplification, with the build-up and concentration of pollutants along the food chain. The fact that man is at the end of this food chain make this phenomenon particularly threatening for humankind (impact on the immune system, allergies).
- other yet-to-be-discovered, understood or explained, biological mechanisms of interaction between living organisms of different species and their environment.

EXAMPLES OF NON-MONETIZABLE IMPACTS

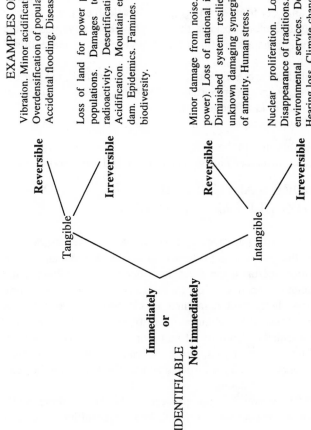

Reversible — Vibration. Minor acidification. Food shortages. Lowered quality nutrition. Overdensification of population. Overfishing and hunting. Accidental flooding. Diseases. War for security of supply. Acts of God.

Irreversible — Loss of land for power plants reservoirs and roads. Displacement of populations. Damages to historic sites. Routine pollutions and radioactivity. Desertification. Poisoning of soil and water tables. Acidification. Mountain erosion. Wrong chemical synergy. Rupture of dam. Epidemics. Famines. Resource collapse. Nuclear accident. Loss of biodiversity.

Tangible

Reversible — Minor damage from noise. Unpleasant smells. Radio interference (wind power). Loss of national independence, of intrinsic and aesthetic value. Diminished system resilience. Accidents. Environmental stress from unknown damaging synergies. Degradation of environment services. Loss of amenity. Human stress.

Irreversible — Nuclear proliferation. Loss of option value and non-use value. Disappearance of traditions. Degradation of the Global Commons. Loss of environmental services. Death of lakes. Accelerated entropy increase. Hearing loss. Climate change. Knowledge of the disappearance of species and human cultures.

Intangible

Immediately or Not immediately

IDENTIFIABLE

NOT IDENTIFIABLE

* Some of the impacts listed here may be compensable damages (i.e. monetizable impacts) via insurance schemes or premium salaries

Table 13.1 Tentative typology of non-monetizable negative external impacts of energy (NMIs) by level of knowledgeability

These NMIs need to be dealt with, prevented or compensated for, using an approach different from the traditional assessment and compensation techniques.

Finally, there are, amongst identifiable and measurable impacts that can be quantified in some way, some which can be considered as not monetizable for ethical reasons.

It is questionable, for instance, whether life or death should be deemed translatable into money terms especially in an ex ante situation, that is, before a decision[3] is taken that will possibly or almost certainly cause the loss of life. As an example, the present conflict between the Northern economists of the Intergovernmental Panel on Climate Change (IPCC) and Southern analysts[4] reveals a deep perception gap with moral overtones.

Obviously this type of ethical outcry will not stop insurance companies, nor cost–benefit analysts from quantifying the 'invaluable', but it stresses also appropriately one more obstacle this time to global governance: the impossibility of using the assumption of a homogeneous 'manageability' of spaceship Earth.

It is obvious that the more the globe becomes 'one world', the more it reveals its complexity and the importance of hitherto neglected sources of value. With increased knowledge, therefore, we can expect a further increase in the awareness of non-monetizable aspects of human and economic development.

13.3 CATEGORIES AND IDENTIFICATION OF NON-MONETIZABLE IMPACTS (NMIS)

We consider here mostly negative externalities because we assume that most, if not all, the positive impacts are somehow already taken into account in the price and/or in the investment decision that triggered the impact and cannot compensate for the negative externalities. These impacts have been listed and combined in categories as logically as possible to allow a clear differentiation of all types of NMIs ; see Table 13.1 illustrating a tentative typology of non-monetizable impacts by level of knowledgeability. Some NMIs, however, can fit into several slots according to the degree of damage inflicted and to whether or not they can be reversed to the previous state.

Let us explain now how we can proceed to categorize some NMIs according to their respective level of knowledgeability. We can distinguish first, among identifiable impacts, those which are observable immediately and appear in a way that permits us to link them directly to their cause. Others, not measurable immediately, will reveal themselves after a period of latency which can be of long duration even though the triggering event may have been very short, as a single accident. In this category of NMIs can be found several deadly diseases.

The impacts identifiable but not observable immediately may be so because not all of them are tangible, that is, physically apprehended. The intangible NMIs can be visible, like a pall of brown air on the horizon, or simply felt, like the loss of aesthetic value, the change of taste in some food or feared like the disappearance of some ethnic groups (altruistic value) or the possibility of a nuclear accident. The perception of most intangibles can be considered subjective and their valuation will differ with persons and regions.

Impacts can be reversible or irreversible, according to the type of burdens and to their strength and spread as well. Irreversibility has been classified into weak and strong forms (Birnbacher, 1994). The best example of strong irreversibility is, of course, the disappearance of species ; other cases may be the damming of rivers when it requires flooding and changes the whole watershed, turning rivers into lakes. By comparison some run-of-the-river hydroelectric dams can be installed reasonably harmlessly and removed without the same irreversible changes.

Irreversibility also occurs when a threshold of tolerance is transgressed, knowingly or unknowingly. At some point, the resource or the service provided is irreversibly damaged and no longer available. Irreversible damages are by definition impossible to compensate,[5] non-monetizable, since no amount of money can bring back the earlier state of affairs.

External costs are sometimes predictable with some accuracy when the state of environmental knowledge is adequate, that is, allowing NMIs to be known in advance and forecast. Other impacts that cannot be predicted at the moment may become known and undergo analysis, so that at a later time this improvement in the information market will make them wholly predictable.

We know very little for instance about threshold values and the degree of tolerance manifested by different milieux. It took scientists a long time to realize for instance, that radiation is cumulative and harmful even at low doses, and that various polluting substances interact in multiple ways in the atmosphere and in water tables for instance. These synergies are still poorly understood and little studied. We cannot forecast their exact impacts on human health or on the environment as these effects are sometimes counterintuitive. This is why these NMIs can be considered unpredictable and unpreventable.

Some identifiable, tangible and predictable NMIs can be recognized as insurable risks. They are the only category of impacts seen in Table 13.1 likely to ever be compensated appropriately through negotiations, even when they are irreversible. Some impacts may also be recognized as giving right to compensation on an ad hoc basis.

For policy purposes, it is useful to recast NMIs shown in Table 13.1 in terms of spatio-temporal categories. Table 13.2 reflects the categories adopted by the Externe Project and distinguishes between local, regional and global impacts according both to their time of appearance and to the span of time they are likely to last: a year or so (short term), over one or two generations (medium term) or longer (long term). This classification may help define the urgency of the threat and the level of responsibility at which it should be treated.

Table 13.2 Spatio-temporal typology of non-monetizable impacts

	Local Problems	Regional Issues	Global Threats
Short Term < 1 year	Flooding. Poisoning of wells. Destroyed harvests.	Famines. Acidification of soil. Poisoning of aquifers. Ecological refugees.	Nuclear proliferation. Climatic events. Ozone depletion.
Medium Term	Erosion. Uprooting of population. Epidemics. Forest degradation.	Destruction of habitat. War for resources. Unrest from unsustainable development. Nuclear routine and accidental releases.	Climate perturbations. Increased background radioactivity. Resource depletion. Nuclear accident.
Long Term > 100 years	Overdensification.	Desertification. Nuclear wastes disposal pollution.	Disappearance of species. Climatic change. Nuclear winter

Externalities can occur in a fairly subtle manner and only become known or noticeable when they are too serious and widespread to still be readily manageable. This is why some of the major environmental problems we have encountered so far became noticed only when they were already threatening the earth global mechanisms: acidification of soil and water, high atmosphere ozone depletion and untractable climate change.

One serious flaw to our approach to improving knowledge which may explain the way we have overlooked some early warnings also has to do with the way scientific research is structured, as has been exposed by Mark Jaccard (1992): 'Most scientists report cases in which they reject the null hypothesis at a certain level of confidence (95 per cent). However, they generally fail to apply the equally important concept of statistical power to interpreting cases where they fail to reject the null hypothesis.'

Unfortunately they are therefore more likely to reject the consideration of existing impacts than to consider possible illusory impacts. This may render research funds cost-effective in the short term, but somewhat unprepared to deal with NMIs.

In other words, our knowledge of NMIs and therefore the attention given to them by policy-makers is, in a first instance, closely dependent on the keenness of attention paid by researchers.

13.4 EVALUATION AND INTERNALIZATION OF NMIS

Since NMIs cannot be valued in any market, how can they be taken into account? The typology of Table 13.1 and the spatio-temporal delineation of Table 13.2 can help devise a framework to deal with NMIs. We can now distinguish NMIs in terms of the time and energy needed to reverse the damage, single out the broad-ranging damaging NMIs to be avoided at all costs (those which are irreversible) and the NMIs which fate and the present state of knowledge leave unpreventable.

To evaluate them at least in a qualitative manner we can distinguish two different approaches, the first one technical, building on existing measurement methods, the other one more social and institutional. As the method of internalization is likely to be closely associated with the method of evaluation, we will deal with both exercises at the same time.

Table 13.3 presents a classification of impacts on the environment, on health and safety, on the energy system, on the economy and on the political sphere. Such a matrix need not be filled with numerary or quantity indicators, but using alternative qualitative types of valuation, some of which are reviewed below. In this table, we make a distinction between the technical approach currently used for lesser impacts and the institutional approach which is definitely needed for larger or more subtle impacts and everywhere there is a possibility of conflict. In most cases, both approaches can be considered complementary.

13.4.1 The Technical Approach[6]

The methods used for the evaluation and internalization of monetizable impacts can sometimes be transposed to assess NMIs. The whole process is even more subjective than for quantifiable impacts, and therefore a consensus on internalization policies will be difficult to achieve. Nevertheless the attempt deserves to be made if, otherwise, such impacts would be occulted and therefore remain totally absent from the decision-making process.

The multicriteria analysis of costs and advantages could be used for some types of NMIs. In comparing options, NMIs can be compared also up to a point and some decision can emerge in favour of the least uncertain or of the least threatening technology, without requiring actual quantification of the impacts.

Table 13.3 Matrix for the evaluation of non-monetizable impacts

Examples of the Technical Approach: Institutional Approach					
Category of Methods	Multicriteria ACA	Acceptance Meth.	Delphi Cons.	Collabora- tive	Referendum
IMPACTS ON:					
The Economy					
Developmental					
Employment					
Growth					
Investment					
Patterns					
Trade Patterns					
The Environment					
Natural					
Ecosystems					
Cultivated Ecosyt.					
Built Environment					
Global Regulation					
Resource					
Depletion					
Health and Safety					
Occupational					
Health					
Public Health (at					
large)					
Accident					
Syndrome					
Future					
Generations					
Overdensification					
The Energy System					
Level of Tech.					
Resilience					
Senst. to Planning					
Errors					
Balance of the					
System					
The Political System					
Power Structure					
Part of Future					
Generations					

Delphi consultations, that is, getting the point of view of experts in the field of the NMI being considered, would yield useful information for action as well as on the choice of instruments to be used to deal with the problem.

There are also the threshold or acceptance methods. Once it has been established that a certain type or level of impacts leads to irreversible damages unacceptable in a certain environment, this verdict can act as a veto.

To give an example, Sørensen (1992) has developed a ranking system which does not necessarily require quantification. He has elected to list impacts one by one, rank them on a scale of acceptance, stipulating that an energy technology with one 'fundamentally unacceptable' judgement on one of its economic, environmental or social impacts would be excluded automatically from the planning process. This veto power awarded to every single type of damages allows an equitable treatment of all impacts, whether monetized or not.Another approach uses case studies to help track down some NMIs and it is used in particular to assess the impacts of energy decisions on the economy (Connor-Lajambe, 1996). Case studies can investigate all aspects of a question and signal the presence of NMIs without necessarily having the constraint of giving precise and quantified assessments. Lessons learnt in other times and places can be usefully analysed to prevent, or better manage, unwanted impacts.

Table 13.4 Dealing with non-monetizable impacts in different situations and timeframes

Type of Situation	Short-Term Policy	Medium-Term Policy	Long-Term Policy
If business as usual prevails	1. Shrink the Share of Shadow (SSS): technical approach	1 + 2. Institutional approach (that is, stakeholders' collaboratives)	1 + 2 + 3. Initiate research on identification and elimination of NMIs
If precautionary approach is needed	1. SSS + Add a precautionary premium	1 + 2. Institutional approach (i.e ; stakeholders' collaboratives)	1 +2 + 3. Define and enforce a policy (threshold) to prevent NMI's occurrence

The above-mentioned methods can contribute to shrinking the share of shadow around the NMI (the SSS approach on Table 13.4) in the short term, assuming that we are in a business-as-usual situation, that is, that the NMI is not of a threatening nature and will not trigger major changes. If it carries the potential of some threat, a precautionary premium should be included prominently in any consideration of the importance of this NMI according to the precautionary principle.

The ecological science is still young and large spans of ignorance are regularly exposed: the assessment of the likely impacts of technology should therefore also include a reasonable margin of contingency — a precautionary premium — which in extreme cases can translate into a ban.

To deal with the long-term threat, the SSS approach would require not only the measures taken to cope in the short and medium term, but also increased research funding to investigate the case. The precautionary approach would impose not just a premium, but require also the setting-up of collaborative structures and a threshold which could ban the harmful activity, as soon as it is suspected that it may have complex and far-reaching adverse repercussions.

13.4.2   The Institutional Approaches

Used alongside the SSS (technical) approach, the institutional approach calls upon refinements of the decision-making framework and has a better potential of going to the roots of the problem — which is more often than not a past decision. As mentioned earlier, NMIs appear mostly because nature and the market operate according to different rules. The market is somewhat observable, but natural phenomena are far less understood and need to be spoken for.

Since nature cannot talk and has not yet been acknowledged as a juridic entity in the way institutions and corporations have been, it is the people who benefit from her presence or from her services who can represent it for the present and for future generations (option value). These disinterested[7] persons could control the process and take decisions in a consensual manner: the way ancient tribes, remote from proprietary civilizations, deal with their own affairs. Democratic elections could bring such people to power if they cared to seek power.

Experiences in Scandinavia and North America have shown that one of the best ways to identify and deal with possible problems is to involve all stakeholders very early in the decision-making process and to keep the statu quo as a possible option. In stakeholder collaboratives, possible NMIs are brought to light and dealt with by the very people likely to be saddled with them. This approach where all interests are represented and well-informed (right of access to information and equivalent expertise) usually improves the quality and the chances of success of a decision taken by consensus. NMIs are therefore automatically internalized.

The organization and the holding of a referendum can also bypass formal quantification and deal with particularly important NMIs. Referenda have been held for instance in the past on nuclear issues in most countries using nuclear power, and now on solar planning (the Canton of Geneva's Solar Initiative in Switzerland).

Other institutional arrangements are voluntary agreements into which industrialists enter freely. They are deemed preferable to taxes and regulation. They orchestrate a simultaneous effort of all competing industries to diminish the polluting burdens they impose on the environment. Voluntary agreements are a way of internalizing externalities by trying not to create them in the first place. This formula started in Canada with the chemical industry in the mid-1980s and has been quite successful, or so it seems. It is very popular in some OECD countries where some governments tend to shy away from intervening in business activities.

To conclude on these two approaches, we should stress that both the technical and institutional approaches to dealing with NMIs remain anthropocentric and 'presentist', as we decide not only for ourselves hic et nunc, but for nature and for future generations as well even if the status quo situation prevails.

Among the various ways of dealing with NMIs, institutional solutions,[8] and in particular the setting up of collaboratives, are more commendable and logical than the justification by the traditional 'invisible hand' of the market; they represent a definite progress replicable at every level of decision-making and they have the power of enlisting government decision-makers. As an added benefit, it is an approach that can be implemented immediately or at least in the medium term and it is already operational in several countries at different levels of responsibility (principle of subsidiarity).

By improving the decision-making process, the establishment of collaboratives may also be the only way suited to internalize NMIs as it holds the potential of dealing with nature or with society on their own terms, as distinct entities, instead of trying to make them fit into the logic of the market.

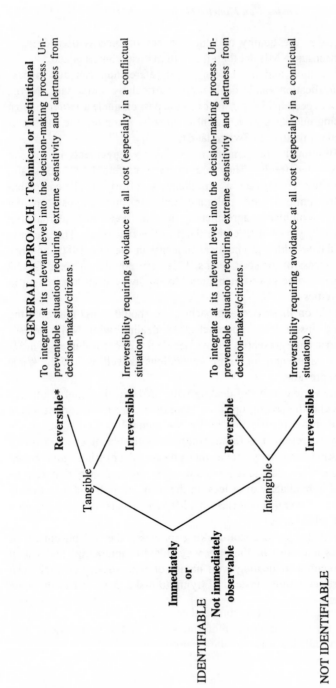

GENERAL APPROACH : Technical or Institutional

Reversible* To integrate at its relevant level into the decision-making process. Un-preventable situation requiring extreme sensitivity and alertness from decision-makers/citizens.

Irreversible Irreversibility requiring avoidance at all cost (especially in a conflictual situation).

Reversible To integrate at its relevant level into the decision-making process. Un-preventable situation requiring extreme sensitivity and alertness from decision-makers/citizens.

Irreversible Irreversibility requiring avoidance at all cost (especially in a conflictual situation).

Tangible

Intangible

Immediately
or

IDENTIFIABLE **Not immediately**
observable

NOT IDENTIFIABLE

* Some of the impacts listed in this category may be compensable damages (i.e. monetizable impacts) via insurance schemes or premium salaries.

Table 13.5 Dealing with non-monetizable negative external impacts

13.5 COUNTING ON NMIS TO TEST SUSTAINABILITY AND SELECT VIABLE TECHNOLOGIES: THE CASE OF ENERGY

Now that we have suggested how to identify and integrate NMIs into policy-making, let us see how this approach could work in real cases, for instance in the design of a sustainable energy strategy.

Energy sources and technologies damaging to the environment will remain in use for years to come, despite the increasing importance of renewable energies. Their external costs which are fairly well known are often taken care of somehow and even sometimes compensated for. Some, however, remain unidentifiable and/or unmonetizable and are listed in Table 13.5 by level of knowledgeability.

These NMIs appear in Table 13.6 by source of energy or end-use with an indication of their timescale (impacts in the short, medium or long term) and spatial range (local, regional or global) in order to introduce the policy recommendations listed in the fifth column under 'minimization of NMIs'. In some cases, the only viable decision for sustainable development is to stop the damage at the source and institute a ban. We see thus how taking NMIs into account can constitute a preliminary selection of sources and of technologies. Starting with fossil fuels, the main energy source affected by the 60–80 percent CO_2 reduction recommended by scientists, minimization of any impact would require a radical revision of our ways of managing and using energy going far beyond presently discussed improvements in energy efficiency. A ban on the burning of the most damaging fossil fuels (coal and oil) would therefore be in order.

Their past, present and future contribution to other environmental and health damage justify extreme caution. They are used intensively all over the world and most of the time are subsidised at one stage or another of their cycle. These declared or hidden government supports should have to be explicitly transferred to the implementation of appropriate renewable substitutes.

Nuclear energy has the widest array of NMIs as:

(a) its fuel cycle is particularly long and complex,
(b) it is a heavy technology requiring huge bulky installations and machinery, all damaging to the environment and most of them also emitting greenhouse gases,

TECHNOLOGY	SELECTION OF NON-MONETIZABLE IMPACTS	TIMESCALE (IMMEDIATE, MEDIUM OR LONG TERM)	SPATIAL RANGE (LOCAL, REGIONAL OR GLOBAL)	MINIMIZATION OF THESE NMIs
Power, Heating and Cooling				
Coal	Contribution to yet unknown pollution and health problems. Agent of climate change.	I – M – L	L – R – G	Elimination of 'dirty' coal uses and cleaning-up of past damages
Oil	Contribution to yet unknown pollution and health problems. Agent of climate change.	I – M – L	L – R – G	Gradual mandatory elimination and cleaning-up of past damages
Gas	Fear of gas explosions. Agent of climate change (methane leakage).	I – M – L	L	Gradual elimination. Improved training of the workforce to prevent leaks and accidents
Biomass	Long-term erosion due to monoculture.	L	L	Improved agricultural practices
Nuclear Fuel	Genetic impacts of low-level radiation. Nuclear pyschosis. Long term infilitration of wastes.	I – M – L	L – R – G	Ban on construction and mothballing existing facilities. Responsible caretaking
Mega-Hydropower	Reduced biodiversity. Ethnocides. Creation of microclimates.	I – M	L – R	Ban on construction
Mini-Hydropower	Possible modification of site.	I – M	L	Choice of benign consctruction without dams
Windmill	Possible radio interference.	I – M	L	Consultation

Table 13.6 Identification and treatment of non-monetizable environmental impacts of some energy sources and technologies

TECHNOLOGY	SELECTION OF NON-MONETIZABLE IMPACTS	TIMESCALE (IMMEDIATE, MEDIUM OR LONG TERM)	SPATIAL RANGE (LOCAL, REGIONAL OR GLOBAL)	MINIMIZATION OF THESE NMIs
Wind Farm	Possible conflictual situation.	I – M	L	Consultation
Solar Plant	Possible visual impact.	I – M	L	Consultation
Solar Photovoltaics	Possible pollution.	I	L	Retention of effluent
Heat Pump	Noise.	I	L	Distance
Transport				
Fossil-Fueled	Contribution to yet unknown pollution and health problems.	I – M – L	L – R – G	Gradual mandatory elimination and cleaning-up of past damages
Electric	Impacts to be studied where the electricity is produced.			
Biofueled	Impacts to be studied where the biofuel is produced.			
Hydrogen-Fueled	Impacts to be studied where the hydogen is produced.			
Airways	Contribution to the thinning of the ozone layer.	M – L	R – G	Limitation of air transport. Fuel substitution
Waterways	Displacement of sport and pleasure boating on river sections.	I – M – L	R – G	Limitation of goods transport
Power Transmission				
Electric Lines	Contribution to environmental and human stress.	I – M – L	L	Decentralisation of eletricity generation
Pipelines	Risks to be considered according to the terrain, the climate and politics.	I – M – L	L	
Gas Facilities	Fear of explosion at gaz facilities.	I – M – L	L	Gradual elimination of the need for such equipment. Improved training of the workforce.

Table 13.6 continued

(c) this is an unforgiving technology with the greatest uncertainties and risks (reflected in the spread of nuclear psychosis),

(d) it is so far the only technology whose proponents are so little trusted that it has had to be submitted to several national referenda.

Its impacts have an unlimited timescale by human standards and their range is all-encompassing. In countries like France its overcapacity prevents the emergence of renewable energy and this crowding-out has created a lack of diversity in the system which is itself a NMI, and could have far-reaching impacts.[9]

Dealing with such NMIs requires and justifies the creation of a number of sophisticated new institutions: collaboratives, extensive public concertation with adequate intervenor funding for counterexpertise, and taking great care in preventing the same people from being judge and party to the debate.

Massive renewable power production sites, hydro or solar, can be construed as also having non-monetized impacts, which are the costs of centralized structures generally. Their timescale can extend over one or two generations, but the impacts remain local. These can be dealt with by the fragmentation of the project in smaller units, or using different devices.

Transportation is still massively fossil-fueled and this is the major environmental problem created in this sector. In the rush to find alternatives to road transport, environmental impacts may end up being underestimated. A more intensive use of waterways in some developed and populated countries could prove disastrous. The status quo is nevertheless now unbearable in most countries, as well as in third-world megacities.

Impacts are seldom monetized to their actual costs, even in countries where gasoline is highly taxed, because nobody knows yet the final cost of climate change. At one time local, these impacts are therefore now understood as being global, with an immediate effect, that may last for a very long time.

Solutions are expected to come more from local governments struggling with everyday problems, than from national administrations, even though both will have to be attuned in order to yield tangible positive results.

Transportation of power and energy fuels is more insidious. Even though transmission lines and gas mains are part of everyday life and decor, as well as a multitude of electric devices and appliances, no one seems concerned by the level of stress created by the magnetic fields and the fluxes of negative ions. Anything invisible tends to remain unnoticed, unmeasured, non-monetized. They nevertheless contribute to the increasing amount of risks people are taking or stresses they are suffering, knowingly or not, when they benefit from technical progress.

If, however, we accept one of the apparent conclusions of the Externe Project that externalities are generally dwarfed by costs routinely included — with the exception of the impacts of global warming which the analysts decided not to include given their wide range — our main recommendations for further research on the identification and treatment of non-monetizable impacts would be:

- to refine the ways of dealing with NMIs using in particular the institutional approaches,
- to improve the understanding of the mechanisms of global externalities and in particular of climate change and its regional variations as undertaken by the Intergovernmental Panel on Climate Change (IPCC).

In the meantime, taking non-monetizable impacts of energy into account requires the measures mentioned above in order to fully respect the precautionary principle and the polluter pays principle, that is;

- a ban of nuclear energy and of any other 'unforgiving' technology,
- the speedy elimination of the burning of fossil fuels,
- the creation of institutions and other mechanisms enforcing energy efficiency policies and promoting clean and, wherever possible, renewable forms of energy.

Such measures and mechanisms should therefore be explicitly incorporated in the assumptions of sustainable development strategies. They are part of the 'price' to pay for sustainability.

13.6 CONCLUSIONS

It will be noticed from this study that NMIs constitute some of the worst and most real threats to human survival, whether it be the impacts of the thinning of the ozone layer, the rapid degradation of water sources everywhere, or global changes in climate. These impacts can usually be traced to energy use or production and they all are:

- environmental in nature, but with deep social and economic consequences as well,
- only recently 'discovered' (in the past ten to fifteen years) and 'caused' (in the last hundred years or so),

- still contested in powerful quarters,
- going to leave everybody worse off,
- ultimately non-monetizable: there is no market to buy a new climate, a new ozone layer or to compensate for the change of direction of the Gulf Stream.

Any sensible energy planner has therefore no other recourse than to adopt the institutional, proactive, strategic approach described here to deal with NMIs 'upstream', that is, 'during the early planning and design stages of the project cycle'(Goodland and Ledec, 1987), and to call upon citizens' collaboratives to:

- require the provision of improved local and global environmental knowledge,
- downsize drastically the use of unsustainable energy,
- weigh the cost of inaction in all possible domains,
- systematically foster energy and materials efficiency and develop renewable energies allowing the design and implementation of sustainable energy strategies.

This is the price of sustainability and only such practices have a chance to prevent NMIs from excessive 'damage overruns' and from one day blowing monetized impacts into oblivion.

ENDNOTES

1. The polluter pays principle (PPP) adopted in 1972 by countries of the Organization for Economic Cooperation and Development (OECD) states that the polluter should be charged for the damages created by his activities. The main objective of the generalization of the PPP was to insure fairness between countries, some having more stringent pollution regulations than others, which created a commercial handicap for their nationals compared to producers in countries without such controls.
2. None of these countries, however, are actually dedicating the product of these receipts to the restoration or the protection of the environment. Most economists will argue that earmarking is inappropriate.
3. Let us say, however, that not putting an explicit value on a 'statistical life' does not mean that value is not imposed implicitly. By building nuclear plants or road infrastructure to a certain level of safety, the governments already put a de facto value on life, even if they did not say so.
4. The willingness-to-pay methodology — 'how much people are willing to pay for a better environment — used by this group of (Northern) economists resulted in 15 lives in the poor South being equated to one life (valued at $1.5 million) in the rich North'. Quote taken from the article by Chakravarthi

Raghavan, 'Southern lives are cheaper, say climate change economists', in *Third World Resurgence*, N°64, 1996.

5. Even when successful, negotiations between the winners and the losers remain keyed to the present and do not take into account the wishes or the condition of future generations. It is also unlikely that all the losers and winners will be included.

6. Sometimes called the SSS approach as it 'Shrinks the Share of Shadow', that is, it improves the state of knowledge in a relative manner.

7. Several commentators, extrapolating arguments developed by J. Rawls, have suggested that people could decide for future generations if they themselves were 'covered by a veil of ignorance' of their own position in society. *Theory of Justice*, Harvard University Press, Cambridge, Mass, 1971.

8. As an example to better integrate policies, during its last Meeting of Environment Ministers, the Organization for Economic Cooperation and Development considered creating a consultative body made up of environmental non-governmental organizations alongside the business, industry and trade unions advisory committees, BIAC and TUAC. See also the institutional changes suggested in the OECD Progress Report on Environment–Economy Policy Integration, pp. 47–9, November 1995.

9. For instance if generic defects are detected in a system that provides an important proportion of the energy budget.

REFERENCES

Birnbacher, Dieter (1994), *La responsabilité envers les générations futures*, pp. 60–62, Presses Universitaires de France.

Connor-Lajambe, Hélène (1996), 'Societal impacts of utility overinvestment: the case of the james bay hydroelectric project', in *Utilities Policy*, 1 (1).

European Commission Directorate-General XII (1994), *Externalities of Fuel Cycles 'Externe' Project, Economic Valuation,* Volume 9.

Funtowicz, S.O. and J.R. Ravetz (1994), 'The worth of a songbird: ecological economics as a post-normal science', in *Ecological Economics*, 10, 197–207.

Goodland, Robert and George Ledec (1987), 'Neoclassical economics and principles of sustainable development', in *Ecological Modelling*, 38, 22.

Goodland, Robert, Herman Daly, Salah El Serafy and Bernd von Droste (1992), *Environmentally Sustainable Economic Development: Building on Brundtland*, UNESCO.

Jaccard, Mark (1992), 'Abatement cost and energy resource planning: revealing social preferences' in OECD/IEA (1993), *Life-cycle Analysis of Energy Systems, Methods and Experience*, Proceedings OECD/IEA Expert Workshop, 21–22 May 1992, Paris, p. 279.

OECD/IEA (1993), *Life-cycle Analysis of Energy Systems, Methods and Experience*, Proceedings OECD/IEA Expert Workshop, 21–22 May 1992, Paris.

Passet, René (1979), *L'économique et le vivant*, Paris: Petite Bibliothèque Payot.

Sørensen, Bent (1992), *What is Life-Cycle Analysis*, in OECD/IEA (1993), *Life-cycle Analysis of Energy Systems, Methods and Experience*, Proceedings OECD/IEA Expert Workshop, 21–22 May 1992, Paris, p. 49.

14. Towards an Integrated Understanding of Environmental Quality

Tim Jenkins and Peter Midmore

How much nature can humankind destroy without destroying itself? We know now that both Bates' (1961) question and the answer are more complex than then realized, but the extent of that complexity has yet to be fully appreciated. Quantitative and qualitative measurements can be made which indicate some elements of the interdependent processes involved in human–nature interaction, but there are considerable problems in combining these into an integrated understanding. Within limits an aggregate measure of manufactured capital depreciation is possible, but an analogous measure of changes in the potential economic services provided by natural resources has not been devised.

This chapter explores potential for such a measurement approach, within the emerging framework of ideas concerning sustainability. We commence with a review of relations between individual and composite biophysical indicators of environmental quality and of the mainstream understanding of the environmental processes which they can be used to monitor. We then set out a more integrated framework, examining socio-economic, ethical and pragmatic political considerations. We conclude that setting environmental quality in a social and cultural, as well as biophysical, context provides scope for a less instrumental approach towards natural resources and contributes to their more sustainable use.

14.1 ECONOMIC SUSTAINABILITY AND ENVIRONMENTAL QUALITY

All activity by humans transforms the surrounding environment. Carson (1963), Hardin (1968), and Meadows et al. (1972), now much cited as major portents of increasing public concern for ecosystem quality and its human welfare effects, suggested that economic development and environmental protection could not coexist and fostered environmentalism that advocated no-growth societies.

Comparatively recently, 'sustainability' has emerged as a key concept governing human activity (IUCN–International Union for Conservation of Nature, 1980; WCED–World Commission on Environment and Development, 1987): environmental protection is no longer seen as an obstacle to development but as an aspect which needs to be reflected in policies if development is to be sustained. The WCED's definition of sustainability ('development which meets the needs of the present without compromizing the ability of future generations to meet their own needs') was specified in the context of arguments against seeing environmental problems as separate from other aspects of human and environmental interaction.

The continuation of WCED work by UNCED–United Nations Conference on Environment and Development has resulted in commitments to a range of processes following the UNCED Rio de Janeiro intergovernmental meeting in 1992. Of these, Agenda 21 (an international action plan for achieving sustainable development) describes sustainable development in terms much wider than the conservation of natural resources. The focus is on the needs of humanity and the importance of maintaining quality of life, and a number of themes can be identified:

- an emphasis on people, communities and non-governmental organizations, encouraging a concern for individuals;
- the need to protect natural resources and fragile ecosystems — the integration of environment and development in land use planning is seen as crucial;
- an essential need to strengthen major social groups through implementation of participatory democracy;
- the means of implementation are considered in detail.

Table 14.1 incorporates some interacting issues relevant to the multifaceted concept of sustainable development. The health of economy and society is seen as dependent on the environment, and economic, social and environmental systems operate within an overall ethical perspective which is not always clearly articulated or understood. In order to examine environmental quality in an integrated way, we must consider whether the needs of society are being met as well as the long-term integrity and diversity of natural systems (Opschoor and Reijnders, 1991). We give the generic term 'sustainability analysis' to methods designed to aid decision-making in this context, and environmental indicators provide one source of baseline data for use within such methods (Dalal-Clayton, 1992).

Although sustainability has commonly been adopted as a post-Rio policy, few clear operational criteria have yet emerged as standards by which to judge the outcome of efforts to secure it. In particular, there is a need to develop practical tools that can guide the management of local resources and provide information to assess progress. Use of composite and individual indicators is explored in this chapter to determine whether the environment can be defined in a holistic way and whether an all-embracing measure of environmental quality is either desirable or feasible. The roles of socio-economic and ethical considerations are examined with the aim of identifying practical ways in which community participation can help define and manage environmental quality. Ultimately, our conclusion is that an holistic conception of environmental quality is undesirable because the perspective required is too reductionist in character. Consequently, we propose promotion of integrated understanding of environmental quality that emphasizes interconnections between processes and improves the informational basis on which decisions are taken.

Table 14.1 Sustainability: issues and dimensions

Dimensions Objects	Environmental	Economic	Socio-cultural	Ethical
Sustainability	Integrity, quality, diversity stability	Livelihood, carrying/harvest capacity	Sustainability	Futurity, eco-centrism, ideology
Resources	Land, air, water, energy, ecosystems	Use of resources. exploitation, renewables	Human resource, education, population	Enhancement, access, conservation, preservation
Community	Carrying capacity, biodiversity, natural amenities	Needs, choice, poverty, livelihood, consumption	Identity, cognition, aspirations, conflicts, empowerment	Values, equity, coexistence, trust

Source: after McKenzie, 1994

14.2 COMPOSITE INDICATORS AND THE SOCIO-ECONOMIC PERSPECTIVE

In the broadest sense, a high quality environment is one that enables human flourishing in terms of health and well-being (such is also the ultimate goal of intergenerational sustainability). It has not commonly been considered appropriate to measure human well-being directly as a basis to draw conclusions about environmental quality. Rather, it has been common to identify characteristics that make an environment high quality, and focus measurements upon those characteristics for a comprehensive assessment, taking into account a wide range of processes related in terms of time, space and scale, and which combine to form unique outcomes. Interacting factors include water and air quality, land management and use, landscape and mineral resources, natural phenomena, biodiversity, levels of waste and toxic substance accumulation, social and aesthetic conditions, population, health, economic losses and pollution controls. It has been argued (van Ierland, 1991) that the lack of an aggregate target for environmental policy, analogous to principal economic policy target variables, has led to misuse of resources, ill-informed policy decisions, and less attention to the maintenance of environmental quality.

A number of different kinds of indicator have been developed, some measuring changes in individual environmental components and others providing a composite indicator from aggregation of individual component measures. Individual indicators do not necessarily give a clear-cut message, for example, moving in different directions as economic activity increases. Shafik's (1994) international statistical comparison has demonstrated three separate kinds of effect: some indicators improve with growth of national income; others worsen; still others worsen and then improve — with turning points at different levels of GDP. Recent indicators for most industrialized nations (OECD, 1993) compiled into an index by the New Economics Foundation (NEF, 1993) reflect this disparate performance: Turkey, the poorest OECD member, has the worst waste water treatment but also the lowest carbon dioxide emissions per person.

14.2.1   Composite Indicators for Points or Localities

Most of the issues surrounding evaluation of the overall condition of a geographically specific natural resource are exposed in the construction of an environmental quality index for the Great Lakes (Steinhart et al., 1982). This was designed to provide a tool for the assessment of management efforts to protect water resources and to enhance the ability of the public to deal with the large amount of data difficult to condense into accessible information. The selection of variables for inclusion, often influenced by how easily data can be obtained, is the first and most crucial stage in the compilation of such indices: since it is not possible to measure every component of the environment, characteristic parameters are chosen. Subsequently, each variable needs to be normalized so that all are in a comparable form; a weighting scheme is necessary to reflect the relative importance of the processes which the variables represent; and the normalized weighted variables need to be combined by means of an aggregation function.

A number of criticisms at each stage of this method illustrate some of the more general problems associated with composite indicators. First, detailed scientific understanding is necessary for each process represented by an element of the index. If there is incomplete understanding of the way in which processes interact to either reinforce or offset each other's impact, elements may be chosen which, when combined, misrepresent the true depth of environmental quality changes. Second, there are problems in reducing all elements incorporated into the index to a continuous scale, and this tends to favour discrete measurable pollutants for which a safe minimum standard has been established. An alternative (Cluis et al., 1988) is to normalize around maximum and minimum values measured, but this is unsatisfactory with respect to the issue of biodiversity (a crucial component of environmental quality). Third, weighting of variables is essentially a subjective process, tending to put value decisions into the hands of technicians rather than democratically elected decision-makers.

Reaching a scientific consensus may itself be remote from the concerns of the community that has to live with environmental quality changes. Provided that the people involved are directly aware of the circumstances being evaluated, the incorporation of their views is helpful in focusing concern on the appropriate processes and variables. One difficulty lies in ensuring awareness of the potential effects of quality changes: Uusitalo (1990) suggests that public conception of the most important environmental features relates to those most recently given a high media profile. Odemerho and Chokor's (1991) index combined professional and public questionnaire ratings of the seriousness of environmental problems. But if there are significant differences, whose views should count? It is also not clear how far the relative intensity of individual preferences, as opposed to their ordering, can be incorporated.

The questions of weighting and aggregation receive considerable attention in the index number construction literature, partly because it is in these stages that value judgements can dramatically affect the outcome. The relative importance of the diverse social and ecological processes represented by individual elements in the overall index is difficult to determine in practice, especially if interactions that alter their impact occur between them — typically, such processes cannot be modelled in an entirely predictable, mechanistic way. Aggregation through summation can mask the extreme effect of one element included in the index. Kung et al. (1993) propose a fuzzy clustering method in cases where subjectivity is felt to be a problem and where the dividing line between different environmental quality classes is unclear, but it is not apparent by what standard the outcome of the process is to be judged. It merely provides a different categorization from that obtained by standard methods, and neither can be evaluated against an external, objective criterion setting overall quality (however, see Munda et al. (1995) for a description of a multicriteria evaluation model using combinations of crisp, stochastic or fuzzy measurements of performance without the need for traditional weighting of criteria).

The key issues here are that the characteristics of environmental quality are the result of diverse and complex processes, and that judgements about their respective importance and about appropriate representative indicators require both scientific and social inputs. On the one hand it is difficult to describe processes satisfactorily in a single aggregate variable; yet, on the other hand, without condensation the ability to assess management effectiveness or convey information about quality to the wider community is compromised.

14.2.2   Composite Indicators at Regional or National Level

Environmental quality at regional or national level is an even more obscure concept. Some measures are intended to inform and guide policy-making in a manner similar to macroeconomic aggregates. Indicators (such as the National Wildlife magazine's environmental index for the US) are non-quantitative, self-consciously subjective and in effect are discursive summaries of changes in key areas of the natural environment. In a more formal context, Hope and Parker, (1990) and Hope et al., (1993) have argued for and constructed a pilot environmental quality index for the UK in the 1980s which includes nine (out of a potential set of 26 identified) components, chosen on the basis of monthly data availability and on the priority accorded to problems by public perception.

There are obviously a number of problems with such measures, such as concentration on monthly availability as a major criterion for the selection of data and the use of a single set of public opinion results for weighting purposes (Bayliss and Walker, 1993). The use of an arbitrary linear progression of weights to stress concern about issues might also be questioned: why should greatly worried respondents be judged to be only 50 per cent more concerned than fairly worried ones? Such aggregation procedures allow spatial eclipsing of hotspots of poor environmental quality, in exactly the same way as aggregate GDP figures disguise variations in income and employment opportunities. Weighting by national average responses to public opinion questionnaires compounds this problem by disguising the effects of local worries about specific environmental problems.

14.2.3   An Ethical Approach to Environmental Quality

Much of the disagreement between environmentalists and others lies in the relative emphasis to be given to instrumental and intrinsic values of nature. Disregard for non-utilitarian ethics in an evaluation of economic activity leads to the environmental problem being reduced to a catalogue of unwanted impacts, lacking conceptual confrontation of the productionist paradigm which has led to them. A non-utilitarian ethical evaluation, on the other hand, suggests there is more to environmentalism than such a 'rearrangement of the furniture' and seeks to understand why unwanted impacts arise. Aldo Leopold's (1966) land ethic represents a fertile departure point for environmentalism, since its concerns about conservation cannot easily be incorporated into the optimizing calculations of economic decision-makers without placing money values on nature's importance. Leopold insisted that decisions must be ethically right as well as economically expedient. Schumacher (1974) also saw declining metaeconomic values as the reason why the economic calculus tends to take over environmental decisions.

However, ethical theories of the environment are less satisfactory at handling the environmental impact of production itself. For some (Berry, 1981; Passmore, 1974), the concept of environmental stewardship (which can be expanded beyond agriculture into a general ethical norm for society) is a solution. However, stewardship is centred around the human values of use and production, neglects wild nature, and represents a non-altruistic ethic rather than conservation for nature's own sake. As a result, most environmental philosophers follow Leopold in attributing moral status and intrinsic value to nature independent of human use.

For certain environmental ethicists, Leopold's maxim ('a thing is right when it tends to preserve the integrity, stability and beauty of the biotic community') also lies at the root of holism. The various meanings of holism suggest that an ecosystem has value in itself rather than being an instrument for the flourishing of its individual constituents. Thompson (1995) provides two instances of holism in action: Savory's concept of holistic resource management (primarily for livestock production), and Jackson's Kansas land institute: these are holistic in the sense that as nature is (sustainably) adapted to human needs, human communities in turn must adapt to their ecological environments. An holistic view of nature suggests patterns of practice that specify the operational content of Leopold's maxim and promote behaviour consistent with it, on the assumption that change in philosophical beliefs will change behaviour. Systems theory is also holistic in that it seeks to put together the pieces produced by reductionist analysis and apply the scientific method to whatever is systematic about ecosystems. However, Botkin's (1993) account of modelling forest ecosystems suggests a tension between the reference notion of ecosystems in equilibrium and the modeller's ability to predict. Systems theory may be holistic in that it portrays a complete set of discrete objects and relationships between them, within the limits of what is accessible to scientific enquiry, but the fundamental philosophical question 'what are we managing nature for?' is unanswered.

This section began by examining the need for an aggregate measure of environmental quality, a policy target strengthening the position of resource conservation measures in relation to conventional economic targets. Considerable operational problems exist in their construction, they are potentially ambiguous, they may eclipse important trade-offs and they are technocratic in character. This does not necessarily imply that indicators should not be used, rather that an appropriate suite of linked measures of aspects of environmental quality may more usefully promote integrated decision-making, involving acceptance of multiple disciplinary perspectives. In terms of the 'post-normal' perspective on science espoused by Funtowicz and Ravetz (1993, 1994), something more than traditional multidisciplinary research is required:

> This plurality of perspectives and commitments does not deny the special competence of people with special expertise ... (h)owever, it does mean that there is a mixing and blending of skills, partly technical and partly personal, so that all those engaged on an issue can enrich the comprehension of the whole. There is no sharp line dividing the 'expert' constituency from the 'lay', particularly since each expert will be 'lay' with respect to at least some of the others. (Funtowicz and Ravetz, 1994, 204.)

14.2.4   Out of the Impasse

The multifaceted nature of environmental resources and the multiple economic and non-economic linkages between them must be taken into account when assessing environmental conditions. However, the summarization which is necessary for this assessment to be taken into account by policy-makers disguises problems affecting individual processes, disregards interactions between different processes and neglects spatial variations which affect them. Numerical indicators (even those consisting of economic valuations) best describe states, although it is clear that human (as opposed to narrowly economic) environmental interaction is a dynamic, coevolving process (Norgaard, 1992), with consequences for succinct, effective communication of priorities.

One possible solution is to increase the number of useful dimensions available to convey information about environmental quality. This can be achieved through the use of AMOEBA diagrams (this Dutch acronym stands for 'a general method of ecosystem description and assessment' concerned with the biotic component of the environment), which provide comparison data in an accessible visual form (Brink, 1991). A representative range of species is selected and a reference position (for instance, the population size that would be expected in a largely unmanipulated ecosystem) is determined for each. A circle on a diagram represents the reference positions and the current population sizes are then plotted radially from the central point for each species. The diagrams can then be used to visualize the potential impacts of human activities or ecological objectives. However, while useful for relating ecosystem management to sustainable development, the tool does not allow recognition of the other environmental components needed to provide an integrated appraisal. Liu et al. (1992) offer an approach which incorporates quality of life indicators (social, environmental, health and welfare components along with traditional economic measures) into a decision support framework to portray progress or retrogression of society for environmental and natural resource management purposes. The attempt to cope with these non-market aspects of human well-being is designed to assist economic policy formation at aggregate level, but it is insufficiently detailed for integrated environmental quality evaluation.

A more powerful tool for carrying out environmental impact assessments would link complex submodels of environmental processes (Cramer et al., 1987), allowing a simplified description of processes without losing the sense of their underlying complexity nor an illustration of the occurrence and vitality of ecosystem components. This general approach of illustrating environmental quality and guiding its enhancement might best be accomplished through the use of geographic information systems (GIS) which combine spatial attributes and other information from a range of databases. A GIS, linking relational attributes to coordinates, allows several processes of environmental and human interaction to be illustrated by 'overlaying', creating a map showing coincidence in space of different types of environmental process. The technique has the advantage that it can work at any scale appropriate to the quality issue at stake, incorporating local effects of processes that also work at more general levels. It is also able powerfully and immediately to illustrate the severity of economy–environment interaction. Because of the visual character of GIS, its use could facilitate the involvement of wider communities in the process of environmental quality evaluation. GIS systems have involved communities in planning processes in the built environment (Inskip, 1987), and similar iterative interactive process could be used to empower of communities in the environmental quality context. Determining processes which affect their local natural environment and their and others' interaction with it would provide communities with information resources which lead to an enhancement of its qualitative state.

14.3 CONSTITUENTS OF ENVIRONMENTAL QUALITY

One of the major conclusions of the previous section was that, due to the complexity of processes which result in changes in environmental quality, there is a need to extend the dimensions of an integrated descriptive measure. This section explores implications of this conclusion for the way different descriptive elements are selected and analysed. The initial focus is on environmental indicators; subsequently, we consider psychological, social and community conceptions of environmental quality.

14.3.1   Environmental Indicators

The UK government has published a national strategy for sustainable development (DoE, 1993). Local authorities are expected to develop their own Local Agenda 21s, stating how they intend to meet the Rio requirements. At both national and local levels it is recognized that performance needs to be quantified and monitored. Current monitoring of the environment does not always provide the information needed to feed back into the policy-making process and is not targeted at measuring performance against the criterion of sustainability. A variety of new indicators are being developed to quantify changes, identify relevant policies for monitoring, and above all, detect environmental changes. Indicators must also be easily comprehensible, have public appeal, and be sensitive to changes in time, space, social distribution, reversibility and controllability. Important elements of environmental quality probably include ecosystems' integrity or 'naturalness', diversity and stability — features that should be quantified to determine the quality of an environment and its likely response to perturbations. Often, however, indicators do not measure environmental quality but simply attempt to quantify the environment: to use an economic analogy, indicators are generally used to express the initial stock of capital, the pressures upon that initial stock, and the results of those pressures.

Environmental indicators (Dalal-Clayton, 1992) measure the change in an environmental component over time. This involves quantification of components and changes in environmental parameters to define and describe the 'state of the environment'. Changes over time may be due either to the natural dynamics of environmental systems, or to human perturbations, policy-induced changes in behaviour, or the use of incentives or disincentives. The focus on human activities has led to the separation of environmental indicators into pressure indicators and environmental effects indicators. Pressure indicators (for example, the annual rate of deforestation) measure anthropogenic pressure on the natural environment, allowing causes of degradation to be tackled and choices in decision-making to become explicit. Environmental effects indicators (for example, threatened species as percentage of species known) measure effects of these anthropogenic pressures on specific receptors over time that cause shifts in relationships between environmental components. Development of both types of environmental indicators is occurring at international, national, regional and local levels (see OECD, 1994 for international indicators; RSPB, 1994 for a national set of Green Gauge indicators). A comparison is also provided in Table 14.2.

Table 14.2 A comparison of Green Gauge and OECD environmental indicators

Component of Environment	Green Gauge	OECD
Air	CO_2 emissions, NO_x from road traffic	CO_2 emissions, greenhouse gases, SO_2, NO_x
Soil		Use of nitrogenous fertilizers
Water	River quality, bathing water quality	Use of water resources, river quality, waste water treatment
Ecosystems	Species in decline, hedgerow loss, fish stocks, timber imports	Use of forest resources, threatened species, fish catches, trade in tropical wood
Landscape	Hedgerow loss	Land use changes, protected areas
Cultural Heritage		
Human Beings	Lost land	Waste generation, municipal waste, industrial accidents, public opinion
Climate		Stratospheric ozone

Sustainability indicators (for example, the proportion of beaches failing EU bathing water directives) are intended to show a change in the environment relative to a specified reference situation deemed sustainable. Their aim is to help orient policy-making by explicitly indicating the state of the environment in relation to environmental quality objectives usually related to emission standards, carrying capacities or critical loads. Sustainable development indicators (for instance, renewable resource use rates within renewal capacity) measure the distance to the wider goal of sustainable development, as viewed from an international and intergenerational perspective. As sustainable development is not only concerned with the natural environment but also with human quality of life, such indicators may include the degree of participation of communities in decision-making. If decisions to preserve the environment have a significant detrimental effect on other dimensions, sustainable development is not attained, so these indicators should be considered in decision-making processes alongside the more obvious indicators of environmental quality.

14.3.2   Psychological Aspects of Environmental Quality

An integrated conception of environmental quality needs to embrace not only the state of the natural environment, but also the human activity that induces changes within it. An integrated set of indicators should embrace key human–environment interfaces, and this suggests the need for a consideration of environmental quality from the viewpoint of psychological well-being. There are many different approaches in environmental psychology. Whereas stimulus–response models of investigation put emphasis on humans as agents of environmental impact or simply as biological organisms experiential perspectives develop analyses of the relationships between people and environments as a transactional connection, in which each contributes to and gains from the relationship (Gee, 1994).

Cognitive psychology involves sequential pattern recognition: we look at objects or states of affairs and assess them by considering relevant attributes, then we take account of correlation between those attributes, and finally we weight those attributes in terms of the assessment objective. An overall assessment is obtained, in effect producing a single measure based on a variety of attributes. This could (in principle) be computer-modelled, given full understanding of attributes, correlations and weightings. The problems of averaging that occur in such a process have been considered above, and some single measures may be based on a misleadingly incomplete list of attributes. Yet this cognitive psychological view is sound: the psychology of well-being with regard to the quality of the environment means the appraisal of a range of environmental attributes, the result of which forms the dimensions along which environmental quality is understood. Each aspect of environmental concern is allocated to an evaluative position on the dimensions, and the process is influenced (and possibly manipulated) by the way information is selected and disseminated through society. Concern about environmental quality involves the dimensions along which such concern is understood, the dimensions of meaning used by individuals and social groups to understand environmental issues, and the dimensions along which decisions are made about support for, or involvement in, issues of environmental concern (Hackett, 1992). Multiple dimensions are used concurrently by individuals and society to rate the importance of environmental conservation issues, and not all issues and activities are seen socially as equally important. This lends support to the ideas, outlined earlier, of extending the dimensions of analysis of environmental quality by using AMOEBA diagrams or GIS techniques to aid decision support.

The psychologists' account of environmental preferences that we develop here is two-dimensional (Knopf, 1987): evolutionary, according to which environmental preferences reflect the operation of evaluative capacities developed in the course of human evolution within the natural environment; and cultural, according to which response to the environment depends on attitudes, beliefs and values shaped by personal experience and social conditioning. Response to nature is thus a mixture of innate tendencies and learning, and this allows psychologists to replace an interactional view of human–environmental relations (concerned with impacts of discrete natural features and environments on psychological variables) with a transactional one focusing on temporal and spatial convergence of people, activities and settings and embedding experience of nature in the pattern of relationships among people, places and psychological processes. Psychology thus supports an integrated approach respecting the essential unity of organisms and their environment.

Psychology provides further insights into policy towards environmental quality. The standard policy approach is objectivist, focusing on tangible goods as carriers of utility and observable preferences as measures of utility. A psychological approach views interpreted objects and events as carriers of utility and experience of pleasure or satisfaction as the measure of utility, and sensory psychology holds that an experience depends on adaptation levels determined by exposure. This holds for pleasure and displeasure with environmental conditions: such pleasure and displeasure are qualitatively separated by a neutral value that shifts with adaptation. Any beneficial effects of improved environmental circumstances may therefore be cancelled by adaptation — people are relatively insensitive to steady states but highly sensitive to changes from neutral adaptation levels which separate positive from negative, gains from losses, and advantage from disadvantage. Part of the adaptive process involves aversion to loss — an asymmetry in response to change. The perceived value of environmental quality lost will exceed the perceived value of equivalent gains in environmental quality, as value functions attach greater weights to losses than to gains. In sum, most decision theory values options in terms of final states, and the objectivist approach of most environmental policymaking neglects adaptation, aversion to loss and relative coding of experiences (Kahneman and Varey, 1991). From a psychological viewpoint, however, gains and losses are given much more importance in subjective experience, and response to steady states is muted by adaptation.

'Pro-ecological education' (Vitouch, 1993) is another area in which policy can learn from psychology. At the epistemological level, our knowledge base develops through further understanding of evolution and ecology; at the metaphysical level, we come to see the world differently as a result of extension of knowledge; and at the ethical level, our behaviour and practices change because we see the world differently. In environmental education, causal progression through these three stages takes place, and the implication for those seeking to promote an environmental ethic is that knowledge of nature should be expanded in order to change views and behaviour. This contrasts with the practice of environmental economists who conventionally envision their task as simply becoming better at protecting particular environmental entities or heading off undesirable impacts.

There are a number of other lessons for pro-ecological education. Changes in behaviour should be promoted in a stepwise fashion to overcome comfort renunciation, perceptions of unrealism, reluctance and helplessness. Anti-hedonism should be avoided. The problem of lack of temporal contingency between behaviour and enjoyment (reinforcement) means that it must be possible to anticipate goals. Planners, for example, might model and show the public what a car-free city would actually be like. There is also a need to counter apparent conflict between economic and ecological values: this might be done by developing the concept of 'ecological prosperity' as a counterweight to conventionally-understood 'economic prosperity', reducing undesirable combinations of economic affluence and ecological squalor noted in many industrialized and industrializing economies.

This examination of ideas of evaluation of quality and of environment, from some viewpoints offered by psychology, discomforts and challenges the objective status of the perspective of natural science with its (often unstated) assumptions concerning the superiority and accuracy of the expert view. The relativism of psychology insists on environmental quality not as an objective property of the physical world but as something arising and evolving with and through human relationships with the natural environment. This need not necessarily lead to pessimism about productiveness of our enquiry into environmental quality, rather the reverse: broader understanding of human–environment coevolutionary interaction offers possibilities of influencing the trajectory of coevolutionary change and of release from behaviour locked into unsustainable patterns of environmental resource use.

14.3.3 Community Involvement in Determining Environmental Quality

Psychological analysis brings awareness of subjective and intersubjective aspects of environmental quality. An examination of the way in which individuals influence community behaviour and the environment in which it exists can contribute further understanding. Human needs are not all individual; many are satisfied through interaction with the wider community, and consequently the quality of this interaction contributes to well-being. Having a say through representative or participatory mechanisms in communities, in this light, becomes as important as expert analysis: the effort required to acquire scientific understanding, not normally diffused evenly throughout communities, becomes more worthwhile if each individual's stake is acknowledged. That, in turn, can lead to better management of natural resources and, more importantly, of the conflicts that arise from their use.

Maslow's hierarchy of human needs (Davis, 1994) illustrates varying levels of requirement for individual needs — obviously, our need for a basic minimum level of shelter and food is greater (or perhaps more immediate) than our need for self-fulfilment. Discussion of the meaning of well-being can assume that minimum standards require satisfaction of physiological and security needs, and equality should be reached in these areas as a priority. Increased opportunities (including education) should allow movement up the hierarchy, at the higher levels at which the concept of sustainable development can be appreciated. This pyramid can be extended to encompass human relations with the natural environment (Table 14.3). The lowest four environmental roles require degrees of appropriation and economic expediency to be the norm; the highest four environmental roles require increasing degrees of holistic appreciation, sensation without appropriation. Hence moral consideration takes increasing precedence over expediency.

In defining their environment and interpreting its value, local communities are ultimately defending their own well-being. Social inequality leads to environmental inequality, as it is the 'poorer' communities that have least opportunity to voice concerns (Blowers and Leroy, 1994). The primary requirement is that communities should have an understanding of the value of the network they comprise, recognizing the need for self-preservation. Developing an understanding of their environment and of the long-term implications of their actions upon it, they should then be provided with the power to influence decisions which directly affect their environment.

Table 14.3 Maslow's pyramid and human relations with the environment

Maslow category	Role of environment	Example	Demands on environment
Transcendence	temple museum	spiritual persons persons as	harmony, beauty rarity, exoticness,
Self-fulfilment		Intellectuals	antiquity
	refuge	solitary walkers	space, limited isolation
Self-respect	sportsground health & recreational resort	Climbers Tourism	wildness, obstacles comfort, limited beauty
	productive partner	organic farming	biological processes
Belonging			
Security	warehouse	mining, conventional farming	raw materials
Physiological	waste tip	polluters, consumers	absorptive capacity

On occasions, community involvement has demonstrably worked in favour of environmental improvement. In an account of transport issues in twinned cities in the UK and Germany, Vidal (1995) shows how the relative success of the latter in creating an environmentally-friendly transport system is based on very different approaches to local government and civic responsibility. In the UK traffic decisions are not made at city level and cities are legally and financially constrained to a narrow range of tasks allocated to them by central government. German cities have far greater tax autonomy, control utility companies and operate public transport networks, and they implement most national environmental standards. They make 70 per cent of Germany's environmental investments, having a direct mandate to take full environmental responsibility.

14.3.4   A Fresh Approach

The arguments examined in this section suggest that, as a result of incorporation of the ideas relating to sustainability, environmental psychology and community development into an overall conception of environmental quality, a fresh strategic approach is required for its evaluation and improvement. The most important conclusion is the need for partnership as the organizing principle of environmental quality, evaluation and improvement. The paramount importance of involvement of local communities in caring for and ameliorating their own natural surroundings can be fostered by careful management of information, advice and arbitration in the inevitable conflicts of interest which arise in heterogeneous communities. Such circumstances provide the best chances of influencing the dynamic evolutionary process that constitutes the evaluative relationships between people and ecosystems, in a way that allows maximum realization of the potential of both. Four principles follow from this:

- education and promotion of environmental awareness, to establish and support pro-ecological behaviour;
- focus on, and action in, areas that currently offer the least in terms of psychological well-being, so that when considering the impacts of development on the environment their contribution to the overall level of well-being is taken into account;
- empowerment of individuals and communities;
- development of interpretation and dissemination of environmental information.

14.4 A FRAMEWORK FOR THE MEASUREMENT OF SUSTAINABILITY

14.4.1 Sustainability Analysis

This section provides a conceptual link between principles and practice in the evaluation of environmental quality. We propose 'Sustainability Analysis', a generic term devised by Dalal-Clayton (1992) to describe methods designed to aid decision-making by consolidating information relating to durable coevolution prospects for social, economic and ecological systems. This can be applied to review the extent to which maintenance, restitution and improvement of natural environmental quality are being achieved (Figure 14.1), and it provides a framework where predictive tools may be used to determine sustainability of proposed activities. Starting with a systematic review of human activities to determine their environmental impacts, it then determines the capacity of the various natural systems involved to absorb them without long-term change. By working through this sequence and enhancing understanding of the processes involved, a certain amount of feedback will modify human activity itself. The range of analysis extends over spatial dimensions (local–regional–global) and across disciplinary domains (environmental – socio – economic – cultural – aesthetic). Sustainability analysis encompasses the use of a variety of tools, such as integrated resource management, social cost–benefit analysis and resource accounting. The systematic, flexible nature of the environmental impact assessment process, as used at project and strategic levels, makes it appropriate for use as the central tool, with others being integrated where necessary to enhance its capabilities.

14.4.2 Strategic Environmental Assessment

Strategic environmental assessment (SEA) is a powerful extension of environmental impact assessment (EIA), favoured because the project-focused nature of the latter tends to ignore broader contexts and policy backgrounds. Although SEA involves the same kind of steps as EIA, it is used to determine the impact of policies, plans and programmes which affect geographical regions or economic and social sectors as a whole. It begins with a screening process to determine whether an analysis is justified: this is normally an administrative decision, although it can be initiated as a result of external pressure. The next stage is scoping — identifying anticipated environmental impacts, direct and indirect, assessing the likely probabilities attached to each effect, and assessing the degree of significance of effects. Environmental analysis then predicts the environmental consequences of each of the alternatives. An environmental database may be set up to describe the state of the environment and provide the basis for the analysis of potential impacts.

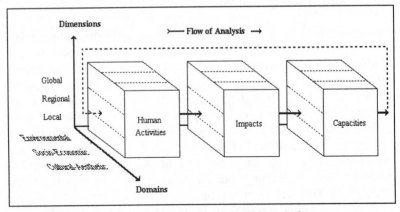

Figure 14.1 A diagrammatic view of sustainability analysis

The determination of the significance of these impacts should involve the public, as evaluation of importance is not merely a technical decision, but also involves social perceptions of environmental quality. A focus for the processes of scoping and environmental analysis is a documentary report. The review stage then exposes the assessment process to critical study, testing whether methods used are appropriate, accurate and comprehensive. As with scoping, the current tendency is not to involve the public interest at this stage, although considerable potential benefits may be lost. Post-decision analysis encompasses questions concerning the extent to which implementation occurred as envisaged, the verification of predicted environmental impacts, and the effectiveness of mitigation and control measures.

The SEA model appears to provide one potential framework for the first two and part of the third component of the sustainability analysis process, as described above. By encompassing the synergies between several different strands of human activity and relating them to different spatial scales, it deals with the first major area of concern. The second component is satisfied through the environmental analysis. The use of techniques for predicting impacts and allowing for uncertainty is well developed for project-level EIA and can be applied to this more extensive domain, though typically in less depth and detail. The first two components of the sustainability analysis process in principle allow for participation by the wider community.

14.4.3 Environmental Capacity

If SEA as currently conceived (by, for example, Therivel and Partidario, 1996) is to provide a complete framework for sustainability analysis, it must be extended to cover environmental capacity. To some extent this already occurs, as the evaluation of impact significance should require community involvement and impact significance directly relates to environmental capacity. However, the explicit consideration of capacity is currently lacking. The capacity of the natural ecosystems to absorb the impact of human activities is of fundamental concern for the maintenance and improvement of environmental quality. Consequently, consideration of it must be undertaken in the light of understanding of human activities and their environmental impacts. The notion of environmental capacities can also be consciously fed back into decision-making and activity in order to reduce its environmental impact and thereby establish a virtuous circle of improvement. Capacities could be recognized and incorporated into the environmental quality evaluation process using two separate approaches:

(1) 'Pristine' ecosystems (such as, for example, some rainforest areas), as yet only indirectly affected by human activity and thus relatively unchanged by human management, exploitation and degradation can offer high potential capacity for sustained human activity. One way of measuring such capacity could locate local environments within a spectrum ranging from complete naturalness to irreversible degradation. Earlier reference has been made to the idea of an

environmental capital stock, which provides a source of materials and services to the human community. However, environments differ widely in terms of their fragility and consequent vulnerability; conversely, there is ample evidence that renewable natural resource stocks, for example fish populations, can benefit from a certain level of exploitation. Management of the natural environment has always been a corollary of human presence; ecological change is a dynamic process, and conceptions of naturalness are bound up with human culture and its contemporary evolving perspectives.

(2) The nature of environmental capacity is bound up with the idea of safe limits or thresholds. However, apart from the fact that a focus on threshold standards distracts attention from less easily measurable qualities, there are other objections to this approach to environmental capacity. One is that progress in the understanding of biochemical interactions often leads to revisions, as new feedbacks, extending the damaging effects of impacts, are discovered. Consequently safe minimum standards do not reflect the social need for a substantially higher quality of life than these imply, since the minimum conditions under which human survival can be maintained are qualitatively different from those which are considered morally acceptable.

Neither of these approaches is adequate for the determination of environmental capacity. Both have shortcomings with relation to social and cultural dimensions, yet it is essential that these interests are expressed and incorporated into environmental quality evaluation. This is where feedback becomes important: informing and involving people in decision-making processes extends and improves the quality of institutional capacity to respond to environmental change. There seems to be no alternative to the effective decentralization of decision-making to protect and enhance environmental quality.

14.5　CONCLUSIONS

A number of different but strongly linked themes run through this chapter. The basic issue is an exploration of the ideas of sustainability, how they may be consolidated into policies, and an indication of how progress towards more sustainable human activity may be judged in terms of improved environmental quality. The idea of a single holistic measure of environmental quality, an aggregate score that can be directly compared between localities, has been rejected. Despite this, many of the reasons for attempting to construct such an aggregate measure also underlie our alternative proposal for a suite of integrated environmental indicators. It is important to assess the significance of different environmental processes that arise on different scales and interact at different levels. Equally, it is important to reduce the vast flow of information that this integration implies to a manageable level that does not disguise the complexity of the processes and their interaction.

A more sustainable society requires changes reaching parts of its institutional structure which are sometimes viewed as outside of, or peripheral to, the major issues involved. To foster and encourage an institutional culture encompassing a more integrated approach to the environment, we advocate recognition of community interaction with environmental change and a jettisoning of attitudes based on passive acceptance of expert advice in favour of interactive participation and empowerment. We also strongly support the development and use of a set of indicators to monitor changes in environmental quality at both regional and local level.

Another theme, which has frequently emerged, is of the primary importance of communities in determining the ingredients of environmental quality, and their responsibility for acting on information about it. This, currently, is the weakest link in the process of understanding environmental quality. If it were more explicitly incorporated, it should result in the development of a set of indicators, integrated from the point of view of social, economic and cultural processes as well as taking into account the natural systems with which they interact and on which they are founded.

REFERENCES

Bates, M. (1961), *Man and Nature*, London: Prentice Hall.

Bayliss, D.H. and G.P. Walker (1993), 'UK environmental index', *Energy Policy*, 21 (1), 3–4.

Berry, W. (1981), *The Gift of Good Land: Further Essays, Cultural and Agricultural*, San Francisco: North Point.

Blowers, A. and P. Leroy (1994), 'Power politics and environmental inequality: a theoretical analysis of the process of peripheralisation', *Environmental Politics*, 3 (2), 197–229.

Botkin, D.B. (1993), *Forest Dynamics: an Ecological Model*, Oxford: OUP.

Brink, B. (1991), 'The AMOEBA approach as a useful tool for establishing sustainable development', in O. Kuik and H. Verbuggen (eds), *In Search of Indicators of Sustainable Development*, Dordrecht: Kluwer Academic Publishers.

Carson, R. (1963), *Silent Spring*, London: Hamilton.

Cluis, D.A., Y. Lefebvre and C. Laberge (1988), 'An environmental index for monitoring water quality and measuring local impact factors', *Canadian Journal of Civil Engineering*, 15 (3), 323–33.

Cramer, W., E. de Greef, H. Leenhouts, D. van der Meent, T. Olsthoorn, R. Reiling and B.C.J. an Zoetman (1987), 'The use of mono- and intercompartmental methods in environmental impact assessment', paper presented to the UN Economic Commission for Europe Seminar on Environmental Impact Assessment, Warsaw, September 1987.

Dalal-Clayton, B. (1992), 'Modified EIA and indicators of sustainability: first steps towards sustainability analysis', in Proceedings of the Twelfth Annual Meeting of the International Association for Impact Assessment.

Davis, J. (1994), *Greening Business, Managing for Sustainable Development*, Oxford: Blackwell.

DoE (1993), *Sustainable Development: The UK Strategy*, London: HMSO.

Funtowicz, S.O. and J.R. Ravetz (1993), 'Science for the post-normal age', *Futures*, 25 (7), 739–55.

Funtowicz, S.O. and J.R. Ravetz (1994), 'The worth of a songbird: ecological economics as a post-normal science', *Ecological Economics*, 10 (3), 197–207.

Gee, M. (1994), 'Questioning the concept of the "user"', *Journal of Environmental Psychology*, 14 (2), 113–24.

Hackett, P.M.W. (1992), 'The understanding of environmental concern', *Social Behavior and Personality*, 20 (3), 143–48.

Hardin, G. (1968), 'The tragedy of the commons', *Science*, 162, 1243–8.

Hope, C. and J. Parker (1990), 'Environmental information for all: the need for a monthly index', *Energy Policy*, 18 (4), 312–19.

Hope, C., J. Parker and S. Peake (1993), 'A pilot environmental index for the UK in the 1980s', *Energy Policy*, 20 (4), 905–16.

Inskip, R. (1987), 'The Marigold System: a Case Study of Community Planning Networks and Community Development', Halifax, Nova Scotia: Dalhousie University School of Library and Information Studies.

International Union for the Conservation of Nature and Natural Resources (1980), *World Conservation Strategy*, Gland: IUCN.

Kahneman, D. and C. Varey (1991), 'Notes on the psychology of well-being', in J. Elster and J.E. Roemer (eds), *Interpersonal Comparisons of Well-being*, Cambridge: Cambridge University Press.

Knopf, R. (1987), 'Human behaviour, cognition and affect in the natural environment', in D. Stokols and I. Altman (eds), *Handbook of Environmental Psychology*, Vol. I, New York: Wiley.

Kung, H.T., L.G. Ying and Y.C. Lui (1993), 'Fuzzy clustering in environmental impact assessment: a complement tool to environmental quality index', *Environmental Monitoring and Assessment*, 28 (1), 1–14.

Leopold, A. ([1949] 1966), *A Sand County Almanac*, New York: Ballantine.

Liu, B.C., G.H. Tzeng and C.T. Hsieh (1992), 'Energy planning and environmental quality management', *Energy Economics*, 14 (4), 302–7.

McKenzie, S. (1994), 'Community Participatory Stewardship for Sustainability', MSc Thesis, University of Wales, Aberystwyth.

Meadows, D.H. et al. (1972), *The Limits to Growth: a Report for the Club of Rome's Project on the Predicament of Mankind*, New York: New American Library.

Munda, G., P. Nijkamp and P. Rietveld (1995), 'Qualitative multicriteria methods for fuzzy-evaluation problems — an illustration of economic–ecological evaluation', *European Journal of Operational Research*, 1995, 82 (1), 79–97.

New Economics Foundation (1993), *The Green League of Nations*, London: New Economics Foundation.

Norgaard, R.B. (1992), 'Coevolution of economy, society and environment', in P. Ekins and M. Max-Neef (eds), *Real Life Economics*, London: Routledge, pp. 76–86.

Odemerho, F.O. and B.A. Chokor (1991), 'An aggregate index of environmental quality — the example of a traditional city in Nigeria', *Applied Geography*, 11 (1), 35–58.

OECD (1993), *OECD environmental data — compendium 1993*, Paris: OECD.

OECD (1994), *Environmental Indicators*, Paris: OECD.

Opschoor, H. and L. Reijnders (1991), 'Towards sustainable development indicators', in O. Kuik and H. Verbuggen (eds), *In Search of Indicators of Sustainable Development*, Dordrecht: Kluwer Academic Publishers.

Passmore, J.A. (1974), *Man's Responsibility for Nature: Ecological Problems and Western Traditions*, New York: Scribner.

RSPB (1994), *Green Gauge*, Sandy: RSPB.

Schumacher, E.F. (1974), *Small is Beautiful*, London: Abacus.

Shafik, N. (1994), 'Economic development and environmental quality — an econometric analysis', *Oxford Economic Papers*, 46 (Supp.), 757-3.

Steinhart, C.E., L.J. Schierow and W.C. Sonzogni (1982), 'An environmental quality index for the Great Lakes', *Water Resources Bulletin*, 18 (6), 1025–31.

Therivel, R. and M.R. Partidario (1996), *The Practice of Strategic Environmental Assessment*, London: Earthscan.

Thompson, P.B. (1995), *The Spirit of the Soil. Agriculture and Environmental Ethics*, London: Routledge.

Uusitalo, L. (1990), 'Consumer preferences for environmental quality and other social goals', *Journal of Consumer Policy*, 13 (3), 231–51.

van Ierland, E.C. (1991), 'Environmental quality as a target of economic policy', *International Journal of Social Economics*, 18 (4), 14–24.

Vidal, J. (1995), 'No visions, please — we're British', *ETA Bulletin, Going Green*, 20, 6–8.

Vitouch, O. (1993), 'Environmental psychology — moving towards the principles of responsibility', *Studia Psychologia*, 35 (4–5), 343–6.

World Commission on Environment and Development (1989), *Our Common Future*, Oxford: Oxford University Press.

15. Institutional Solutions for Sustainable Management of Global Genetic Resources – A Constitutional Economics Approach

Dorothee Becker Soest and Rüdiger Wink

15.1 INTRODUCTION

Human activities on earth are changing ecosystems in many ways. One consequence of humankind's interference with ecosystems is the dramatic loss of genetic diversity (see, *inter alia*, Global Biodiversity Assessment, 1995; UNEP, 1993). Wild species, the bearers of genetic resources, are endangered by large-scale human-induced change in, or even complete loss of, their habitats. The resultant extinction of species, most of which are still unknown, is bound up with an irreversible loss of options for future use of their genetic potential. Aspects to be taken into account in the management of genetic resources are the interrelationships between genetic resources and the stabilization of ecosystem processes as well as their relevance for the satisfaction of human needs, on the one hand (Reid and Miller, 1989), and, on the other, the uncertainty and limited knowledge about cause–effect relationships and their potential reversibility in ecosystemic processes and the future substitutability of natural genetic resources. Decisions on the future management of the global gene pool must therefore be seen as major challenges facing the international community. Any society seeking to coordinate the systemic interrelationships between ecology and economy in an intergenerational context must find solutions to this problem (see, *inter alia*, Costanza, 1989).

The necessity of changing human lifestyles raises a number of critical issues concerning the appropriate contribution and methodology of economic science within an ecological–economic society. A dominant focus on mathematical and physical laws resulted for a long time in highly artificial models and deterministic visions of the optimal pathways towards the collective objective of sustainability. The complexity of social interactions between humans worldwide, whose values, habits and ideas vary enormously, was neglected in this process. A lack of concrete options for the design of practical implementation processes in the political sphere is the result. The aim in this article is to show that economic research must focus primarily on the rules governing decision-making procedures. We illustrate this argument in the context of prospects for achieving sustainable use of genetic resources within a liberal and pluralistic society. Proceeding from the basic normative assumption that values originate in individuals,[1] the analysis will centre on the decision-making process at the individual level, and assumes a bounded rationality of the individuals (Simon, 1959). The generation of constitutional rules based on liberal and pluralistic decision-making procedures is legitimized, however, by considerations of expediency (Hayek, 1960) aiming at sustainable use of genetic resources. The article therefore begins by analysing decisions on sustainable uses of genetic resources as a problem of coordination, and identifies the requirements to be met by scientific models of sustainable pathways. The second section discusses the limits of mathematical models for deriving a constructivistically determined, generally binding objective of sustainability within a pluralistic society. In the third section a constitutional economics approach based on principles of procedural justice is described, as an alternative to constructivist models. This approach is based less on a general sustainability objective but focuses more on liberal discourse and divergent individual preferences and lifeworlds within a society. The article ends with an initial application of this approach to the problem of sustainable use of wild genetic resources.

15.2 SUSTAINABLE USE OF GENETIC RESOURCES: A PROBLEM OF COORDINATION

Ecological goals enter political thinking when the scarcity of natural resources becomes apparent. Expressed in economic terms, scarcity is the result of competitive demand between humankind and nature for the global gene pool. Given the limited availability of genetic resources, coordination of the various users is needed if irreversible losses are to be prevented and, from the intertemporal perspective, if the living conditions of future generations are not to be jeopardized. As demand is not for environmental resources per se, but rather for the functions they perform in the context of specific activities (Hueting, Bosch, and de Boer, 1992), coordination should be clearly differentiated according to the specifics of the single function groups. For the global gene pool the following groups of functions can be distinguished (Pimm, 1994; Prescott-Allen and Prescott-Allen, 1986; Tisdell, 1990):

- *regulation functions*: as shown by biological studies being interrelated with the stability and resilience of ecosystems,
- *production functions*: contributing to the satisfaction of human demand for agricultural and pharmaceutical products, and
- *carrying functions*: the potential to absorb and process the material or immaterial results of human activities.

Differences between the three function groups in respect of spatial cause–effect relationships produce collectives of different size and scope, in which demands for the various function groups are coordinated. Yet, the three functions are interdependent, in that regulation functions constitute an indispensable prerequisite for the availability of production and carrying functions. Although regulation functions are only of indirect use for humans, they are affected in their functional potential by human activities. Regarding production and carrying functions, there is a growing need for international coordination because the areas of greatest genetic diversity are in tropical regions, whereas the specific industrial know-how about gene technologies and the necessary financial means are to be found in OECD member countries. The latter are therefore interested in maintaining the ecological conditions on which the availability of wild genetic resources depends.[2] Given our present limited knowledge regarding the potential future usefulness of genetic resources, it is essential to focus awareness on the intergenerational, sustainability-oriented dimension so that future generations with a greater knowledge base can keep their options open and use wild genetic resources in hitherto unknown ways (see for option valuation in general Arrow and Fisher, 1974; Fisher and Krutilla, 1974; Bishop, 1982; for an application on genetic information see Polasky and Solow, 1995).

The international and intergenerational conflict over the allocation of genetic resource functions to competing users illustrates the need for institutional action to achieve sustainable use of genetic resources. In economic terms, this global coordination problem and the concomitant high level of uncertainty calls for valuation of the benefits to be derived from conserving genetic functions compared with the related (opportunity) costs, as well as analysis of the inter and intragenerational distribution issues relevant to achieving sustainability. Three conditions must be met if the right decisions are to be implemented:[3]

- objectifiable scientific knowledge about cause–effect relationships in ecosystems, and about technical and traditional know-how and

Valuation and the Environment

    research activities concerning the use or substitution of genetic resources;
- normative judgements regarding the degree of confidence in scientific statements; general risk attitudes; intra- and intergenerational values; the future availability of genetic information; and
- concrete action to protect genetic resources for the future.

In Figure 15.1 these necessary steps to realize uses of genetic information compatible with sustainability-oriented objectives are illustrated.

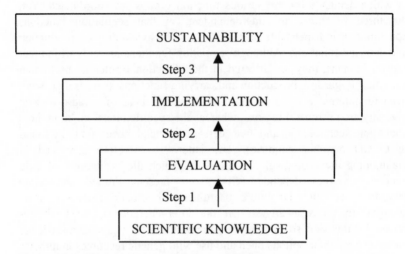

Figure 15.1 Three steps towards sustainability

However objective scientific data may be, the sheer variety of scientific paradigms and the permanent growth of human knowledge generate a high level of uncertainty concerning the actual need for protection over time and the available options for coping with the risks of genetic resource loss (Faucheux and Froger, 1995). Because of this uncertainty, normative decisions have to be made regarding the acceptability of scientific results and the implications for protective action. There is great variation in values due to the international, individual and intergenerational differences in sociocultural, economic and personal backgrounds. Even if the need for protective measures is accepted, the final step, namely practical implementation, will depend on the specific conditions operating in each single case. Neglecting these factors may lead to opposition in the regions affected.

In light of the basic assumption of methodological individualism, this brief look at the necessary conditions for sustainability-oriented decisions underscores the indispensability of integrating information available only at the individual level. Taking these aspects into consideration, it would thus be the task of an institutional framework for social coordination to promote the expression of individual preferences and the exchange of information, and to provide incentives for generating, disseminating and applying knowledge. The solutions to the allocation problem provided by certain models will be examined in the following section.

15.3 THE 'FATAL' CONCLUSIONS FROM DETERMINISTIC MODELS

Scientific literature based on the neo-classical *economics of renewable resources* provides several approaches which use mathematical models to determine pathways to the sustainable management of genetic resources[4] (see for example Wilen, 1985). If one examines the methods applied in these models with respect to the coordination problem described in the previous section, one can identify a certain misunderstanding on the role of scientific advice in designing institutional frameworks. This misunderstanding produces 'fatal' consequences (in the sense of Hayek, 1988), endangering rather than promoting sustainable pathways. The main problems associated with deterministic models are that they:

- neglect the need for incentives to disseminate existing and develop new (scientific and technical) knowledge;
- concentrate on valuation assumptions without providing solutions to the corresponding conflicts within pluralistic societies; and
- place excessive demands on political systems seeking to attain constructivistically determined and generally binding social goals.

Two categories of deterministic models can be distinguished in this context. The first is directed at maximizing profits from a specific resource (Hartwick and Olewiler, 1986), with possible correctives in the form of risk deductions or surcharges. The results depend, among other factors, on the assumed time preference rate (Williams, 1978; Boehm-Bawerk, 1961). The second category, based on principles of ecological economics, rejects the assumption of positive time preference rates and stresses the need to consider intrinsic values as well as irreversible effects on ecosystems without monetarizing (Page, 1977; Sen, 1992; Callicott, 1986). To ensure sustainable availability of genetic resources, demands are formulated to ensure the conservation of genetic diversity (Gowdy and

McDaniel, 1995) or to implement safe minimum standards (Ciriacy-Wantrup, 1971; Bishop, 1978).

Despite differences between the models, some common methodological aspects prevail. Both model worlds take the required information as exogenous. They analyse neither the processes leading to the development of knowledge, nor the valuation processes within individuals that result in specific preference schemes. The research focus is on calculating the results of implementation. Implementation itself is seen as a mechanistic process in which politicians use socially advantageous instruments and individuals adapt to political guidelines in a 'predestined' way.

This lack of focus on the development and use of knowledge means the necessary scientific discourse and the ensuing competition between competing paradigms, ideas and recommendations are neglected. On the contrary, the exogenous introduction of normative values — for example, concerning risk acceptance, time preference, or the substitutability of genetic resources — degrades scientific debate to ideological conflicts rather than scientifically objectifiable disputes.

If one analyses the steps actually taken to achieve the objectives derived from these deterministic models, it can be seen that the mechanistic approach towards formulating guidelines for individual behaviour involves an elitist pretension of knowledge by particular societal groups, on the one hand, and lack of attention to the problems caused by political processes, on the other. Given the variety and complexity of interactive social processes, what is needed is openness towards individual lifeworlds and decentralized communication structures in order to ensure that the peculiar features of specific cases are taken into account in policy decisions. Deterministic models lack this openness and therefore run the risk of neglecting a variety of individual solutions to social problems. Furthermore, they will not only induce individuals to find ways to circumvent the centralistically formulated guidelines, but also harbour the risk of suppressing the wide-ranging research activities on technical, organizational or social problems (see O'Hara, 1996, on discursive ethics), which might otherwise produce the requisite future-oriented innovations.

In addition to these aspects, it is necessary to study political processes and their influence on practical results. Politicians, as individuals pursuing individual rational aims, direct their activities towards maintaining or increasing their sphere of influence and power. Since they depend on support to implement centralist regulations and policies, they will accept the cooperation and influence of effectively organized lobbies (see for example Olson, 1982). As the support of these groups can only be expected in return for obvious benefits, politicians have incentives to orient their programmes towards objectives which will produce at least short-term benefits for specific interest groups. The integration of intergenerational aspects into concrete policymaking, however, is unlikely given the difficulties of organizing intergenerational interests effectively. An analogous argument may be put forward for the official representatives of interest groups, who also follow the interests of their most influential members. Therefore, it must be assumed that instructing interest groups and politicians to strive for sustainability and to take action to attain such objectives will lead to ongoing distributional conflicts within society, and an imbalanced capacity for well-organized societal groups to achieve their aims at the expense of groups that are difficult to organize. It is doubtful whether such a strategy can lead to sustainability. Moreover, it implies abandoning the principle of equal opportunity on the part of all members of society to attain their individual goals in life, as well as the intergenerational advantages of a permanent and pluralistic discovery process.

Constitutional economics provides an alternative to such excessive focus on concrete objectives. In this field, the task of economists is not to produce models for maximization and optimization, but to create procedures for resolving the social conflicts arising from differing value orientations and competing interests in connection with scarce resources (Buchanan, 1975a; Barry, 1973).

15.4   A SKETCH OF THE CONSTITUTIONAL ECONOMICS APPROACH

The remarks in the preceding section indicate firstly, why determining specific quantitative goals relating to sustainable use of wild genetic resources on the basis of model theory will not lead to objectifiable social objectives, and secondly, the problems involved in implementing the resultant policies. In contrast to these modelling approaches, we elaborate a twin line of argument by stressing the following:

- the importance of constitutional rules for achieving procedural justice rather than defining an 'equitable', that is, sustainable, allocation of resources; and
- the recognition that these constitutional rules require a liberal and pluralistic society in order to conform to the requirements of sustainability objectives.

The constitutional economics approach proceeds from the observation that, due to the multifariousness of specific living conditions, values and technical knowledge, individual concepts of sustainability will differ too greatly to permit a generally accepted quantitative goal. Constitutional economics implies switching the focus of research to the analysis of how different life concepts within a society can be coordinated in a way that each participant will accept the result of the interactive process. The outcome is liable to be accepted when the participants assess the rules of the decision-making procedure to be just. Justice, therefore, does not refer to the results themselves, but to the procedural rules instead (Buchanan, 1975b; Rawls, 1971; Barry, 1973). The achievement of sustainability implies an integration of efficiency and distributional aspects in an intergenerational context. On this basis, the research programme of constitutional economics focuses on general, abstract, future-oriented and equally binding rules which are accepted as leading to efficiency and distributional objectives. This approach does not aim at answering the question as to the specific details of a sustainability-oriented objective, because the composition of the latter will depend on the preferences of the individuals involved. Therefore, objectives are expressed in concrete terms only at the level of the individual, whereas at the social level it is only possible to predict in outline what the outcome of the coordination process will be.

Different approaches can be distinguished within constitutional economics. The main differences concern the way in which constitutional rules are developed. Whereas some researchers, such as Buchanan, Rawls and Barry, focus on the legitimation of a social contract on the basis of individual calculations, Hayek and Nozick concentrate primarily on evolutionary processes leading to permanently developed spontaneous orders (Hayek, 1973; Nozick, 1974). Despite the differences, the strong emphasis on liberal concepts can be seen as a common theme (see, *inter alia*, Hayek, 1960; Rawls, 1993). Liberal constitutions are not taken to be the 'pseudo-liberal democracies' in Western countries (for critiques, see Hayek, 1979; Brennan and Buchanan, 1985), which are characterized by a strong bias in favour of successful pressure groups within society (see also Dryzek, 1994; Demirovic, 1994). Liberal constitutions in this context are defined through subjective freedom of action limited only by the freedom of others (Mill, 1859/1969), which is attained by guaranteeing basic individual options to decide and act freely. This freedom may not be seen as a value for itself but serves to achieve three goals that are essential for sustainability:

- to identify the wealth of individual knowledge pertaining to potential uses of genetic resources;
- to provide scope for generating procedural rules enabling coordination between conflicting normative conclusions concerning the sustainable use of genetic resources; and

- to overcome the dominant problem of political implementation by instituting competitive procedures that produce incentives in support of individual creativity and which increase willingness to adopt new technologies.

The characterizing features of the liberal constitutional approach can only be understood in terms of a complete openness of the social process by which sustainability objectives are identified. In contrast, other (guided) constitutional approaches use constitutional frameworks to realize pre-given societal principles, such as dematerialization of the economy or minimization of human interventions into ecosystems. Accordingly, these approaches proceed from collective normative evaluations, developed from discursive proceedings that may be dominated by opinion leaders. The resulting guidelines are used to influence the search process for scientific knowledge as well as to reeducate people towards socially beneficial behaviour using 'market' instruments. Liberal concepts, however, do not contain any concrete sustainability objective. They are oriented towards rules for social processes where everyone has the opportunity as well as incentives to reveal his or her knowledge, values and abilities, and to make available as much information as possible about science, norms and implementation options. Table 15.1 illustrates the differences between the deterministic and constitutional approaches.

Table 15.1 Comparison of different approaches to sustainability

	Scientific knowledge	Normative values	Implementation
Deterministic approach	Exogenous assumptions	Exogenous assumptions	Mechanistic processes, based on political decisions
Guided constitutional approach	Search process according to societal guidelines	Collective values, developed in discursive procedures	Reeducation of individuals by economic incentives
Liberal constitutional approach	Competition of ideas, diffusion channels and adoptions	Individual values, coordinated through procedural justice	Decentral competitive procedures

According to this aim, liberal constitutions correspond to a preference for market forces and competition as social coordination procedures. This does not imply a naive expression of market philosophy, but refers to the larger potential of market processes accompanied by constitutional rules as a means to achieve sustainability, compared to other types of social coordination procedures (see for example Becker Soest and Wink, 1994). The advantages of market processes relate to the use and creation of information — scientific knowledge as well as information on implementation options — and openness towards diverging normative values of distributional justice. Due to the highly efficient processing of information via the price mechanism and the incentives of pioneer gains associated with a monopolistic position as a result of product or process innovation, market processes are efficient in both a static and dynamic perspective. They thus lead to a constant increase in knowledge within a society, a crucial prerequisite for coping with forthcoming challenges.

Furthermore, any anonymous information that results in a willingness to pay can be integrated.[5] This ensures an equal consideration of individual interests and counteracts the risk of societal discourse being biased by the particular power of well organized pressure groups and their representatives (see Habermas, 1981, on ideal discursive processes). Therefore, a variety of individual value judgements and knowledge can be considered, which would otherwise overtax the potential of a central coordination process and perhaps engender an impression in affected regions that a goal is being presented and imposed in an 'imperialist' fashion.

Within liberal systems, the task of the legislature is to formulate, within the constitutional framework, a set of general and abstract rules that permit future predictability. These rules will indicate to the individual whether, by exercising individual freedom without paying any compensation via market processes, he or she is limiting the rights of others. Confining the need for political decisions to the formulation of abstract constitutional rules will reduce the costs for organizing decision-making procedures and implementing regulations. Current examples showing that a coordination of interests on private markets is possible are provided by contracts between private companies, especially from the chemical industry, and countries with high genetic diversity, or by efforts to enforce intellectual property rights in the field of genetic knowledge (for examples see Simpson, 1992; Coughlin, 1993).

The orientation towards individual coordination — mainly through market processes — is often criticized for failing to consider that the interests of future generations are not taken into account when determining market prices and that individuals are dominated in their negotiations by short-term perspectives. From this point of view, a sustainable management of scarce resources would therefore have to be induced by a political correction of market results, for example through taxes on resources, or by a ban on the depletion of certain resources. The point of view informing this opinion can be contrasted with two qualifying remarks:

- The failure to give full consideration to future scarcity in current prices for resources is mainly a consequence of strong political forces in the countries of origin, where state-run companies are instruments to serve short-term fiscal interests.
- The lack of consideration given by individuals to future concerns is partly a result of uncertainty within the political framework. Whereas at the private level people in all parts of the world try to make provisions for the future, at the level of larger collectives individual action is dominated by the risk that this action, for example restraint in using resources, may be counteracted by the action of other members of the collective and therefore would not be rational. This fear is enforced by the short-term perspective of political measures, often connected with a strategic, rent-shifting management of scarce resources, which may not be compatible with sustainability-oriented allocation (see in detail Brennan and Buchanan, 1985).

The advantages derived from private coordination on markets reaches its limits when individual property rights can be neither defined nor allocated. This aspect is especially relevant for the regulation functions of genetic diversity, where a collective decision concerning the protection of regulation functions is necessary, and a requirement for subsequent coordination of all competing intergenerational interests in any of the interrelated functions. This implies a need to add procedural rules to a market constitution. These rules would support market processes and therefore have to comprise the three steps towards sustainability already mentioned.

Collective coordination decisions concerning ecosystem functions must address the question as to the acceptable level — from a human point of view — of pressure and pollution on ecosystems. Production and carrying functions can be allocated on private markets because the incentives induced by market procedures will produce a stronger orientation towards economic efficiency and the consideration of intergenerational challenges than political procedures will do. Whether or not the potential of market procedures can be fully developed depends on whether or not the need for global coordination of regulation functions is met.

In the following, implications of the constitutional economics approach for the concrete problem of sustainable management of global genetic resources will be outlined.

15.5 STEPS TOWARDS A CONSTITUTIONAL CONCEPT FOR SUSTAINABLE MANAGEMENT OF THE GLOBAL GENE POOL

The management of global genetic resources has already been the object of several international treaties. By presenting the shortcomings of existing regulations, the aim of this chapter is to analyse how to implement internationally accepted constitutional rules which safeguard the potential role of liberal concepts in achieving sustainability. The key impetus in this context is the realization that, in keeping with the specific problems involved in developing generally accepted constitutional rules within a social contract, the main focus must now be turned to evolutionary processes, firstly within single countries, but also aiming at the establishment of liberal procedural rules at the global level. These rules must assure openness to different lifeworlds and to new ideas and incentives by which individuals can express and adopt sustainability principles.

A major criticism of existing agreements like the 'Convention on Biological Diversity' is that they lack instruments for asserting and enforcing their objectives against national interests (for a critical discussion see Stähler, 1994; Swanson, 1994). Conflicts stem from the contrary interests of prosperous countries, on the one hand, and countries with high genetic diversity, on the other. Existing negotiation procedures for global conventions fail to resolve this conflict; instead, they circumvent it by allocating to single countries the authority to implement strategies for the conservation of genetic information. Despite the need for binding rules governing the use of globally relevant regulation functions such that the interests of *all* users worldwide as well as future generations are taken into account, existing allocation mechanisms lead to conservation measures based on the costs and benefits of only *one* country in each case.

When applying the principles of constitutional economics to tackle the shortcomings of existing regulations, it is important that the objective of an institutional process is not seen in quantitative terms, for example as the number of areas that need protecting in order to conserve wild genetic information. Needed instead are procedural rules accepted by all affected parties on the basis of intra- and intergenerational fairness and the general economic and ecological advantages they offer. It is then necessary to create a competitive framework within the scope of these rules. This framework must provide incentives for *creating* and communicating scientific and technical knowledge, through competitive structures based on quality of argumentation, equitous integration of divergent normative decision patterns by securing equal access to decision-making procedures within society, and decentralized processes to implement protective measures that also respond to the specific circumstances involved.

Affected parties require clear prospects of economic and environmental benefits before they are likely to accept liberal constitutional rules. All participants can gain from cooperation if companies in the EU and other OECD member states are given access to 'wild' genetic resources, enabling them to make use of the options they provide for their part. Compensation for opportunity costs could be offered to countries with high genetic diversity, as well as further benefits from exchanging and developing knowledge about more efficient conservation measures. The readiness of countries to participate in effective international regimes could be boosted by linking single issues (for a game theory interpretation and analysis, see Folmer et al., 1993). Regulations leading to a protection of natural habitats as well as to implementing individual rights for the exclusive use of genetic information by certain — foreign — companies in countries with high genetic diversity may be reached if these agreements are linked to other incentives such as trade benefits or support in capacity building, for example education and research relating to genetic resources. Protection of genetic information can be effected by negotiating 'package deals' involving different extents to which human use of protected areas is prohibited or waived. The higher the degree of protection and/or the expected value of the available genetic information, the higher the compensation for the receiving country will be. Achieving sustainable use of globally relevant genetic information will therefore depend on the rules governing this negotiation procedure.

There are no short-term prospects of sustainability-oriented rules being implemented through a global convention. Despite the possible gains from cooperative behaviour in the negotiation processes, the costs of implementing effective, economically efficient and sustainable rules might exceed the potential benefits. Key factors determining the level of these costs are

- the intensity of political interest on the part of OECD countries in using genetic resources,
- the initiation of negotiations in which all participant parties are willing to reach a compromise by cutting back on their initial demands, and
- sustained and dependable implementation of these rules.

The roles played by political representatives in international negotiations are primarily shaped by the consequences of potential agreements for their personal aims, and are therefore intimately bound up with the need to support the specific interests of powerful pressure groups. Given, first, that the immediate benefits to be derived from protecting genetic resources are rather uncertain ; second that some interested parties have already signed private contracts in certain countries with high genetic diversity ; and third, that further negotiations might possibly involve concessions in certain economic fields that will be difficult for OECD politicians especially to justify *vis-à-vis* their voters,[6] it is unlikely that politicians in institutional negotiation processes will assume a more active role. Within the population, major deficits of information concerning the relevance of genetic resources are evident; this means in effect that only a very small percentage of voters would support the requisite political efforts, especially if these policy recommendations require moderation of individual lifeworlds or consumption patterns (see, *inter alia*, Spash and Hanley, 1995). In this context, scientific publications and environmental pressure groups at local and international level have an important task to create a public awareness of the values inherent in genetic resources.

The initiation of negotiation processes, within which each of the parties will cut back their initial demands to reach a generally favourable compromise, is impeded because many countries are involved, and because a 'wait and see' attitude prevails, with each of the parties delaying action until other parties take the initiative. Coalitions between different nations with common interests as well as bilateral solutions between countries which are strongly interested in quick results, or which can fall back on already existing bilateral rules, might speed up the process (for treatment of this aspect from a game theory perspective, see Barrett, 1992; Carraro and Siniscalco, 1992). Unilateral actions by one country in the form of self-binding contracts, for example the offer of non-conditional preferential regulations in trade for countries with high genetic diversity, might accelerate the process of finding compromises, but due to the high risk of other countries not cooperating, this solution may also produce the reverse effect (Hoel, 1991).

The likelihood of global agreements being reached can be improved by linking controversial issues. However, the greater the complexity of negotiation packages, the higher the risk that some of the parties involved will try to circumvent less favourable regulations. In order to sanction such infringements, instruments for controlling and disciplining non-cooperating parties are necessary. This question poses problems insofar as only few, economically strong countries have the potential to impose sanctions, thus engendering unfavourable structures of dependence (Becker Soest and Wink, 1994).

It seems clear as far as these problems are concerned that effective global agreements can be achieved only after protracted negotiations and at high cost to the participants. As costs might then exceed any benefit of the agreements, there are two possible outcomes. First, participants might refuse to participate in negotiation processes. Second, agreements might be found which do not require complex negotiations because the sovereignty of the single countries is not really affected. But — as with existing agreements — these contracts are generally without effective consequences and therefore do not contribute to the achievement of sustainability. Economically advantageous results might not be realized as a result.

Two problems arise in connection with the effects of global agreements on incentives for individuals to achieve a dynamic growth of knowledge. First, protracted negotiations and 'wait and see' tactics often block single initiatives to exchange scientific and institutional knowledge. The uncertainty about the stability of regulations and the expectation of stronger support from the political sphere in future might lead to a deferment of investments involving high risks. Second, international agreements often involve subsidies for private investments, favouring certain economic sectors, research projects, and so on. This implies formulating a certain direction that has to be taken into consideration when developing new knowledge. As the generation and application of successful new ideas depends to a critical extent on the existence of a broad range of diverse thinking, any concrete formulation of directions for research and development will cause loss of information for the future.

In order to create sustainability-oriented institutions at the global level, this development must be based from a constitutional economics perspective on several steps, leading only in the final analysis to a globally accepted constitutional framework for surmounting the realization and incentive problems just mentioned. The focus must first be directed to the motivational patterns of individuals and their actions, because these are the sources for the necessary information, and only with the help of their awareness and creativity can institutional changes for all three steps be achieved. The realization of individual freedom and equal capacity to act according to self-defined long-term objectives are a precondition for any evolutionary process, starting from decentralized networks, initiating demands for scientific and technological information, gained by fair competition, as well as a discussion about how to deal with divergent normative concepts, and leading, ultimately, to liberal constitutional rules on the global plane.

Accordingly, it is necessary to investigate why people use resources without regard for the implications this has for future generations. In many cases, economic pressures — due in many cases to increasing population — and political failure can be identified as central causes, for example when regarding the strongly politically influenced world food market and its consequences for subsistence farmers in tropical countries.

Many proposals call for strict standards for realizing certain lifestyles and production techniques, for example 'sustainable' agricultural methods (see, *inter alia*, WBGU, 1995) or limitations on population growth (Ehrlich and Ehrlich 1970), especially in countries with a high share of — partially unidentified — genetic resources. However, we would argue that institutional measures which primarily serve to alleviate the pressures and which are geared to flexible capacity-building will pave the way for individuals to develop adaptation pathways to the challenges of natural scarcity, which due to the possibility of original thoughts will create more knowledge about genetic resources than central standards. Corresponding measures refer in particular to an educational and social framework in which NGOs might play a key role. They could facilitate future-oriented family planning, for example, or enforce the implementation of a reliable institutional framework in which agreements between local farmers and companies interested in the availability of wild genetic resources will be developed. The framework strives to offer preconditions for the individuals to develop individual plans for using natural resources in a way that enables their values of sustainability to be satisfied. This may lead, for example, to the establishment of local networks for managing natural resources on a collective basis, or to complex bargaining processes between companies and local authorities or private organizations on the use of wild genetic information.

OECD countries could provide incentives to enforce institutional developments by offering preferential trade conditions or research cooperation to the respective countries during the adaptation process. Furthermore, future institutional developments aiming at sustainability, for example within the EU, will be most important because they might serve as models for the evolutionary change of institutional structures, leaving more space for an individual and self-responsible orientation towards the future. These changes could involve:

- the elaboration of measures in the field of liability, such as for users of genetic material;
- a renunciation of support for specific activities, for example, agricultural practices using genetically uniform crop plants;
- support for creative exchange between research and organizational processes by means of intellectual property and competition laws; and
- a review of the existing tax system, taking into account its consequences for the individual and social provision for the future.

15.6 FINAL REMARKS — THE ECOLOGICAL–
ECONOMIC SOCIETY AS AN OPEN SOCIETY

The aim of this article was to consider how sustainability objectives can be pursued within an ecological–economic society. Global genetic resources were taken as an example in order to analyse the different aspects of institutionally coordinating competing demands on natural resources. This task is characterized by a high degree of uncertainty about future developments and by globally and inter-individually differing preferences about the protection of genetic resources. By distinguishing mechanistic from constitutional approaches, the focus of the analysis was shifted from quantitative management objectives towards the social procedures leading to decisions on the use of resources. From procedural justice principles the idea of rules was derived that induce individuals to act in such a way that socially desired objectives are achieved. The objective of the constitutional approach is to make use of individual knowledge and creativity as comprehensively as possible by creating a liberal and open community, where the freedom of the individual is given priority as long as it does not limit the freedom of others. The challenges of uncertainty and complexity of social and ecological processes in an intergenerational context show the limits of human possibilities to determine concrete sustainability aims and lifestyles, and the necessity for open social structures that induce permanent research and discovery of new techniques and rules. This openness leads to less certainty when formulating concrete visions of social processes, lifestyles and economic production techniques. It requires time to achieve the step-by-step evolution of a corresponding framework, leading in turn to undetermined societal development based on the preferences of the individuals. Yet, threats which are not acceptable for society according to its own rules can be eliminated. Thus, an ecological–economic society will be developed which actively faces the challenge of sustainability by implementing structures incrementally adapted to new information and through individuals who are eager to learn.

ENDNOTES

1. For more details on the methodological individualism debate see, *inter alia*, Brennan and Buchanan, (1985). See Fisk, (1975) for a more critical analysis, and Vanberg (1975) for a description of the collectivist approach.
2. Due to the importance of evolutionary pressure, information derived from wild genetic resources cannot be substituted by genetic information from gene banks, botanical or zoological gardens.

3. See Popper (1984) on the distinction between 'three worlds' — physical subjects, subjective consciousness, and man-made interactive theories.
4. Sweeney (1993) views endangered species, and their function as bearers of genetic information, as non-renewable resources. A detailed discussion of certain models will be of less interest in the following than a general evaluation of the usefulness of theoretical models for deriving political policies, so models of non-renewable resources will not be explicitly examined.
5. Criticism is based on the contention that certain value components — for example intrinsic values of genetic resources — are not reflected in market prices because the related preferences are not revealed and a willingness to pay is not formulated, thus leading to 'distorted' demand and supply structures. These criticisms can be refuted by pointing out that market mechanisms will lead to less 'distorted' results once a corresponding framework enforcing a revelation of preferences is implemented. A possible alternative, the consideration of option and existence values within coordination processes by political decisions, might lead to worse biases than market processes due to the dependency of political measures on the influence of well-organized pressure groups.
6. An example would be the liberalization of trade rules in the field of agriculture in a way that puts pressure on prices for agricultural products in OECD countries.

REFERENCES

Arrow, K.J. and A.C. Fisher (1974), 'Environmental preservation. Uncertainty and irreversibility', *Quarterly Journal of Economics*, 88, 312–19.
Barrett, S. (1992), 'International environmental agreements as games', in R. Pethig (ed.), *Conflicts and Cooperation in Managing Environmental Resources*, Berlin et al.: Springer, pp. 11–37.
Barry, B.M. (1973), *The Liberal Theory of Justice*, Oxford: Clarendon Press.
Becker Soest, D. and R. Wink (1994), *Vision und Wirklichkeit des globalen Bodenschutzes. Effizienzorientierte institutionelle Ansätze auf marktwirtschaftskonformem Boden*, Bochum: mimeo.
Bishop, R.C. (1978), 'Endangered species and uncertainty: the economics of a safe minimum standard', *Journal of Agricultural Economics*, 68, 10–18.
Bishop, R.C. (1982), 'Option value. An exposition and extension', *Land Economics*, 58, 1–15.
Boehm-Bawerk, E.V. (1961), *Positive Theorie des Kapitales*, Meisenheim: Anton Hain.
Brennan, G. and J.M. Buchanan (1985), *The Reason of Rules. Constitutional Political Economy*, Cambridge, Mass: Cambridge University Press.
Buchanan, J.M. (1975a), 'A Contractarian paradigm for applying economic theory', *American Economic Review*, 65, 225–30.
Buchanan, J.M. (1975b), *The Limits of Liberty*, Chicago: University of Chicago Press.

Callicott, J.B. (1986), 'On the intrinsic value of nonhuman species', in B.G. Norton (ed.), *The Preservation of Species. The Value of Biological Diversity*, Princeton: Princeton University Press, pp. 138–72.

Carraro, C. and Siniscalco (1992), 'The international dimension of environmental policy', *European Economic Review*, 36, 379–93.

Ciriacy-Wantrup, S.V. (1971), 'The economics of environmental policy', *Land Economics*, 47, 36–45.

Costanza, R. (1989), 'What is ecological economics?', *Ecological Economics*, 1, 1–7.

Coughlin, M.D. (1993), 'Using the Merck-INBio agreement to clarify the convention on biological diversity', *Columbia Journal of Transnational Law*, 31, 337.

Demirovic, A. (1994), 'Ecological crisis and the future of democracy', in M. O'Connor (ed.), *Is Capitalism Sustainable?: Political Economy and the Politics of Ecology*, New York: Guilford Press, pp. 253–74.

Dryzek, J.S. (1994), 'Ecology and discursive democracy: beyond liberal capitalism and the administrative state', in M. O'Connor (ed.), *Is Capitalism Sustainable?: Political Economy and the Politics of Ecology*, New York: Guilford Press, pp. 176–97.

Ehrlich, P.R. and A.H. Ehrlich (1970), *Population, Resources, Environment: Issues in Human Ecology*, San Francisco: Freeman.

Faucheux, S. and G. Froger (1995), 'Decision-making under environmental uncertainty', *Ecological Economics*, 15, 29–42.

Fisher, A.C. and J.V. Krutilla (1974), 'Valuing long run ecological consequences and irreversibilities', *Journal of Environmental Economics and Management*, 1, 96–108.

Fisk, M. (1975), 'History and reason in rawls' moral theory', in N. Daniels (ed.), *Reading Rawls*, Oxford: Basil Blackwell.

Folmer, H., P.V. Mouche and S. Ragland (1993), 'Interconnected games and international environmental problems', *Environmental and Resource Economics*, 3, 313–27.

Global Biodiversity Assessment (1995), published for the United Nations Environment Programme, Cambridge: Cambridge University Press.

Gowdy, J.M. and C.N. McDaniel (1995), 'One world, one experiment: addressing the biodiversity-economics conflict', *Ecological Economics*, 15, 181–92.

Habermas, J. (1981), *Theorie des kommunikativen Handelns*, Frankfurt: Suhrkamp.

Hartwick, J.M. and N.D. Olewiler (1986), *The Economics of Natural Resource Use*, New York et al.: Harper & Row.

Hayek, F.A.V. (1960), *The Constitution of Freedom*, London: Routledge & Kegan Paul.

Hayek, F.A.V. (1973), *Law, Legislation and Liberty, Vol. 1: Rules and Order*, London: Routledge & Kegan Paul.

Hayek, F.A.V. (1979), *Law, Legislation and Liberty, Vol. 3: The Political Order of a Free People*, London: Routledge & Kegan Paul.

Hayek, F.A.V. (1988), *The Fatal Conceit: The Errors of Socialism*, London: Routledge & Kegan Paul.

Hoel, M. (1991), 'Global environmental problems: the effect of unilateral actions taken by one country', *Journal of Environmental Economics and Management*, 20, 55–70.

Hueting, R., P. Bosch and B. de Boer (1992), *Methodology for the Calculation of Sustainable National Income*, Gland: WWF.

Mill, J.S. (1859/1969), *Über Freiheit*, Frankfurt: Europäische Verlagsanstalt. (Original: On Liberty).

Nozick, R. (1974), *Anarchy, State, and Utopia*, New York: Basic Books.

O'Hara, S.U. (1996), 'Discursive ethics in ecosystem valuation and environmental policy', *Ecological Economics*, 16, 95–107.

Olson, M. jr. (1982), *The Rise and Decline of Nations. Economic Growth, Stagflation, and Social Rigidities*, New Haven: Yale University Press.

Page, T. (1977), *Conservation and Economic Efficiency*, Baltimore, London: Johns Hopkins University Press.

Pimm, S.L. (1994), 'Biodiversity and the balance of nature', in E-D. Schulze and H.A. Mooney (eds), *Biodiversity and Ecosystem Function*, Berlin u.a.O.: Springer, pp. 347–60.

Polasky, S. and A.R. Solow (1995), 'On the value of a collection of species', *Journal of Environmental Economics and Management*, 29, 298–303.

Popper, K.R. (1984), *Objektive Erkenntnis*, Hamburg: Rowohlt.

Prescott-Allen, R. and C. Prescott–Allen (1986), *The First Resource*, New York, London: Yale University Press.

Rawls, J. (1971), *A Theory of Justice*, Cambridge, Mass.: Harvard University Press.

Rawls, J. (1993), *Political Liberalism*, New York: Columbia University Press.

Reid, W.V. and K.R. Miller (1989), *Keeping Options Alive. The Scientific Basis for Conserving Biodiversity*, Washington: World Resources Institute.

Sen, A. (1992), *Inequality Reexamined*, New York: Basil Blackwell.

Simon, H.A. (1959), 'Theories of decision making in economics and behavioral science', *American Economic Review*, 49, 223–83.

Simpson, R.D. (1992), *Transactional Arrangements and the Commercialization of Tropical Diversity*, Washington: Resources for the Future.

Spash, C.L. and N. Hanley (1995), 'Preferences, information and biodiversity preservation', *Ecological Economics*, 12, 191–208.

Stähler, F. (1994), 'Biological diversity: the international management of genetic resources and its impact on biotechnology', *Ecological Economics*, 11, 227–36.

Swanson, T.M. (1994), *The International Regulation of Extinction*, Houndmills: Macmillan.

Sweeney, J.L. (1993), 'Economic theory of depletable resources: an introduction' in A.V. Kneese and J.L. Sweeney (eds), *Handbook of Natural Resource and Energy Economics*, Vol. III, Amsterdam: Elsevier, pp. 759–854.

Tisdell, C. (1990), 'Economics and the debate about preservation of species, crop varieties and genetic diversity', *Ecological Economics*, 2, 77–90.

UNEP, United Nations Environment Programme (ed.) (1993), *Global Biodiversity*, Nairobi: UNEP.

Vanberg, V. (1975), *Die zwei Soziologien. Individualismus und Kollektivismus in der Sozialtheorie*, Tübingen: J.C.B. Mohr.

WBGU (1995), Scientific Advisory Council on Global Change, *The Threat to Soils*, Annual Report 1994, Bonn: Economica.

Wilen, J.E. (1985), 'Bioeconomics of renewable resource use', in A.V. Kneese and J.L. Sweeney (eds), *Handbook of Natural Resource and Energy Economics*, Vol. I, Amsterdam: Elsevier, pp. 61–124.

Williams, M.B. (1978), 'Discounting versus maximum sustainable yield', in R.I. Sikora and B. Barry (eds), *Obligations to Future Generations*, Philadelphia: Temple University Press, pp. 169–85.

16. International Environmental Issues: Towards a New Integrated Assessment Approach

Nuria Castells and Giuseppe Munda

16.1 INTERNATIONAL ENVIRONMENTAL ISSUES: A SYSTEMIC PERSPECTIVE

Increasingly, environmental issues are to be solved on the basis of international cooperation, due to the many different geographical scales that characterize ecosystem behaviour. Local level actions may be ineffective if they are not coordinated in a wider framework of collaboration among the different actors (countries, regions, industries) which together contribute to the environmental disruption. In this context, more and more institutional arrangements are emerging to define and coordinate the implementation of international strategies to mitigate pollution or to prevent further damage.

The decision-making process towards the definition of international environmental policies requires inputs from several disciplinary backgrounds. This diverse information can be articulated through the use of integrated assessment approaches (IA).[1] As an analytical approach, the so-called integrated assessment relates to the complexity of the issues at stake, since it intends to link and integrate the different dimensions of the system which must be taken as a whole even if not commensurable.

From systems theory it is possible to draw the distinction between systems which are simple or merely *complicated* on the one hand, and those which are *complex* (that can also be complicated). Among complex systems, defined as those which cannot be captured at all by a single perspective, the *reflexive systems* (formerly called 'emergent complex' in Funtowicz and Ravetz, 1994a; O'Connor et al., 1996) are those with the properties of awareness and purpose. In ordinary complexity, characteristic of biological systems, there is an absence of full self-consciousness and purposes. In order to better understand *reflexivity,* Funtowicz and Ravetz (1994a) use a mathematical metaphor from chaos theory, that of a multidimensional phase space. The dimensions include those of the relevant mechanistic attributes (space, time, measurable properties), the ordinary-complex attributes of structure and function, and in addition those of the technical, economic, societal, personal and moral realms. These higher dimensions relate to knowledge and consciousness, and of course do not have the same type of metric relations as the lower dimensions. We may use the term 'topology' to indicate the difference: the lower dimensions have a 'harder' topology, permitting measurement and quantitative gauges while the higher dimensions have a 'softer' topology, in which the more qualitative properties are described.

The particularity of reflexive systems is that some of the constituents of such systems are self-aware subsystems and elements. When dealing with international strategies towards the mitigation of environmental disruption, the analytical framework is the one of reflexivity, since the actors involved and the interests at stake are totally interrelated and conflictive.

In this paper, we will first discuss the characteristics of IA in the framework of reflexive systems, then we will examine an empirical example to show the relationships between theory and practice and finally the main features of a new IA approach will be outlined.

16.2 INTEGRATED ASSESSMENT: A PROCESS OR A MODEL?

First, we would like to clarify what we intend by integrated assessment (IA). The literature on the topic is ambiguous, since there is often no clear distinction between the process of integrated assessment, and the computer tools used *to support this process*. Integrated assessment is not a 'computer model', but an analytical approach for understanding the issues at stake: it is *integrated* because it links together the different relevant components and actors of the problem to be tackled, and it is an *assessment* as a result of the systemic perspective in which different subsystems are apprehended and analysed to produce a comprehensive dynamic scenario. IA approaches should allow the decision-makers' progressive awareness of their preferences and the expression of these (we might say a kind of learning process as in Socrates' *majeutics*).

IA deals with reflexive phenomena since an effective assessment, in order to be realistic, should consider not merely the measurable and contrastable dimensions of the system that even if complicated may be technically simulated. It should deal as well with the higher dimensions of the system, those in which power relations, hidden interests, cultural constraints, and other 'soft' values, become relevant 'variables' that heavily but not deterministically affect the possible outcomes of the strategies to be adopted. Thus, Integrated Assessment is understood as cross-disciplinary in the horizontal axis, integrating disciplinary perspectives on the issue at stake, and as pluri-participatory on the vertical axis, integrating the perspectives of the different stake-holders and social actors concerned by the issue (see Figure 16.1).

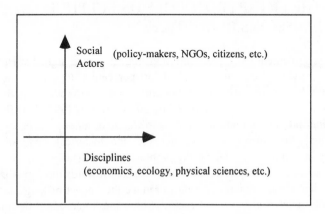

Figure 16.1 Vertical and horizontal integration in IA

Integrated assessment models, such as the RAINS model[2] or others dealing with acid rain and, more recently, with greenhouse gas emissions and absorptions bearing on global climate change, have become essential technical tools used to simulate ex ante the potential effects of alternatives abatement strategies of pollution (Sorensen, 1994). The performance of such tools has facilitated the development of much more detailed international agreements, since their results save time and discussions around what would be the possible consequences of alternative strategies; they provide alternative scenarios for several time horizons in each country, and different hypotheses on cost-abatement functions. Nonetheless, these integrated assessment models (IAM) are not able to, and they are not supposed to, apprehend the reflexive properties of the systemic issues at stake when defining environmental policies.

The distinction between IA as a process to support decision-making and IAM as technical tools in this process is essential. Integrated assessment models may reproduce biased perspectives in their design, that pre-determine some trends or some preferences toward particular technologies or strategies. *The lack of transparency* from the conception and design of these models may lead to the transmission of built-in values in the assessment process toward the political decision.

Some consequences of conflating the role of IA models (IAM) with the role of integrated assessment (IA) are illustrated in the following section. We describe the case of the second sulphur protocol to the LRTAP Convention,[3] in which the use of RAINS has played an important role (Castells and Funtowicz, 1997).

16.3 THE LRTAP PROTOCOLS ON SULPHUR EMISSIONS REDUCTION

The first agreement on sulphur emissions reduction was signed at Helsinki in 1985, giving rise to the so-called '30 per cent Club', since the goal stated by the first protocol on sulphur emissions was to reduce the Sulphur emissions for each country involved by 30 per cent in 1993. This flat-rate reduction did not take into account the differences among the ecosystems concerned, the current level of damage, the historical trend of each country in facing or not facing the problem of acidification, and so on. It was nonetheless highly relevant as the first step towards the formalization of an international strategy aiming to reduce the impact of long-range air pollution across Europe. The relative arbitrariness that could be inferred from such a flat-rate reduction facilitated the defection from the agreement from some countries, such as Poland or the United Kingdom (Wuster, 1992). In June 1994, the second protocol to the Convention on LRTAP on Further Reduction of Sulphur Emissions was open for signature at Oslo. This international agreement on air pollution was the result of a previous process of negotiation among the parties involved. For the first time an integrated assessment model was used to provide scenarios to the policy-makers as the basis for discussion. Although RAINS was the official model, two other IAM were used to compare results, CASM[4] and ASAM[5].

The negotiation process involved policy-makers and scientific experts in the field, who were recursively interacting in order to build an effective strategy for air pollution abatement, both from the technical and political point of view. The RAINS model was used to simulate the transport of air pollutants and their impact on the ecosystems, on the basis of the critical load concept. The critical load (Nilsson and Greenfelt, 1988) is the threshold upon which an ecosystem may suffer irreversible damage from the pollutant concerned (there are critical loads for sulphur, nitrogen, acidification). The use of the critical load concept has facilitated the design of a country-target scenario, since the IAM (RAINS, CASM and ASAM) have been generating ad hoc targets of emission reduction for each country involved in the agreement. According to the data on sulphur deposition, the matrix of transport of pollutants, and the maps of critical loads, the IA models were used to generate the so-called '60 per cent Gap Closure' scenario (Amman et al., 1993). This scenario was designed for reducing by 60 per cent the excess on critical load by the year 2000. This means that the abatement strategies were designed in order to reduce the emissions that are affecting ecosystems over the threshold of the critical load, and that are provoking irreversible damage.

Table 16.1 presents a comparison between the targets agreed at Oslo, and the RAINS scenario on which the negotiations were based. It can be observed that when considering the first time horizon, year 2000, the coincidence between RAINS scenario and the final protocol is more the exception than the rule. Only Austria, Belarussia, Finland, Luxembourg, The Netherlands, Norway, Russian Fed., Slovenia and Switzerland have signed for the percentage of reduction issued from RAINS. Two Southern European countries, Portugal and Greece, have signed for targets more restricted than those proposed by RAINS, but in both cases the model scenario figures allowed for an increase in their emissions. Spain has signed for a reduction of 35 per cent, which is nearer to their own Spanish calculations[6] (37 per cent) than from RAINS results (55 per cent). Seventeen countries are missing the 'first appointment' to meet the targets leading to the 60 per cent Gap Closure scenario. In the year 2005, Italy joins the group of 'equal to RAINS'. Finally, in the year 2010, Czech Republic, Poland, Slovakia, Ukraine and United Kingdom are also committed to meeting or surpassing the RAINS scenario requirements. Longer timing has been conceded to some countries to allow them to fulfil the requirements to implement abatement strategies. The following countries are not committing themselves to RAINS scenarios at any of the time horizons: Belgium, Bulgaria, Croatia, Denmark, France, Germany, Hungary, Ireland, Spain and Sweden.

A priori, the achievement of the 60 per cent Gap Closure scenario may be put into question, since the uncoordinated changes in national targets do not ensure the coherence of the whole scenario. Furthermore, since the RAINS simulations have been made to the year 2000, and the Oslo Protocol postpones in many cases the time horizon, the results are that the implementation will not take place as was envisaged in the simulation exercises.

What we want to emphasize is that at the practical level, when the final country targets are negotiated, the reflexive properties of the negotiation process emerge: the commitments take into account the 'soft' constraints under which the policy-makers are deciding and committing the countries they represent. The cost-effectiveness of the joint abatement strategy that is assumed to be the result of the model at the international level is not preserved when down-scaling to the national level. Clearly, there will be relative winners and losers in the cost-sharing of the abatement costs, and these were not considered in the simulation process. This is particularly evident in the case of Spain.

During the negotiation process leading to the Oslo Protocol of Sulphur Emissions, some countries submitted the request to be allowed to use different integrated assessment models to generate the final scenario. In particular, Spain asked to be allowed to define its country target on the basis of the ASAM scenario. In the process of negotiations, three IA models used to define the final scenario for the agreement, all constrained by the same goal, that is to reach the '60 per cent Gap Closure' scenario, and all running with the same input data on critical loads of the territory and of emissions. But the ASAM scenario asked only 41 per cent reduction for Spain instead of 55 per cent from RAINS. This means that according to the different design of these models, the cost-sharing of the final implementation of the abatement strategy will differ.

In the Spanish case, the level of protection of the ecosystem in terms of area, before even applying the abatement strategies to reduce sulphur emissions, is already 98 per cent. Typically the higher the initial protection level, the more expensive it becomes to reduce pollution in the territory (Castells and Martinez Alier, 1995). Furthermore, Spain has to reduce the emissions in relation to two cells out of the 35 that constitute its territory in the maps used by the models.[7] Thus, the aggregation process from the regional level to the national one penalizes this country where the pollution is concentrated in just two cells. The difference between the RAINS scenario and the ASAM one is mainly due to the different aggregation processes (Ministerio de Obras Publicas Transportes y Medio Ambiente, 1993a,b).

What we illustrate with this example is that on the one hand, the models are useful in order to anticipate the potential impact of hypothetical policies during the negotiation process. But, what is at stake is the *transfer of legitimacy from the technical tools to the policy-makers*. If the biases embodied in the modelling tools are not clear to the decision-makers, they can argue that they are taking objective and neutral decisions based on scientific assessment, while really they are not.[8] Scientific tools do reflect in their results the premises of their design, and the design *may not be neutral*. Furthermore, these tools were developed in the countries that were first to have been concerned and aware of the issue at stake — namely acidification in our example — and it may be the case that they reflect the particular conditions (climatic, distribution of pollution, technology) of those pioneering countries in the field. If these models are applied to countries that differ from those where they first were conceived without appraising the suitability for these different cases, the scenarios may be a source of unequity since some situations are better represented than others.

Table 16.1   *Comparison between RAINS scenarios and the final agreement for the second sulphur protocol (Oslo, June 1994)*

	RAINS scenario (% of emission reduction)	Final agreement Oslo 1994			Relation between reductions agreed at Oslo and RAINS scenario
		2000	2005	2010	
Austria	80	80			=
Belarus	38	38	46	50	= > >
Belgium	77	70	72	74	< < <
Bulgaria	50	33	40	45	< < <
Croatia	40	11	17	22	< < <
Czech Republic	72	50	60	72	< < =
Denmark	87	80			<
Finland	80	80			=
France	80	74	77	78	< < <
Germany	90	83	87		< <
Greece	+ 49 (Increase)	0	3	4	> > >
Hungary	68	45	50	60	< < <
Ireland	41	30			<
Italy	73	65	73		< =
Luxembourg	58	58			=
The Netherlands	77	77			=
Norway	76	76			=
Poland	66	37	47	66	< < =
Portugal	+ 11 (Increase)	0	3		> >
Russian Fed.	38	38	40	40	= > >
Slovakia	72	60	65	72	< < =
Slovenia	45	45	60	70	= > >
Spain	55	35			<
Sweden	83	80			<
Switzerland	52	52			=
Ukraine	56	40	45	56	< < =
United Kingdom	79	50	70	80	< < >

Notes : < means that the reduction accorded at Oslo is inferior to the reduction suggested by RAINS (emissions will be reduced less than it was suggested by the model)
> means that the reduction accorded at Oslo is above the level suggested by RAINS

Source: Own elaboration based ECE/EB.AIR/40, Protocol to the 1979 Convention on LRTAP on further reduction on sulphur emissions (Oslo Protocol), onAgren (1994) and Amman et al. (1993).

16.4   TOWARDS A NEW INTEGRATED ASSESSMENT APPROACH

16.4.1   IA in a Post-Normal Science Framework

Global environmental issues present new tasks for science; scientists now tackle problems introduced through policy issues where typically, *facts are uncertain, values in dispute, stakes high, and decisions urgent* (Funtowicz and Ravetz, 1991). Thus Funtowicz and Ravetz have developed a new epistemological framework called 'post-normal science', where it is possible to use two crucial aspects of science in the policy domain: uncertainty and value conflict. The name 'post-normal' indicates that the puzzle-solving exercises of normal science, in the Kuhnian sense (Kuhn, 1962), which were so successfully extended from the laboratory of core science to the conquest of nature through applied science are no longer appropriate for the solution of environmental problems.

As a post-normal science, ecological economics recognizes the presence, importance and legitimacy of different value-commitments for the appropriate management of *uncertainty*. It does not claim ethical neutrality, nor an indifference to the policy consequences of its arguments. According to Funtowicz and Ravetz (1994b), the traditional analytical approach, implicitly or explicitly reducing all goods to commodities, can be recognized as one perspective among several, legitimate as a point of view (and as a reflection of certain aspects of real power structures) but not the whole story.

To choose any particular operational definition for value involves making a decision about what is important and real; other definitions will reflect the commitments of other stakeholders. As a consequence, the validity of a given integrated assessment depends on the admission of the plurality of legitimate perspectives as well as the non-omission of the reflexive properties of the system, even though these latter are not easy to deal with. Once the premises of a particular IA approach are known, the decision-makers are more able to be aware of the consequences of the assumptions. This requires transparency in relation to two main factors:

(1) mathematical and descriptive properties which make the models used conform to given requirements;
(2) the way such models are used and integrated in a decision process.

Is it possible to improve the quality of a decision process? When science became used in policy, it was discovered that lay-persons (for example, judges, journalists, scientists from another field, or just citizens) could master enough of the methodology to become effective participants in the dialogue. A basic principle of post-normal science is that these new participants are indispensable. This extension of the peer community is essential for maintaining the quality of the process of resolution of reflexive complex systems. Thus the appropriate management of quality is enriched to include this multiplicity of participants and perspectives. The criteria of quality in this new context will, as in traditional science, presuppose ethical principles. But in this case, *the principles will be explicit and will become part of the dialogue.* This call for a democratization of science and the respect of cultural diversity is shared with the concept of coevolution (Norgaard, 1994). According to Norgaard, in environmental management local knowledge and expertise (being the result of a long coevolutionary process) sometimes are more useful than experts' opinions.

Post-normal science can be located in relation to the other, complementary classes of assessment practices, by means of a diagram (see Figure 16.2). On it, we see two axes, 'systems uncertainties' and 'decision stakes'. When both are small, we are in the realm of 'normal', safe science, where expertise is fully effective. When either is medium, then the application of routine techniques is not enough; skill, judgement, sometimes even courage are required. Funtowicz and Ravetz call this 'professional consultancy', with the examples of the surgeon or the senior engineer in mind. Our modern society has depended on armies of 'applied scientists' pushing forward the frontiers of knowledge and technique, with the professionals performing an aristocratic role, either as innovators or as guardians.

When conclusions are not completely determined by the scientific facts, inferences will (naturally and legitimately) be conditioned by the values held by the agent. If the stakes are very high (as when an institution is seriously threatened by a policy) then a defensive policy will involve challenging every step of a scientific argument, even if the systems uncertainties are actually small. Such tactics can become incompatible with the values of scientific enquiry and of open government, when they are conducted covertly, as by scientists who present themselves as impartial judges when they are actually committed advocates. Partly for this reason, there are now many initiatives, increasing in number and significance all the time, for involving wider circles of people in decision-making and implementation on environmental issues.

In the next section, we will discuss the formal and descriptive properties of some multicriteria methods useful in IA.

16.4.2   Multicriteria Analysis in Integrated Assessment

We now want to discuss some methodological options for the organization of information and assessment in a post-normal science perspective. Evaluation of objects under different descriptions invokes not just different practices and perspectives, but also different criteria and standards for evaluation associated with these. It presupposes *value-pluralism*. Appeal to different standards often results in conflicting appraisal of an object. Thus there is a need for mathematical tools able to tackle situations where there is no solution optimizing all the dimensions at the same time. This is the aim of multicriteria evaluation.

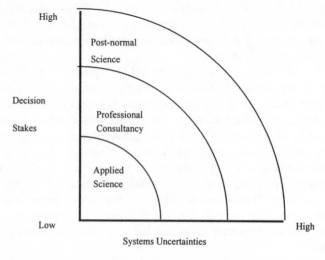

Figure 16.2 Graphical illustration of post-normal science

In the framework of IA, it is clear that in policy-relevant economic–environmental evaluation models, a variety of socio-economic and nature conservation objectives are to be considered simultaneously. Consequently, multicriteria methods are in principle an appropriate modelling component for environmental decisionmaking issues: prospects for a compromise solution taking into account different conflictual values can in principle be identified.

A great number of multicriteria methods have been developed and applied for different policy purposes in different contexts. As a first example, we take into account the linear aggregation rule. This methodology is quite relevant since it is widely used in many empirical applications in environmental management (above all in the form of the so-called 'weighted summation method'). Here, we will show that it is not an adequate aggregation rule for environmental policy.

The linear aggregation rule is a particular case of an approach called MultiAttribute Utility Theory (MAUT). This theory is based on the following hypothesis: in any decision problem there exists a *real valued function U* defined on the set *A* of feasible actions, which the decision maker wishes, consciously or not, to examine. This function aggregates the different criteria taken into consideration, so that the problem can be formulated as max $U(g_i(a))$ (where *a* belongs to the set *A*) where $U(g_i(a))$ is a value function aggregating the *m* criteria (therefore a multicriteria problem is replaced by a monocriterion one). The role of the analyst is to determine this function. The most usual functions are the *linear* or the *multiplicative* form.

The Linear aggregation rule can be expressed as follows:

$$\sum_i^n v_i(g_i(a))$$ (16.1)

(where $v_i(g_i(a))$ represents a normalized value between 0 and 1 of the criterion score). If weights (W_i) are used, the formulation becomes

$$\sum_i^n W_i * v_i(g_i(a)).$$ (16.2)

This formulation is called the 'weighted summation method'. For *IA* applications this method presents the following main problems:

(a) The aggregation of several dimensions implies taking a position on the problem of *compensability*. The way each aggregation procedure transforms information in order to arrive at a preference structure can be called its aggregation convention, which is generally well illustrated by the numerical transformation used. Clearly, the convention underlying the linear aggregation rule is completely compensatory ; for example, if environmental and economic criteria are to be taken into consideration, complete compensability implicitly means complete substitution between man-made capital and natural capital (weak sustainability). Or, as in the case of acid rain, if different countries' actions are being compared, complete compensability would mean that stronger abatement action by one country is presumed to compensate for lesser abatement by another.

(b) One should note that the linear form can be used only if the condition of preference independence holds (Keeney and Raiffa, 1976). This condition implies situations like the following: one's preference of red wine over white wine would be independent of whether the meal is meat or fish!

Let's take into consideration the following case. A and B are two different social scenarios, where

M represents an amount of money income,
S represents a measure of social degradation, and
E represents an indicator of environmental degradation.

Formally, the preference independence condition in our case, is:

$$\forall \ (M(A)_0, M(B)_0),$$
$$(M(A)_1, S(A)_0, E(A)_0) \ \mathbf{P} \ (M(B)_1, SB)_0, E(B)_0) \Rightarrow \qquad (16.3)$$
$$(M(A)_1, S(A)_1, E(A)_1) \ \mathbf{P} \ (M(B)_1, S(B)_1, E(B)_1)$$
$$S(A)_i = S(B)_i \ \text{and} \ E(A)_i = E(B)_i \ \forall \ i.$$

In this framework there is a need to accept a strong implicit assumption, that is, that society is willing to substitute one sort of degradation for another (that is, a 'trade off' is possible whereby more environmental degradation can be compensated by a reduction in social degradation, other things equal). The possibility that some levels of environmental and social degradation are unacceptable cannot be taken into consideration.

Moreover, as a consequence of the preferential independence condition, an additive value function permits the assessment of the marginal contribution of each attribute separately so the marginal contribution of each can then be added together to yield a total value. In the case in which environmental dimensions are involved, the use of a linear aggregation procedure then implies that among the different ecosystemic aspects there are not phenomena of synergy or conflict. This appears to be quite an unrealistic assumption (Funtowicz et al., 1990). For example, laboratory experiments have made clear that the combined impact of the acidifying substances SO_2, NO_X, NH_3 and O_3 on plant growth is substantially more severe than the (linear) addition of the impacts of each of these substances alone would be (Dietz and van der Straaten, 1992).

Now we will briefly describe, as an example, three multicriteria procedures we think more useful for real-world environmental policy applications: outranking, mixed qualitative and quantitative methods, and fuzzy information.

Outranking methods (Roy, 1985) consist of aggregating the criteria into a partial binary relation aSb (outranking relation) and then of the 'exploitation' of this relation; each of these two steps may be treated in a number of ways according to the problem formulation and the particular case considered. As an example, in ELECTRE 1, the proposition aSb is accepted if the concordant coalition $C(aSb)$ composed by all the criteria for which action a is equal to or better than action b is sufficiently important (condition of concordance) ; and if on the other criteria the difference $g_i(b) - g_i(a)$ are not too large (condition of non-discordance). The importance of a coalition is represented by the sum of the weights (w_i) of the criteria belonging to that coalition. As an example, for a Parliament, the concordant coalition can be considered as the summation of the votes of the members in favour of a given option; according to the majority rule of democracies this option will be approved if it obtains more than the 50 per cent of votes. According to the normative tradition in political philosophy, all coalitions, however small, should be given some fraction of the decision power. One measure of this power is the ability *to veto* certain subsets of outcomes. This explains the use of the condition of non-discordance. One should also note that in the concordant coalition the number of criteria are counted, that is, only ordinal information is used. In the computation of the discordance index, the 'intensity' of such a discordance is considered.

A common property of the outranking methods is that they are completely or partially non compensatory. From an empirical point of view, outranking methods are relevant since they allow, in a perfectly consistent framework, the application of weights as 'coefficients of importance', which is the most natural way of expressing weights. In its applications to IA, an important consequence of noncompensability is that it is possible to operationalize notions of multiple critical properties or thresholds (such as air and water quality, energy supply, food distribution). This is desirable in, for example, sustainability scenario studies where many different system performance properties must be portrayed. In the case of acid rain, such threshold criteria and weightings could be used to portray limits to acceptable economic burdens (by country or by sector) or strategic considerations such as domestic production of energy, as well as the ecosystem critical loads.

Turn now to another aspect of the multiple dimensions of complex systems assessment. It has been argued that the presence of qualitative information in evaluation problems concerning socio-economic and physical planning is a rule, rather than an exception (Nijkamp et al., 1990). Thus there is a clear need for methods that are able to take into account information of a 'mixed' type (both qualitative and quantitative measurements).

An example of a multicriteria method that may use mixed information is the so-called REGIME method which is based on pairwise comparison operations; from this point of view it has something in common with outranking methods (Hinloopen and Nijkamp, 1990; Nijkamp et al., 1990). Its point of departure is an ordinal evaluation matrix and an ordinal weight vector. Given the ordinal nature of the evaluation criteria, by means of pairwise comparison of alternatives, no attention is paid to the size of the difference between the impacts of alternatives; it is only the sign of the difference that is taken into account. Ordinal weights are interpreted as originating from unknown quantitative weights. A set S is defined containing the whole set of quantitative weights that conform to the qualitative priority information. In some cases the sign will be the same for the whole set S, and the alternatives can be ranked accordingly. In other cases the sign of the pairwise comparison cannot be determined unambiguously. This difficulty is circumvented by partitioning the set of feasible weights so that for each subset of weights a definite conclusion can be drawn about the sign of the pairwise comparison. The distribution of the weights within S is assumed to be uniform and therefore the relative sizes of the subsets of S can be interpreted as the probability that alternative a is preferred to alternative b. Probabilities are then aggregated to produce an overall rating of the alternatives, based on a success index or success score.

Another problem related to the available information concerns the uncertainty contained in this information. Ideally, if a 'best' choice is to be identified by calculation, the information should be precise, certain, exhaustive and unequivocal. But in reality, it is often necessary to use information which does not have those characteristics so that one has to face the uncertainty of a stochastic and/or fuzzy nature present in the data. If it is impossible to establish exactly the future state of the problem faced, a stochastic uncertainty is created; this type of uncertainty is well known and has been thoroughly studied in probability theory and statistics.

Another framing of uncertainty, called fuzzy uncertainty, focusses on the ambiguity of information in the sense that the uncertainty does not concern the occurrence of an event but the event itself, which cannot be described unambiguously (Zadeh, 1965). This sort of situation is readily identifiable in complex systems. Spatial-environmental systems in particular are reflexive complex systems characterized by subjectivity, incompleteness and imprecision. For example, in the cases of soil and water pollution from acid rain and land cover changes that might be induced by an enhanced greenhouse effect and consequent climate change, the cumulative effects of pollutant and climate 'forcing' on the ecological processes are quite uncertain. Fuzzy set theory is a mathematical theory useful for modelling situations of such a sort, that is, it aims to portray in terms of fuzzy uncertainty some of the indeterminacies of the socio-ecological system under study (Munda, 1995).

Zadeh (1965) writes: 'as the complexity of a system increases, our ability to make a precise and yet significant statement about its behaviour diminishes until a threshold is reached beyond which precision and significance (or relevance) become almost mutually exclusive characteristics'. Therefore, in these situations statements as 'the quality of the environment is good', 'the unemployment rate is low' are quite common. Fuzzy set theory is a mathematical theory for modelling situations, in which traditional modelling languages which are dichotomous in character and unambiguous in their description cannot be used.

A new multicriteria method, based on some aspects of Roy's 'partial comparability axiom', called NAIADE (Novel Approach to Imprecise Assessment and Decision Environments) has been developed (Munda, 1995). It is a discrete multicriteria method whose impact (or evaluation) matrix may include crisp, stochastic or fuzzy measurements of the performance of an alternative a_n with respect to a judgement criterion g_m, thus it is very flexible for real-world applications. From an empirical point of view, this model is particularly suitable for economic–ecological modelling incorporating various degrees of precision of the variables taken into consideration. From a methodological point of view, two main issues are then tackled:

- the problem of equivalence of the procedures used in order to standardize the various evaluations (of a mixed type) of the performance of alternatives according to different criteria;
- the problem of comparison of fuzzy numbers typical of all fuzzy multicriteria methods.

In environmental and resource management and policy aiming at, say, ecologically sustainable development, many conflicting issues and interests emerge. Particular attention has to be given to the problem of different values and goals of different groups in society. Equity issues and, more generally, conflicting values in multicriteria decision aid are traditionally introduced in two different ways:

(1) by weighting the different criteria. A disadvantage of this approach is that in public decision-making a single point-value solution often tends to lead to deadlocks in a decision process because it imposes conditions that are too rigid to permit a compromise; and
(2) by taking into consideration a set of ethical evaluation criteria. A weak point of this approach is that it could lead to an excessive number of evaluation criteria. Furthermore, to identify ethical criteria and give them an operational specification may be not an easy task.

In NAIADE there is a third possibility proposed, the use of conflict analysis procedures integrated with multicriteria evaluation in order to allow policy-makers to seek 'defensible' decisions that could reduce the degree of conflict (in other words, in order to reach a certain degree of consensus), or that could have a higher degree of equity for different social groups. Starting with a matrix showing the impacts of different courses of action on each different interest/income group, a fuzzy clustering procedure indicating the groups whose interests are closer in comparison with the other ones is used.

16.5 CONCLUSIONS

When dealing with international strategies towards the mitigation of environmental disruption, the appropriate analytical framework is one of reflexivity, since the actors involved and the interests at stake are totally interrelated and conflictive.

Integrated assessment Models (IAM) in themselves are not able to, and they are not supposed to, apprehend the reflexive properties of the systemic issue at stake when defining environmental policies. As a consequence, any attempt to fit the real world in a closed model leads to a simplification, to a violence to the description of reality.

Appropriate IA approaches thus require transparency in relation to two main factors:

(a) mathematical and descriptive properties which make the models used conform to given requirements;
(b) the way such models are used and integrated in a social evaluation and decision process.

This way of looking at rationality implies a new concept of quality in analysis, communication and decision support. The focus is placed now on the process leading to a given decision, not just on properties of the final decision. A basic principle of post-normal science is that extension of the peer community is essential for maintaining the quality of the process of analysis and conflict resolution for the management of reflexive complex systems. Our attention to the social context and process of working with models can be understood in this light.

We have emphasized the property of multiple dimensions in analysis of complex systems; and that the multiplicity is irreducible. In this context, it is important to add that incommensurability, that is, the absence of a common unit of measurement across plural values, does not imply incomparability. However it permits (if not presupposes) value-pluralism. Appeal to different standards often results in conflicting appraisal of an object; thus there is a need for mathematical tools able to tackle situations where there is no solution optimizing across all the dimensions at the same time.

ACKNOWLEDGMENTS

The helpful comments and suggestions of S. Funtowicz, M. O'Connor and J. Ravetz are gratefully acknowledged. Responsibility for the arguments of the paper is the authors' alone. G. Munda acknowledges financial support from the European Commission, J.R.C. under contract 12243-96-10 F1EI ISPE.

ENDNOTES

1. We could also use the term integrated environmental assessment, but we will keep using IA, assuming that we are discussing its application in the field of environmental policy. This is to simplify the presentation and not to introduce more confusion in this already confused terminology.
2. RAINS: Regional Acidification INformation Simulation model. Developed at IIASA, International Institute for Applied Systems Analysis, Laxenburg, Austria, it has been applied for simulating abatement strategies for acidification.
3. The Convention on Long Range Transboundary Air Pollution, Geneva, 1979.
4. Coordinated Abatement Strategies Model, Stockholm Environment Institute, York.
5. Abatement Strategies Assessment Model developed at Imperial College, London.
6. During the negotiations process, the Ministry of Environment in Spain carried out its own calculations with a simulation model using the same input data and constrained in order to reach the same 60 per cent Gap Closure scenario. According to these calculations, this could be reached by reducing the emissions by just 37 per cent.
7. The grid-cells for the RAINS are 150 km^2.
8. This is an important issue in operational environmental policy. For example, David Pearce claimed that his work for the intergovernmental Panel on Climate Change (IPCC), where lives of people in rich nations are valued up to fifteen times higher than those in poor countries, is a matter of scientific correctness versus political correctness! (*New Scientist*, 19 August, 1995). Is it really a matter of value-free scientific correctness to use valuations based on assessments of a community's willingness and ability to pay to avoid risks of death?

REFERENCES

Agren, C. (1994), 'The making of a protocol', *Acid News*, 1, 10–14.

Amman, M., G. Klaassen and W. Schopp (1993), 'Closing the Gap Between the 1990 Deposition and the Critical Sulfur Deposition Values', Report to UN/ECE Task Force on Integrated Assessment Modelling, IIASA, May 1993.

Castells, N. and J. Martinez-Alier (1995) 'Problemas Distributivos para la armonizacin de la politica ambiental en la Union Europea', *Papeles de Economia Española,* No. 63, 358–70

Dietz, F.J. and J. van der Straaten (1992), 'Rethinking environmental economics: missing links between economic theory and environmental policy', *Journal of Economic Issues,* 26, 27–51.

Funtowicz, S.O., G. Munda and M. Paruccini (1990), 'The aggregation of environmental data using multicriteria methods', *Environmetrics,* 1 (4), 353–68.

Funtowicz, S.O. and J.R. Ravetz (1991), 'A new scientific methodology for global environmental issues', in R. Costanza (ed.), *Ecological Economics,* New York, Columbia, pp. 137–52.

Funtowicz, S.O. and J.R. Ravetz (1994a), 'Emergent complex systems', *Futures,* 26 (6), 568–82.

Funtowicz, S.O. and J.R. Ravetz (1994b), 'The worth of a songbird: ecological economics as a post-normal science', *Ecological Economics,* 10, 197–207.

Hinloópen, E. and P. Nijkamp (1990), 'Qualitative multiple criteria choice analysis, the dominant regime method', *Quality and Quantity,* 24, 37–56.

Kuhn, T.S. (1962), *The Structure of Scientific Revolutions,* Chicago: University of Chicago Press.

Ministerio de Obras Publicas Transportes y Medio Ambiente (1993a), *Calidad del Aire en España,* 1990, Monografias, Madrid, Spain.

Ministerio de Obras Publicas Transportes y Medio Ambiente (1993b), *Consideraciones sobre el Segundo Protocolo del azufre,* Madrid, Spain.

Munda, G. (1995), *Multicriteria evaluation in a fuzzy environment. Theory and applications in ecological economics,* Heidelberg: Physica-Verlag.

Nijkamp, P., P. Rietveld and H. Voogd (1990), *Multicriteria Evaluation in Physical Planning,* Amsterdam: North-Holland.

Nilsson, J. and P. Greenfelt (1988), *Critical loads for Sulphur and Nitrogen,* Miljorapport 1988, 15, Nordic Council of Ministers, Copenhagen, Denmark.

Norgaard, R.B. (1994), *Development Betrayed,* London: Routledge.

O'Connor, M., S. Faucheux, G. Froger, S.O. Funtowicz and G. Munda (1996), 'Emergent complexity and procedural rationality: post-normal science for sustainability', in R. Costanza, J. Martinez-Alier and O. Segura (eds), *Getting Down to Earth: Practical Applications of Ecological Economics,* Washington D.C.: Island Press/ISEE, pp. 223–48.

Roy, B. (1985), *Méthodologie multicritère d'aide à la decision,* Paris: Economica,.

Sorensen, L. (1994), 'Environmental Planning under Uncertainty', PhD thesis, Technical University of Denmark, Lyngby, Denmark.

United Nations Economic Commission for Europe (1994), Protocol to the 1979 Convention on Long-Range Transboundary Air Pollution on Further Reduction of Sulphur Emissions, ECE/EB.AIR/40.

Wuster, H. (1992), 'The convention on transboundary air pollution: its achievements and its potential', in T. Schneider (ed.), *Acidification Research: Evaluation and Policy Applications*, pp. 221–239, Elsevier.

Zadeh, L.A. (1965), 'Fuzzy sets', *Information and Control*, 8, 338–53.

Index

Index